S0-APN-342

About *Scars That Can Heal*

"In the twelve years I've spent working with youths who were
raised in the system, I've heard many horrible stories, but none
more grueling than David's. His courage, strength, and
determination to deal with his past and help others is truly
inspirational. I applaud him for finding the courage to expose
the system for what it too often is: inept, powerless, uncaring,
and filled with holes. I know this book will have a positive
effect on countless children, whether in the system or not."

> Lori Kezos
> Program Director,
> Independent Living Skills,
> Boys Republic

"I'm awestruck by this book, and amazed that David had the
courage to write it. In America we've become complacent about
orphaned and abused children, telling ourselves the government
has everything under control. David is here to tell us that things
are not as they seem. This young man's story is a must-read for
healthcare providers, teachers, parents, counselors, and anyone
who cares about children. I found it both informative and
inspiring. I literally couldn't put it down!"

> Sammie Justesen, R.N.
> Author of *Common Threads*
> and *A Patient's Guide to
> Surgery*

"[David's] writing style evokes a vivid presence as you walk
alongside an orphaned boy trying to find his place in the world.
I highly recommend clinicians, clergy, and academia use this
book. We must help our young people get the message their
lives can be different and they can chose a better path for
themselves; I have never seen this message conveyed better
than in David's book."

> Lisa L. Hartwell, Psy.D., R.N.

"David has a powerful command of the English language and a gripping voice. It's hard to believe this is his first offering as a writer. His story of tragedy and triumph is a real page-turner. I'm confident that you will achieve your goal of helping many children with this book."

William Hoffman,
distinguished novelist and true crime writer, author of *Tough Guy*

"When I arrived at Boys Republic, the awards ceremonies happened about a week later. You stole the show. You have no idea how much of an impression you left on me. Just knowing who you are now is really incredible. You are one of the reasons that I succeeded so well at BR. You are one of the reasons that I took BR seriously. You were my first impression of the program, and the best one, in my opinion. Truthfully...over the many years, your face has come to mind and I have had to think to myself...if I didn't see you win those awards, I might not have become who I was at BR, let alone who I have become today. You have no idea how much you inspired me to push forward in my life. It has been a GREAT pleasure hearing from you, David!"

Cory Brown, Graduate, Boys Republic

Scars That Can Heal

Does every life have value?

David Louis

Aloha Joe,
Thanks for your
dedication to our youth in
crisis.

Warmest Regards,

Copyright © 2006 David Louis

All rights reserved. No part of this publication may be reproduced, stored in a retrieval system, or transmitted in any form or by any means, electronic, mechanical, recording or otherwise, without the prior written permission of the author. Printed in the United States of America. This book is available for promotions, trainings and conferences. For more information address: scarsthatcanheal@yahoo.com. http://www.myspace.com/heartgalleryhawaii

ISBN-10 1-60145-053-2
ISBN-13 978-1-60145-053-1

Booklocker.com, Inc.
2006

Cover Design by Camilla Skold of Maui Publishing
Photographs by Heidi Anderson of Keiki Photography
www.keikiphoto.com

FIRST EDITION

This book is dedicated to Terrell Peterson, I will never forget you brother.

Table of Contents

Acknowledgments

This book would not be possible without the emotional support of my wife and best friend, Dove. My children were also a constant source of inspiration and comfort. My little family helped to pull me out of the terrible space I often fell into as I was writing by saying the three words that I never heard growing up: "I love you."

Daveda Lamont, my editor at WordsArt, Inc. Her heart, dedication, and patience was a real blessing. She is a true wordsmith.

Thank you to all the staff that cared. Those few that decided to "see" me and treat me with dignity.

Thank you to Boys Republic and congratulations on your 100 year anniversary in 2007. I speak for thousands when I say thank you for your excellence and dedication to children in crisis.

Foreward

I am honored to write about an amazing young man. David is one of the most insightful, bright and competent young men I have ever met. In the twelve years I have worked with youth aging out of the system, there have been many horror stories of children raised by the state, but none that I have heard more awful than David's. I am impressed that he survived physically and mentally. It is incredible that he was able to not only adapt to the different and often difficult situations he was placed in while growing up, but that he was able to assimilate the good and leave the bad. He was able to focus his fears, anger and frustration towards positive goals as he excelled in school and received many academic awards. Through his strength and determination, he has broken the cycle of abuse and neglect that plagued his childhood and patterned his relationships with his wife and children in a manner exactly opposite of what was modeled towards him.

Most of the 500 youth placed every year at Boys Republic have at least an extended family member or family friend to transition to after completing the program. David was the first young man referred to me who had lived in out-of-home-care for most of his life, a true "system kid." The fact that he had been left in the custody of the state meant that any relatives that might exist were deemed unfit to raise him. There was no one to care for him. As bad as I felt about his past, I was grateful that his 30th placement was in a program that could make a difference in his future.

Many kids don't have the same opportunity. It is difficult to comprehend the struggle that thousands of adolescent boys and girls face as they contemplate leaving placement. "System kids" have numerous problems placed on them that kids raised by a family never have to deal with. Being raised by programs or staff members creates an artificial environment where it is difficult to know whether what is being told to you is truth or a lie. There is often no clear sense of right or wrong—different staff have different values. There is a strong awareness of not being loved, wanted or needed. If a foster family or group home doesn't like you or your behavior, they simply call your social worker and have you moved. It doesn't matter how valid it is. Practical things like getting a driver's license, renting an apartment or buying a car without a co-signer become almost impossible. In addition, all the things a child normally learns growing up, like how to cook or budget money, are not taught in many programs. "System kids" are not even allowed to spend time alone and unsupervised. Sometimes the first time they are in a house alone is the first night they spend in their own apartment.

The deck is stacked against these youth. Most young adults raised in a family have a place to return to, if only temporarily, when they need it. "System kids," on the other hand, have no place to go during breaks at college when the dorms are closed, when they lose a job and have no income to support themselves, or after a divorce, etc. David and thousands of young people like him don't have that. The psychological impact of knowing there is no one to turn to for help after you've "aged out" is staggering. I don't know if I could have survived such isolation.

The most difficult aspect of caring for him was in how to offer hope. As a staff member I knew that Boys Republic would do whatever was necessary to help him transition safely and successfully, but as a kid who had been routinely disappointed by adults, he had no real way of knowing what was in his future.

This book is a valuable contribution. It offers the first-hand perspective of an individual receiving services (or lack thereof) as a ward of the court. Almost all that has been written about treatment, delinquency or teenagers comes from the professional point of view and describes theories, the process being used and the interpretation of the impact on the client through their own eyes. This book is evidence that much of the professional interpretation of their impact, if not inaccurate, is highly distorted. There is much to be learned directly from someone affected by the "treatment" provided.

I appreciate the perspective David has given me on what he was going through during his stay in our program. It has helped me understand what others in his position are going through, and makes it possible for me to help the many I have seen since develop hope for the future and acquire the experiences that increase self-confidence and a sense of security and trust.

It has been wonderful to watch David grow and mature and have joy in his adult life. I appreciate that he has maintained contact and allowed me to be a part of his life. It gives me great satisfaction to know that my commitment and dedication were recognized and valued.

From great tragedy has arisen great promise. David now has the opportunity to help people understand what he went through, provide a voice for others in similar circumstances, and hopefully create change so that future children will not have to endure the same pain and obstacles. He also has the ability to help children in the system through his current job. He has a true understanding of what they are going through, what is possible for their future, and how to help them get there.

David is dedicated, capable and a very hard worker. He is extremely passionate about the family he has created for himself and the young people he works with. I am proud of who he has become and his willingness to open up his life to help create a sense of understanding about life as a dependent of the state. I wish him the peace and happiness he truly deserves.

Lori Kezos
Program Director,
Independent Living Skills Program, Boys Republic

Preface

Burning, fire, brightness,
She towers over me swinging, swinging, screaming.
The whip snaps against my flesh and I can't get away.
Sweating, shaking I awake,
Pulse ripping through my chest as I curl up. It's over.
Is this ever going to end?
I pray for release from shaking legs and sheets soaked in
sweat and urine.

I was just a face in the crowd to the U.S. Social Service system. Since its inception, perhaps a hundred million children have passed through the System. Today, there are millions of former foster children all over the country. Every year, around 19,000-25,000 teenagers "age out" of foster care, never having found a family to adopt them. In 1994, I was one of thousands who turned the magical 18, and was remanded to my own custody. Nearly every one of us has found it a daunting task to suddenly become a well-adjusted, mature and worldly educated adult on one specific day and face the world, all alone. I am saddened to report that many in my "graduating class" have had a very hard time fending for themselves, and the majority of aged-out foster children are struggling in every possible way. Many are in jail, mentally or physically, and some have passed away, by their own hands or otherwise. I was one of the auspicious few who used my skills and life lessons to build a home inside my heart. But then I did something unique. I took my diploma from the school of hard knocks and reached back to help the children who now sleep in my old bed.

I close my eyes to hold back the immediate rush of emotion that takes me over as I do my first room check. Abused, neglected, and starved for emotional and physical sustenance— that was my every day for 18 years. I grew up an orphan, a foster child, and a lost boy as a ward of the courts. I blink hard once or twice and I am anxious and intimidated by what my eyes take in: I hold the keys now. I am the staff, the counselor, and often, hope embodied to the lost and hurt children I now care for. Diligently, I complete my check of drawers, paintings, and bedding for illegal contraband and sharp items. As I begin to move on to the next area, I pause. My hand on the open door, I look back and take in the whole room very carefully. A deep breath and then a solemn oath:

I swear that I will do whatever I can to be an advocate for my kids. I will use all of my training, my years of experiences, and, if necessary, will reopen the wounds of my heart to heal others. I will not fail any of them the way that I was failed; I will not be a part of, nor party to, any crack in the System.

A rush of warmth through my body affirms the pact I have made with myself. I acknowledge the feeling with a nod and close the door.

I should begin with a name—the only thing my parents gave me: Louis Alberto Martinez. The police found my siblings and me in a home full of drugs and prostitutes. At two, I was turned over with my little brother Anthony to the Department of Public Social Services (DPSS), battered from head to toe, drugs in my system, burn welts on my arms and chest, and the world to face.

My mother, Abbie Keafer, was 13, 14, 16 and 18 respectively when she had each of her four children. A father? I was told that an immigrant from Guatemala, Luis Alturo

Martinez, married her to stay in the country. I read his name on my birth certificate and I saw a picture of him once—I'll explain later. Our "parents" were now the courts of California, and without any biological family to return to or look out for us, Tony and I looked to each other. One of my first memories is from just before my fifth birthday. I can see myself sitting on a red brick fireplace hearth while dangling my feet from side to side. I nervously traced the outline of the bricks as the adults spoke. I remember them talking about Tony and me as if we were invisible, like we weren't even there.

After the mumbling between the adults ended, they turned our way and looked us over, all nodding their heads in some agreement. Then, with just an instant of eye contact, the lady who drove us there smiled, waved, and was gone. We slept in bunkbeds with the glow sticks that they had given us. Bewildered and scared, I busted mine open and splashed the green glowing liquid on the ceiling and door. I lay next to my brother, who was shaking and crying. He was curled into a tight ball, gripping the sheets. His sobbing lessened as he rolled over to me. "What's happening Louie?"

His question hung there for a moment as I took in its meaning. I will never forget that night, when my little brother looked to me for security, for answers. I knew I had little to offer but innately I took the post. I responded, "We are going to stay here a while."

Tony nudged a little closer to me before quietly whimpering himself to sleep. I swore then, at just under five years of age, that I would protect him—that I would stop any pain that attempted to enter his life. I stared up at the spattered, glowing ceiling. My eyes filled with tears, but I refused to cry aloud—I wouldn't let Tony know I was as scared as he was. I was his strength, after all, and I could be strong, at least for him. Tears covering my face, I fell asleep to the vision of a blurry, glowing ceiling.

It has been ten years since I was under the "care" of the social service system. And finally, only after living enough normal time in the real world, do I feel I have prepared my heart enough to write this book. Frustrated for years at the lack of action by my "parents," a.k.a. "The System," at my reports, I thought that this endeavor might be futile. But I've been encouraged to endure, through remembering my considerable pain, so as to give others hope by sharing insight, informing and hopefully raising awareness. The events I will tell are not rare by any means—just rarely brought into public light. I desire to bring the shame that is the national tragedy of child abuse and neglect, especially among those in the foster care and social service system, to the public forefront. I desire to make you, the reader, a witness to the painful and unjust events of my childhood—details that are heard echoed in the lives of the 650,000 children in the system today, and in the five million annual reports of child abuse throughout America.

Yes, I *did* suffer and languish in government care, but so have countless others. This book is not just about my story; it is about hope and awareness. I want this memoir to shine a ray of light on the 150,000 children waiting to be adopted in America today. These children need to be recognized as real people, with little hearts that want your help.

There is another result I dream will come out of the work I have put into this book, and it coincides with the one wish that every orphaned child makes every night—to find true parents and a real home to be part of. I want you to look at yourself and ask, "Is there a place in my heart, and a space in my home, to adopt?"

About the People in this Book

This is a true story. This is how my file should read. I was blessed (or cursed) with a semi-photographic memory and I recall the exact names and locations of every one of my placements and all the adults in my life. However, I have purposefully changed most of the names in this book. After a few of my close friends, to whom I've only given general details of my childhood, read it, they wanted to seek out some of the perpetrators. I do not wish harm on any of these people; that is part of forgiveness and being a survivor. I hope that in the ten to twenty years that have passed, they have reflected on their actions and made changes for the better.

Part I

THROUGH THE HEART OF LOUIE

Have you ever held a small child in your arms? It is an amazing experience. Whether you have or not, I have a small request before you begin reading. It is a request that I hope you return to each time you pick up this book: Hold a small child up, look into their huge beautiful eyes, so full of light and hope, and embrace them. Take a little time to soak in how their little body feels in your embrace, how soft their hair is, and how warmly your embrace is returned. Try not to lose that magical feeling of connection as you journey with me through my childhood. Thank you.

Chapter 1 - More Than A Stray

"Loneliness and the feeling of being unwanted is the most terrible poverty."

—Mother Teresa

Usually the best thing about childhood is merely having the opportunity to be a child. The gift of a childhood is priceless—and irreplaceable. Being someone's number one means you get to soak in all the offers of life while your experiences are filtered and you have a soft place to land. Under the umbrella of a parent, a child gets to succeed, explore, play, daydream—and get caught in some of life's storms without getting too wet. But for those of us who have never been offered the love of a parent, we don't get to soak in life; we are forced to endure it and face all its challenges alone. It is truly unfair for any child to have to navigate adult experiences by him or herself. A child's memories should include raising his arms to catch a ball, not to block an attack. Little hands should be filled with ice cream cones, not suitcases. However, that is not the reality of this world. My arms flinched upwards to protect myself more times than I can remember, and I was first given my suitcase at age two.

Somehow the most traumatic events seem to be those we recall most easily. My very first recollection is one of such severity; although I'm not sure if it was my initial removal from my mother when I was two, or merely another instance in which I was being moved around, I do remember a car seat. I remember brown harness straps that prevented me from reaching out to my little brother Tony, who, little more than an arm's length away, was strapped in his own light blue car seat. I clearly remember crying, yelling and pressing against the straps. I can see Tony's face, flushed as he wailed. The car stops. I am startled as the car door my feet were pressed against gives way and swings open. I remember being engulfed in a woman's oversized sweater as she lifts me up and sets me right next to my little brother. And I remember that, for a moment, we stop crying.

It's not until I was four that I could start stringing together events, people, and feelings. By this age, Tony and I were being shuffled to our eleventh or twelfth foster placement. The thing that stands out most from these first memories is a feeling that I endured throughout childhood: I was abandoned, and therefore an unwanted intrusion.

I don't remember any faces, at that age, as we were being bounced from home to home. But I do remember that my priority was to protect my little brother. He was the only thing familiar, the only person who never left me. As long as we were together, I knew that there was a small amount of love in my life. I remember touching my little brother's hand, and how it helped to quell the torrents of anxiety and fear for moments, sometimes minutes—but the feeling of abandonment never left me entirely.

I don't blame my first foster parents for being only stepping-stones for Tony and me. I can reason out why so many of them handed us back—we came with a lot of baggage. A case file stated that we had been removed from our 16-year-old mother, Abbie, while she was distracted by a recreational drug-induced stupor. The report said that there were three of us—the eldest, a girl a year older than me, myself, and my little brother, a year younger. My sister Terry had been placed with our biological grandparents, who had room for only one child. The file reported that there was a fourth child who had died a week after birth—a crack baby. If you were brave enough to turn the pages in the file after reading that, you would find out that

Social Services had forcefully removed the three children because of torture-like conditions imposed by drug addicts and perverts. It would tell you that Abbie kept her three children with her in a crackhouse and sedated them with narcotic leftovers.

After a foster parent put the file down, they only had to look us over to see what they had gotten themselves into. I had scars from severe burns on various parts of my body and had been sexually assaulted. Tony and I were sickly and malnourished. I can see having compassion for children in this state, but realistically, I can also understand what a challenge it would have been trying to help two severely abused babies go through drug withdrawals as they filled the hours with screaming and forced you out of bed with their night terrors.

Before I could put words to it, I still always had the feeling that I was imposing on my foster homes. My first inclination when placed in a new home was to remain as still as possible and refuse anything offered, so I didn't take anything away from someone else. My response was often met with resentment by System providers, who took those actions personally or as ingratitude. No matter the efforts the best-intentioned foster parents tried to make, it would be nearly impossible to bond with children dealing with our level of posttraumatic stress, abandonment, and separation anxiety. Then add to this the scenario of our biological parents trying to reunite with us or visit, perhaps forcefully, and I don't think anyone would blame those first foster homes for providing us only a temporary solution. I don't know much about any of these first foster care providers, and prefer not to disclose the hearsay I was later given. I'm sure that they provided adequate care, as my memory isn't scarred by any one incident that early. And I think that once you've read the details of the rest of my System life, you'll agree that, by comparison, those early placements comprised a trivial part of the defining events of my childhood.

Instead, I begin with the first foster home seared into my memory, Henry and Karen's. I was nearly five years old when we arrived. The two-bedroom home was tucked away in rural Corona, California, three houses down from a set of train tracks. All the houses on our street were at least twenty to thirty years old and none of them had even slightly manicured yards.

Our new parents were an odd pair. Karen was an obese woman about five and a half feet tall. She was of Latin descent with bold features, long black hair, and a slight accent. Her husband Henry was almost a head shorter than her. He was a thin, pale Caucasian with sandy-blond hair and a handlebar moustache. Tony and I would later be showered with many comments about how we were a perfect match for them because we had Latin blood in us but appeared to be completely Caucasian.

The inside of the home was tidy, and Tony and I settled on the couch, easily sharing one cushion. We sat as close to each other as possible, fearful of moving away from each other, and waited for the adults to nod to each other and the social worker to leave. I'm sure that this process of moving was explained to us as we shuffled from home to home, but I can't put a name or a voice to any one time. I just always knew that we weren't with our own family, and that we were visitors to someone else's. Tony and I sat quietly and waited for the adults to show us our room. When they took us there, we shoved our plastic bags of clothing into the dresser, my bag always in the top drawer and Tony's in the middle or bottom. We never unpacked for obvious reasons. We didn't speak during the process; we understood only that we were to follow orders, and we couldn't have really comprehended much else. After a short tour of the property, we were officially settled in.

Karen was all smiles for the first few weeks. *They always are.* Henry, on the other hand, was rarely there, always at work or "out." Karen wanted children so badly that she had persuaded Henry to foster the two of us, with the intent to adopt.

For me, barely older than a toddler, arriving in a stranger's house was nerve-wracking. We got dropped off and told to "stay"—like when you tell a stray dog to quit following you. All at once, I got lost in how big everything was. It is impossible for your eyes and ears to take in everything. Having a strange adult give detailed explanations about the house rules added to my disorientation. Full of confusion and tension, we sat in a new home, with strange people, and then were left to figure out where we fit in. Most of the time, those receiving us wore a smile and did things to try and compensate for our unease. This first foster parent I clearly remember did exactly that; Karen was very concerned at first, bathing us, feeding us and fussing over our every desire. But then the honeymoon ended.

Foster Parent/Guardian Rule No. 1: *It All Starts with the Right Motive.*

Check your heart closely. Do not look towards social services or parenting a foster child as a means to fill any void in your emotional life. Every child in the System wants a family of their own, but that doesn't mean it is going to all be "golden times."

Our System fears—those that accompanied us wherever we went—were quadrupled by the dynamics of our new foster home. Henry and Karen would constantly bicker and argue with one another, and in short order their struggle would be taken to the next level. Their first fight was a wake-up call to my brain's survival mode. It was late in the evening and Tony and I lay in front of the TV with our pajamas on. In the living room, we shared their bedroom wall, and could hear their yells gaining volume. The pounding of a body against the wall startled us both. The sounds from the television seemed to disappear as I strained to take in every note of chaos. I didn't know what to think about what was going on. Terrified, I took Tony to the

bedroom and opened the football toy chest, grabbing a Pan Am
jumbo jet model plane. I handed it over to him, but he sank
back. He kept backing farther and farther into the corner as
Karen's cries grew louder, accompanied by Henry's yelling. I
kept trying to distract him; I didn't like seeing my little brother
scared.

Tony's survival instinct pushed him to take refuge under
the bed. I tried to make a game out of it and dumped the rest of
the toys out of the chest and got inside, closing the lid over
myself. I called out, "Tony, come and get me!" to no avail. A
few more attempts and I got out and went over to the bed. "I bet
I can find you!" I could hear Henry's approaching feet pound
the hardwood floors. Swiftly, I managed to get under the bed
before he reached our room.

When the door burst open, Henry stood still, staring at
the toys I had dumped out. A few seconds passed before he
started kicking at the toys and yelling, "What the f*** happened
here?! Louie, Tony where are you?!" Henry left, calling for us
in the other rooms. I pushed Tony as far back as I could,
towards the corner of the room under the bed. He was shaking
like a leaf behind me, and so was I, though I hoped he hadn't
noticed. Henry entered the bedroom again and even more
loudly, demanded that we come out right away.

The order was repeated and we crammed ourselves as
far back into the corner as our little bodies would allow. Henry
first checked the closet. Then his bare feet moved over to the
bed and his hands appeared. Once he spotted us, he got on one
knee and reached far back toward us. With escalating speed and
volume he ordered, "Get-out-of-there-right-*now*!" Pressing
myself harder against the wall didn't help; he got hold of my
ankle and dragged me out. My crying was mute in comparison
to the shrill shriek that Tony released. As Henry went back to
pull him out, I grabbed his leg and bit as hard as I could. He
wheeled around and picked me up by my neck. Screaming, I
tried to look into his eyes but they bored right through me. He
gave me a quick backhand to the stomach and dropped me. As I

hit the floor, Karen rushed into the room and began pulling on Henry and crying, "Leave them alone!"

Henry shoved her back and started again for Tony. I could barely breathe and was helpless to stop him. Henry pulled him from under the bed and smacked him across the face, yelling, "You boys don't hide from me!"

Karen announced, "I called the police!" and fled the room. Henry chased after her and they ran right on out of the house.

Tony came over to me and tearfully asked, "Are you okay?"

"Let's go," I whimpered. We went out to the backyard and began to climb a huge pomegranate tree. Up as high as we could go, we clung to the tree, covered in foliage. Still crying, we stayed there until we saw the police lights. "Come on, let's go tell them." The only thing I remembered our social worker drilling into us was to find a police officer when you're scared. And in the middle of the night, twenty feet off the ground, I thought this counted.

We approached the back of the police cruiser and saw Henry in handcuffs, sitting on the curb. We walked over to Karen who bent down to us and softly said, "Let's go inside."

In the policeman's direction I voiced, "Daddy's being mean."

Karen smiled and pushed while commenting, "Don't worry, the nice policeman are going to talk to Daddy. Everything's gonna be okay." She led us by the hand and sat us at the dinner table. In a meek voice, she began to try and explain. "Daddy is having a bad day. You know he loves you, right, boys?" She continued further with how sorry Daddy was, and how, if he said he was sorry, we should forgive him. *We were being set up.* She had made up a story to cover for him and didn't press charges—no sooner had she finished speaking, than he walked back into the house, with no police and no apology. He went straight to his room and shut the door. We could hear the click of the lock and that was all.

With uneasy hands, Karen poured us warmed chocolate milk and set down a plate of cookies. She continued to try to convince herself aloud, repeating how we all make mistakes and how he really didn't mean it. I just stared into my mug as the bubbles in my chocolate milk slowly swirled, trying to understand what was happening in our new home. When I broke my stare and looked up, Karen was checking Tony's face and putting a bag of frozen peas over his cheek. I looked up at her as she started toward me, hoping that she was going to explain what was going on, but she didn't. She checked for a mark on my stomach and began rubbing my belly. She started crying. I put my head on her lap and she took in a deep breath before suggesting that we go lie down. I got in the top bunk and Karen got in the bottom with Tony. She embraced him and began a soft song that comforted us to sleep.

Days went by without a word from Henry, until one night, while watching the Dukes of Hazzard, Tony nudged me to look back. I turned to see Karen face down on the couch with Henry on top of her, moving around. He saw us. "What the f*** are you looking at?!! Turn around or go to bed!" I quickly complied, not knowing why he was so upset. After all, I was only five years old.

But it wouldn't be long before I would find out. One night I got up from bed to get a drink of water. I made my way to the water cooler next to their doorway, placed my mouth over the faucet and pressed the button. I could hear them making noise, so I peered around the doorway. I could see them clearly by the light of a candle. Henry was on top of Karen, moving around again. He was holding her wrists against the headboard and her face said she was in pain. I wasn't going to try to understand their actions; the sight just made me more fearful of Henry.

There were many incidents of a sexual or sensual nature that occurred while we stayed with them, and each of these occurrences made it harder for us to figure out our place in our new home. They didn't show discretion in their sexual lives; at times we were made to wait in our bedroom while they used the living room for their encounters. It was only a short while before the sexual appetite in the home moved in Tony's and my direction.

First there was bath time. Karen insisted on being in the bath with us and made us wash her after she washed us. She had us wash her everywhere and vice versa. Tony and I both knew that we were doing something wrong, and we were too ashamed to say anything to each other about it. Then one day Henry came home early from work and popped his head into the bathroom. At the sight of us all bathing together, he began yelling that we were too old to need to be bathed by her. The baths stopped.

The less we saw of Henry, the more experiments started taking over our afternoons, usually after she had finished a small bottle of something. She would still be in her nightgown and take it off right in front of us, telling us to rub her. It quickly became the custom for us to earn the right to go outside and play in this manner.

Then there was the kissing. Karen had made a game of getting us to French kiss her. We both complained that it was gross, but she offered us pastry rewards and the like for the one who would do it the longest. She fondled us and made us lie naked with her on the couch. She directed our small hands to the places she wanted, laughing, giggling and cooing all the while. Although it is unhealthy to contemplate, these intimate times became my most cherished thoughts of our mother figure. These were the only kind attentions that we received from her. While we never talked negatively about these incidents or afternoons, we never talked positively about them, either. Our special time with "Mommy" was always followed with the threat, "Don't tell Daddy or he'll get mad again."

While Henry hit us first and hardest, Karen hit us most often. She went right from our intimate sessions to swinging paddles at our backsides before her boredom could set in. As soon as Henry halted our baths and the kisses weren't satisfying anymore, the intimate sessions were completely replaced by her pointing out our errors, physically. We would be hit for almost everything, from leaving the toilet seat up to not putting our toys away. We couldn't keep up with all of her directions, and missing one earned us a physical reminder. I'm sure she also felt she could purge her conscience for the inappropriate touching if she was a good disciplinarian.

It is strange how often adults have such high expectations of children that they didn't raise. They almost always demand that you call them "Mother" and "Father" immediately, as though we could recognize their insecure need for instant gratitude. Or they expect you to heed every word the first time and *never* forget the rules about where everything goes in their house. And it was always *their* house. Never was the terminology or ideology of "Our Home" used to actually help us bond with our current parents. Always on the back burner was the fact that you were expendable and all they had to do was make a phone call to get rid of you. Often we were even told that there were many other children waiting for a home who could take our place. Hearing this puts you on eggshells, trying to do whatever you are asked and accept whatever happens, so that you can stay. The penalty for breaking the harmony that *surely* existed before we arrived was always paid in full by the little children who were unable to grasp the rules and intimidated against standing up for themselves.

Karen often hit us until she was out of breath, then stuffed us into the hall closet, next to the ironing board and the vacuum cleaner. After that we inevitably faced two fates: Either she would let us out and tearfully apologize, then let us go out to play, or two, she would try to persuade us how we had brought it upon ourselves. We would stand there, swaying on sore legs, as she droned on about how we were at fault. After a while, she would ask us to repeat what she had said, and inevitably it wasn't accurate enough for her. Then entire process would be repeated until she gave up or let us go outside.

There was a time Karen fell asleep on the couch with an empty glass at her side, after hitting us and putting us into the closet. Tony and I began playing with the ironing board, rubbing our fingers up and down its perforated length to make music. Realizing she hadn't responded to our melody, I checked the closet door, which she often locked, and opened it, to see her passed out. I grabbed Tony's hand and led him outside and up the pomegranate tree. We stayed there until long after dark. We vented our feelings about our situation and talked about running away.

We waited for what seemed like forever for something to happen. Finally Henry's car, an old, dusty, mid-70's station wagon, pulled up. As his engine stopped and his door creaked open, Karen emerged from the back door, calling for us. *The horror of the next few hours burns my brain even today.* After they found us and got us back in the house, they took turns beating us, Henry with his belt and Karen with her wooden paddles. Yes paddles, plural, because in the process of hitting me she broke her favorite paddle over my butt and grew even more enraged. They handed us from one to the other, taking turns with their teaching methods. I learned something all right that night—to stay in the closet, no matter what.

As we went to bed without lunch or dinner, I couldn't help feeling responsible for Tony's beating. I repeated over and over in my mind how Tony wouldn't hurt right now if I had only stayed in the closet like we were supposed to. I had let him down.

Can you imagine? A five-year-old boy taking responsibility for the abuse dealt to him and his younger brother by their "mother and father." More confusing than that was trying to cope with how far they would take things. We never knew to what extent we would be beaten. What was their threshold? When would these strangers be satisfied and stop hitting? Many times, instinctively, I feared they would keep striking us until we *had* to stop crying, because we'd be dead.

That day above all others I feared for Tony and me. We should have stayed in the closet.

Henry didn't usually get involved in our ritual of discipline unless Karen had left a visible mark. If Henry took his eyes off the television long enough to play father and noticed a bruise, welt, or cut, the trouble really began. He would question her about the marks and the events leading to our discipline. Karen embellished the account to justify her actions, meaning that she always failed to mention any amount of alcohol she had consumed before her overreaction to our *grave sinful acts.* This would work him up to take off his belt and begin his turn. He would proclaim his rage at us for making her day so difficult. His hits were as vicious as his booming voice. "Little man's syndrome," I've come to recognize. You see, Henry was a mere five foot three—but to a five-year-old he was a giant. He swung with no regard to our size ratios, and the marks he left lasted days—long after the welts Karen made had vanished.

Did we tell? Tell whom? Up to the date of writing this book, in most states, there was no mandated continuous training for people who became foster parents. And with only the lame excuse of, "There isn't enough time in the scheduled workday," most social workers have a very poor record of keeping up visits with children on their caseload. Our social worker visited only a few times a year—maybe. An extra visit might be warranted if our foster parents needed more money than had been allotted them for food and clothes. It was only then, when they made the request for more money or to complain that their check hadn't arrived on time, that our social worker remembered Tony and me and came for a visit.

We would either be accidentally "gone" when the social worker arrived, or professionally prepped. If they decided to face the social worker—*or were just bold enough*—Henry and Karen would take us out to dinner the Saturday and Sunday before the scheduled visit, and to the arcades, parks and on shopping trips. I had no idea why we were being buttered up;

we were simply happy to be doing something fun. All of a sudden, we would hear a knock on the door, or a *request* to come downstairs for company. Karen and Henry would bring up the weekend events and report how we were only getting into mischief occasionally. When the worker turned her few minutes of attention to us, what could we say? "They have been beating the mess out of us and we want a new home, *NOW!*" We didn't even know that was an option. Besides, there was no way a child, in fear of what they thought was normal punishment for their bad behavior, would say anything negative right in front of the perpetrators and possibly incur further punishment. Playing expertly on our short-term memory, one of them would ask a rhetorical question such as, "Did you have fun at the pizza parlor?" or "Tell the nice lady about your new clothes." *And you already know it worked.* Just as they planned, we sang about our weekend, which had been bliss compared to our typical days in their home.

Riding on a cloud of what seemed like parental affection after these visits, reality would set in within a matter of days. Inevitably, Tony or I would fail to meet the house expectations and the pattern would be repeated. How I wish just one social worker had pulled us to the side and explained that we had a choice, explained that this didn't have to be our reality. Our social workers left us under the impression that this was our permanent living arrangement and that we were lucky to have foster parents who would take us both in. Add to that the way Henry and Karen constantly reminded us of their generosity and of how "good" we had it. After all, we could be living on the street with no one to feed us. So they had us believing.

More terrifying than our first summer in their home was our first autumn, when I was enrolled in school. I constantly ran away from school and back to their house, only a few blocks away, concerned for Tony's safety. Imagining the abuse he must be enduring by himself was too distracting. Even though deep down, I knew that I couldn't really prevent anything, I'd rather they focused on me than him. I loved him so much. He was all I had and I was willing to take any beating in his place.

Much of the school year went this way. Karen and the school officials had meetings to discuss my potential, as observed by the teacher. They discussed ways to keep me in class. I wanted to yell out, to report my pain to the teacher. But what would come of it? Would we get hit for telling? Or would their threats come true; would they throw us out on the streets to fend for ourselves? It wasn't hard for them to toy with our child brains and keep us guessing. Karen would explain away any visible marks or bruises to the teacher, and there was never any follow-through. She even had me moved to a different school in the middle of the year; maybe it was for convenience, but more likely it was to avoid potentially damaging inquiries.

In frustration, I misbehaved, fighting, swearing, and running away from the school officials, getting myself marked as "that troubled foster kid." I had no schoolmate friends, and didn't try to make any. I was the new, weird kid with thick glasses and generic clothing. My schoolmates pointed fingers, ridiculed and excluded me. Most of them had grown up together and stood as one in pointing their fingers and humiliating me. Sometimes I would build the courage to respond to them physically, and that behavior brought down the wrath of Henry and Karen. I hardly remember a time with them when I wasn't being hit or locked in that damn closet.

The benefit was that Tony was sometimes hailed as the "good one." His beatings became infrequent and eventually rare—and for me, it was worth every blow I took. I would've taken a hundred more if I could have taken back the ones he had received. And it was in my small way of shielding my brother that I learned a measure of self-sacrifice. But even with the intent of keeping Tony out of harm's way, my actions managed to overspill to him at times.

Awakened by the sounds of Henry and Karen's sexual regimen, I would routinely get a drink from the water cooler and go to the toilet. One night, Henry had left his blue jeans on the bathroom floor. I searched the pockets and found his wallet, and in a leather case attached to the belt, a folding knife. My attention turned first to the knife. I quickly opened it up. The blade mesmerized me. I ran my finger slowly up and down the cold metal. It was so heavy! I stabbed the air. I froze as I thought I heard footsteps. I strained my ear. Nothing more. Then again the faint sound of their continued session. I climbed into the bathtub and with the utmost precision, drew the shower curtain.

I opened the wallet and found two bills—a ten and a five. I thought I was so smart! I reasoned I would take the five, leaving the larger bill, so that my withdrawal would go unnoticed. I slipped the bill in my underwear, placed the wallet back in the jeans and grabbed the knife out of the tub. The blade had locked into place and I struggled to force it shut. I laid the back of the blade on the sink and pushed down with all my strength without any success. My eyes started to tear up in frustration. I knew that if I couldn't close the knife I might as well walk in their room and yell, "I was playing with your knife!" I began to fear the thought of Henry's tireless hand against my body. My eyes welled up so that I couldn't even see the job at hand. I wiped my tears and held the knife up. I examined it, desperately searching for a moving part. I flipped it over and over but couldn't see anything. I squeezed my eyes shut; hoping I could wake up from this nightmare. Nothing.

I filled my chest with air and then opened my eyes with a determined optimism. I again felt the length of the contraption. But this time I found it—the locking counter metal screamed out to me. I pushed as hard as I could down on the metal but lacked the strength to depress it enough to close the blade. I pushed and pushed until my tug of war was finally over—the knife gave in to me. I closed it and had to pee again.

In the morning, I showed Tony our spoils, though I left out where I had gained our new fortune. We went to the corner mom and pop store and quickly located the one-cent candies. And you can be sure we did our best to count out five hundred candies. We argued over who was going to pay the clerk, thinking she would be suspicious. It took both of us to carry the candy to the counter and I tossed the bill to her, hoping she didn't notice my shaking hand. The clerk didn't even bat an eye as she counted the candies and helped us fill the order.

We hid behind an abandoned, rusted out car behind my school. We opened the candies with blazing speed at first, devouring the tiny jelly-filled fruit drops as fast as we could tear their wrappers off. Sharing laughter, I made a joke of how close we were to the school. We peeked over the metal carcass and ducked back quickly, thinking the buildings were going to report us. We stayed there for hours. When we got thirsty, we sneaked onto the playground and drank from the fountain. When we had to pee, we went behind the car. We shared an idea or two of staying safe behind our car forever. We thought we were free that day.

As evening fell, hunger and anxiety took over and we gave in to going back to the house. Karen was in the kitchen and once she heard the screen door shut—cursed screen door—she stormed into the living room. She grabbed my arm and swung me across the room, then got hold of Tony and pinned him against the wall. I ran toward her and was leveled with a backhand. She turned to me and began yelling. As she started toward me, Tony ran down the hall and into our room, darting under the bed. She snatched the phone off the wall and called Henry. The wooden paddle was next and she placed a call to my backside.

She wailed until she was out of breath, dangling me by one arm and swinging at me with the other. All I could see was her long black hair swirling around me as I twisted in her grip, being hit from side to side. I fell to the floor when she finally let go. She strolled back to the bedroom to retrieve Tony. "Don't make me pull you out of there!" I could hear. She returned with him, then locked away her troubles in the closet, waiting until she could muster a second wind. For a child's hour we waited, sweaty and cramped, for her, but it was Henry who opened the door next.

He yanked us out and pulled us to the middle of the living room. I lay dormant, exhausted and out of tears. He gave the order to stand, and when I did, he sat on the couch, belt in hand, and began the interrogation. "Who took the money from my wallet? There is nothing I hate more than a thief and a liar!" My plan hadn't worked and he must have noticed the withdrawal right away, or maybe at lunchtime. I know now that if you're living from paycheck to paycheck, you know where every dollar is. He didn't mention our absence, just the money. Didn't he know we had been gone all day? I was completely terrified as I stood in front of him. My legs tingled from being stacked in the closet under Tony for so long and it took all my strength to keep from falling over. I wanted to lie down and stretch so badly. I had dropped to the floor during a previous "lesson" and was kicked for doing so. Again the question rang out, but I didn't respond.

Henry grabbed Tony forcefully, his frustration at our silence obvious, and started swinging. Immediately I began yelling out that I was to blame. But it was too late, Henry had to be satisfied before he would stop. Karen came over and lifted me off the floor by my shoulders to prevent me from interfering with him. I kicked and yelled, but I was powerless. My tears found their way back to my eyes as I cried and screamed to attract his rage.

Henry released Tony, who collapsed into a puddle, and turned toward me. He swung with no regard to where his belt would land. He continued swinging and slapping me while yelling, "Stupid!" "Liar!" "Thief!" Karen let me go and finally I fell. Henry continued to strike and began kicking me as I lay on the floor, unable to gather enough strength to tense my body or ball up. He yelled, "I'll teach you to steal from me!" Each blow felt fainter and fainter to me, as its impact became more a sound ringing in my head than a blow to my nerve endings.

Sent to bed without first aid or food, hours later I craved death for the first of many times. I didn't know of an afterlife, but desired silence and relief from my throbbing body. But I had to stay...for him. My voice shook as I held my little brother and whispered, "I'm sorry, Tony."

Little did we suspect then, that before long, our "home" was to be replaced with another. Karen had recently started a new job at the local gas station. While serving dinner one evening, she let Henry in on a little secret of hers. Since she had started her new job, she had met and fornicated with her new love, a fellow Quik Stop clerk. Henry didn't take this at all lightly. He yelled and slapped her across the dining room. Karen got up as if nothing had happened, and began to fix our dinner plates, then sat down next to me at the head of the table and began her meal. But Henry wasn't done. He grabbed her long black hair and pulled her backwards in her chair. She hit the floor with a gasp and a loud thud; then there was silence. She had been knocked unconscious. But Henry began kicking her and voicing his disapproval with long strings of profanity.

Thinking she might be dead, I got up and shielded her body with my own. I don't know why my instinct was to protect her. Maybe I subconsciously recalled our first month in her care, when we basked in her affections. My actions gave Henry a new target—one that moved and would make the noises that pleasured him. Henry vented on me for a minute, then turned to command Tony to stop crying. He paused, catching sight of Karen's motionless body, and was stricken with her reality. Hoping he hadn't killed her, in a purely ironic gesture, he tried to revive her by slapping her across the face and swearing at her.

She revived in a minute, in pain and disoriented. Henry threw her arm over his shoulder and assisted her to their bedroom. You could hear their pathetic apologies and promises clearly, since he hadn't shut the door completely. He hugged her, more, I'm sure, in relief than sincere concern.

Late that night we were awakened to what I now understand to be "You're mine and I'll prove it" sex. Tony asked what was going on, and not hearing any screams or punching, I simply replied, "It's okay. Mom and Dad are making nice. Just go to sleep." We fell back asleep quickly, as the sounds of their session was nothing new to our ears.

The next few days were the longest and loudest we had ever spent in their custody. They went back and forth from snapping at each other over every little thing to cuddling on the couch. And you can believe they didn't exclude us from their roller coaster. Punishments either doubled or we received no consequences at all. They would send us out of the house often, so that they could have private time—namely, rough sex that could be heard anywhere in our yard.

Church now became a weekly activity. Tony and I often fell asleep on the long, padded wooden benches. Henry and Karen would get handshakes and hugs, once people found out that we were their foster children. Remarks of "How sweet," and "You boys sure are lucky to have such a nice Mommy and Daddy," haunted our ears as they were often echoed. This, of course, gave them immediate acceptance and involvement in the inner circle of the churchgoers. Henry played bass guitar in the church band and Karen started assisting with the Sunday school class. But their new-found religion didn't change a thing on our home front, and the roller coaster continued.

Tony and I had constantly wet the bed and began having incontinent episodes while we were outside, because we were afraid to go in the house to use the toilet. Naturally, this was a punishable offense, because it had developed in their home and could therefore reasonably be beaten out of us. The fact that my social service file said that I had been sodomized as a toddler, causing immeasurable damage, wasn't taken into account. We were smacked around and sent to bed without lunch or dinner for our transgressions. Frustrated after cleaning our underpants several times, Karen made me wear them, full of feces, on my head and sent us outside. I was the older one so, she reasoned, Tony would stop if I did, right?

We climbed the pomegranate tree, known to us as our "safe" tree, and I climbed up higher than I ever had before. Tony started to get scared for me and told me to come down. The treetop swayed in the wind and I held on in sheer panic. Eventually, we were called to come in, but I was too afraid to move. Tony got down and told Karen where I was and she came out to talk me down. Once inside, she told me how upset she was that I had been so high in the tree. *Probably just worried someone might see me and then she'd have to explain.* She slapped me on the head and knocked me off balance, forcing me to bounce off the wall and fall to the floor. She yelled at me for being so stupid, and again got down her paddle. About a dozen swings or so was all her obese body could rally before she was out of wind and sent me to the closet, soiled underwear still on my head; alone this time. I sat in there balled up, whimpering to myself. I had lots of time to think about what I could do to make her happy so she would stop hitting us. I made promises to myself to be a good boy and not a stupid one—promises that, if my life with Henry and Karen so far meant anything, I was surely not going to be able to keep. When Henry got home, not a word was spoken about the tree and we were directly sent outside so they could indulge in their intimate session.

Wanting to escape the jungle, Tony and I often visited a neighbor's house to play with his son. Marbles was the neighborhood game, and I practiced enough to become a capable player. One day I soundly beat my neighbor and began walking home with his marbles and my own, so in anger he sent his German shepherd after us. We ran hard, but our short legs were no match for the large dog. I threw the marbles down behind me, but he kept coming. The animal lunged at my backside and sank his razor sharp canines into my leg. After snatching a souvenir, the beast turned around and returned home for his master's praise.

I got up slowly and was bewildered by the lack of pain. Tony and I walked into the house cautiously and went straight to our room. I pulled my pants down and could only see a bloody mess. My leg began shaking rapidly. Tears began to stream down my face and my skin started tingling all over, then a rush of pain swept through me in a wave. Tony wanted to go tell Karen but I wouldn't let him, thinking of how mad they'd be if he knocked on their door. I pulled on Tony's arm but he got loose and I lost my balance, falling to the ground.

Tony came back in the room with a half naked Karen in tow. She immediately shrieked, picked me up, and carried me to the bathtub. The second she turned on the water, the all-over pain turned into a fire at the bite. Henry casually walked in, wearing only underwear and scratching himself, and once he was briefed he, as expected, got angry at us; not for the bite, but for not telling them right away. He again reminded me how stupid I was and then went away. Karen poured peroxide over the bite and dressed it, sending us off to bed.

The next day at school I complained of the pain in my leg and was sent to the nurse. The nurse took my pants down and gasped at the sight of my wound. I was immediately rushed to the hospital and my social worker was called, as well as the police. I talked to them after getting a rabies shot and some stitches. I never had to go back Henry and Karen's house again. I met up with Tony while waiting at the pharmacy with a cop.

The official story was neglect, and when asked if they wanted us back, they said they were separating and neither would be able to take us. An uncontrollably enormous smile raced to my face where our new orphanage director thought a frown belonged. After a year, we were free of them.

We brought an assumption of peace with us to the orphanage. After all, nothing could be worse than what we had just been through, right? Although worried about what would happen next, we found some serenity in just being with each other. Because of that bond, we were able to sleep deeply, happy to be away from them and happy to be together. That night we had a safe bed, but our search for a home wasn't over, it was only beginning.

Chapter 2 - Smoke and Mirrors

Within a few weeks of our recuperation at Father Matthew's Home for Boys, Tom and Donna showed up and took us out for an afternoon. They were related to Karen and Henry and had seen us during the holidays. Social workers, although well intentioned, mistakenly thought that this was an optimum placement for us, since we were familiar with them and they were willing to take us both. Tom and Donna found out about some of the abuse from our orphanage director, and reported that Henry had checked himself into a drug rehabilitation center. We learned this by overhearing a conversation the couple had with the social worker before taking us on a home visit. But it apparently was not enough of a problem to deter another placement in the same family circle. In a rush to move us, we were promptly sent home with Tom and Donna.

Carried out with such swiftness, it was impossible that this decision was made with serious inquiry or a thorough check of Tom and Donna's living arrangements. Being tossed around like a piece of meat or an inanimate object plays hard on your self-esteem. You feel like you should be grateful, no matter where you land—as though you have no value. We were only asked what we wanted after a decision had been made. But we wouldn't have argued anyway. We wanted to be part of a family, even if we didn't really know what that meant. We did know that we'd rather move than stay in the boy's home at the mercy of aggressive older peers. So we moved from placement to placement, never thinking to say, "No, we don't want to go live with them."

Foster Parent/Guardian Rule No. 2: *Offer A "Home"*

Check the boat! Take a close look at the hull, deck, and cabins before adding passengers. See if you really are up to the commitment; acknowledge both your own and the child's emotional precipitating factors and make sure that the fit is right. Don't be part of another pit stop or "placement failure."

We sat in another living room with all that belonged to us in traditional System suitcases—black plastic lawn bags, filled with clothes and a few toys. The silence was broken with an offer to show us our room. Unlike Henry and Karen, Tom and Donna didn't try to assume the role of the traditional Mom and Dad; they continued to remain Aunt and Uncle.

We were mostly in wonder of their whereabouts. Tony and I hung out in the streets and spent long hours playing together. We danced together when a good song came on the radio, and had fruit-throwing fights with the neighbor kids. We visited the homes of our neighbors and sometimes they offered us treats. A large Mexican family across the street shared unusual dishes with us and even taught us a little Spanish. Days flew by between playing, sleeping and smiling. We wrestled, explored, and chased each other in all sorts of games. We were so happy then. Tony and I were all the family we needed.

We were almost always being watched by a babysitter—one of their two real teenage kids. We mostly saw Tom and Donna at dinner or when we all went to church. We did things that deserved discipline, but rarely got any. Tom wasn't aggressive like Henry. He wasn't small like him either, being somewhere around six foot eight. His responses were unemotional and predictable; and we began sharing information with him, good and bad.

Telling on each other or relaying something about school became easy with Tom. My attendance improved dramatically and I was getting all outstanding marks, often bringing home assignments with a gold star on them. At home, I was looked to as Tony's responsible older brother, and Tom explained that it was my job to look out for him. I wholeheartedly accepted the assignment that before had only been internalized.

While playing one Sunday after church, Tony was almost stuck by a car while chasing after a ball. I ran after him and pushed him further across the street. The car swerved, missing both of us, and Tom ran out of the house. Man, if I didn't just about piss my pants as he towered over me. When he reached down, I flinched, curled up, and hoped that my spanking would be over with quickly. But Tom just picked me up like a large basketball and placed me next to Tony. He checked to see if we were okay and in his deep, soothing voice, told us to be careful and play only in the yard. He even commended me for pushing Tony out of the way! No swinging, no belts, or being locked in a closet. Just always calm Tom.

His wife seemed to be of the same temperament. Donna never snapped at us or even raised her voice. Every now and again she could be relied on to tuck us in or give us a good night kiss (without asking for tongue). Her nurturing way stood out the day I got stung by a bee. As I carried on like it was the end of the world, and Tony lent his support by crying for me, she applied a patch of mud and made funny faces. When the trauma was over, she kissed my wound and assured me that I would live. Tom and Donna made us feel safe and secure. Our lives had a consistent calm while we were with them and it felt good. I dared to think that maybe Tony and I had found a safe place, a place to call home.

The only pain that came was from their dog, a Doberman. While crawling around the floor pretending to be a dog, I made the mistake of pretending to share her meal with her. She didn't find me amusing and proceeded to bite at my skull a few times. I was very frightened of being eaten alive, and I struggled with her under the dining room table until Donna came in and called off the dog. I bled some, and was left with a few tiny bald spots. Needless to say, I learned my lesson and have never played with the food of canines again.

Like the whirlwind that brought us to this pleasant home, it came to an end just as abruptly. Donna tried to kill herself with an overdose of prescription pills and Tony found her passed out in a pool of her own blood. She had hit her head on the bathtub. Tony was very shaken and wasn't speaking. No matter how I tried, he wouldn't tell me what happened; he just clammed up and cried to himself. Without a clue, I was told that we were going back to Father Matthew's Orphanage. Going from what seemed like family harmony one day, to being told that it was over the next, I was caught off guard as reality smacked me in the face. It had only been a couple of months with them. The same two thoughts kept cycling in my head: *We would always be let down. We would always be abandoned.* We went to bed filled with anxiety, not understanding or knowing what was next.

Late into the night I stepped over into anger. *"What did we do?"* I thought. *"Why are we being moved?"* Believing that we were being betrayed, I worked most of the night on persuading Tony that we should run. Otherwise, who knew where we could end up? Maybe another home like Henry and Karen's, or worse. So we packed a few things in a trash bag, punched out the screen to our window and waited for morning's first light. (We were too afraid of the dark to leave sooner). I couldn't shut my eyes, trying to think of what I could do or where we could go. All night I played out scenarios in my mind, but I couldn't answer any of the basic questions that concerned being able to care for Tony and myself. So when morning came, I told Tony we weren't going anywhere. He kept pleading for me to get up so we could run away. I lay there, tormented by his pleas, but knowing that we were better off with a roof over our heads. I felt responsible for him. His safety was still my priority, and I knew that I couldn't feed him, clothe him, or protect him from the big bad world out there.

His requests finally ceased and we were roused by Tom to get ready to go. Off to Father Matthew's again with no physical pain, but twice the emotional disquiet.

Chapter 3 - Incarcerated Because our Family Deserted Us

Invisible Children. If you had to live in a state-funded placement, you would know why these two words are the perfect description for your position in life. You have no choice in what to eat, where to sleep, or even how to dress. Adults walk around you with an occasional look down to check that "the System" is humming along. For the most part every orphanage, every group home, and every institution is the same in this regard. So finding one staff or one social worker that steps out and chooses to see you is a miracle. You would marvel the instant another human reassuringly touched you, made eye contact, or acknowledged your existence. The wonder of being noticed. *I am six years old now, and today I am three-feet-something inches of invisible human child.*

Foster Parent/Guardian Rule No. 3: *Do No Harm.*

If all you do is provide a child a roof and a hot meal, you have done something good. But if you want to help, give them some space to release and express their emotions without taking it personally, and respond with empathy and compassion. No matter what, don't add injury to the insult and shame of not having a family.

This return to Father Matthew's felt somewhat familiar and I was lulled into a state of security (as defined by my life's experiences to this point). The house was a huge 1-story, 9-bedroom stronghold. Everything was locked and a large wooden fence reinforced by thick, tall hedges and trees surrounded the place. The youths there were pretty much the same as before, teasing, tattling, fighting and so on. The strong smell of pine cleaner and bleach filled the halls. All the furniture and appliances were in the same places as when we left only a few months ago. Finally, the sight of the large "Peanuts" mural that spanned the entire hallway confirmed that we were somewhere we had lived before. You probably can fathom how two young orphans retreated into themselves every time they were bounced to live with each new set of strangers. But for once, we were returning somewhere we could remember. The familiarity, the uniformity of everything, really gave the impression that my brother and I would be okay here—at least until they found us a new family.

Although some out of the scores of names of all my foster siblings have faded, every detail and nuance of my stay at Father Matthew's is still with me. Clyde Peabody was in his late twenties or early thirties, was about five foot nine and proudly displayed his potbelly. He often wore teal or pink colored polo shirts, with tight khaki or white shorts. His hair was always slicked back and he loved telling little jokes, or, I should say, pointing out everyone else's insecurities or inadequacies to gain the older kids' acceptance or garner another staff's laughter. He was the most outstanding of the staff, and the only one that seemed just a little off. One example was the way he would walk up and down the hallway talking to himself and doing a two-handed snap fist-clap. He played a lot of games with the boys and constantly whipped the snot out of them. However, if you could prove yourself an adequate adversary, then you were put on his special "favorites" list and received preferential treatment, from extra desserts and privileges to the more coveted position of finger pointing with Clyde and being exempted from having any of Clyde's "jokes" played or told on you.

"Mean Gene the Restraining Machine" was a slender man, about six foot four with short, oily black curly hair. He had a natural tan and a large nose, exaggerated by his beady eyes. He was very muscular and would often take some of the older kids to play racquetball with him.

Augie was Clyde's right-hand-man. Short, pudgy and very round, his long hair and dark Mexican skin made him stand out from the other staff. He taught Clyde how to say curse words in Spanish and basically went along with whatever Clyde did.

And finally, out of those of any note, there was Richard, the director. He was of average build, stood six feet tall, and had reddish pale skin. A shiny bald pate protruded from brown hair that puffed out around his ears and joined with sideburns that connected to a full beard. It was hard to read his eyes, which were tucked behind his semi-thick, round-framed glasses. He seemed indifferent toward us, but we tried to stay near him because it was obvious that the other staff feared him. The rest of the staff rotated frequently, getting hired, fired, or quitting.

Upon our arrival, it seemed as though we were being greeted warmly. We were familiar with these people. But this perception didn't last long, mostly because we didn't have anything to offer. That means that we couldn't compete with the older kids in this 16-bed unit who could play Dungeons and Dragons with Clyde and Augie or break dance, among other things, for all the staff's entertainment. Rather, we and the other younger kids became quite the opposite—objects for ridicule and playthings for the staff's amusement. The older kids would prompt us to say curse words if we wanted to be their "friend," or would have us fight with one of the other young ones— almost like fighting chickens or dogs, each older kid had a younger one as their "animal." Then, if the tide turned too much in favor of one competitor, the older boys would jump in to equal out the abuse. This jailhouse living arrangement was anything but safe.

A few of the kids placed there were those who had taken their family's love for granted—"the spoiled brats." They fought school officials and/or their families and were placed at

Father Matthew's for a drastic discipline. Others were behavioral health cases—"the crazies"—who were deemed uncontrollable and were there for a respite until their new medications had made them normal again. The majority were Child Protective Services (CPS) abuse cases—"the punks"—and the probation department placed a rare few delinquents—"the criminals"—there at that age.

Most of the stories that could be told in that building would make your blood boil. There were boys who had been exploited, molested, raped, demoralized, browbeaten, severely battered, tortured, or had been forced into some form of child prostitution. Many of the children had displayed violent behavior in reaction to what had happened to them. Nearly all of our roommates had come from poor families, but the vast majority of our housemates had some member of their family still looking out for them. This made for the one thing that they could always stand together and look down at Tony and me for—we didn't have any family "on the outside."

As I shoved our plastic bags into our locker closet, I told Tony not to worry, "They'll find a good family for us soon." It is staggering how fast a child can acclimate to his circumstances, good or bad, and face the new reality with some type of order. I don't recall when I first became aware that our "real" mother and father were never coming to get us. So I offered Tony the only hope I could—that we would be placed with another family soon. I felt it was my duty to digest any information and spoon-feed reality to my little brother. Maybe I thought I could somehow make his transition easier. We had been moved, processed, and given a room. After putting our clothes away, I knew all that was left was to try and figure out where we would play into things this time around, where or if we fit in, until we moved on. As we waited for that to happen, I knew it was on my shoulders to protect my little brother and myself.

The staff functioned exactly like corrections officers. Although our only crime was that we were the spawn of the degenerates and irresponsible of society; we found ourselves grouped with the "bad" kids who needed therapy and treatment to redirect what was called "oppositional" behavior. A giant board tracked literal pluses and minuses for every action or offense committed every day. We had a very specific schedule to follow and had to ask to eat or use the bathroom. Our speech was monitored and our possessions were regularly searched. Many of the staff made something of a game of the power they wielded over us. And the "bad" kids learned the rules quickly; prospering much the same way adult prisoners do.

Besides lists of chores, our small tortures—behavior modification treatments—ranged from five-hundred to a thousand sentences of "I will not talk back to staff or swear," to standing at the wall for hours on end, to the ultimate punishment, being restrained. The "game-playing" staff gave us demeaning nicknames, manipulated the older kids against us, or made us eat a plateful of our most loathed food. The "head" or older boys would take turns holding us down and farting on our heads, giving us wedgies or committing other such indignities on us. Small fights with other kids always landed us in early beds or without the fifty-cent to two-dollar allowance that was part of our behavior incentive program.

Two fights in particular come to the forefront of my mind: one with Tim and another with the twins, Byron and Myron. Tim was one of the older boys, and while I was finishing a chore, he had been trying to force Tony to give up one of the few toys we had. I came into the room and was immediately enraged at the sight of Tony pinned up against the wall by Tim. I jumped the bed and landed on his back. His head caught the corner of the closet door and split his cheek open.

Staff rushed the room at his cries. I found myself on the floor being crushed by two staff while another attended to Tim. Tony explained later what had happened, but that didn't get me out of standing at the wall for an hour staring at the giant Snoopy, or the thousand sentences of "I will not fight with my peers." However, the explanation, as well as Tim's bandages, had gotten me acclaim and embarrassed Tim far beyond words in group-home land.

For these reasons Tim, being the big tough guy, decided to ambush me in the hallway. He waited in the alcove by rooms 1 and 2 right before school time. Poised with a sharpened pencil, his first strike stabbed my ear and my wrist blocked his second. Staff rushed him and held him up against the wall. I lay on the cold linoleum floor, watching the staff hold Tony back and looking at the blood on my hand. I remember being terrified as, due to shock, my hearing seemed muffled. I feared never being able to hear again. As I was picked up and ushered to the dining table, I could see Tim in tears and apologizing. I don't think he truly understood what his actions could result in, and was either in fear of being locked up or utterly shocked that he had made someone else bleed.

They took me to the emergency room and got me on an operating table right away. As the doctor was pulling broken graphite from my ear, I was plotting revenge. It happened that the pencil didn't penetrate my eardrum, but only pierced the cartilage.

I returned with a few stitches to find Tim gone. He had been arrested and wouldn't be coming back. Clyde Peabody didn't like this much as Tim was one of his favorites. I had to put up with Mr. Peabody looking for any opportunity to punish me within his means for the rest of my time there. He didn't stop any of the older kids from hitting me or committing any of the other normal tortures. In fact, I'm sure he probably had a hand in telling them to focus on me. His big opportunity came soon, as yet another squabble arose, this time with the twins.

Byron and Myron were not older or much bigger than me, but there were two of them. They used this advantage to push around the younger kids and ally themselves with the older ones. On top of that, the staff favored them because these two little black boys could break dance better than Turbo from the movie "Breakin'." In the course of lobbying for power, Myron targeted Tony and was trying to take his snack from him. He had pushed him into their room and had him cornered. I looked around for Tony, once I had gotten my snack, and one of the other younger kids eyed the Twins' door.

I sped into the room and commanded, "Leave him alone!" Myron flashed a fierce brow my way and told me to shut up. Byron got up on the bed and kicked toward my head. He missed and I threw a wild kick his way. It landed right at his knee and it folded, sending him plunging backward off the bed. Myron darted toward his brother and yelled out for staff. I grabbed Tony by his arm and raced down the hallway, into our room and shut the door behind us.

Staff entered our room shortly after and asked us what happened. Tony quickly blurted out the truth, focusing on Myron's role. Tony was visibly shaken and his snack was still in the twins' room. But Clyde found a way to turn matters around and told us that Byron had been knocked unconscious for a few minutes. True or not, I don't know, but with his axe to grind, I didn't put it beyond him to add a little extra to make sure I got some punishment.

Clyde flexed his power and had Tony and me separated, giving us each a new roommate. I didn't take this lightly and threw a fit, which in turn gave him a reason to restrain me and deal out even more consequences. Now let me explain the technique involved in the "restraining procedure": I was made to stand at the wall, often well into the night, and every thirty minutes or so was "restrained." Clyde would come up behind me, take hold of my wrists, cross both of my arms in front of me and then pull them together behind my back. He would hold them like this for thirty seconds to a minute, depending on how long it took for your arms to go numb, which was marked by your lack of strength to struggle. When he released, you had better stay standing or he would restrain you again and add time to your sentence.

Tony refused to watch me cry without some intervention; so he kicked Clyde in the leg during my first restraint—a fly trying to bully a hippo. Clyde let me go and I fell to the ground and tried to catch my breath. Clyde chased Tony to his room and sent Augie in to take care of him. I could hear my little brother's cries and it tore me up. Clyde started toward me and I quickly rose and faced the wall, crying. It didn't help and he grabbed me and restrained me again. He held on for eternity and I couldn't breathe. It felt like a fire had erupted in my head and I began kicking, trying to get loose. I pissed myself and some must have gotten on him because he dropped me.

I laid there barely conscious of anything, seeing the world in a blur. My head was swimming; I could see Clyde's lips moving but couldn't make out a single word. He pushed me onto my back and then sat me up against the wall. When the room stopped spinning, he put me in a chair at our large dining table. He shook my shoulders repeatedly and eventually I made out that he was saying, "Are you okay?" In an almost raspy whisper, he kept repeating himself until I nodded my head affirmatively. He then got me up and said I could go to bed.

As I stood up, Richard grabbed under my arm and asked if I was okay. Clyde had the look of a ghost on his face and was sent to the office. Richard took me to my room and told me to "be a good boy and you won't have to be restrained anymore." Augie left my crying brother behind with me and was ushered out by Richard. I hadn't the sense or time to ask Tony if he was okay—my head was throbbing and I was lightheaded. I laid my head on my pillow and fell asleep very quickly. I recall a staff waking me up a couple of times during the night with the question, "Louie, are you okay?"

Chapter 4 - A True Orphan

"Without love ...children tend to die."
—Love and Its Place in Nature, by Jonathan Lear

How can I possibly relay what it is like to be an orphan? Do the words exist that can give you an inkling of what it is like to absolutely not have one soul on earth to look to for love or comfort? Can you imagine never having your father hold you up in adoration; or your mother never encouraging you? What if your brother or sister were taken away? I think it is possible, if you really meditate, to at least get an idea of the sheer panic I felt as a child orphan. I hope that you can really soak in this next chapter, and not just say, "How horrible for that little boy."

Every week the house psychiatrist, Dr. Sandler, would take the kid with the most behavior points out to dinner at Bob's Big Boy—a very coveted prize. I didn't have the most points, but Dr. Sandler rationalized that I had made the most improvement and he was changing the rules this time. Now, I thought he was being truthful because everyone knew that the kid with the most points *wasn't* the best behaved, but rather the favorite of the collective staff. I didn't question why because I understood that going with the doctor meant that I wasn't going to be invisible, at least for one meal.

Oblivious to any other possible motive behind this outing and full of excitement, I went to Bob's Big Boy and ordered the Big Boy Combo and hot fudge sundae, which all

boys he brought had bragged about. We talked about Father
Matthew's and the other boys. I told him how the older boys
picked on Tony and me. I began to relate my heartfelt
commitment to my brother, why I felt it was my duty to look
out for him. He refocused the conversation on my feelings, the
fights and the points system. I freely offered him whatever
information he wanted; after all, today he was my best friend.

Dessert came and such a treat tasted like pure heaven
compared to my normal fare. I asked for a doggie bag for half
my hamburger, fries and sundae with the intention of sharing it
with Tony. Dr. Sandler convinced me to finish the sundae
because it would melt, but I wouldn't budge on the rest. I got
back to the house late and was directed to take a shower and go
immediately to bed. Gene took my food and promised to put it
in the refrigerator for Tony. I took a shower and went to bed
feeling like a million bucks. I slept soundly, content with the
taste of the hot fudge sundae playing over in my memory.

For an orphan, just one little extra event, like going out
to dinner, would make all the difference in the world to you. A
small individual activity like that could be enough to keep you
uplifted for a week, maybe two. Although my wish was that
Tony and I could have shared the experience, we understood
that it just didn't work that way. But when I found out the real
reason why I was chosen to go to Bob's Big Boy, I wasn't
uplifted for a week, or even a day. Instead, the weeks that
followed were going to be the most arduous I had consciously
ever faced.

I went through the morning rush of chores and went off
to school without realizing that Tony was gone. When I got
back to the group home and didn't see my brother, I was
outraged. My world swirled around me as I asked every staff
and kid for my brother's whereabouts but got no answers. The
staff kept trying to pacify me by passing the buck to the house
supervisor, "—who," they said, "will give you the answer when
he gets in."

"Why won't *you* tell me?!" I demanded.

I only got the same lame response: "I wasn't told everything; you'll have to wait for Richard." Richard didn't "get in" for another day and in that time I managed to get restrained almost non-stop. I refused to stand at the wall and threatened to run away. I futilely struck out at whomever was around, in severe desperation to have something happen, to find out something. All I wanted to know was where my little brother was, if he was okay, and if I'd see him again, but the most I got out of any staff was that he was all right and Richard would be in to tell me the rest soon. I refused to eat and found every opportunity to swear at the closest person. At school, this got me sent to the office, but I was shown leniency once I told the principal what I was so upset about. At the house I barely slept a moment while waiting for Richard to show.

On the third morning after Tony's disappearance, something changed. I didn't awake to staff's demands to get out of bed as usual. My eyes were wide as they took in the room; it was a school day and my roommate wasn't there. The sun wasn't supposed to be shining brightly when I woke up and I became worried about not being where I was supposed to be. *Had they forgotten me?* I got up and started toward the office. Richard and a female social worker directed me to the dining room to eat breakfast. The woman introduced herself and I knew then that Tony and I were going to get a new home. That was what the appearance of a social worker always meant to us.

She began with all the normal distractionary pleasantries. "You're quite a good looking young man," and "You must be very smart to get so many points on the board." Then came the lead in, "Tony is visiting with a family to see if you guys would like it there." The shock on my face must have been profound, because she paused for a few seconds.

"Why didn't we go together?"

"We think it would be better if this family saw you one at a time." She then started in on who these people were and how Tony would be back in a few days to see me. She sat next to me with a smile on her face and began to put her hand on my shoulder. *She sat there with a smile on her face!* Richard chimed in and corroborated her story. He told me not to worry, and reassured me that Tony was safe and in good hands. They continued to try to distract me with television and even took me out to the movies. Over and over I was told not to worry. Reassured constantly, my heart was somewhat tranquilized into trusting these words; I decided to wait to join Tony in our new home.

Only after a few weeks of impatience did I finally meet Tammie and Edward and their two pre-teen children. They brought me some small gifts and were very obviously nervous while speaking with me. *They'll get used to me.* I had a plan set in stone before they arrived. I would (1) hug my brother, (2) gather my belongings, and (3) go home with my brother and our new family. One, two, three— easy, right? Of course, there was no way I was going to let them separate us again.

Tony came up and I embraced him and put my arm over his shoulder, asking a flurry of questions. I didn't really listen to his answers; I was just relieved to finally be holding my little brother again. We walked back to my room and he showed me the new watch they had bought him. He reported on how nice they had been and how much fun he had been having. I showed him my packed plastic bag and excitedly reported, "Richard told me that I can go with you. I can't wait to see our new room." And before my sentence had weighed in Tony's mind, Tammie emerged and interrupted. She asked to talk to me in private and directed Tony to go ask "Dad" a question.

Recalling her words still sears my ears today with pain far greater than Tim's pencil ever produced. I was expecting Tammie to start telling me her house expectations or something of the like. I was utterly blown away when she told me what was to be my future reality. With staff filling the doorway behind her, she began trying to explain how Tony was having "bad dreams" and that they weren't ready for me to come and live with them, yet. She tried to reason that I should give him "some time" to adjust. *Just a thought, but maybe he was having bad dreams because you stole him away from his big brother!*

I immediately began to argue that Tony needed *me*. "I'm his brother!" Aggravation turned into hysteria at the thought of Tony living with them, apart from me, away from his big brother's protection. I repeatedly blared out, "No, you can't take him. I can help him, not you! He's *my* brother!"

The staff began ordering me to calm down. I flatly refused and began crying, screaming, and yelling, "She is going to take my brother away!"

Tammie backed out of the room and left, with Tony. They all left. When I was finally let out of my room, I ran down the hallway only to be stopped by Richard, right before the front door. I tried to squirm free, but the more I moved the tighter his grip grew. He wrestled me to the ground; lying on top of me he kept repeating, "Calm down, calm down."

My whole body burned as I tried to get free. I struggled and struggled without success. I screamed and tried to bite and scratch him. But my arms kept getting tucked under and my head pushed down against the hard floor. Knowing the other boys were watching, I wouldn't allow myself to cry out loud and instead let out a low, deep growl. I tried again and again to push for my freedom, but could barely feel my arms, and gave in. I fought in vain until I had no strength left. After a while, I lay still in defeat, sobbing, and Richard released his grip. I was powerless and my heart was turning as cold as the linoleum floor my face rested on. Richard hovered over me with one hand on my back and the other next to my head.

"It's going to be alright. They'll come back. Don't worry." Did he think I was a total fool? I *knew* they had taken him from me. I *knew* what the peace offering gifts were for—so they could bring Tony to visit without it being a fiasco. How could they think I could be bought off? They took my little brother! I was only six and a half, and they took him, *knowing* I couldn't do a damn thing! I let in to unstoppable tears until they ran out. Eventually, I was let up and directed to the staff office.

Richard apologized for having me pack my bags. "We were told that you were going to visit their home." Then some staff behind me offered that I had scared them away by raising my voice and demanding to go with them. Richard cleared his throat and shook his head. After that, I blocked a lot out. It was a while before I started to take in their words again. They tried to con me into thinking that it would be only a matter of time before this nice family came to sweep me off my feet as well. *If I was good, they would come back sooner.* And on and on, their words began blending with the hum in my head that cried for my little brother. The only family I had, the only person I cared about, the one I watched out for and would die for. They plucked him up like he was for sale, like I was an option—the older, ugly puppy left behind for the younger, cuter one.

Did I even get a chance to say goodbye? Was I given the dignity of being let in on their decision to separate us? Couldn't I have been at least told or prepped for such a drastic change to my daily life? Absolutely not. I was to endure this shock and pain by the skin of my teeth. And to add insult to injury, I was lied to and given false hope! Given the line of bull crap that I would soon be with my brother again, which was proven false in my mind by the fact that I wasn't even allowed to write or call him until *they* were "ready."

Was I good after that? *What the hell do you think?* I spent most of my evenings isolated in my room, staring out the window and counting the boards of the brown wooden fence. I plotted to run away and find my brother. The rest of the time I took every opportunity to release my rage. I got the crap kicked out of me by every big kid in the house, because I was the perfect target and I wouldn't back down. Clyde and Augie got several opportunities to restrain me and took many. They would send me to bed without dinner and with hundreds of sentences to write. I got put on house restriction—not allowed to go on activities. I didn't care and wouldn't relent. I threw whatever blows I could but was always overwhelmed by them in one way or another. Staring out the window, my eyes crimson and full of tears, the bruises they gave me seemed not to exist. I was a shell of a child. At six years old, I knew the true meaning of loss and loneliness.

Years later I would come to find out that my aggressive behavior was the excuse used to keep Tony and me separated. Ironic, or merely disgusting and unjust? Not that anyone had the intention to reunite me with Tony anyway, and this "reasoning" seemed to be adequate enough for the paperwork shufflers who never bothered to ask me. They simply read reports and made decisions about how my life was going to go. Months later I was still without contact from my brother, and the possibility of my living under the same roof with him began drifting away in my head.

What would you do if someone took your family away? At six and a half years old, I was blindsided and shoved down a path on a journey that I was powerless to prevent. There is nothing that I can write to accurately relay how empty my heart was, so please, do whatever helps you to feel. Put on "that one song" that reminds you of the lowest time in your life; meditate on the loss of someone special in your life. Whatever you do, reflect on your own experience and soak in those feelings before continuing on. I know that the next thirty or so pages are going to be the most difficult to write. My hands are trembling at the thought of having to put words to this part of my life.

To have my brother ripped away from me was in itself excruciating. But stack that on top of that my existing feelings of abandonment, and I was left feeling entirely worthless. With my head hung low, time passed slowly. Lost in depression and group home activity, each minute was as vague as the next, and every day brought a new set of problems that had only changed because of who was involved. Fighting over toys and food and disrespectful behavior occurred hourly. I tried to conceal myself in the chaos of activity and consequences. I was desperate and alone.

Weeks and months went by before I found a friend in my new roommate, Chris Peterson. His teenage mother had moved to Virginia and orphaned him. We shared loneliness together and that created an unspoken bond between us. We sat in quiet understanding, both having a very clear definition of what being an orphan was. We never fought and didn't try to push the other into saying anything that might hurt. As the holidays approached, we grew closer, trying to make a joke of being the only ones without a family visit or home pass.

My whole body ached every time I passed the group home holiday decorations and tree. I would do all I could to find a reason to be alone in my room. I was just tall enough to set my chin on the windowsill and rest my forehead on the cold window. I spent countless hours in front of our bedroom window, watching my warm breath dance back and forth on the pane as I cried and made wishes. I held onto toys that Tony and I used to share and hugged them, remembering the imaginary worlds he and I had created with them. I cradled them gingerly, and often would slowly trace their outlines, wishing with all my might for my brother's return. Every time someone would come in or a staff did a body count, I would wipe my eyes, afraid of the ridicule I would receive if I were caught crying by either staff or other kids. Sometimes I tucked myself behind my bed or balled myself in the closet and shut the door, so I could be alone with my sorrow. This was the only time I didn't have to worry about wiping away my tears. I wouldn't answer when called, and sometimes even fell asleep in the cold, absolving darkness.

Nothing helped. For many years I would endure unbearable depression as I waited to be reunited with Tony. But no amount of tears brought him back or mended my heart. I limited my verbal interactions to yes and no. I stayed in bed when I was given the option and wouldn't participate in any of the house activities. When I was forced outside for an activity, I would sit alone in one corner of the yard and stare at the blades of grass. If the sun was shining my way, I would find a small bug and watch as it crawled over my hands. Sharing internal dialogue with an insect was about the only thing that would nearly bring a smile to my face; providing a small respite in an unconditional friend. With Tony gone, I was forced to look more closely at my own life. He had been my family and so, also, a distraction from where I was or where I was going. He had always been my first priority. Without him I was lost and, at this age, it would be a long time before I could find myself again.

In the months of materialistic buildup during Christmas and Thanksgiving, I was always hit the hardest that I had been left behind and that I had no family. My defense mechanisms took many forms, from fights with my peers to denial of my feelings; I pretended to ignore my Orphan's Reality. I even created a game of denial to play in the early mornings—a game that I would return to for many years. I would keep my eyes closed as tight as I could and tell myself that today would be the day I woke up from my nightmare. I persuaded myself that all I had to do was wish or pray hard enough and I would be reunited with my brother and we would both be happily living in our own parents' home. I would strain to avoid thinking of any of the facts of my existence so that I could hold onto this fantasy as long as possible. And with painstaking efforts, at times I was able to convince myself that I had never really known what an orphanage was. For a few moments, I believed that my life had been a dream— that my imagination had gotten the better of me. There truly was a small peace in that. But reality would set in as a staff would flip on the light and give the orders to get up and complete our morning tasks. When I opened my eyes and looked over to see that my brother wasn't there, I had to cry. I didn't care; even if only for a little while, I needed my mirage to keep my mind in some small defiant state; refusing to accept that my life could be so empty. And in the thick of the "family" part of the year, I held onto whatever I could.

Thanksgiving Day came, and even though Chris and I were the only ones left in the house, we were separated. He went with one staff to his home and I went with another.

Because one staff didn't want to shoulder the responsibility of handling us both, I was again separated from the closest person in my life.

Please believe me that having a staff take you home with them to celebrate a holiday with their family *isn't* a good thing. Imagine losing your only connection by blood, being ripped apart by the System, and then taken to a home full of the family and loved ones of a staff person and expected to be on your best behavior. And the sight of their closest friends would be the cherry on the cake to remind you of their power to separate whomever they wanted, whenever they wanted. Can I even begin to describe how uncomfortable I was? Gene had drawn the lot, I suppose, and as I sat on his couch amidst his family and friends, my chest burned and my eyes welled up.

I took a fancy cookie stick—the kind with chocolate only on the tip—and began to nibble. I tried to focus on the TV, even though I hadn't a clue about the rules of football. Could I be left to just lay low and eat? Hell no. Everyone has to ask, "Where is your family?" And then *tell me* how awful it must be not having one. They kept on, saying what a great guy Gene must be for taking me home with him, and repeated the empty promise of how I could be part of *their* family.

How could anyone think that any of this would be helpful or make me (or *any* orphan) feel better? *Family for a day?* I nodded my head and gave half smiles until they left me alone. I went to the bathroom and tried to hide there for a while. I began sobbing deeply, only getting a moment or two of solace before someone knocked to see if I was okay. *NO, I wasn't okay!* I was an orphan, depressed and missing my brother. The sight of their family and all the *genuine* hugs and kisses they exchanged, something I had yet to experience, didn't soothe me. I was enraged and then depressed in cycles. They talked of experiences that brought smiles and laughter to each other. And there I was, in a daze without a clue. I had nothing to share, no one to reminisce with, no funny stories or jokes to tell.

We ate dinner and they gave me the token inclusion in their prayer over the turkey. Right before the prayer was directed toward someone who had died or needed some type of health aid was my inclusion. "Thank you for letting Louie spend this day with us, we pray for your blessing upon him," and blah blah blah. How was this supposed to make me feel like a part of their family—by bringing up that I was an intruder or someone unexpected and in need of a special blessing? Nonetheless, I ate in silence, and after finishing my plate, I asked to be excused. They sat there for hours reminiscing and laughing, and it just prolonged my feelings of utter inward emptiness. I kept wondering what Tony was doing that day and if he was happy, all right, and safe—answers that I knew wouldn't be given to me.

I was allowed outside for a short time and I chose to crouch behind a small shrub and begin crying. My small body wailed uncontrollably at first, and then I began letting out that low whimper that had grown so familiar. I sat and stared at the leaves of the plant in front of me, plucking them one by one. I traced the veins in each leaf and tried to pull it apart by the outlines. So I sat there with my leaves and my tears. Gene came out of the house a few minutes later and called out to me. I dried my face and stood up. He came over and placed his hand on my head and said, "Don't worry, everything is going to be okay."

Wasn't that great? This guy who, to me, seemed then to have the perfect life, was going to tell me not to worry. I grew *so sick* of staff uttering that same line of crap—as if they were doing anything to ease my pain. I'm sure they felt like those words were going to accomplish something, but maybe a little thought into the matter would have helped them to see what an empty phrase it was. Where was the ray of hope in that sentence? Was I to believe that the person speaking was going to take it upon himself or herself to make things go well for me? Did they ever mention a *plan* to make everything okay? Yet this very empty phrase was repeated to me countless times in a band-aid effort to make sure I didn't make the sayer uncomfortable with my sorrow.

Does that mean that there wasn't anything he could have done for me? Not at all. He could have offered the one thing I had lacked for so long: someone to talk to. If he had had the skill or insight to simply ask me about my feelings instead of trying to smother them, then I would have had a real solution. But most staff remain in "job" mode when they look at their "clients." But what many staff need is the perspective of a family approach rather than the required clinically therapeutic relationship. If Gene had only seen me as a kid who needed a hug, a child without any family or affection, then maybe it would have prompted him to rethink his trained standard response to a depressed client. Maybe then he would have let his guard down and really talked to me. And maybe then I would have had a real opportunity to vent and connect with another human being—something every child in the System desperately searches for.

With Thanksgiving over, it was time to rush to Christmas. Every boy at Father Matthew's received a grab-bag toy at the grand get-together with the three other 16-bed homes. Many of the boys used this as an opportunity to brag to one another what they had gotten or had been promised by Mommy and Daddy. Chris and I hung out in the back of the room with a handful of others, trying to hide our discomfort and changing the subject whenever possible. We all knew the action figure in our hands was going to be the only present we received. Regardless of that fact, we threw them away in a united front against the hypocrisy of our gift-giving staff, who had only made our lives hell.

In the days that followed, one kid after another would go on home pass until it was down to Chris and me. And again we were divided up to go home with a staff person to watch their families share each other's love. The same scenario played out with the conversations, trying to include me with intrusive inquiries, food, prayer, and so on. Oh yeah, and to make matters orderly, they would take a present from one of their children, take the tag off and give it to me! I knew, the kid knew, and they even announced that they had been expecting me—a very warm holiday experience indeed! Again, I found the corner of the house, tucked myself in it, and watched as they gave each other presents and thankful embraces. Tony, I thought, was surely having a good Christmas with his new family. My eyes began to strain, trying to hold back tears. Eventually I got up and went to hide in the bathroom.

Upon returning to the group home, I was informed of a very special visit I was to have. No amount of prodding or whining got me an answer other than to get dressed up. A short while after I dressed and began watching TV, I was informed that my visit had arrived. You can imagine my shock to see Tammie and Tony standing in the front door.

Please don't let this be a dream. I froze, with tears filling my eyes. I thought for sure, finally they had come back to get me—my only Christmas wish come true. I couldn't contain my excitement as I darted down the hall, smiling ear to ear. I grabbed Tony and squeezed him hard enough to make his head pop off his shoulders. He smiled and laughed and held up a bag in front of him full of presents. I wiped my face, thanked him and told him that I had something for him.

I raced back to my room and searched for anything in sight. The cheap piece-of-crap action figure would have been useful at this time, but I had thrown it away with Chris. I dumped out my closet and grew frantic at the sight of all the toys we used to share. Surely I couldn't give him one of these. I went into the game closet and pulled a puzzle off the top shelf. It was opened but I didn't care, I had to give him something. I wrapped it sloppily with a brown paper bag and rushed back out to see my little brother.

Tony was sitting in his van with his new older brother and sister, playing with some new toys. I remember pausing, being stricken with a pain in the pit of my stomach at this scene. I had been replaced and he had bought in. My run changed to a cautious walk, and as I approached, I took note that it was a few long seconds before Tony turned his attention back to me.

We exchanged gifts and I opened mine to find Garfield stationery, pencils, a roll of stamps, and a Bible. When Tony got his gift unwrapped, it looked as though he'd been struck with confusion. His older brother sneered, "It's a used puzzle!" I couldn't have been more embarrassed, and I wanted to crawl back into my closet. "Eddie," Tony's new dad, told the boy to shut up and he did.

But I had no confusion about my presents. I knew exactly what the stationery was for. Did they let it go at that? Of course not! Tammie had to explain and *show me* how each of the letters had their address on it. "You can write anytime you want to!" *What a gift, I'm allowed to WRITE my own brother now!!* With a smile on her face she continued on about how I should pray, and told me to read from the Bible every day. She commented negatively on Father Matthew's being a Catholic home. *Can you believe the audacity of this woman?* Not only had they taken my brother away from me months earlier, but now they were giving *me* permission to write my own flesh and blood! And then telling me about God and directing me how to pray. "God isn't with this family," I thought. I held back from exploding all over them, knowing full well that the staff were watching me and they would end my visit. With no smile or thank you, I placed the bag on the ground and turned towards Tony.

We walked around the yard of the group home and he gave me a picture of himself on a brand new He-Man bicycle with Tammie and Eddie standing behind him in front of a big house. He talked of how he got to ride up and down the street and how he had his own room, his own TV, and on and on. I loved my little brother with every fiber of my being, but I couldn't *help* but feel jealous at hearing about all his new belongings. When he asked how I was doing, I spared him any discomfort and said everything was okay.

His visit was brief. A quick thirty minutes clicked away, then they said they had to go. Caught off guard, I snapped, "Where?" then feared for what my response could incur.

"We have to go to Grandma's house for dinner, and we don't want to miss *Santa.*" Either Tammie was rubbing it in, or she was the dumbest, most insensitive woman on the planet. I wished with all my heart the next sentence was going to be, "Go get your stuff so we can leave," but I got a goodbye instead. She never took my feelings into consideration with her plan to lure my brother away from me by offering him a special event. It was obvious that none of them cared.

Before leaving, Tony asked if I liked my presents. I offered a fake smile and nod. Shame prevented me from asking the same of him. Tony's new family started piling into their shiny Chevy Custom Cab Conversion van and Tammie told Tony to say goodbye. He seemed reluctant to hug me—I couldn't feel my strong grasp being returned. My eyes began to tear up as pangs of sorrow overcame me.

Richard had been cued outside and put his hand on my shoulder to give an authoritative squeeze to let me know I had to let go. *To hell with that—I wasn't about to let go!* His touch only prompted me squeeze harder, as my body gave way to sobbing. Richard's grip tightened and he started pulling on me. Tammie now started to pull on Tony as well. My six-year-old body cringed under Richard's painful grasp and I was forced to release Tony.

As I looked at Tony, I saw that his face had only a faint hint of emotion on it, and it crushed me. His trip to go see what Santa had gotten him was more important than my obvious suffering. He got into the van with Tammie and they both smiled and waved goodbye. I dropped to the ground as the van turned the corner and let go what I had been holding back. Crying deeply, I became lost in my sorrow. My glasses fogged up, and eventually slid on my tears to the ground.

When my gut allowed me to force out a word, I asked, "Why?" Why had they left again without me? Why wasn't

Tony crying or sad to be leaving me? Why, why, why? Richard wasn't about to answer—as if he had an answer anyway. He just kept repeating the cure-all phrase, *"Everything's going to be okay."* He tried pulling me up by my arm, but I wouldn't cooperate. I had nothing left for my legs at the time and wanted to stay where I had last held my brother. He used a simple psychological ploy, saying, "I guess you can stay out here all day. I'm going in to eat some ice cream and watch TV. You can join me whenever you want to." Wasn't that nice. *"Go ahead,"* I thought.

I lay there in the driveway until I cried myself dry. I stared at the bag left for me, then looked over to where their van had been parked and imagined them driving back up to get me. I was frozen on the spot, paralyzed. I rubbed the ground, yearning for a sensation in my fingers that resembled Tony's corduroy jacket.

Eventually Richard came back out and told me that I had to come in *now* or he would be forced to call the police and tell them I was AWOL. I got up and embarked on the longest walk I'd ever taken to my room. Every step away from the place I last saw Tony was harder and harder, like each one was a metaphor calling out to me that I was permanently drifting further and further away from him. In my room, I lay motionless on the bed and began sobbing. Richard came in after a few minutes and placed the bag of "gifts" at the doorway. I remained still as I stared at it. Running back and forth in my head was the self-blame that I hadn't been a good enough brother. I began crying again, as I told myself that I was being targeted because I wasn't handsome enough or had too many personal flaws of character or of the mind to deserve a family. I twisted into this blaming session, searching to make sense of everything, and I lay there for hours, wallowing in self-hatred at my own existence. Anguish and tears overtook me again and again and I cried until it was dark. I refused dinner and stayed in bed. Eventually I cried myself to sleep.

That was probably the hardest day of my life. I knew for sure that there was no hope for me. I realized that Tony's family didn't want me and that I would have to face being alone now. I pondered possible reasons why this had occurred, but no excuse came to my rescue. I was lost, stripped of my only family without apology or consolation. I started to imagine a life without Tony, without a little brother who needed me. It was clear he didn't need me anymore. My heart was empty.

In an almost catatonic state, trying to deal with my traumatic separation, I lost track of the days. At first I didn't use the stationery I had been given; I didn't know what to write. Eventually I did write—and write and write, but got no response. Finally, after months, I got a thick envelope that had two letters in it, one from Tony and one from Tammie. Tony's letter was a short one with a small drawing on the bottom. It said, "How are you? I hope you are having fun. I got a new dog. Write me back. Love, Tony."

Tammie's letter was very long and far more detailed. It informed me of what I should write and why it should lead Tony to believe I was happy, and blah, blah, blah. I thought, *Forget her, I'll write whatever I want. He's my brother and I can say anything I want to, especially the truth!* What I failed to realize then was how easy it was for her to screen his mail. I found out years later that he never received any of my letters.

Affection was absent in my life and sorrow dominated my existence. It seemed everywhere I turned someone else was receiving love. My peers returned from home pass with new toys, and had birthdays and dozens of other holidays calling for their parents to show up and hug them and take them out for a day or weekend. In my orphanage home, this was one of the underlying tortures. My "home" really made you focus and compare what everyone else had against what you didn't. And for me, that was a long list. Even when my birthdays rolled around, all I got were empty glares from my peers, who simply wanted me to hurry up and blow out the candles so they could

have dessert. I was slapped in the face with the fact that I had
nothing; and there was never going to be a holiday just for me.

I stayed at Father Matthew's for over two years, waiting
for a family or for contact from Tony. I visited with one foster
family who gave me a box full of toys and had me stay in my
prospective bedroom for the weekend. After a couple of visits,
it was obvious that they weren't interested in me and probably
were more interested in a tax-free state check. From my vantage
point, if I moved in with these people, it would be like
completely shutting the door on any chance of living with my
brother again. I tried very hard to be difficult and demanding,
but my behavior didn't seem to bother them. I really didn't
expect to feel loved by these people and I refused to read
anything into their smallest family-like gestures. I finally got
their attention with a small fire in the yard and was returned to
the home, never seeing them again. Clyde had made a point of
telling me that no family would want me because I was too
ugly. Pale-skinned with 1-inch-thick glasses and a bedwetter, I
let myself believe him. I sank forever into self-loathing,
thinking that maybe he was right—I was ugly and unlovable.

So I quit on myself, and dug an even deeper hole for
myself with my behavior. What could they take from me? What
could they do to me? I was unlovable, unwanted and already an
object for ridicule in this home. I retaliated in a childish way to
"prove" that I didn't need any of them. I got up in the middle of
the night and changed everyone's points on the board with a
stolen grease pen, or stole someone's favorite shirt or toy and
planted it in one of the older boy's closets. Sometimes I would
get caught and restrained, but many times I got away with it.
My biggest "crime" occurred after we had received a donation
of Keebler Almost Home Soft Batch cookies.

Clyde Peabody had quickly grown attached to this
donation, which was supposed to be for all the boys, and
handed them out only to the ones who played Dungeons and
Dragons with him or who made him laugh—meaning they had
to do something "funny" to one of us younger kids. We sat at

the large 18-place dining table and Clyde and Augie threw cookies to their favorite boys. During our meal, I had made the mistake of asking one of the older kids if they wanted my green beans, because I didn't like them and he said he did. He told Clyde and it was a matter of minutes before I had a huge plateful of green beans in front of me. They all laughed and snickered at his game: namely, don't let it out that you don't like something or you'll get a triple portion.

Clyde stood over me and ordered me to eat the beans or he'd feed them to me. Most of the boys laughed in support of his entertainment offering. Those who remained quiet looked down at their plates, remembering when the same "trick" had been pulled on them—a plateful of cottage cheese for Jaime, mushrooms for Darrin, and so forth. Clyde had made them eat every last bite. I had no illusions about how my evening was going to be spent. He grabbed my hand holding the fork and shoveled a heap towards my mouth. I chewed the mouthful and gagged, spitting the half-chewed beans out.

"You better finish every bean on that plate," he threatened. "If you throw up, I'll make you lick it up." I sat there frustrated and intimidated by Clyde and the ranting of the other boys. So I ate three or four beans at a time, stopping every now and again to choke back my gag reflex. Eventually, everyone became bored with me and moved on to taking showers and watching TV, but not Clyde. He set up his Dungeons and Dragons game on the other end of the table, eating the donated cookies and snapping at me between turns. I tried to eat the beans, but they had grown very cold, and I had already picked out most of the unchewed ones and eaten them. I knew he wouldn't be satisfied until I had swallowed every last cold mushy bean, and so I sat.

Lights began to go out in the house as kids went to bed. Clyde obliged me with his threats of what would happen if I didn't finish: I would be restrained for wasting food and the beans would be saved for my breakfast. He tried to force another forkful into my mouth but my throat refused to cooperate. I gagged and the beans came back out. He pulled my chair out, lifted me up, and pushed me to the wall. My restraint came next and his frustration was obvious—he had to win. He made me stand there for over an hour, marked by two age groups' bedtimes, staring at Charlie Brown. My legs felt like jelly and I kept shifting my weight between them every two seconds or so, looking for relief. When he came back and offered to let me back to the table to finish my beans, I thought he was being actually merciful. My legs tingled as I sat down and I was relieved, until I remembered the other obstacle I had to conquer. I put a small amount on my fork and tried to eat them. I gagged again and spit the mush out. Clyde threw his hands up in frustration. "I don't care if it takes all night Louie."

Gene had come in for night shift, which was at 10 p.m. He gave me a once over, and then kept on toward the office. Dinner had begun at 5 p.m., so it didn't take a genius to figure I had been at the table for about 5 hours. After a brief shift-change meeting, Clyde and Augie walked by and on out the door without a look or a word. My blood boiled when I heard their laughter as the door shut. Gene came out shortly afterwards and excused me from the table. I got up and watched as he threw my affliction away and mumbled something under his breath.

I went to my room with renewed energy as I lay down thinking of Clyde's laugh. I had to get him back. *But how?* Chris asked if I was okay and we talked about Clyde and his power trips. I don't remember who brought it up first, but in a matter of minutes we were talking about stealing the Soft Batch cookies. The key hung over the locked pantry door, out of range from anyone without a six-foot reach. We planned that he would climb the counter top and I would support his legs as he leaned out for the key. We woke up the other young boys in the room across from ours and told them our plan.

Everyone was pumped and no one had reservations. We waited for Gene to sit in front of the TV and begin to zone. Mustering our courage, we sneaked through the dining room and into the kitchen without a collective peep. I gave Chris a boost onto the counter and he reached for the key. He leaned and leaned until he got it, but my grip failed as he jerked to get the key and he fell off the counter. I lacked the strength to catch him and we both fell down. I thought for sure it was over and Mean Gene the Restraining Machine would come in and inflict some severe group home justice. We lay completely still, anticipating the inevitable footsteps, but they never came. I pulled myself by my arms across the floor and peeked around the counter. The coast was clear and I waved to the boys to get up.

I got the key from Chris and with the utmost precision slid the key into the pantry lock. With my other hand I grabbed the knob and turned it and the key slowly at the same time. I pushed the door open a centimeter at a time, ever so mindful of the slightest creek. Once I had it ajar enough to get us through, we left the door cracked and squeezed in to look for our prize. Two huge boxes, both already haphazardly dug into, lay on the floor with the flaps open. We reached down and grabbed three and four packages each, then left. We sneaked across the hall and placed our treasure on the far side of our beds before going back for more.

One of the other boys dropped a package and the sound reverberated down the hallway. We jumped into our beds and covered ourselves. Expecting the lights to come on, I threw my blanket over my head. Yet again nothing. I got up after a few minutes and went down the hallway, to find Gene sleeping in front of the glowing television screen. I raced back to the kitchen and grabbed another armful of cookies, then went to another room and woke up Roger, another of the younger kids. I showed him my trophies and offered him some. He was half asleep at first, but once I made the motion to hand him the packages, his eyes opened wide up. I directed him to stuff them in his closet behind his clothes, which is what everyone else had done.

I returned to the pantry with Chris, shut the door, and we managed to get the key back on the hook. Boy, did we have a party that night. We each sat by our doors with a package each and stuffed our faces. Every now and again, one of us would peek our head around the corner to see if Gene had awakened, but our feast remained uninterrupted. We ate and laughed with our hands covering our mouths. When our respective packages were finished, Chris and I collected them and snuck them outside to the dumpster through our bedroom window.

I slept soundly, with sore legs and arms, but with victory on the brain and contentment in my stomach. And the thought of Clyde having fewer cookies to eat, take home, or give to his stooges gave me a peace I hadn't known since Donna had tucked Tony and me in for the night.

Morning came and everything went as usual. Gene woke us up at 6 a.m. and we did our chores, cleaned our rooms, made our beds, ate breakfast, grabbed our stuff for school, and waited by the front door with our shoes in hand. When we returned from school, Clyde and Augie were sitting at the table playing Dungeons and Dragons and eating Soft Batch cookies. My stomach hit the floor at the sight of the red packaging, immediately thinking of the worst: that they had found our stashes and were sitting there rubbing it in our faces. I surely gave Mr. Dungeons and Dragons more credit then he deserved. But paranoia in a kid's brain spreads like wildfire.

We checked our stashes and found that nothing had been touched. Unlike before with Henry's wallet, my withdrawal had gone unnoticed this time. That evening I did everything to stay out of Clyde's way, isolating myself in my room. Chris hung out with me and we played cards and made little jokes about our cunning. This had probably been the most that we had spoken to each other in over a year, usually just respecting each other's right to be depressed. But now we laughed and played and I almost felt like I had a brother again.

Night came, and during the little celebration at our doorways, Roger approached our alcove. Tagging along with him was his roommate, Garret, one of the older boys. "I heard you guys scored some cookies?" he inquired. He wanted in, and the cookies in his hand told me we had no choice. So again we went for the pantry, letting Garret get the key this time and only taking two packages each to replace the ones we had already eaten. As Garret and Roger were on the way back to their room, Gene intercepted them. Garret dropped his armful of cookies to the floor as Gene lunged toward them. Still hidden by in darkness, we ran to our rooms, jumped into our beds, and flung the covers over ourselves. Paying no regard to the hour, Gene yelled at the boys. "What the hell are you guys doing? Where did you get these cookies?"

Gene started in on Roger first, sure he would break quickest, but he kept his mouth shut. Gene demanded that they face the wall, then separated them. He put Roger at the end of the hallway by the office and Garret by the kitchen, within earshot of our rooms. He turned on all the lights to find the pantry door open, then growled at Garret before retrieving the key from him. Gene restrained Garret and then went down the hall and restrained Roger. Gene's demands for information bellowed down the hall but went unmet. Roger let out another shrill burst as Gene restrained him again. On his way back down the hall we heard his thundering footsteps come to a quiet stop in front of our door. We heard Gene mumbling something to Garret, then the lights in our room were switched on.

I played like I was asleep, as did Chris. Gene ordered us to get up but I didn't move until his second command. I did my best to give the half-awake, eyes barely open, mumbled, "Yes, sir?"

"Get out of bed" he demanded, and then started tossing our closets. Within seconds he found the evidence. He grabbed us by our arms and pulled us out of our room, leaving us in front of the Snoopy wall. He threw our packages on the dining table with the rest of them. I whispered over to Garret, "Snitch!" Gene heard the utterance and turned around.

"What was that? Who said that?" Garret piped up and once more reported on me. Gene paced right over and restrained me. "Mean Gene the Restraining Machine," I found, was justly earned name. He lifted me off my feet and pulled my arms so far back I thought I might be able to touch the opposing elbow, literally. He released me and ordered me to stand at the wall and shut my mouth. He asked if anyone else was involved and I interjected with a tearful and convincing "No." He believed me, and the others were spared.

He turned off the lights and left us standing at the wall most of the night, making rounds to restrain us every half hour. Swaying back and forth in this endless night, all I could think of was how I would get Garret for his cowardice. When finally allowed to go to bed, my hot head couldn't stop my exhausted body from falling into a quick sleep.

Wake-up call seemed to come almost instantaneously after I closed my eyes and slept. Gene didn't say a word to any of us and went through the morning routine as usual. We were sent off to school, so we thought maybe it was over and there wouldn't be further mention of our crime. Nothing could have been further from the truth.

When we got back from school, Clyde, Richard, Augie, and Gene were at the dining room table with the boxes that held the rest of the Soft Batch cookies inside. Everyone was directed to sit at the table and we listened to each of them talk about stealing, and how we took from our own house brothers. They demanded that we stand up and tell everyone what we did. Richard commended Garret for telling the "truth" and allowed him to sit down. Then he handed out cookies to all the sitting boys and the staff and told them to eat them in front of us. Clyde thought he was so clever in adding to our torment by commenting how good the cookies were, and then offering milk and soda to everyone. While they were devouring the cookies, Richard asked the group what they thought we should get for punishment. Chalk in one hand and a cookie in the other, he wrote down possibilities on the chalkboard behind him. "Early bed," "5000 sentences," "KP duty," "Yard Duty," "Bathrooms for a month," and the list grew until he didn't have any more room to write.

"These look about right" and Richard threw the book at us. We rotated the various consequences between Chris, Roger, and myself, while Garret got off without so much as a sentence to write. Clyde had a field day administering our consequences, telling the boys to not pick up after themselves and to dump their leftover cereal milk in the trash instead of down the sink so the bag would burst. He even came in and ripped up the first 8 pages of my sentences because he caught me writing all the I's first, then the will's, then the not's, all in rows down the paper. He *required* that I write each sentence out in its entirety before moving onto the next one. 27 sentences could fit on one side, 54 per page, so he had just ripped up about 482 of my required 5000 sentences and told me to start over. If you have ever had the pleasure, then I don't need to lament on how sore your wrist, hand, and fingers get writing the same thing over and over hundreds (in this case thousands) of times.

Within two weeks we each had our sentences done and had only two more weeks of the extra chores. Chris and I wanted to get Garret back for snitching us out, but we knew he had Clyde's protection. But with all the other crap in our lives that had happened to us, Chris and I weren't deterred by the possibility of more restraining or more consequences. We waited until the weekend when most kids were outside playing or in the Rec Room with the staff, and found Garret alone in the bathroom. He was brushing his teeth and I threw a towel over him as Chris pushed him over. We punched and kicked as hard as we could. I grabbed the shampoo and dumped it all over him and Chris emptied a tube of toothpaste on him before we ran to our room.

Garret was too embarrassed to tell anyone that two of the smaller kids, including Louie, who wore the thick glasses, had just got done kicking the crap out of him. We didn't care about his reasons as long as Clyde wasn't going to find out. But his silence didn't matter; our guilty faces were evidence enough for the staff. Chris and I kept our mouths shut even though we had to stand at the wall all day, were restrained every thirty minutes and not allowed to eat. But the consequence that followed were far worse than 5000 sentences or even a million; they separated us and gave us new roommates; both being Clyde's favorites.

It wasn't long after that Chris's mother came back into the picture and started taking him on passes. I was happy for him, but torn between my selfish needs at the same time. Chris left with his mother shortly after her reappearance and I had again to endure loss—the loss of my first friend, what some might call a soul mate. As his transition date grew closer, he made comments like maybe his mother could take me with them. I knew the reality and simply gave him the smile that was meant to make him comfortable and let him understand it was okay if he went home. As young as I was, I appreciated the facts and was willing to let him go gracefully. I wanted his torment to end; I wanted him to have a chance at happiness. As for going with them, I knew better than to allow my hopes to rise. I understood that we weren't allowed to make plans about where we could live, and, after the experience of losing Tony, especially not be allowed to choose with whom.

Chris gave me all of his toys and some of his clothes before he left. When his mother arrived to take him home, he embraced me harder than my brother had; he even allowed his eyes to water as he got in her car and said goodbye. I could see that he took into account what leaving me behind meant for me. My heart didn't completely empty out like when Tony had left with his new family. This time there was something left; a piece of honor that Chris gave me by showing that he cared. We hugged each other good-bye the same as anyone who was moving away from a cousin, and I knew that his promise to not forget me wasn't an empty one.

Chapter 5 - I Decided to Leave Tony

With my best and only friend gone, melancholy found me. I sat alone in my room, thinking of Chris and my brother, mulling over and over what I had to live for and why this was happening to me. It was so cold and empty inside. My heart weighed a ton, and I stayed in my room away from the chaos of the house. Nothing changed among the boys, and the fact that my friend had gone made me even more of an easy target.

Clyde and his boys kicked into double time with their tortures. I think also, because I had been there so long (the average stay was 4-8 months), Clyde had grown comfortable in tormenting me. He made up new names for the other boys to call me on a regular basis. He made fun of my glasses, calling them "coke bottles" and saying "tell me the future." I often walked on my tiptoes (and habitually still do, subconsciously expressing that I spent my life walking on eggshells) and was labeled "faggot." His boys punched me or held me down and rubbed their groins in my face, chanting, "Get the faggot! Faggot, faggot!" All this degradation was carried out before they went on home pass for the weekend. Clyde just laughed, as did Augie, and I only got a break when they had their two days off.

My frigid existence during this time was marked by their torments and trying to hide in the closet to be alone and cry. When I got really pissed off, or they triggered me with anything about my brother, I tried to verbally retaliate. Sometimes we would fight and other times they would jeer, "*At least I have a family!"* I dreamed of having Chris back, but especially of being with my brother again. Not even the first smiles and attention of the new staff could bring me out of my despair. They would just go along with the senior staff and made no objections. Besides, it was a game right? It was all in fun right? Everyone was laughing except for me and the few other younger ones that were rotated in the Games.

As the holidays again approached, I had to go through watching everyone go home again, except this time I didn't have a friend. In its climax, I idolized the affections that the other boys were receiving. In my mind, it seemed that everyone had a family except me, and this was a heart-wrenching perception. I was the house humiliation and going to be totally alone when Thanksgiving arrived.

When The Day finally came, I dared not leave my room. I sat on my bed and stared at the multicolored construction paper turkey I had made at school only a few days before. I was meticulous in its design, obviously trying to distract myself from what it represented. All the days leading up to Thanksgiving were always full of family talk, especially at school. It was hard listening to my classmates' answers to the "What are you thankful for?" question. It was harder still hearing the plans their family made for their special day. I never answered. I was always quiet and made an excuse to go to the restroom or the nurse's office.

I broke my stare from my paper turkey when I was finally informed that the last kid had gone home and I was sent on my way to Gene's home again. Everyone was nice and said they were glad to see me. It seemed a little easier this time, although I never forgot that I was a guest to their celebration. Gene had grown a little fonder of me and allowed me time for myself; I spent it behind the same shrub, practicing what was fast becoming my holiday tradition.

The arrival of Christmas amplified the previous holiday's feelings. At the big group home get-together we were forced to sing "Silent Night," and its melody haunted me. I didn't understand the words, but the tune and peace in its chorus seemed to grab me by the heart. I stared at the Christmas lights on the tree and lost myself in their soft glow. We were forced to watch traditional holiday cinema—the kind where the main character comes to find the meaning of love and family through Christmas—and my heart broke over and over again. My mind wove between thoughts of Tony and Chris and my body tried to force tears. I had become a master at holding them back at such rushes of sadness, but this time I was unable to fight them off. I turned away from the silver screen and went to the bathroom to get rid of my body's expression before anyone could notice.

When I came back, Father Matthew had on his Santa hat and beard and was handing out toys to the kids. In tribute to Chris, I didn't even open my toy and threw it away when no one was looking. I listened in silence as the other boys made exclamations to one another of what they got or were promised. And even though they were all expecting gifts far grander than the small cars and action figures, they protected them. In fact, at the close of the party you could hear them arguing over someone touching their toy or someone else's being stolen.

Crazy how these boys who were placed in this home because of their "bad" behaviors were the ones who got the most presents from Santa Claus. I was better than these kids; I didn't pick on the little ones that arrived after me who were five or six. In fact, I often jumped to their aid to divert one of the bigger kids away from smacking them around or taking their toys and snacks. Where were *my* gifts? *Was* I unlovable, was I too ugly, was I naughty? My face rested in my palms and I shook my head. These questions had no answers, and I told myself they didn't matter. I wrote off "Happy Holidays," whatever that meant. There wasn't an ounce of hope left in me at this seasonal apex of goodwill and family.

As the boys left, one by one, I couldn't dare to dream that maybe a family would show up for me. Would buy me a new watch or bike and give me a home. I watched in dejection as they each left with their loved ones, their families, and I was left with Melancholy.

When Christmas Eve finally arrived in my ninth year of being on this planet, I was completely alone. I shared the silent 16-bed home with one staff—not one child was there with me. I hummed Silent Night in my room while staring out the window, counting the wooden boards with eyes swollen from crying. I wonder what Tony was doing. I wondered if he'd come again. I wished and prayed. "If there is a God, please let me see my brother again." I wished the day away.

Clyde had come in for the evening shift. I thought, "Oh great, I get to spend the saddest day of the year with the jerk that'll point out that it is my fault I'm alone and then laugh at me." I tried to hide in my room and stay away from his razor tongue. But he wouldn't let me be, and insisted that we play some game together. We passed the time with Monopoly and it happened that the dice rolled my way and I won. A gleam of light amidst this terrible day. Clyde was noticeably agitated by my victory, but didn't lash out.

We had dinner in front of the TV and watched a movie he had brought. Bedtime came and I cried myself to sleep as Clyde's radio softly played classic holiday tunes by Bing Crosby and the like. I didn't harbor any hope for Santa's visit and was doing my best to put Tony out of my mind. I'm sure he was getting plenty of affection and presents and I hadn't heard from him in longer than I could remember. Clutching my thin orange blanket, I cried myself to sleep. I would remain totally alone.

I was awakened in the middle of the night to find Clyde and Augie in my room and my bed full of presents. I didn't know how to feel. There was a load of toys on my bed but my nemesis and his sidekick were in the doorway. Augie had on a Santa hat and greeted me with "Merry Christmas" and began handing presents to me. I opened them quickly and discovered a bunch of cars and action figures. I know I'm going to sound ungrateful now, but these were exactly the same types of toys that were handed out a couple of weeks before at the grand party. Did they expect me not to notice that they were giving me the extras or leftovers from then?

Oh well, do I chalk up one for effort, or should I feel patronized? Regardless, they rushed me out of the house and we went somewhere to look at some celestial thing happening. That was as close as I got to having a decent time while under Clyde's supervision ("care" would not be appropriate).

When the rest of the kids came back over the next week, they all had an array of new toys and gadgets. They clung to them with pride and could be seen everywhere in the house showing off to one another. My roommate had gotten an oversized bear, radio headphones and many Christmas cards that evidenced his family's love. He shared what he could, and sometimes let me sleep with the bear or let me borrow his headphones. I would take the bear and put it under the covers with me and wrap its arms around me from behind. I tried to back into it like it was a mother's embrace, snuggling me. I would close my eyes and hold the stuffed bear's stubby arms with my hands. After a solid moment, tears would begin their descent down my cheeks and I would drift asleep. Once, while I was trying to feel like I was getting a hug, Augie shone a flashlight on me and said, "That's enough." I don't know how, not even today, but I knew what he meant—that I shouldn't try to get a hug from the bear. Maybe I thought then subconsciously that I still didn't deserved to be loved, not even from an inanimate object.

When I borrowed the headphones, I tuned in the easy listening station to hear songs of love and loss. I tried to use them to figure out what I needed to do to be loved. I memorized the station's entire play list. I didn't find any answers, but stayed attracted to the sounds of "I love you," or "forever, I miss you," or "someday we'll be together," and so on. To merely tease my heart with these words was enough to get me through a few lonely nights.

The intense separation anxiety I should have been dealing with was pushed under in an instinctual attempt at denial. I was so afraid to lose another friend that I refused to let anyone get close to me. I was an expert of hiding my emotions and the king of isolation. I did my all to control any little part of my life that I could. And all that was left was that—to not be hurt by someone else leaving me behind.

In the final week of Christmas vacation, I read dozens of children's books on just about anything to kill time. Whenever possible, I hid in the closet to avoid having to explain my teardrops to anyone. After three years, despair had gotten the better of me and I didn't feel I had anything left—no brother, no family and no friend. Every house outing pushed this further in my face. I would stare blankly out the cargo van window as we were carted off to the beach, park or a museum. As all the other kids played, I would look over and yearn to be part of what was all around me: families. A father playing with his children. A mother sharing a meal or a treat. I died a little inside as I watched siblings play and laugh. But the lowest I felt was the time I witnessed an entire family showering affection on their dog. They ran, laughed, and played with the golden retriever and the animal seemed to be smiling with them. *I wish I was a dog.* After getting back from one of these grueling excursions I decided to make a dark effort. Pondering how hard it was going to be to face my classmates, who had real families, and listen to their holiday reports, I took my shoelaces and went into the bathroom on a desperate mission. I volunteered to be last to shower and no one argued because that meant you were responsible to make sure the floor was dry and everything was clean.

I stared into the mirror for long minutes. I examined my face. My "coke-bottle" glasses, my pasty-white skin, my dirty brown hair. *I'm ugly.* Both my aqua-blue eyes appear larger than my nose and wider than my mouth. *I'm a freak.* I looked at the deep scars on my face, arms and chest. *Everyone hates me.* Finally, all of those unanswered prayers. *Even God doesn't care.* I took off my glasses and turned toward the shower. It was an enclosed shower with a small basin floor and a frosted glass door. I stood up on the ledge of the doorframe and leaned over to wrap the shoelaces around the showerhead, holding onto the corner of the wall to support myself. I wrapped the shoelaces around the showerhead numerous times and then tied them around my neck. I coiled my wrist in the cord near the spout, pulling on the laces to check my knot. One jerk and my foot slipped off the ledge. The string tore into my wrist and then snapped.

An icy burn surged around my wrist and blood began spreading down my forearm as I stared in disbelief. I panicked, thinking not only of the humiliation I would have to face from everyone, but also what could happen if they knew I was trying to kill myself. I stood, turned on the water, and tried to rinse the evidence down the drain. My wrist burned continuously and I wrapped my washcloth around the wound. I teared up so much and couldn't wipe my eyes enough to keep my vision clear. Being half blind, literally, I'm sure the rip in my skin wasn't as bad as it seemed, but I truly thought I was going to bleed to death. Although that had been my initial plan, I feared having to die so slowly.

I pressed on the cloth and eventually the sharp pain was replaced by a duller, consistent one. I unwrapped my wrist and the blood had stopped rushing out and was now just exiting in waves. I ran the water as cold as it would go and raised my wrist to the showerhead.

A knock came on the bathroom door and an inquiry, "Are you almost done? Your time's up." My eyes began to tear up because I was sure I was going to be discovered. I answered, trying to sound as normal as possible, "Almost done."

I shut off the water and tied the washcloth to my wrist. I started drying myself and then put on my underwear. No sooner as I had them pulled all the way up, the door opened and bumped into me. "Hurry up" and it shut. My stomach was in knots. I started to retrieve my shoelaces and again slipped in the shower basin. I got up and tried again; now with angry frustration. I got the strings down and wrapped them in my towel, then sneaked into my room with my damaged wrist wrapped in the towel and clothing. As I placed my clothes inside, the lights flashed on.

Clyde said in an annoyed voice, "We called lights out, get to bed." My heart stopped for a second and I leaked a little into my underwear as I heard his voice, dreading that I hadn't got away with it. But he just turned off the light and walked away. I closed the closet door and crawled into bed with the wet washcloth still wrapped around my wrist. I waited for shift change and after the first checks, climbed out the window and got rid of the shoelaces. I stayed up most of the night with the throbbing in my wrist pulsating in my ears, while shockwaves coursed through the rest of my body. Finally, the rhythm of the pain lulled me to sleep.

I got up the next morning to the typical lights-on greeting that prevailed in all group homes. I rolled out of bed onto the floor away from the door and began to unwrap my wrist. It was moist and all white and wrinkly from the wet bandage. I hid the cloth under my mattress and got dressed, cleverly donning a long sleeved shirt and my jacket. I was, of course, asked to take my jacket off in the house, but it was winter and I replied that I was cold, so I was allowed the jacket. Night staff were almost always more lenient with the rules, probably because of the sleep deprivation and not wanting to have an argument when they were just ready to crash. I did my chores and got out of the house with my washcloth. I hid it in an empty cereal box and threw it in the dumpster.

Then I made it out of the house and went to school with no one the wiser. As a matter of fact, I was initially so careful that it was a day or so later, during PE, that my teacher noticed the wound and sent me to the nurse's office. I panicked, and on the way with note in hand, I veered off my path to hide in the bathroom. I paced back and forth trying to think of a plausible excuse. I hid in the stall and racked my brain for anything that could free me from the consequences of the truth.

I went to the nurse's office and told them that I had tied a string to the jungle gym and tried to swing across like Tarzan. It worked—they didn't ask for evidence but simply started treatment. They put on some ointment and wrapped it for me. I confided in the nurse and explained about Clyde and how I would be ridiculed if they found out and she made a deal with me. She said as long as I came in two times a day, before school and after lunch, that she wouldn't send a note home. I happily agreed and kept my promise for the couple weeks until she said I didn't have to come anymore.

My PE teacher was let in on our secret and complied with our arrangement. I had become quite fast on my feet, and because I had become so accustomed to my black depression, was good at running long distances. I would come out of long runs with lungs ready to burst, and sometimes cough up blood, but didn't feel any of the onsets until I hit the finish line. This got me a little positive attention from her and a small ray of happiness to my dreary existence. Happy as I was winning races and gaining recognition from my classmates, the colored ribbons and certificates didn't replace a family.

January, February, and March came and left with me falling deeper into a black void of depression and emptiness. To make matters worse, I caught the chicken pox from my roommate. I watched as his parents brought him gifts to comfort him. I could only look on and dream of what that might be like. My comfort came in the form of Clyde and Augie coming around now and again to snap or yell at me for scratching myself. I felt so alone and entirely worthless—just a "thing" the staff only dealt with so they could get a paycheck.

I suffered enforcement of scores of their strict rules every day. Everything was labeled or marked off with masking tape on the walls and/or floors. Everything was always locked, and everything was off limits. "Don't cross the line." "Knock on the office door before you speak to a staff." "Don't go in another peer's room." "Don't go in the kitchen." "Ask to use the bathroom." "No horseplay." "No yelling." "No running." "Dinner is at five." "Level 1 bedtime is 7 o'clock." "Push in your chair." "Don't go outside." "Your bed will always be made unless you are sleeping in it." "No pens." "No sharp objects." "Stay in your room until you are called out." "Chores are to be finished by 6:30 a.m." "Only staff turns on the TV." "Phone time is..." "Study hour is..." "Don't." "No." and on and on; there was a rule or restriction for every possible detail of every day. I hated it. I hated every day, every rule. And I especially hated all of the ways in which we could be punished for any infraction.

I began to think of different ways to kill myself. Maybe I could climb a tree or jump off the roof head first into the sidewalk. I thought of putting my head through the plate glass window in my room. I plotted out the most opportune time to jump off a freeway overpass as we crossed. I knew that whatever I tried, I needed to succeed; my staff would ensure that there would not be a second chance.

As I built the determination to carry out the simplest and, to me, most painless of the options, something happened that promised to change the course of my life at the anniversary of my birth. Be it positive or negative would remain to be seen.

This April 17th would mark my 10th birthday and well into my 3rd year at Father Matthew's. My case file had grown to a cumbersome rubber-band-clad pair of 3-inch folders that dwarfed all the others. I had been, by far, the longest and most troublesome resident—or inmate, if you will. Around dinnertime, everyone was called to the table early to present me with the typical institutional-sized birthday cake. It had a black and white checkerboard frosting and read, "Happy Birthday Luis." Three years and they couldn't spell my name correctly on a cake that I knew was made there. I blew out the candles and looked around at all the expressionless faces; I didn't even bother to make a wish.

When the "celebration" was over, the staff told me to put on my nice clothes to go out for dinner. I allowed the thought to enter of my brother coming to visit me. I started getting dressed faster and faster, speeding toward the possibility of seeing Tony again. Richard rapped on the doorframe and told me that my visitors had arrived. I eagerly asked, *"Is it Tony?"* but he didn't answer.

I peeked down the hall to see two women standing by the shoe racks looking right back at me. I thought, *"Who are those guys? Where's Tony and Tammie?"* Richard prodded me down the hall and introduced us. "This is Jackie and this is Shirley. They are going to take you out for your birthday." I sized them up. Shirley was a broad shouldered five foot nine with long wavy raven black hair; she had sharp features and a bold brow. Jackie, a head shorter, about five foot four, had long straight brown hair, wide blue eyes and a friendly smile.

Jackie started first with the questions, and asked if I could eat anything in the world what would I like? My first impulse was to think that they were social workers. Last year on my birthday, a social worker had taken me miniature golfing, so I thought this was going to be my consolation present from the social workers this year. Anything would have been better than to spend my birthday at Father Matthew's. It didn't take but a moment to digest her offer, but disappointed at the absence of my brother, I answered, "Anything is okay." Jackie gave a look to the staff and said, "Don't worry, we've got something special planned for Louie." She opened the door and we were on our way.

They took me to Fudruckers and ordered me the largest banana split in the world. Shirley said very little, and being the authority on the fake smile, I reasoned that she hadn't been paid enough to tag along. I got to play arcade games and run around almost like a real kid. I didn't care who these people were, I was merely glad to be out of my regular house and get to do something without competing with 15 other kids for the adults' attention. The night sped by and before I knew it, we had to

return to Father Matthew's. Jackie gave me a small package in
the driveway once we arrived. I opened it to find a gold
necklace with a little golden shark pendant. I thanked them, still
believing they were social workers. I went inside without a look
back and went straight to bed. I hung the necklace on the
doorknob and stared as the hall light reflected off it.

My thoughts began to wander towards Tony and what
my little brother was doing. I thought of what it was like to have
a birthday with a real family. I knew his birthday was a month
before my own and I envisioned him sitting at a table with his
family, blowing out candles, surrounded by school friends and a
table piled with gifts. My eyes began to burn as I thought I
would never feel that much affection. The burning gave way to
tears and I soaked my pillow on my way to a deep sleep.

I didn't wear the gold chain to school the next day
because I looked at it as a reminder that only people who were
paid or ordered gave me positive attention. Not really knowing
the value of gold, I actually tied the necklace to some shoelaces
and used the mixed cord to lock my closet. But right when I
thought the meeting with Jackie and Shirley was a one-time
thing, they appeared again. I allowed some hope to well up
when they offered to take me on a "home pass."

It is very hard to relay the desperation of a young
orphan, especially after being left behind by my younger
brother. In the world of orphans we all understand that with
each passing year, your chances to get "picked" grow slimmer.
Most people don't want an older adoptee; they want a baby or
someone so young that they will grow up seeing their adoptive
parents as their actual or only family. You can somewhat
understand this, even while watching parent after parent test
drive a kid for the weekend, although it remains very hard to
swallow. After reaching my tenth birthday, I thought that my
chances to be "picked" had been blown out with the candles.
Me, the ugly one with the thick glasses, the one the other boys
labeled faggot and saw as a freak for not having parents. How
many times had I stared at the door and hoped that when adults

came through it they would take me on a home pass instead of one of the others. Almost three years had gone by with only one potential family visit. Could these two be the ones who would take me out of Father Matthew's forever? God, at this point I would have taken Freddy Krueger for a parent. Unfortunately, what I got eventually turned out to be fruit not far from the same tree.

Jackie did most of the talking, as before, and kept making small talk to kill the uncomfortable silences. I accommodated her with brief responses, afraid to say something wrong. We stopped at a donut shop and Jackie told me to pick anything I wanted. I reported that I was undecided between two large donuts and she told the clerk to wrap them both. I first ate an apple fritter larger than both my hands, and next, the biggest chocolate donut ever made, covered with chocolate frosting and sprinkled with chocolate chips. I didn't care that I was starting to feel sick as I gulped down the second donut, and I refused to leave a crumb.

They brought me to Quail Valley, a tiny outlying town in the arid district of Lake Elsinore. Jackie drove us up to a large twenty-foot gate that opened to a five-acre ranch. The property, which was partitioned into three fenced sections, cascaded down into a valley and was complete with a large house, barn, horses, cows, and dogs. I was overwhelmed, as this was a far cry from the urban jungle I was accustomed to in Redlands, San Bernardino, where Father Matthew's was located. Everything seemed so open and all the animals given so much space to run. My senses were confused and in shock, having never seen the country before, or horses and cows either for that matter. Just the inside of the home was so large that my mind gave up on trying to remember everything as Jackie gave me the tour.

Jackie and I went through the living room, dining room, kitchen, hallways, closets, laundry room, and a home office, where they sewed and welded trampolines. Jackie then began showing me the bedrooms. She started by showing me Shirley's room and explained how Shirley lived with her as a ranch hand, meaning she broke the horses, tended to all the animals, and cared for every aspect of the property. Shirley helped Jackie in exchange for room and board. I didn't really understand how this information would impact me, and at the moment, I didn't care. Jackie went on to the enormous master bedroom—her room. And then it happened. My heart jumped out of my chest when I was shown my room. It was decked out with framed pictures of cars, toy planes hanging from the ceiling, my own stereo, desk and bed. *Was this it? Was this the perfect home that every orphan dreams of?*

Shirley showed me around the grounds and not-quite-completed barn. Two sets of stairs 100 feet apart led down to the horse and barn area. Inside the barn structure, there was a tool for everything. I was amazed, impressed and awestruck at the amount of equipment hanging on the walls, shelves, or locked in a small overflowing room. There were professional grade metal and woodworking machines, leather-crafting tools and all the oils, solutions, and cleaners for every type of job imaginable. *Anything is possible here!* My senses were so overloaded that I often tried to pause, to just try and take in the utter joy of these moments. I can't remember any time before that day that any adult spent so much time talking with me and showing me things. I felt so important, special, and wanted. But my extraordinary day wasn't near over; Shirley next saddled the horses and offered her knee so I could mount.

When I was on top of a horse for the first time, I truly thought that I had to be dreaming. *This can't be real!* I rode half the day away and then learned how to bathe and brush the horses; I relished every minute. I got to stay up all night and had ice cream, popcorn, and soda while watching movies I had chosen from the video store. I was in kid heaven. I woke up the next morning thinking that it had all been a dream and was afraid to open my eyes and see Clyde again. When I did get up, I was lured to the kitchen by the smell of a five-course breakfast. That second day was more of the same, and even though my thighs were sore from riding the first day, I pushed past it and went for round two.

As the weekend came to a close, I dreaded going back to Father Matthew's. On the ride back, we had a lot to talk about and I kept thanking Jackie and Shirley for taking me on pass. It was at this time that hope began to flourish. Shirley interjected, "You know, Jackie is looking to adopt a son." *I sat still on pins and needles. What did she say? Were they offering me a home?*

Then Jackie offered directly, "What do you think about coming to live with us?"

I was taken aback and stumbled over my own tongue. What else could I say? What would any orphan say when faced between an orphanage and a horse ranch? Without pause I gave an enthusiastic "I'd love it!"

We got back to Father Matthew's and I went in and reported my weekend to the staff. A couple more visits and I was directed to grab my stuff after the weekend report. Richard came out of the office to say good-bye and Gene came up and gave me a hug. It was the first real hug from a human since Chris left; it almost made me want to stay. *Almost.* I walked down the hall and saw Clyde with the boys in the TV room and he taunted, "Don't mess it up." My strong desire to leave came rushing back.

When we got back to Quail Valley, I looked at the house differently. I saw the horses and couldn't believe that this was going to be my reality. My thoughts raced to where my little brother might be and what he would think of this place. *I wish Tony was here.* I hated that I was moving without my brother; but I knew that there was no other way. I decided to leave the dream of living with Tony behind and move on. I opened the gate for the car with a newfound vigor and sense of direction for my life. I had found a family!

Chapter 6 - Is This L'amour?

"It's not his job to love you; it's your job to love him."

—Dr. Phil, 2005, talking to adoptive parents who were having trouble connecting to their new son, and wanted to send him back.

Can a child who has never known love, not even his own mother's love, show or express it? I could show gratitude, kindness, and the willingness to cooperate, but is that what is in a mother's embrace? I don't think that I had the skills at 10 years old to show my love, and I was confused and frustrated by that. I wanted so badly to leave all my misery, desperation, and angst at Father Matthew's. I wanted to use my new home to the fullest—to really become a son, to learn what love is, feel it, and learn how to express it. For a child, it is easy to make fantasaical plans about how this placement is going to go, but it is an overwhelming task for a child, especially an orphan child, to carry out even the smallest detail.

Here I am again, transferring my clothes and toys from my black trash bag to an unfamiliar set of drawers. Every movement struck a cord in my heart that I was leaving behind the hope to be part of a family that included my little brother. *I would make this home work.* I didn't have a clue about what I was going to do, but I figured it couldn't be that difficult—my brother had done it successfully, right? Instantly, I put that responsibility, and the challenge, on my shoulders—*if I was moved again, it would be my fault, my failure.* I followed every direction to the letter as best I could. I smiled even when I didn't really know why; I just wanted to make my new family comfortable. This is often referred to as the "honeymoon period"—a time when everyone was on his or her respective best behavior, when everything was near euphoric. It was also a time when no matter what anyone did or said, it was brushed over as merely a folly in human connection. The "real" experiences were to come later; the fighting and talking back were what my record told them to expect from me. So from their standpoint, all they needed to do was humor me during my "honeymoon phase" and brace for the other shoe to drop.

At 10, I didn't know or care about these dynamics; I simply wanted a family and was open to however Jackie defined that. I was wholly unprepared to switch from institutional life to a home environment, but I refused to allow my new freedoms to overwhelm me. My first priority was to be accepted in my new home and find the love that I had never felt in my life…yet.

I wasn't enrolled for the last eight weeks or so of school because everyone agreed that it would be an unnecessary burden and we could use the time to bond. *No school? Fine with me!!* Jackie was a phantom Monday through Friday, having to drive around 100 miles in LA traffic to and from UCI Medical Center every day. I didn't miss her much because Shirley took it upon herself to be a teacher to me. Shirley wasn't physically affectionate, but what she lacked in hugs, I felt she made up for in concern for my personal growth. She showed me how to feed the animals and then gave me some of the responsibility. She patiently showed me all sorts of things, saddling a horse, tying knots, and something I thought was cool, building small weapons from scratch. We made slingshots, spears and rubberband guns. Jackie got home late, but we always shared dinner together, finally ending the evening watching some sitcom—as a family. I knew my prayers had been answered, and I had been given the perfect family. Content, I wallowed in my happiness. In bed, I closed my eyes tightly and let three words dance on my heart: adoption, son, and family.

In the beginning, my social workers visited to check on how I was getting along. I remember one taking me to an Angel's baseball game, and another bringing me on a shopping trip to the mall. I reported every detail of my wonderful new home over and over, especially the details of my own bedroom. My social workers arranged for all of us to attend meetings for foster parents. Shirley had to come because she lived under the same roof with us and she had to babysit me so often. Jackie and Shirley went in one room, and I went with all the foster kids into another. I remember one activity that was supposed to help us bridge our old lives with our new ones. We were given biological data from our births and any pictures they had, then told to make a new baby photo album. We put a tape measure in it to show our birth length and drew flags that represented the nationalities of our parents, as according to our birth certificates. Next, we were helped to measure a bag of oranges to represent our birth weight, and then told to cradle them.

"Here Louie. Be careful while you hold the baby." Those words flared up in my head because for years I had seen burn marks and scars on my face and arms and knew that I had been abused as an infant. I had been questioned by a psychiatrist about molestation, physical abuse and probed about any reactions because of the serious illegal drugs I was fed. I truly wasn't interested in glorifying my infancy stage. I grabbed the sack of oranges at one end and began swinging them. Appalled, the social workers called out, "What are you doing? That is a little baby!"

"This is how I was treated as a baby." The other kids started swinging their "babies" around as well and they had lost control of the room. I think back and laugh at this, but also feel fury at the social workers who didn't think that perhaps I had something that needed to be talked about with a professional. Instead, they reported to Jackie and Shirley that I had caused problems. Nobody wanted to *discuss* these problems or the related factors. I got a stern talk and the issue was closed. I continued to receive a lot of positive attentions in those first months, and started relaxing. Above all, I enjoyed learning new things, working with the horses, and what I read into Jackie's hugs.

Foster Parent/Guardian Rule No. 4:   *Measure Your Expectations.*

Be reasonable. Be patient. Let them adjust, and give them time to accomplish the goals you set. Before you endeavor to teach anything, accept that some things will be easy, some will be more difficult, and sometimes, a child *does* forget.

For a while, I had a steady stream of visits from social workers, but then they started to slow down. I don't know if it was because everything was going so well, or because we simply missed each other. But, a little too conveniently, it seemed to coincide with my first summer at the L'amour Ranch, when things started on a downward spiral. While Jackie was at work, I spent many hours alone with Shirley. It seemed as though she had grown jealous of the affection that Jackie kept showering on me, and she looked for a reason to pick a fight. One night while we were making dinner, waiting for Jackie to come home, she imposed a dreaded question. "Why don't you call Jackie 'Mom'?"

I didn't answer aloud and offered my shrugging shoulders. I had just come through utter living hell on a daily basis, and she expected me to jump to the tune because I had a few new things. That's not how it works, not in my mind. In my thinking, Jackie hadn't proven anything other than she knew how to spend money. I wasn't going to jump on this wagon until I knew for certain that the wheels worked.

When Jackie came home and we sat down for dinner; Shirley brought it up again. "I asked Louie why he doesn't call you Mom."

Jackie smiled warmly and locked eyes with me "It's okay. He doesn't have to call me Mom if he doesn't want to." She was smart like that, always playing with words to manage and shift responsibility away from her, and tack on a little guilt in the process. Shirley didn't get it and wasn't happy that Jackie didn't jump to her side. She rephrased the question and tried again.

"I think that he has had plenty of time to decide if he wants you for a mother or not. He should prove that he wants to stay here by calling you 'Mom' and showing respect for all you have done for him." She turned to me and started asking direct questions that were entirely rhetorical. "You do like Jackie don't you? You like all the things we bought you and gave you, right? So why don't you call her Mom; hasn't she treated you like her son?"

I was trapped and chose to not rebut. Instead, I gave in and agreed to the title. After all, it was only a name and my experiences had proven that titles didn't count if they didn't stand the test of time. "Thank you for tucking me in, *Mom.*" was the first time I used my new word and it didn't feel as misplaced as I thought it would.

Calling someone your mother and understanding what it means to be a family member are two entirely separate things. I was ten years old and had a vague idea of what the word "son" meant, but definitely confusing to me was living with a family that didn't include Tony. I was happy to receive one-on-one attention in my new home, but I still had rushes of emptiness that would take me over. I had severe fluctuations in depression and I would hide in the barn to be alone and mourn my brother among other things. Other times I cried uncontrollably, not really knowing why I would break down.

Shirley had found me several times hiding among the stacks of hay and asked what was wrong. I would routinely

wipe my face and respond with "Nothing." I don't think I was
rejecting her; but maybe I was. I knew that she wasn't the one
that was going to adopt me; she was merely a ranch hand,
Jackie's friend, and my babysitter. So maybe I held back from
saying anything to Shirley while waiting for an opportunity to
share with Jackie—with Mom. Whatever the case, I had never
opened my heart to anyone before and really didn't know how.
Shirley would usually just leave me alone to cry, but then one
day it was different. It became a struggle and she repeatedly
asked me what was wrong. I maintained my silence, answering
only with more shrugging shoulders. She perceived that I didn't
want to share with *her*, and offended, she walked away
mumbling, "I don't give a sh** anyway." I went to pet the
horses and give them some sugar cubes as a way to distract
myself from my feelings.

It was after that rejection that Shirley came back out
pacing toward me fast. I faced her, faintly recalling what
usually followed after a walk like that. She held out a bent horse
bit she claimed to find under a saddle. "What is this? Didn't I
show you how to care for everything? Why did you ruin my
best bit?" I didn't remember leaving a bit under a saddle; I was
actually hypersensitive to doing anything out of order. Before I
could think to deny the allegations, she threw a dozen more
questions at me and frustrated my thought processes.

"If you do something wrong then you have to be
punished. Turn around." I noticed that she hadn't exposed her
other hand but could clearly see the training whip sticking two
feet out over her head. I started to shake and cry, falling back
into the fence looking for safety. She pulled me by my arm and
ordered, "You stand there and take it like a man!"

She snapped the whip twice before I could wiggle out of
her grip and turn around. She continued, "You're going to make
it worse if you don't take it like a man!" I clung to the fence,
but she pulled me off again. She snapped the whip on my butt
two more times and then let me go. I had tried to block with my
arm and felt the sting there far worse than on my rear end. I

stayed there frozen, holding my forearm and crying. *What the hell was she thinking, hitting me with that thing meant to only cut through the air around the horses?* She left me there to my crying and didn't speak to me for the rest of the evening. I was bewildered. *Why was I just treated worse than the animals?* Already dealing with uncontrollable depression, her actions catapulted me back into the constant state of self-loathing and low self-esteem that I had tried to leave behind at Father Matthew's.

Jackie came home around six and Shirley went in her room with her while she changed. I could hear them arguing and it rose to yelling shortly. I heard Jackie scolding Shirley for using the whip and Shirley trying to reason that it was necessary. They stayed in there for thirty minutes or so before emerging.

Jackie called me out of my room and sat us down at the dining table. She asked about the bit and the whens and whys. I didn't have any satisfying answers other than "I forgot."

Shirley insisted, "He just doesn't care. I've shown him a dozen times how to care for everything." Jackie was a serious horse trainer and competitor, she had literally hundreds of trophies and belt buckles in her room in a showcase that entirely covered her master bedroom wall. She didn't take the whole "I forgot" thing lightly, and kept pressing for more.

"Why didn't you put everything back like you were shown? You need to show respect for the horse equipment, it is very expensive." In an effort try and scare out my devious plot she threatened, "Do you want us to take you back to Father Matthew's?"

I grew tearful again and began crying, "I'm sorry," and "I didn't do it on purpose." My words were heartfelt. I was to the point of pleading, as the last thing I would ever want is to lose all the new physical and emotional belongings in my life and be forced to return to "Clyde's" orphanage.

"Do you promise to not do it again?" asked Jackie.

"Yes, I promise."

She turned to Shirley and warned her about using the whip. Shirley argued, "I barely touched him! Look and see if you can find a mark!" Jackie became satisfied, finishing the meeting by giving me another warning and sending me to my room. Shirley, on the other hand, wasn't as easily appeased and demanded more justice, as once again, Jackie hadn't taken her side and rallied against me for ruining the piece of equipment. As I got up, she told me to sit down. Jackie directly opposed her and repeated her orders to me. It seemed obvious to me who I needed to listen to, as only one of them was my "Mom." In recognition of her failed power struggle, Shirley gave us a "So this is how it's going to be" look and went to her room, slamming the door.

The next morning, while Jackie was at work, Shirley was quiet and aloof. She kept a good distance from me wherever I was on the property. At lunchtime, she presented me with a list of tasks I needed to complete in order to pay for the piece of equipment. I had no objection; I felt that I knew the reason for the extra chores. She began disciplining me with more and more chores for any infraction. If I was late to feed the horses, I had to wash the horse trailer. If the horse trailer wasn't cleaned thoroughly enough (rarely was it), then I needed to muck out the horse stalls. And on and on, one chore kept leading to another until they began stacking. It was a small matter of time before I was caring for almost everything on the ranch yet being found incompetent in most tasks.

The physical abuses started gaining momentum too; as no matter what I did, it wasn't good or fast enough. In short order, I became familiar with the training whip. Only when I was falling short of expectations was Shirley willing to interact with me, and only physically. Jackie stopped her objection to the use of the whip, as long as there weren't any serious marks.

Shirley could hold her own against any ranch hand, male or female. She walked, dressed and was forceful like a man. She was strong enough to break horses and throw bales of hay around like they were pillows. Once she showed me how to do something, she expected that I do it just as well. She yelled to get me to do something and yelled some more when I didn't do it just so. While helping her to break her horse, Chris, she took turns hitting the horse with the whip and then me. Chris threw me a dozen times, but I was never as fearful of him as of Shirley's whip. Day by day, Shirley's fuse for my incompetence became shorter and shorter, regardless of the fact that I had no previous experience or training at being a ranch hand. She followed her frustrations by threatening, "I'm going to have you sent back to Father Matthew's!" I would apologize for whatever I had done and beg that she didn't send me back.

All over again, I was living in daily fear of what I would be punished for and how. Only this time I faced it alone. Jackie seemed to almost balance out what Shirley did by spending time alone with me on activities for any tasks that were completed. Conversely, she had also stopped any objection or debate as to my punishment, as Shirley had made me seem like some kind of monster who refused to comply with even the smallest request. Jackie continued in her conclusion that there was no harm in my "spankings" as long as there weren't any severe marks left behind.

I became so afraid of Shirley's presence that I would flinch as she would walk by. Then she would hit me for flinching. "What's wrong with you? Are you a little sissy? Stand up straight! Be a man!" She began demanding more and more of me as time pressed on. I started working on the landscaping, clearing away the five acres with a hoe, pick and shovel. I spent long summer days digging holes for an electric fence, pulling weeds by hand or mucking out the horse and cow stalls. She had me stack the hay when it came in, even though the deliverers did it for free. She was always standing behind me with the men and antagonizing, "I'm making a man out of him." The workers nodded and lent support by telling me what a good job I did after I was finished. Her manipulations were perfect, and I kept jumping at her every order, thinking that everything was my failure, and I *could* please her if I did a job good enough. Time and experience would prove otherwise.

Finally, one evening I said something as Jackie was cooking dinner. She offered, "I got the day off tomorrow and thought it would be nice to go to the batting cages, after your chores are done."

"No thanks." I revealed my blistered palms and fingers, "My hands are too sore."

Shirley came in and heckled, "Aw, can't handle your little chores. After all we've given you, you want to complain and whine. Look at these hands! I do twice the work you do and I don't complain!"

"*Little chores?* I feel like I'm your slave," I snapped back. I don't know where I got the courage; maybe I just thought that 'Mom' wouldn't let anything happen to me. It ended up being a phrase that was used against me over and over again.

"What did you say, you little sh**?!" She squinted her eyes and her thick, dark brow shaped a telling "V." She rushed into the room and slapped me across the face, sending me to the floor. As I hit the ground, she tried to lift me up to spank me some more. When I wouldn't cooperate and did my all to get away from her, she began kicking me across the living room. As her silver tipped boots kept hurling towards my body, I curled up and tried to see her next move through my arms, trying to shield my head.

Jackie bolted over and pushed Shirley from behind and away from me. "Stop it! Stop it! Go calm down." I thought for sure that Jackie had come to my rescue and was going to comfort me. Instead, she turned and snapped, "Don't you ever talk back to her like that!" She reached down toward me, and in order to lecture me, tried to remove my arms from shielding my face. I tensed my body and waited for the next blow. She pulled on my arms and ordered that I get up.

"Go to the bathroom, *now!*" Her voiced lacked the angry tone from before and, afraid of what noncompliance would result in, I started to get up. Right away, I noticed blood all over my right forearm. I thought that Shirley's boots had split my arm. I didn't feel anything and couldn't find a source. I was so scared seeing my blood all over and not knowing where it was coming from. When we got in the bathroom, she turned on the bathtub water and rushed me in, clothes and all. She started splashing my face and I only felt stinging for a few seconds as the water came into contact with the wound. I shook my head as the water was going up my nose and Jackie grabbed me firmly and ordered, "Stay still."

It was the first time I really remember tasting my own blood. The more she wiped and splashed, the more that my mouth and nostrils were filled with water-diluted blood. I endured my nausea until I was satisfactorily cleaned and I was able to drink a few hand cups full of water to wash away the tin and iron taste. During all of this, I heard Shirley demand that I stop crying. Jackie turned and told her to go get the first-aid kit. She came back shortly, still with a sneer on her face, and jabbed the kit forward. Jackie went right to work applying ointment and gauze to my face. When she finished, she sent me to my room, where I stayed, hoping that the storm was over.

I wanted to see what was wrong with my face, so I peeled some of the tape back while standing in front of my mirror. Racing through my mind were the whats and whys. *Had I earned this punishment? Maybe I shouldn't have said what I did.* I took on the blame, already feeling like I was a piece of meat and less than human, unworthy of normal interactions. I justified their actions in my mind, thinking *"If I had only,"* or *"Next time I will be better."* All were excuses, a 10-year-old trying to make sense of these senseless actions. I got the corner of my bandage unstuck and pulled it back to see what looked like a gash along my jawbone. As I examined myself, the door swung open.

Shirley's voiced filled the room, "What are you doing? No one told you to touch that!" She started taking off her belt and I began backing. I fell over my desk chair behind me and clamored to grab something right before I hit my head against the wall. She smiled and said, "Serves you right for not standing up like a man!" At this, I began hating her; how I wished I could have stood up and punched her in the jaw. She was standing there scolding me for looking at the wound she gave me, and then smiled when something else happened! But she wasn't finished; she continued up to me and started swinging. The leather burned my arms as I tried to block my head. She razzed, *"Get up Coward!"* *"Get up Sissy!"*

Again, Jackie came in and grabbed her, pulled her back, and ushered her out of the room. I was crying so hard I couldn't hear. She tried to calm me down, and once I had; started with the excuses. "Shirley thinks this is how you show you care. She just doesn't know her own strength. Her father was very strict and she is punishing you the only way she knows how. She really loves and cares for you." There was no way I was going to be convinced that her extremely abusive roommate cared! To me, it seemed like the professional ranch hand thought that I was an animal that needed to be broken. "You're just going to have to be patient with her and do what she says so you won't have to be punished, *okay?*"

Looking back, I cannot believe that she put the weight of Shirley's temper and physical discipline on my shoulders. But at the time, I just wanted to get back to the place where Jackie "loved" me again, so I nodded my head in agreement. Next, she began to tell me how I shouldn't have talked back to Shirley and that I have to always show respect to adults. *Pure manipulation, pure Jackie.*

My face healed slowly, as I wasn't taken to see a physician because surely they didn't want to have to explain anything. I didn't really know better and assumed that my wound wasn't serious. Shirley backed down for a few days, but only for a few days. She did most of my chores for me while commenting, "Don't want you to feel like a *slave,* do we?"

In addition to our Sunday routine of chores, Shirley had made a habit of bringing me with her to a Catholic Church after something big like that happened. She would give me a rosary to hold while I waited and tell me to pray to God so that He would make me behave. I would wait on the dark wooden benches, staring at the flicker of candles while she confessed and got forgiveness. I used my time to get lost in the glow of candle flames, trying to understand what was wrong with me, and what I needed to do to be loved. Shirley's little routine of finding peace with God didn't ever change her actions, but usually slowed her down for a while until her blessing wore off. She found other ways to torment me until she regained her resolve to hit me again.

In another coincidence of balancing out my trauma, I was told that "my cousin" was having a summer wedding and we were flying out to Denver, Colorado with Jackie's parents who lived about thirty miles away. Jackie took me shopping for a suit and shoes and I gloried in the attentions of Jackie and the salespeople. Sitting in the airport with Grandma and Grandpa and Jackie—my official family—I felt so warm, thinking that maybe the worst was over, and perhaps now I would be treated like a son and not an animal. The truth was that Jackie was insanely jealous of her sister Racine, who was very successful, owning a large trampoline business. But even when I figured that out, I didn't really care; I was content to be in the middle during the next few weeks while they tried to prove to the rest of the family who could be more affectionate to me.

First and foremost there was no hitting in Denver, which would have been heaven enough. But on top of that, Racine had gotten me a gift bag of toys that she presented as I got off the plane. "Welcome to the family!" she said as she pulled me into her bosom. Jackie's mom and dad, Gary and Elaine, were showered with gifts as well. Shirley, thank God, had to stay home and tend to the ranch.

During our visit we were whisked up to Aspen, where Racine had rented out an enormous wooden cabin so the whole family could stay together. Every time that Gary or Elaine would make a comment about how nice it was, Jackie's face grew so grim she would have to catch herself and walk away. I heard from one of the teenage cousins how they had been competing since they were little. Their sibling rivalry was well known and sometimes their verbal competitions turned into small brawls that needed to be broken up.

As I silently sat in the living room among the adults catching up, I got a small taste of their feud. Racine ran her trampoline business out of Boulder, and Jackie had a small franchise in her garage. Racine turned to Jackie and commented on how business was slow. Everyone knew she was baiting Jackie so she could patronize Jackie's very slow business. Jackie's eyes swept around the room in embarrassment and then she gave a fake all-teeth smile and changed the subject. "I've been spending so much time getting ready to help my foster child that I haven't had much time for trampolines." Jackie began to relay facts from my file without regard for my feelings; she just wanted to seem like a bigger person now with all eyes on her.

After comments like "that's a shame" and "poor thing" passed around the room, Jackie was recognized as a good person for taking me in. I was bubbling with embarrassment and my skin felt like it had flushed red-hot. I stared down at the floor, feeling every eye on me, waiting for me to comment. Like my story was to be retold in my own words now for their entertainment. I fidgeted in my seat until Jackie's other sister, Sarah, changed the subject and let me off the hook. That was the last time the subject was brought up in my direct presence while we were on our trip. Except for a few awkward moments, I did have a lot of fun in Denver. Everyone seemed nice and even concerned with me, some asking where I got the cut on my face. Jackie quickly interjected, "Didn't you get that helping me break Chris?" Before I made a choice to go along with her or not, the rest of the family—*who were all serious horse people*—jumped in, saying how I was really part of the family.

"Helped break a horse? Louie *must* be a L'amour" from one aunt.

"That's how to raise a boy!" from Grandpa L'amour.
Then it was all or nothing: "Did it hurt?" a cousin
asked. *Should I buy in or jump out?* Every ear in the room was
waiting for the next words out of my mouth. The rest of the
family seemed so approving that I decided to go along—to fit
in. I shrugged my shoulders, not able to find the words to
validate Jackie's story.

I didn't need to. In short order, a procession of horse
breaking and riding stories ensued. I got pats on the back for
being "tough as nails" and eventually I jumped in with my own
true experiences of breaking Chris. I wished I had taken note at
how masterfully Jackie had maneuvered around the truth.
Instead, it became the first of many times that I looked to Jackie
to explain any marks on me. I was instantly trained that to let
Jackie explain meant that I would be rewarded with family. It
was a horrible trade-off in retrospect, but at the time it seemed
very much worth it.

All my new cousins took me to a small amusement park
and I got to ride a Ferris wheel for the first time. Once the
wedding was over, everyone flew down to Lake Powell to stay
on Racine's houseboat for the weekend. I got to ride her jet skis
and water-skied behind her speedboat. I very quickly started
hanging around Racine more and more to see what we would
get to do next. Which, I'm sure, was her exact plan for mind-
wrestling her sister. She had less of an edge than Jackie and was
more predictable. This was evidenced further when, while I was
riding the jet skis with a cousin, his sank and she didn't even
blink an eye. No blaming, conniving, yelling, swearing or
anything—behavior that seemed very peculiar to me. This
overwhelming, intoxicating dose of materialism had to be what
drove me to stay with Jackie and her family in spite of other
factors.

I returned to Quail Valley after my trip with a new sense
of self. I had been shown in a small way that I was worth
something to someone, and was worthy of consistent positive
attention, regardless if it was a game between sisters. I had

some peace in my heart, having smiled more in those weeks than I had ever smiled since playing with Tony a lifetime ago. When we got home from the airport, the house was empty and I was relieved. I knew that Shirley would be incensed if she found a smile on my face, especially since, to my knowledge, she had not been invited to come.

Shirley appeared the next day, full of attitude. With an obvious chip on her shoulder, she picked on Jackie first, playing "devil's advocate" while Jackie talked about the trip and how Racine had showed off. At times Shirley would demand to know why Jackie hadn't done or said this or that. She reiterated how Jackie looks after her parents without any help from the rest of the family. Shirley's agitation turned entirely onto me once Jackie began reporting the "extra" attention I had received. She started questioning me in a frenzy. "Why didn't you stick up for your mother? Why didn't you stay by your mother? Hasn't she been nice enough to you?" Then came the name calling, "You ungrateful piece of sh**. You're not her son, you'd turn your back on her the second someone with more money came along!"

She ranted on until she began repeating her cycle of questions and hurling her venom all over again. I didn't know what to say. I wished I had had the words to tell her that Jackie didn't treat me like her own son, and how she used me as a pawn in her sibling rivalry, and how she watched Shirley beat the crap out of me so she could play "good cop." But most of all, I wished I could have stood up then and hit her, or told her to go screw herself. I didn't do any of these, of course. I was scared out of my mind, and as she towered over me, my body froze and I remained speechless. She walked over to the water heater, now her favorite place to keep her whip. Once she brandished it, I got up and hid behind Jackie.

Jackie wasn't going to stand up for me this time. "Get away from me. Now you want *me*?" If I had had any idea of the game they were playing, or that Jackie would be so hurt that I was trying to have fun, maybe I would have cut the time spent with my new family in order to stay right by Mom's side. I didn't realize that I was *Jackie's* stray puppy, and only allowed, like a pet dog, to really be a part of the family that was under *that* roof—I didn't know that I wasn't truly welcome to become a member of the whole family. I was no more than a work tool, and if needed, a scale tipper in the battle for ground in Jackie's own family war.

Shirley stormed up and reached for me. Running, I sought sanctuary under the dining room table and grabbed the chair legs so I could block her whip. In a rage, she tossed the table over and started swinging the whip at me. I pulled as close to the table as possible and screamed and cried but she continued. Every blow sent a shockwave through my body and I tried to squeeze myself into a tight ball so that less of me was exposed to the whip. Shirley couldn't hear my cries clearly enough, so she pulled me out by the arm and dragged me over to the living room. She demanded that I stand up in front of Jackie, who was now sitting in her chair. She gave me a three count that I couldn't have possibly known had an end. "One. Two. Three," and then the whip snapped against my back. "One. Two…" I got up quickly and stood in front of Jackie. I tried to keep Shirley in my field of vision but she kept moving around behind me. Then, knowing what I was doing, the whip snapped by my ear as she ordered me to stand still. I gave Jackie a long, sincere, gaze, hoping that she would make this all stop. Even with tears streaming down my face she wasn't moved. Her cold, piercing eyes told me that she was into this game. The "Questions" started again, this time from Jackie.

"Don't I treat you good? I love you like a son, so why don't you treat me like your mother? You have horses and the dogs to play with. A big house and your own bedroom. And this is how you say 'Thank you'; by cuddling up to the first person that offers you more than I can. That is not what *Family* does. I should take you back to Father Matthew's right now and get another boy that will appreciate all that I've done for him!"

How I wish I had had a time machine so as to have the insight to be able to whisper to her, "If you really loved me, then you would have been happy to see me smiling." Surely this would have just drawn more hits, but it might have given her something to think about later. I stood there whimpering and shaking and pushed out, "I... *love you.*" I started buying into her logic while trying to catch a glimpse of Shirley.

"Answer her!" The whip snapped across my shoulders. I fell to one knee and she again commanded that I stand immediately. "One..." and I stood up. My shoulders now aflame, I couldn't hear past the intense burning in my back. Another snap across my lower back and buttocks. I flinched forward but remained standing. This obviously wasn't satisfactory and she whipped me across my shoulders with the tip coming around and snapping my uncovered neck. I fell to the ground again, curled and held my neck, writhing in pain. I could feel the warm blood on my hand and I gave out that silent cry that would've been a shrill scream if my voice box could hit such a note. When the need to cry out had passed, I closed my mouth and began to growl in my throat, trying not to give her the satisfaction of more wailing.

"You think you're tough?" She wanted to hear screams. She began to kick me with her silver-tipped boots. The first strike sent me onto my other side, and the second landed in my gut. "Get up tough boy. Get up now! We're not through with you!" Her demands required an immediate response before the next series of blows inevitably came. I started to get up, but not fast enough for her. As I rose to all fours, her boot came swiftly to my chest, pushing me into the air. I fell to the ground and saw a white flash as I hit the floor; then there was nothing.

I awoke some time later to Jackie's soft voice. I was in my bed, all wet, with an enormous headache. My neck had been bandaged and Shirley was nowhere in sight. She reached for something and turned; I flinched and scooted back in the bed, tensing my body for another strike. Her hand offered a glass of water. "It's okay, your punishment is over. Are you okay? How is your head? How is your stomach?"

Was she for real? She had just witnessed me getting beaten to unconsciousness and had done nothing to intervene. She was no less a monster than Shirley. And even with my blossoming hatred for these abusive actions, I searched for reasons, like so many abuse victims, to understand my responsibility. I hadn't the wisdom to grasp that to be the good cop, Jackie had to act concerned after her abusive friend was done with me. The reason why she let it go so far this time was simple. She wanted to be the only one that got credit for bringing a smile to the face of this orphan. She wanted my happiness to be a reflection of what a "good" person she was. This wouldn't hold up if I showed any appreciation to her sister for all that she offered. And because of her jealousy of her sister, and her desire to play comforter to Shirley's discipline, I had to pay the price.

But without this insight, I reacted emotionally, taking everything at face value. Since I didn't understand the game I had become part of, I took every one of her words to heart. In my mind, there was no greater threat than having to go back to the bleak, dreadful loneliness of Father Matthew's Orphanage— to again be the object of others' amusement, to again endure that daily wait to see if just maybe the next family through the door might choose me to be their son. And who knows what the next family might be like, or if there would even be a next family. I didn't doubt that Jackie and Shirley would send me back, and that was unacceptable. My brain searched for the reason they would want to dump me. Maybe I wasn't good enough; maybe I wasn't a cute enough "puppy" with my thick glasses and bed-wetting. Maybe I had done something really wrong to deserve all my punishments. I had no choice; I had to stay. Where would I go? I needed to prove myself a good son to these women, worthy of this home, this family, and mostly, worthy of their love. I spent the rest of the summer jumping at Shirley's every command trying to prove just that.

Chapter 7 - The Silver Lining

It was now time to start school, and just like moving in with new guardians, I faced all the same fears of being accepted or not. With Shirley having thoroughly taken my self-esteem hostage, I automatically walked around with my head down and minded my own business. I didn't even bother to check the room to see if anyone cared, as the teacher did the whole "Class, we have a new student" routine. I slowly made acquaintance with my classmates. My athletic ability was the key to breaking the ice, and pretty quickly I began getting picked in the top three when we formed teams for recess or PE.

After school, I spent every second outside the house with the animals. Trying to avoid Shirley and understand my new school dynamics, I would inevitably also assess my living situation. After my chores were done, I'd hide among the haystacks, and one time in particular, I recall making a literal resolution to stay with Jackie and Shirley. Sitting in the barn and watching the sunset, a strong wind blew through the structure and the tools, harnesses, and ropes swayed and rapped against the sides of the barn. I didn't look at all of these items with optimism and possibility as I once had before. Now I saw tasks, and had memories attached to these items— how that rope had been swung at me or how sore my hands were from using those hay hooks to stack the deliveries. I hadn't found the perfect family, but to me, it was still better than living at the orphanage. It remained my duty, my responsibility, to make this placement a success, and I was determined to continue to take any "spankings" and move forward. It almost brought a smile to my face that I thought I had control in my life, and I was in the driver's seat. Once I heard Jackie's car pull up, I headed for the house.

"How's school?" Asked Jackie.

"Okay."

"Make any new friends yet?"

"A couple"

Jackie offered to keep her promise to use my trundle bed for a sleepover if I wanted to invite a classmate. At first I jumped at the idea, but as Shirley passed through the kitchen, I thought of what might happen if I introduced one of my friends to her. I didn't decline verbally, but I chose to visit my friends only at their homes.

I had some fun hanging out with the more athletic students of my school, who also ended up being "the cool kids." I stayed after to play sports until their parents came, and sometimes caught a ride home with one of them. This led to stops at fast food restaurants and then to an invitation to spent the night at my buddy Jeff's home. We watched some videos and got into some mischief, which no one ever found out about, that made for a good story to tell our peers. These interactions marked the time in my life when I began to project a tough or jock image so that I could make friends. In my mock toughness I gained some "cool" friends, but I inadvertently pigeonholed myself and couldn't talk about my abuse or how scared, hurt, and often depressed I was. I had lost the opportunity to have a real friend because I was being fake all the time.

As my first holiday season with the L'amours approached, I couldn't help but let depression take me over again. Between periods of abuse and calm I never found the opportunity to relay how important Tony was to me. Not that I thought they would have listened before anyway, but now, seeing the soft glow of Christmas lights in store windows and adorning homes, I began grieving again for my lost brother who had been taken from me nearly five years earlier.

Foster Parent/Guardian Rule No. 5: *Admit What You Bring and How it Will Affect Your Child*

Every day take an inventory of what you bring to the table when interacting with youth trapped in the System. Whether a personal belief, personality trait, or a mood—admit to what positive and negative impacts these will have on a child.

When Christmas came, I was lavished with gifts from Jackie. I don't know if it was out of guilt for leaving me with that monster Shirley all the time, or as a result of direct competition with Racine, who had sent a big-screen-TV-sized container full of presents to our house, almost ninety-nine percent just for me. I didn't care. Racine's box of gifts was so big we had to bring the truck down to the post office to pick it up. Money, toys, clothing, and jewelry emerged out of endless packages that had tags with my name on them. Jackie must have spent a thousand dollars to compete; she bought me a computer, a remote control car, and a new saddle. Even the next day there were more presents by the fireplace with "from Santa" tags on them. "Grandma" and "Grandpa" also had a load of competitive presents from both daughters.

Feeling like I was in a movie, I sat down to a Christmas dinner feast with Jackie and her mom and dad. The family event continued as we listened to carols and opened presents. It did seem peculiar that Jackie was all of a sudden concerned with my happiness and for some reason Shirley wasn't around that night. But I was far too engrossed in the events of the day to ask any questions. It was awkward to be receiving presents—a lot of presents—for Christmas. My child's eye took this overflow of wrapping paper and fancily prepared food dishes as love and affection. It was my first Christmas, and I took every gift as a note of acceptance into the family fold. Maybe I was now good enough to be treated as all the tags and cards called me: Son, Nephew, and Grandson. Maybe.

I got to give presents to the animals, too. Lobo the German shepherd got new chew toys, Aussie the Australian Shepherd and Lucky, the black mutt got new blankets for their beds and treats, and the horses got carrots and sugar cubes with new brushes and shampoos. It seemed that pain had taken a break in the L'amour home, and there was finally a family day. I was almost 11, and I wanted the gifts to mark acceptance. I wanted my life to be devoid of Shirley's lessons now. I wanted to finally have earned a spot in their family. At least that's how I wanted to perceive the abundance of gifts, in my childhood naiveté.

New Years was next, and Racine had flown everyone out from Colorado to see the Tournament of Roses Parade and the Denver Broncos in the Super Bowl. Of course they were big fans, since generations of their family had been brought up in Colorado. They colored their hair orange and all had bright orange clothing on. I flaunted the Christmas gifts Racine had sent me and thanked her a million times. She seemed embarrassed at the gratitude and kept giving me hugs to hush me. Naturally, this motivated me to pay her even more compliments in hopes of getting more hugs, since she seemed to not run out of them. As before, when the family got together, Shirley wanted no part of their visit. Shirley said she hated Racine for how she manipulated Jackie's family. I was glad Shirley excluded herself. I didn't feel totally a part of the L'amour family, but I did feel included, at least when Racine was involved. Again the cousins got permission to take me out and we went to Knott's Berry Farm.

I never knew such a place existed. We were on our feet for hours playing games and going on rides, and the pace never slowed all the way up until it was time to go. I had a great time with them and was glad to be smiling in their company again. In a short time, everything was over and I returned to school. I finally had something positive report when our class shared their Christmas break activities. Riding on a cloud of euphoria, I thought that I was becoming resistant to the pain and depression that had dominated my life for so many years as before. But then there was Shirley.

Once the L'amours left, Shirley returned. She wasn't happy at reports of my participation in family activities. She found reasons to knock me around in the house, and I did my best to be outside whenever possible. She must have thought that I was taking her place in Jackie's life, and not wanting to lose her friend as well as her home; she went on the warpath to find fault in anything I did or was responsible for. She made a routine of using the whip and if not readily available, her belt, boots, sticks, bridles, and fists. I remember her dumping over a bucket of water and swinging it at me. Nothing was off limits so that I would "learn my lesson." But by far her favorites were her whips. She would creep up behind me and snap the training whip in the air by my ear to scare the crap out of me, and before I could ball up and hit the ground, a second strike landed on my butt.

I probably would have broken in two if it weren't for my responsibilities with the animals. They were my friends and a major source of relief for me. I bathed the horses and they allowed me to give them long hugs and rub the soft spots on their mouths. I had gotten to raise the cows since they were babies, bottle-feeding them and petting them. I would let them lick my hand and sometimes their long tongues would reach halfway to my elbow. The dogs were also my companions. Lobo, the German shepherd, had at first been wary of me, and very much Shirley's and Jackie's guard dog. On the other hand, Lucky, so named because she had crawled into our yard as some Vietnamese were chasing her down (Jackie told me this and said they would eat all black dogs), was very fond of me and would follow me around everywhere. And Aussie, a very gentle and smart Australian Shepherd, could always be found close behind.

I spent many hours avoiding interaction with Shirley by tending to and playing with the animals. In an effort to be nice, or perhaps to prevent me from reporting them, Jackie had given

me Otay, a speckled gray and white Arabian mare. The ranch
bordered a large state park, and I was allowed to take her on the
trails there. I would ride all day with her. Most of the time,
Lucky and Aussie tagged along on these rides. To me it felt like
I had a family in them, family members I could spend the day
with without fear. Our securities were found in each other and
we were all relieved to be off the property. Everyone except
Lobo had known the force of Shirley's boot, and Otay shared
the knowledge of her whip with me.

After a few more years, Lobo didn't escape Shirley's
brand of "love" either. There had also been a Dachshund puppy
that hadn't even been given a name yet. She had peed on the
floor in excitement as we entered the house one day, and as a
result caught a boot from Shirley that sent her flying from the
front door to the fireplace in the next room. Jackie explained
that the injury was serious, and how it was the dog's fault for
peeing on the floor. Shirley took the puppy to the back of the
property and I never saw her again.

None of the animals had to worry about me hitting them,
and when I was being hit, I'd often turn to them for comfort.
They would always receive me and lie with me until I stopped
crying. They were my confidants and I could tell them anything,
especially about Shirley, and they were completely attentive. I
loved each and every one of them and felt that they loved me. I
spent as much time as possible basking in the almost
unconditional love of the animals. I craved acceptance by Jackie
and Shirley but was contented with my loving animal friends.

Lobo had eventually put aside his guard-dog prejudices
and began sharing these moments with me, too. Shirley
wouldn't let him off the property when I went riding, but he
started to join our circle of consolement. After months of
watching me work the yard and tend to the animals, he began to
sit closer and closer to me, as if to watch over me while I was
working. I wasn't allowed to feed him—only Shirley was—and
that probably kept him a little hesitant as to what my role was
there.

In March, Jackie told me that I was invited to a skate party for my little brother. I was overwhelmed with emotion and was vociferously grateful. Both Jackie and Shirley took the credit for arranging my visit when the other wasn't around. It was some weird game that I was too elated to focus on. I didn't care who had found Tony for me, I just wanted to see him.

To report that my first visit was a disappointment would be an extreme understatement. I had been torn away from my sibling five years before and all I got was a three-hour birthday party in a music-blasting skating rink. Jackie brought me and sat at the adult table with Tammie until it was time to go. Tony and I shared very awkward exchanges, like we knew that we were family in one way, but not in another. Tony spent most of his time on the skating floor with dozens of his friends and newer family members. It wasn't long before I committed myself to the shadows and subconsciously refused to interact until Tony came over to invite me himself. But he never did.

Our goodbyes were brief and unemotional. There wasn't any talk of future visits and I didn't profess any of my feelings for him. I took it very hard that we had grown so apart. But I never blamed Tony; I blamed the System.

Going back to school, I had a heavy heart that had been crushed by a nine-year-old. My own birthday was only a few weeks away and I would be turning 11. Jackie told me that I could invite Tony out for my birthday and spend the whole weekend with him. I couldn't believe how I leaped at the suggestion. I thought, "Maybe I can impress him and make him want me back again. Maybe it will be different if I get to show him my horse and my room and my toys and show him how to choose blood over possessions." I was going to make it obvious that I cared about him more than anything else and hope that the feelings would be returned.

April 17th came and I didn't really have many friends to invite to my party, and chose not to, remembering how I had felt so left out amongst his. I planned to spend the weekend with only him and me. Jackie went to pick him up on the way back from work, and I paced the yard, waiting for their arrival.

I was getting a second chance with Tony, on less distracting terms. Every time before, when we were together, there was always a lure of presents, or the promise that something more exciting would be available, if he left me. No cousins or exciting new friends this time; just him and I. But I struggled in thinking this would work. Could I prove to him that I was worthy of his love? Could I prove to him that I loved him more than anyone on this planet? Would he accept my love and choose me to be in his heart again? Would any of this be enough for him? Determined to find out, I planned to entice him not with gifts, but with the honest love of his real brother.

As the car pulled up, I rushed the gate, swinging it back as fast as I could. I chased them down the driveway and began opening Tony's door before they had come to a complete stop. I practically pulled him out and lifted him off his feet as I squeezed him. We went inside and put his bag in our room, it would be our room once again and the thought sent a chill through my body. He was here, with me, and I couldn't contain my excitement.

I sat on the bed as he looked around the room. We turned on the radio and played computer games. He stayed at the desk for a while and I sat on the bed behind him, holding onto the excitement that was starting to overwhelm me and bring on tears of joy. Jackie peeked her head in and told me that I should show him around. We walked around the yard with the dogs by our sides. Lobo had been put into his quarantine pen as it was thought that he might bite. I showed Tony the trampoline in the yard, around in the barn and out to the horses and cows. He asked if he would be able to ride one of them and I proudly informed him that Otay was mine. He just about glared a hole through me, in what I have to think was jealousy. Could he possibly be jealous of my home? I didn't have many cousins and friends there competing with him, but I thought maybe he intuitively saw how my relationship with Otay and the other animals as threatening. I didn't understand his look and wanted to put him at ease immediately. In sincerity, I told him that whatever is mine was his also.

We stayed up all night playing video games in our room. We teased each other over who got the highest score and fought in play to decide the ultimate victor. Shirley came in to tell us to stop and sternly asked us not to horseplay because someone might get hurt—an obvious power-play brimming with irony. We followed her direction and Tony soon got tired and went to sleep. I was still all wired at his mere presence and stayed up as long as possible, simply to watch over him. Every minute, I played out scenarios in my mind of him living with me—of me being his protector again and the one he turned to for answers and love. It was surreal to have him lying in a bed next to my own, in the same room again, and I didn't want it to ever end.

The next day I got up and fed the animals without bothering my little brother's rest. I helped Jackie make breakfast and got him up once everything was finished. I made plates for him and me and placed them next to each other at the end of the table. Jackie sat at the head and Shirley, who had slept in, didn't show for breakfast. I watched for the look on Tony's face as he devoured his meal, seeking his approval. By the quickness with which he ate, I figured I got it. After breakfast we went down to the stalls and I showed him how to saddle Otay. Jackie let me borrow her horse, Opinion, a stunning paint stallion. I helped boost Tony onto Otay and took the reins, walking him through the field. I showed Tony basic horsemanship and then got up on Opinion. The dogs followed us over to the state park and we began down a trail.

We spent hours that day on the open trails. I gave no attention to where we were going, just basking in my day, the wind in my face and Tony by my side. I daydreamed aloud, "I wish it was the old west and we could ride wherever we wanted together."

"Why?"

"So we could stay together and live wherever we wanted."

Again this time with true inquiry, "Why?"

I was scared. Was he totally oblivious to what I was saying, or was he sending me a message that he wouldn't want to go anywhere with me? A sledgehammer of silence had been slammed and I didn't know if I had the strength or courage to lift it. Afraid of rejection yet again, I took the easy way out. "It would just be fun, that's all."

"Oh. Yeah." Tony was always prone to one-syllable responses when it came to me, and this pattern made it hard to know his thoughts. So I gave them my best guesses and hoped for implications and actions that I could use to try and draw him close to me.

We made it to the back of Lake Canyon and tied the horses to a tree so they could reach the water. I stripped down to my underwear and jumped in. Tony sat on the side with Lucky and Aussie with a "You must be crazy" look on his face. "Come on in!" I invited.

"What if someone comes?"

"No one ever comes back here. Come on, get in!" I encouraged. A little more needling and he took off his clothes and jumped in. We took turns swinging by a giant rope that hung from a tree. I laughed and Tony laughed. My heart was at peace for those hours. All the time worrying that my brother didn't like me anymore had proved unfounded in our time at the lake. I hopped on Otay and walked her into the water.

"She'll drown, what are you doing?!"

"Don't worry, I do this all the time with her. She loves the water and she can swim."

"Horses don't swim."

"Of course they do, watch." I had gotten her deep enough and had swum away from her in a game that we played. She and I swam to the other side of the lake together. We did it again and I grabbed her reins and asked Tony if he wanted to try. He refused and asked to go back. On the other hand, I didn't want to go back and wanted something more along the lines of us staying there forever—or at least until the sun was about to go down. But I wanted Tony to stay happy, so I reluctantly agreed to go back.

When we got back, we put the horses and saddles away and started jumping on the trampoline. We jumped together, holding one another's arms. Every so often one of us would land a split second before the other and be catapulted. We would fall together laughing and wrestling.

At this, the sliding glass door had opened, and Shirley started her angry pace toward us. The training whip in clear view, I thought that there was no way she going to come over to us. "I told you guys to stop fighting! Now you're getting a spanking."

We were only playing." I explained.

"It doesn't matter. You shouldn't be playing like that on the trampoline." She insisted. "Someone could get hurt. I warned you and gave you guys a chance and you are fighting again anyway."

"We were playing!" I implored. I knew what was coming and didn't want to give Shirley the chance to try and prove herself to Tony. She wasn't backing down and I began to panic. What can I do? I can't protect Tony from this psycho. In an effort to appease her, I got down off the trampoline and bent over for her to strike me. She was in mental ward heaven and quickly took the opportunity to show her authority. I don't know if she was being merciful or calculating, but her hits were nowhere near as hard as they had been before. Two more light hits and there was a pause.

"Okay Tony, it's your turn. Come down and take it like a man." I saw the look of utter confusion on Tony's face. His expression showed shock and disbelief and he didn't move from his spot.

"You can't spank me! You're not my Mom!"

I turned toward her, grabbed her leg and cried out, "Please no. It was my fault. Tony was trying to tell me to stop." It didn't work and she kicked me away.

"Get down here now and take it like a man or you'll get it where you are." Tony climbed down and faced her standing totally upright. Big mistake. Shirley expected every boy or man to cower before her and grabbed his arm and swung him around. "One" and the first strike sent Tony into tears while trying to run away from Shirley. Her grip was too tight. "Two." Tony fell to the ground and cried louder still. Without a second thought I ran over to Lobo's pen and let him go. He ran after Shirley, snapping at my command. She swung the whip at Lobo—big mistake. He lunged at her and began snarling. She backed up and sped up the staircase with Lobo steadfast in his threat to bite. Once she got to the second stairs at the foot of the house, Lobo turned back to me.

I ordered him to sit and he complied. I put my hand on Tony's shoulder and in just above a whisper asked, "Are you alright?"

"No."

"Don't worry, she won't be back." And I motioned toward Lobo. I pulled him by his arm and lifted him onto the trampoline. "I hate her!" came out next.

"Why did she use that whip?" Tony said over his sniffling.

"I don't know. That's the way she punishes me when I do something bad."

Sounding puzzled, he inquired, "She hits you...with a whip?"

I couldn't look him in the eyes, "All the time." I led him over to the hose and we washed our faces off. We sat on the trampoline for an hour or so, with Lobo standing guard in silence. What must he be thinking? I had hoped that he gave me credit for letting Lobo out and finding a way to protect him. In honesty though, I thought that he was probably blaming me for the whole thing.

Jackie finally drove up and I told Tony to follow me to the fence. "What's wrong? Why is Lobo out?"

I informed, "Shirley hit us for wrestling on the trampoline."

Tony added, "With a whip!" Jackie, of course, didn't blink an eye, already knowing full well what I meant when I said "hit us." I continued on to detail the incident and how I had let out Lobo to get her to stop hitting Tony. Jackie tried to look surprised as the story was told. She parked the car and began to lead us to the front door. As she opened it and began to guide us in, Tony stopped ten feet shy of the entrance and refused to step any closer. I walked over and stood next to him in an act of solidarity. Jackie understood and then called out to Shirley, ordering her to come out.

Shirley emerged with the look of murder in her eyes. She glared so intensely at me I thought I'd fall over. My eyes darted to the ground and I squeezed Lobo's collar. Jackie began, "What happened, Shirley?"

Tony interrupted with a rush of words, "She hit us with a whip for playing."

Shirley's threatening look turned to a snicker as she scoffed, "I punished them for fighting on the trampoline. They could have hurt each other, and I had already warned them."

A brick wall blocked her justifications, as Jackie interjected, "You don't hit them for playing around!"

Shirley wasn't finished, "And then Louie let Lobo out and sent him after me!" My heart beamed at the sound of her admitting defeat. I thought of how Lobo chased her up the stairs and then let out a smile in her direction. "He's using that dog as a weapon and you should get rid of it or put it down! Louie doesn't deserve to live here, we should send him back to the boy's home."

Jackie played her role to perfection, as always. "Lobo was only being protective. You had no excuse to hit these boys." Before she could begin her next rebuttal, Shirley walked to Jackie's truck and got in. "Where are you going? We need to talk about this!" Shirley wasn't going to let Jackie be the good guy this time, not at her expense, in front of Tony, and should I mention, Lobo? The truck roared to life and she slammed the gas pedal, leaving a cloud of dust in her wake.

We went inside and Tony asked to use the phone. I recognized the look of sheer panic on Jackie's face. What could she do, hold him hostage until it was time to return him home and try to convince him in the meantime not to share anything about Shirley to his mom? I wish she had, for then her monstrous qualities would have been made manifest. Without any legal option, she just nodded.

Tony got on the phone and in seconds began to recount everything to his mom. I'm sure his mother thought that he was being beaten to death because you could hear her yelling into the phone. Finally, she told him to pack his stuff and wait for her outside our property. Jackie motioned to Tony to allow her to speak to his mother, and he handed her the phone. Tammie must have hung up right away because Jackie began a sentence and then hung up.

Tony waited outside the fence, sitting on the curb. I followed but remained on the inside of the property at first. I couldn't believe my eyes. There was my little brother, waiting for his family to come and protect him from the monster that I lived with every day. Hadn't I done a good enough job? I knew I hadn't, and reasoned that Tony probably didn't even remember ever being struck harder than he just had. I gave up on dignity and began begging.

"Tony, you don't have to go. Shirley is gone and Jackie said she wouldn't be back. I can keep Lobo out with us."

"My mom is coming to take me home and she said to wait out here for her. There's no way I'm staying here." His words ripped through my heart like chainsaw. I had failed miserably, yet again, to protect my brother, but more importantly, to win him back.

Finally, going over to sit next to him, I continued, "You don't have to worry; that won't happen again." I started spouting off what I'd do to Shirley if she had tried anything again but lacked conviction to my threats. He wasn't buying it and only smiled at the thought of my outrageous plans taking place.

"I gotta go." His mom was pulling up. She had made an hour and a half drive in about forty-five minutes. She got out of the car and grabbed Tony's bag, only diverting her eyes from him for an instant to give me the "it's all your fault" disgusted glare. Without a word, she grabbed my brother, whisked him into the car and started pulling away. Tony didn't look out the window or wave.

Again, I was in a driveway watching Tammie take my little brother away from me. Again, Tony had made the choice to go with her. And again, I was torn up inside. The tears so familiar to these events had begun their stinging. I sat unmoving on the curb, and my solitary tears gave way to crying, and that gave way to anger. I took a lot of the blame on myself, but also realized that there was another party responsible. I got up and walked down to Otay's stall. I hugged her and wept, slowly stroking her mane. She stood there calmly, providing a resting place and comforting shoulder.

Then I walked to the barn and lay down in the hay. Aussie and Lucky followed me and Lobo sat ten feet away, keeping watch. I cried over the loss of my brother once more, worrying about what reaction and permanent consequences these events would have with Tammie. My mind swam as I went back and forth from being the victim in Shirley's plot to not being able to protect my brother. I thought of getting back at her—she had spoiled my plans to win my brother back. But my plotting ceased as I came to the realization that I wouldn't be able to do anything to her.

I fell asleep there in the hay with my only real family. Sometime in the middle of the night, Lobo had come over to add to the warmth of our circle. I put my hand on his back and petted him until my arm was sore and I fell back to sleep. A little while later I was awakened again—this time by a human. I didn't quiver, knowing that Lobo wouldn't let anything happen. I slitted my eyes and made out Jackie's shape. She tossed a blanket over me and walked away.

In the morning I got up and fed the animals with Jackie's help. She asked if I would come inside and eat the breakfast she had prepared. The last meal I had had was lunch with Tony at the lake and my body wouldn't allow me to refuse. I went inside, ate, and took a shower as Jackie had requested. I stayed on my bed in disbelief at what had transpired less than 24 hours before. I laid there for an hour or so before Jackie called me out of my room.

"Look out the window," she said excitedly. "No way you got Tony back," I thought. I pulled the curtain back to see a classmate being dropped off. She had prepared a surprise party for me. But I didn't want to see anyone. I wanted to be alone and especially didn't want Jackie to think that having a couple of my friends over was going to make up for the damage her friend had done to my life. What could I do? I didn't want to be rude, but I didn't want her to gain any acceptance either. I chose to bring up the previous day with every one of the kids that came over, retelling what had happened and why my brother wasn't there.

The first time Jackie heard me telling the kids in front of their parents that Shirley had hit us with a whip, she butted in and grabbed me by the arm and pulled me into the room. "That is family information. No one tells family information. We have to work things out ourselves. Shirley was wrong and I'm going to take care of it." Should I believe her? What choice did I have? I took her statement to mean that she was siding with me and agreed to not tell anyone else.

The day was a blur of events. We ate pizza and shared cake and ice cream. They all brought me presents and we played with the horses. Shirley hadn't shown up and it would be days before she would. I know I should have been more gracious to my guests, but I wasn't in the mood for any party. I only wanted to be alone to think. Finally, the day was over and they left. I thanked them as whole-heartedly as I could at the time. I went straight to my room to lie on my bed. My birthday wish was that Shirley didn't live with us and that she had never hit my brother. Being no stranger to wishing, I kept on wishing that I had Tony back, wishing that he would choose me again. Wishing and wishing.

Dinner was interrupted by a phone call that was immediately distressing to Jackie. Tammie was calling to threaten legal action as well as to inform her that Tony would not be allowed over again. But it became obvious that in Jackie's manipulations she convinced Tammie that no real harm had been done and using the "little training whip" was similar to using a belt. (I found out years later that Tammie had no problem with physical discipline.) Jackie's next priority was to put distance between Shirley's actions and herself. She sounded sincere as she pledged that what Shirley had done would not go unpunished. It worked. No part of the context of their conversation implied that Tammie had asked if I was okay, or had made any demands for my safety. Her boy was safe at home and she cared less about me. Jackie let out a sigh of relief as she hung up, knowing that she was still in control.

I reverted back to the aggressive attitude that I had taken on at Father Matthew's once I started to think that I might never see Tony again. I also knew that I could only get away with this at school. I started clowning around in class and not completing my assignments. I began looking for a fight and standing up for myself, both physically and verbally, when kids called me "four-eyes" and the like. My fuse was extremely short, and I rushed to be offended, ready to get into it with any classmate, no matter what age they were. With Shirley again pouting, I gave no thought to what repercussions might come from my behavior at school. I got in trouble for having a rock fight at school, where I nearly blinded one kid. Another time I started a fire with my glasses in the boy's bathroom, but was excused from consequences by the principal, who trusted that it was truly an accident. I received only minor school-based consequences that didn't really teach or redirect me. It was only because I was missing playing sports after school with my buddies that I cooled my jets some in order to get back into that activity.

Tony hadn't called since the episode and, of course, Shirley wasn't going to call him and apologize. After all, we were in the wrong and what difference did it make to her to whom she dealt out the discipline that Jackie had validated as fair? I was delinquent at school oblivious to the connection to my brother and more with the idea that I was in training to rebel against Shirley…when the time came.

One night, Jackie made a point of acknowledging that we had spent a full year together. To me, reaching the one-year anniversary felt more like crossing a threshold than justification for any type of celebration. Although I remained steadfast in my goal to make this home work, I needed some things to change. With Shirley continuing in her "job" of turning me into a man, we had settled into a rhythm of abuse and everyone had a role. I didn't like mine. I thought maybe things could change.

More in anger at what had happened to Tony than in the actual belief that someone would rescue me, I decided to tell my schoolmate Jeff a little about what was going on with Jackie and Shirley. My mistake, of course, was that, out of embarrassment or pride, I held back a lot of information that might have prompted a responder to pursue my story and not give up too easily. The night Jeff's father called the house was a night unprecedented.

Chapter 8 - ADHD, Oppositional Defiant Disorder, or a Cry for Help?

From the System's perspective, psychological "labels" are meant to help you to know possible ways to *not* interact with a youth. They are not to dictate every interaction, or allow you to write off what a child does because of what you heard about some psychological diagnosis. I found out years later that my neighbors had been told that I had severe psychological problems, and this made them unwilling to interfere. Public school officials are also quick to whitewash questionable behavior or even physical marks, as long as there is some stated psychological reason why a student is behaving wrongly or badly. I paid dearly for the ignorance of all these people.

I don't know what Jeff's father said, but I remember being called out of my room. Jackie yelled, "What in the hell are you telling those kids down there at school?" Shirley shouted something to the effect that she was going to really give me something to complain about as she went to get her whip.

"I told you not to share family information. They don't understand what is going on with you!" In her role of abuse-enabler, Jackie was trying to convince me that *I* had the problem. "If you want to go back to Father Matthew's, then go right on ahead and tell more stories about me and Shirley!" I don't know if Jackie was more infuriated or embarrassed, but it was obvious that Shirley was just angry.

Shirley yelled so many things at me that night. But the things that stood out most were: "You have such an easy life!"

"Your mother gives you everything!" and "We can take it all away just as fast!"

Jackie, on the other hand, was manipulative and conniving. She tried to convince me that my mind was "blowing things out of proportion" and "everyone gets spankings when they are young, it's part of growing up." Then she talked about how things could only get better, as long as I was "learning" from my lessons.

Shirley was never good with mind games and looked for immediate satisfaction. With punishment in the forefront of her mind, she beat me and then promised that they would take away my privileges and new possessions. She finished by repeating the threat. "If you ever complain to anyone again, you'll get a whipping like you've never had before." Believing both of them, and blaming myself, I never came forward to report Jackie and Shirley again.

When Jeff asked about his father calling, I told him that everything was okay now. I finished my school year quietly, with good grades that I had to put little effort into achieving. Jackie got me more gifts, keeping the balance and perpetuating the cycle. I trusted her on some small level, but I still feared the thought of having to spend long summer days at the ranch alone with Shirley.

And I was blindsided by a very special contact at the beginning of summer. Once I found out whom I'd get to visit, I began to believe that Jackie was telling the truth and she was always at least trying to make me happy. Through the guidance of some social workers, my older sister Terry had received my location. I had never met her or even seen a picture of her, to gauge what she looked like. I can't even say that I was aware I had a sister before I was told that I was going to meet her. Then suddenly we were together again after nearly ten years.

We met at a small church fair. She was a beautiful little girl with long black hair, fair skin, and a smile that lit up the carnival grounds. She tugged me along through the fair and introduced me to her foster parents. They seemed nice and gave us tickets to go on the rides together. We laughed and played the day away. She stuck by my side the whole day and kept asking me if I was having fun. When the sun set on our laughter, we made promises to call, write and see each other again soon. We hugged and I didn't want to let her go. I wished that I could go with her and stay in her family. Finally, someone cared about me and was as excited to be with me as I was to be with them.

I eagerly asked Jackie, "Am I going to be able to visit her again?"

"Of course, I'll set it up for you to so that you'll never lose contact." Jackie used this event like bacon in front of a dog. With my heart scrambled from the excitement, I instantly concluded that Jackie was the key to reuniting me with my brother and sister—a key that I subconsciously held onto for years.

But just as suddenly as she came into my life, Terry was gone again. Without any explanation, all contact was lost and Jackie was supposedly never able to locate her again. But I always had some hope of seeing her again, and I walked with joy in my heart as I often thought of my family member who had seemed to want me in her family as much as I wanted her in mine. I don't know if Shirley was trying to help or was being malicious, but she told me that my sister didn't want to see me again because my presence was uncomfortable for her. She told me that my social service file mentioned pornographic sexual abuse by my biological mother's boyfriends against my sister and I. She put emphasis on the supposed fact that this would continue to grow inside us and make us weird inside. She explained that seeing each other would be a painful reminder and a torment.

I refused to believe that my presence plagued Terry, and kept waiting for a phone call or letter, but they never came. I stared at the picture we had taken together of our heads in a flowerpot cut-out and carried it with me everywhere I went, doing everything I could to not forget my day with her.

Shirley had made good on keeping everything that had been taken away from me for reporting them to Jeff, and my room was still bare. Jackie's brain kicked in and she told me that I could earn everything back. Conveniently, there was a lot of weeding that needed to be done and hillsides of ice plant to sow. She even went so far as to put together pay rates and a chart. I never received a real or figurative dollar. But I never brought up pay, because nothing I did was good enough and I was happy to just get through most the majority of an assignment without Shirley attacking me. And there were other benefits to my hours of labor. Besides becoming unusually strong for a boy of 11, my neighbor noticed my labor and paid me a visit.

I was startled when a car drove up beside me as I was working on the outside of the fence. To my surprise, I got a job offer from our neighbor up the hill, Bill Cox. He sold rabbits at the swap meet and had seen me spending many hours outside working the fields and tending the animals. "So you're not afraid of getting your hands dirty?" Bill was in his late sixties, an older gentleman with a very large house that he shared with his bedridden wife.

"No, sir." I replied confidently.

"Would you like to help me on Saturdays at the swap meet?"

"Yes, sir!" I could barely contain my excitement.

"Well then, I'll ask Jackie to borrow your services." He dipped his head and waved good-bye.

Jackie thought it was a great idea. I thought, I'm going to get out of the house for the day and have a valid excuse to get the hell away from Shirley.

Our Saturdays went without incident. Bill was a kind, gentle older man who had made a successful life for his family from the underbellies of automobiles. He didn't need to work, but craved activity and sold rabbits on the weekend. He built his own cages and also had an extensive vegetable garden in his backyard. After a day of work he would let me swim in his pool and gave me twenty dollars for helping him. I used the money to buy a mountain bike so I would have yet another means of getting out of the gates. I got to work with Bill for only a few weekends before being called back home to tend to the next big project at the ranch.

For some strange reason, Jackie had gotten the idea of landscaping the driveway and front yard. She wanted to put up decorative cinder block walls around different sections and add fruit trees and grass, a sprinkler system and a fountain. This was a very large undertaking, but she didn't hire any professionals. Why should she? She had Shirley, who had made all kinds of wild promises to handle the project. Shirley handled it all right—she went to town and picked up two illegal aliens standing on the corner and supervised them and myself as we dug up the ground for the walls and sprinkler systems. Every morning she would get me up and send me outside to go work with "my people." She had many slurs for anyone who didn't share her racial heritage, although with me, she was a little more subtle. At times she would sarcastically say, "Time to go to work, Martinez." I had deduced from her beatings and orders that she thought I belonged to the big "them"—second-class citizens in her eyes. She ordered us around while she stayed inside and watched TV, and then took all the credit once Jackie got home. It made me furious, but I knew what kind of thunderstorm I was asking for if I dared to mention anything.

We worked our butts off while she relaxed and occasionally came out to tell us we were doing something wrong. She kept the same two Mexicans working for her and they had grown fond of me. They spoke almost no English and we would exchange lessons over lunch. They could see that I hated Shirley and taught me all the best colorful words to describe her in Spanish. We busted our backs together and they acquired respect for me, as I kept up with them and didn't back down. Little did they know that my motivation wasn't a work ethic, but a fear ethic. And regardless that I had done my best to tow my line, Shirley still found excuses to exact her discipline.

Once the wall was up and the PVC sprinkler system in place, we had to roto-till the soil and add literal tons of mulch by shovel. We planted grass in three large sections and about seventy to eighty fruit trees. Once completed, Shirley gloated at her fine work and of course never once gave me a "thank you" or a nod of approval. As Jackie asked about how I had helped, she diffused the praise by saying that I had only helped minimally, and that I was slow and complained a lot. I wanted to wring her neck; I wanted to tell Jackie that her friend hadn't done a damn thing and to kick her out—but I knew better than to pick that fight.

As it turned out, I didn't end up having to say anything. On the weekends, Jackie would work alongside everyone and she would speak in Spanish to the workers. The Mexicans had said something about my hard work and something else about Shirley not helping and Jackie let her have it. There was a huge argument over the Mexicans' report of Shirley's lack of involvement in her own project. For me, the result seemed like Jackie had a small sense of justice, as she bought me some video games to play with. I say "seemed," because I don't really know if she was playing Shirley against me intentionally or not, but Shirley took everything out on me when she could, scolding me with her boots when Jackie wasn't there.

Jackie reported to me that she was also going to reward me by taking me to a martial arts class so that I could learn self-discipline. She announced in front of Shirley that she had a solution to my behaviors and I would be more mindful if I took up a martial art. The thought of spending evenings (or any time for that matter) away from that house sounded like a gift. The next couple of weeks I was happy that I had gotten a break from doing any extended physical labor around the house. Training in a martial art was the cherry on the cake for me. Another year would pass before I would find out that I was being forced to do work Shirley had promised to do in return for Jackie allowing her to live room and board free. The offer at martial arts training was most likely reality playing on Jackie's mind. I'm sure she realized that eventually someone would ask and I would tell about my horrid experiences while in their care. Learning discipline through a martial art was surely meant to give me a false sense of empowerment or purely be a distraction for me.

At first, Jackie made it a family activity we would all participate in, so we all met Leonard together. He was a sixth degree black belt in the rare form of BOJUKA Ryu. He had trained in Japan, and with others in California; the art was a fusion of boxing, judo, jujitsu, and karate. Leonard was an imposing figure. He stood well over six feet tall and was very muscular. He moved like a cat, and with grace and poise, his movements were sharp and purposeful. He approached me with a warm smile and greeted me in a gentle voice, accompanied by a bow. Then he extended his hand and introduced himself. His hand was so big that it completely engulfed mine. He quickly went into his philosophy about using the art to learn to discipline oneself and that it was to be used only for self-defense. His voice was soothing and commanded respect. He never raised it and had no need to; everyone in this class had deep respect for his skill but mostly for his gentle, respectful, and yet authoritative demeanor. Shirley, of course, was the only exception. On the way home after our first meeting, she couldn't stand to see the happiness in my eyes, and started in on how she thought that maybe this wasn't such a good idea. She protested, "I can teach Louie to be a man better than that n*****." But it didn't matter what argument Shirley gave, Jackie was taken by him and didn't give in.

Since Shirley wasn't going to get me out of my new lessons, she put her all into each class. I can still see her trying to emphasize every block and every strike, trying to get the attention of Sensei. Thursday was judo night; and she would always try to partner up with me. At first she succeeded, but after throwing me to the mat too hard a few times too many, Sensei stepped in and took my place.

He ordered her to show him how to execute the technique and my jaw dropped. I waited in eager anticipation of what she would do. She just stood there at first, not knowing if he was serious, but once the order was repeated with a snap to it, she got in position with her hands on his gee (karate uniform).

She started to pull, turn on her heel and shift her weight, but found frustration in trying to execute. He didn't budge. She started to make the motion again with a lot more effort and let out a loud "Key Aye!" but Sensei reversed her momentum and with blazing speed, lifted her into the air and tossed her on her back. He then scolded her for not breaking her fall correctly. He walked over to me and put his large hand over my shoulder and discussed the importance of technique to the class.

This was the first man in my life who had made me proud to be one. He taught me many invaluable lessons, both physically and mentally. I sometimes went to class alone so Jackie and Shirley could have time to themselves. And after training, Sensei would invite me into his home with his wife and two daughters to spend time with them, to play video games or share a meal. I didn't feel like I was standing on the outside looking at their genuine happiness and order; I felt like a part of a real family, if only for a short while.

Life was starting to take the shape of normalcy. I had a defender at home in Lobo, and in class, Sensei. I enjoyed the seemingly endless affections of the animals. My defenders were exposing Shirley as a tyrant who only preyed on those weaker than her. Her frustrations mounted, but she was powerless to do anything about it in class or while around "my" dog.

Trying to get me inside, Shirley would yell for me to come in to take out the trash, then punch or whip me for letting it get so full. It was during one such incident that my ultimate weakness was exposed.

It was common knowledge that I had loved to run and excelled at being able to maintain speed while running long distances. Shirley had even issued a challenge to me that her horse Chris, the same one I had helped to break, could trot a mile stretch of uphill and downhill road faster than I could run it. Some of our immediate neighbors came out to watch, as she had told them of the challenge. I ran and Chris trotted, and after ¾ of a mile I had a substantial lead. In the home stretch, Shirley, seeing that I was about to claim victory, pushed Chris into a canter, catching up and passing me, then returning to a trot near the finish line. Her face glowed at first, but then everyone teasingly called her a cheater and said I was the real winner. She swore that it was all Chris and she had tried to slow him down, but I knew and she knew what the truth was.

Anyway, with that information surely prevalent in her mind, she swung her whip across the back of my legs while I leaned over to tie and pull up the trash bag. One hit was all it took. I fell to the ground screaming and twisting in pain after just one strike. You see, my butt had almost become numb to pain, having endured Karen's paddles and Henry's belts. Add the blows from Shirley's boots and whips, and sensation was a memory in that region. But not so in my legs, my lean legs that held onto Otay as I rode her bareback; my calves and thighs that had supported me in the fields and while pulling weeds and digging holes. I fell and cried for minutes.

Not believing the sincerity of my reaction, she stood in delight at having so much power over me again. She waited until I quieted down and ordered me to stand again. I refused and stayed on the ground, curling myself around the trashcan. She threatened to go retrieve the bullwhip and give me "something to really cry about" if I didn't comply.

Knowing she wasn't one to bluff, I scrambled to my feet. With psychotic precision she commanded, "Bend over. One more." I slowly bent over, and before I could finish the motion, she exerted the next blow, which felt like she had wielded a torch against the back of my legs. I fell, legs bursting into flames, yelling and crying. I balled up and pushed myself against the refrigerator. The shockwaves would not cease and the pain persisted stubbornly. I caught a glimpse of Shirley's face through my tears and was terrified. She stood there with a smile on her face, knowing what she had found, and knowing where every one of her future hits were going to be directed.

Shirley would either catch me in the morning or after Jackie got home in the evening to punish me for some "unacceptable" behavior. Her measuring scale for correction in relation to the infraction was proven time and time again to be extreme. She wasn't ever known to give a warning or verbal redirection. Everything I did was "on purpose" and had to be dealt with severely. She would often hide around corners, lying in wait for me when she heard me come in and creating a war zone for every second I spent in the house.

Sometimes she appeared from the hallway in a burst and began whipping me to the ground. She would follow it up with actions that were meant to prove that she was teaching me something important. She pulled me over to the living room and sat in Jackie's chair. Her brow was rigid and her face was red and puffy. Jumping out of my mind is one such time when I had to be "taught" over an apple.

Shirley sat with slitted, angry eyes and ordered, "Tell me what you did!" I hardly ever knew the answer. When I couldn't figure it out, and several strikes later, she finally let me know that she saw me share my apple with the dogs. "We don't buy food for you to waste it. The dogs have their own food." The rest of my consequence was to not be fed dinner for a week, so that I would appreciate what they provided. That was the precedent incident that led to many mealless nights and days.

I had wet the bed since before I could remember, and even took medication for it at Father Matthew's. But Shirley knew that I was doing it in their home as an act of outright disobedience. She wouldn't allow me to have water after four p.m., and anytime she saw me heading for the bathroom, she stopped me and made me stand in front of her while she sat on the couch. She would reason that if I could hold it longer, then I wouldn't go in my sleep. She held the whip out and snapped it at me if I started moving or fidgeting. And when I couldn't wait out her arbitrary time period—which was never disclosed—and urinated on myself, I would get the full brunt of her whip or belt for my "opposition."

I spent many long days in the sun working from morning till dusk, cleaning up after the animals or doing yard work, and my thirst was substantial. I would hold out as long as I could, but when I started to get lightheaded, instinct would send me on the mission for water. I tried to get a drink from one of the many water faucets outside, but Shirley would hear the pipes or something and would come out and start swinging and yelling. Next I started getting a drink from the horses' water trough, but within a few attempts was caught.

While I was drinking, I heard her voice, low and methodically eerie, ask from behind me, "What are you doing?"

"Nothing."

"Why is your shirt wet?" I shrugged my shoulders and the nightmare began. With her voice gaining momentum, she mocked, "You want some water? I'll give you some water!" She lifted me by the seat of my pants and tossed me in the trough. Her hands were everywhere and I couldn't escape their orders. She kept pushing me down and all I could do was get an occasional footing and push myself up. I was able to only get a gasp of air before she pushed me under again. I was a small boy, and her dominance was unquestioned. She grabbed hold of my legs and was able to hold me down until I was forced to let out every last piece of oxygen in my lungs. I thought for sure this was it. But right as I started to give up hope, she pulled me up over the side and left me there. Murder wasn't her game, torture was.

My lungs burned and my head tingled and then throbbed. I climbed out of the trough, fully taking the blame for my punishment. I shouldn't have tried to deceive her and sneak a drink of water. I was almost embarrassed to head back in; but when I had gathered myself enough, I headed for the house. I opened the sliding glass door to find Shirley and Jackie waiting on the couch. Jackie sat and scowled at me as Shirley stood and pulled the whip back.

The next day I stayed outside and refused to come in, even for food. This was my way of trying to prove that I didn't need them, that I would make them sorry for my beating by refusing to eat. I was only a child, and this was childish reasoning. I stayed by Lobo and the horses. When night fell, I lay down in the hay with my dogs and started crying myself to sleep.

Chapter 9 - Misplaced Hopes

**"...when I look up at the sky, I somehow feel that
everything will change
for the better, that this cruelty too shall end..."**

—The Diary of Anne Frank

After the more serious events of abuse, there was always a lot of talk about finalizing my adoption. Now I'm sure most of you are thinking, "Dear God, surely any kid would at least be bright enough to not want to be adopted by such cruel people!" And maybe a normal kid wouldn't have thought twice about saying "hell no," running away, or telling other family members that they didn't want to go live with "Aunt So and So" because of... etc. But I wasn't a normal kid. I was first an orphan, looking at the world from inside a tornado. Secondly, I was a foster kid, and for as long as I could remember, I had spent every hour of every day wishing to be part of a family. So I was excited over any talk about adoption, the candy of being someone's son too enticing for the little child that ruled my heart.

Everyone experiences ups and downs when growing up. For an orphan, every peak and valley is magnified by a child's desperation to be loved. After the lows of summer, I sheepishly began a new school year hoping that I could prove myself to my adoptive parents and earn the affections of their "family" promises. In my first weeks of school, there were a lot of highs.

A momentum of positive experiences occurred, as in addition to continuing in martial arts, I got to join the local Little League with Jeff and my other friends. I was in a school play and was again winning ribbons in P.E. for running track. As before, the more comfortable I became, the more Shirley tightened the screws. Weekends became hell and I couldn't wait until Monday mornings. When the holiday break approached, I knew to expect some windfall of events, and I was mindful to keep my distance and conceal my feelings.

When Shirley and I were alone on the ranch, reality was subjective. Sometimes she was nice to me, sometimes she ignored me, and still others she became violent at the drop of a hat. My first goal was to not be a factor in her day, focusing on exchanging affections with my animal friends. There were many days that I couldn't accomplish that goal. As her apparent distaste for my presence grew, staying out of the way became a minute-by-minute goal. My harshest interactions with Shirley usually came if I failed to switch gears fast enough from being happy with the animals to becoming an elusive shadow around her. I was so happy coming in after a ride that sometimes I forgot myself. I knew that I always needed to be somber in Shirley's presence, or there would be a price to pay. One time in particular that price was very steep.

After the holidays were over and I was waiting for school to start, Shirley gave me a powerful reminder that she was still very much in control of my life. I had taken care of the animals, completed my chores, and was allowed to go for a ride afterward. During these times, I often felt that I'd made progress in finding a niche in this household. I felt some pride in my small accomplishments. I would gain some of Jackie's respect, but only in hindsight; I would never conquer Shirley's jealousy. Passing her on the way to the shower I made the mistake of leaving a skip in my walk and a smile on my face. I got in and began washing the trail dust out of my hair and flinched at the sound of the curtain being jerked back.

Shampoo in my hair, and now in my eyes, I saw the first snap of her wrist. She tagged my wet skin and I thought that the leather would cut right through my flesh. The hits kept coming and I tried to escape. I slipped, slid, and then crawled out of the tub frantically, as she kept yelling words that were drowned out by her actions. In pure survival instinct, I scampered past her and headed for the back door. Gaining distance was a mistake as it gave her more room to swing, but I got out the door.

It was dusk, and intuitively I searched for safety with the horses on the opposite end of the property. Lucky and Aussie had immediately come to run at my side. I made it to the stalls without another lash and jumped in behind Otay. Straining to hear the smallest sound, I didn't catch any note of Shirley making her way to me. The rumbling of a sliding glass door startled me. A minute later, her silhouette filled the barn thoroughfare and I could see that she had exchanged the comparatively "small" training whip for the bullwhip. She paced straight towards me, as the dogs had inadvertently given my position away, and ordered, "Get out of there, boy. Come take this spanking like a man or it's gonna get real bad." I didn't budge. She vehemently swung the dividing gate and opened up the pen. One taunting snap of the bullwhip and a wide-eyed Otay ran around the stall and then out, knowing what damage could be done.

I cornered myself in the stall and tried to tuck myself behind the feeder attached to the fence. Shaking, crying and naked, I pushed my head behind the hollowed out barrel, and tensed for the first hit. She struck the barrel and it tolled out the force behind her arm. I looked around and saw her winding up for the next blow, which surely wouldn't miss. I darted out of the stall and towards the back of the horses' area. Shirley charged after me and wound up for another blow. In two movements I was up and over the fence as the whip viciously met the top pole. As I ran back up toward the house, her whip cut me off. She finally connected and the bullwhip tore into my flesh, sending me writhing to the ground. A glance up at her yielded the sight of a second strike coming, which wrapped around my back and chest. I screamed and tried to produce the strength to move away from the next blow, but only managed to crawl.

But it wasn't necessary. Lobo jumped her from behind. Caught totally off guard, she was knocked to the ground and Lobo had grabbed her arm, as if to take away her weapon. His head shook back and forth, tearing away at her forearm. She tried to push and kick him off, but he just kept coming and moving around her, skillfully keeping his target attainable. She managed to stand up and kicked out at him, but she missed—he dodged the blow like a boxer. Hunched over and coddling her arm, she walked up toward the house while Lobo put himself between her and me and stood there snarling.

All the other dogs responded to my whimpering and came over to sniff and lick my wounds. I got up soon after I heard the sliding glass door open and close. I stumbled to the barn and opened the front compartment in the horse trailer and crawled inside. I lay there for hours, shaking and waiting for Shirley to come back out. Crunched up, filthy, and bitterly cold, I waited in an awful fear rather than go in and give Shirley a target to swing at again. I dared not move, and pissed myself rather than risked leaving. In my mind, I knew she was waiting just outside the barn, whip in hand, waiting for me to appear. I covered myself with the burlap sacks that were stored there and tried to hold back from crying out loud so as not to give away my position. I found out later that she had gone to the ER to get her bite treated.

A few endless hours later, I heard the dogs get up from guarding the trailer and run barking toward the front gate. A car had driven all the way down to the horse stalls and the dogs escorted it. I heard Jackie clapping and kissing at the horses and calling out, "Get, get." The horses had been wandering around the property, as the gate had never been closed. I started to move out of the trailer to see if "Mom" would be a comforter this time.

As I approached her, she stared in shock, mouth frozen open. Aussie and Lucky walked me over, wagging their tails and licking me on the knee. "What happened?"

"Shirley."

"Why?"

I shrugged my shoulders and replied, "I dunno." She tugged at the burlap sack over my shoulders and I winced in pain. She pulled it away and stared at my back, allowing herself a small gasp. "What the hell happened?" I didn't dignify it with a second response. You know what happened. Your psychotic friend with an axe to grind had literally struck again.

Jackie walked me to the house and sat me on the couch, calling out for Shirley all the while, but there was no response. She approached with the first aid kit as she kept calling Shirley. She gave me a large round pill and wrapped me in a towel. She opened the first aid box to begin her routine of patching me up, finding that most of the vital supplies had been used up from previous "lessons."

Jackie began pressing about Shirley's actions and her whereabouts. I gave shrugs and refused to speak, glaring at the dried blood veining around my body. She wiped the trails away with a warm cloth and apologized for Shirley's actions. She started using leading questions as to prod me along to discover why Shirley had done this, and to find out where my fault was. She was looking for what triggered Shirley's actions so she could justify them. I continued my refusal to speak. She warmed a can of soup for me and offered another pain pill before sending me to bed. I couldn't find a comfortable position and tossed for at least thirty minutes trying to avoid the burn and throb. Eventually, the medicine kicked in and I fell asleep.

I was greeted in the middle of the morning with both of them filling the doorway. "Get up and come out here." I wearily stood and tottered out. Jackie told me to sit on the couch next to Shirley, but I stood still in refusal. Jackie got up and offered me her Laz-y-boy, and sat next to Shirley. I took the seat and stared at the floor. "Shirley said you were being disrespectful and giving her 'attitude.' Is this true?"

I shook my head.

"But you did run away from a spanking? And Shirley had to chase you all over the property, while you screamed your head off." Although her facts lacked degree, I nodded affirmatively.

Shirley reached behind the couch and pulled out a double-barrel shotgun; I pissed myself for the second time that night. My fingers dug into the arms of the chair and I stared at the double-barrel, paralyzed. She stood up and approached me with it. I didn't know what to do. Should I try to run? There's no way I could outrun a shotgun blast. What then? I froze and looked back down toward the brown carpet, thinking, this is it.

"If a dog bites his master than he has to be put down." She put the gun in my lap and stepped back. How I wish that I had had the courage to pick it up at that moment and point it at her. If only I hadn't been so terrified, I might have, and then I could have seen what it was like for her to be the one cowering.

I pushed it down off my lap with my elbows. Jackie leapt to catch the falling weapon. She had apparently not been made aware of Shirley's scheming to kill Lobo. Lobo had been Jackie's dog first, and she had raised him from a pup. "Lobo was just doing what he thought was right. Look at his back! You went too far. Lobo was just protecting Louie." I had felt the same thing as I was crouched in the trailer. "Lobo is not at fault. You shouldn't have been chasing him around the yard with a bullwhip! What if the neighbors saw? It doesn't matter what is happening, discipline should be dealt out in the house."

I didn't know how to take this revelation. She had protected Lobo, scolded Shirley about chasing me in the yard, but it didn't really seem like she was taking my side, because she was referring to what just happened as discipline. She defended the dog's life but hadn't banned the beating I just took. Shirley huffed and puffed but failed to win any part of the argument. At the end of their tennis match she conceded defeat and, pouting, said she wouldn't feed Lobo anymore. Then, as she usually did when taken down off of her power pedestal, she stormed to her room and slammed the door. Jackie produced a shopping bag full of first aid supplies and told me to sit by her so she could tend my wounds.

For the first time, I had hate in my heart for them both. Hate for the cold-hearted witch trying to cover over her friend's twisted and fraudulent method for raising a "man." Hate for the absolute maniac that rested in her bed, frustrated that she didn't get to see me kill a dog I loved, and surely still scheming for retribution. The anger burning in my head was trite compared to the agony of my skin as she pushed it around to sanitize and dress it. But even though I was focusing on my utter hatred, Jackie's next words enticed me to invest in this home again.

"I want you to take care of Lobo. And let me know if Shirley tries anything to hurt him, okay?"

I know I was a sucker then, but I bought into this hook, line, and sinker. In my young hot head I only saw acceptance and power. I was being given the responsibility of the family guard dog, and a small measure of authority over Shirley! I fantasized about how Jackie would respond if I had told her that Shirley kicked Lobo. I answered her with vigor, turning to make direct eye contact, "Okay!"

For the next few weeks Shirley lay dormant, either completely frustrated or just waiting for her perfect opportunity. Either way, I didn't care as long as she was off my case and pouting again. I stayed by Lobo and would brush him, play fetch with him and even began taking him with me on trail rides. I would now lie next to him in the evening and pet him and talk to him while waiting for Jackie to come home.

I stayed home for a few weeks because I was "sick." I wanted to go to karate class, and thought of telling Sensei what happened, but I was held back. Shirley fell into her role of threatening, with Jackie manipulating and conniving, and when I did go back, I had been convinced that we had to deal with our own problems. When I was sent back to school, I was moved to a school in Anaheim. I was allowed admission by telling them I was a new foster child and by using one of Jackie's workmate's addresses to put me in the district.

I spent most of my time at the new school as a ghost drifting through the hallways. I knew that back at my old school there were parties and special events for my graduating 6th grade class. There were special events here too, but I often chose to keep my head down and hide.

In March, it was again arranged for me to visit Tony for his birthday. I was informed that Tony wasn't allowed over by Tammie because of Shirley trying to teach him a lesson with the training whip. Shirley had tried to make it seem like Tammie was being unreasonable, since in her mind, she hadn't really done anything wrong. "Better make the most of your time Louie, since our house isn't 'good enough' for your brother." I sincerely planned to do just that, "make the most of my time" with my little brother, my only real family. I was overwrought with joy at the prospect, and kept watching the clock, trying to make it go faster.

Then I was again in his life, in his house, and getting to see firsthand what I had always envisioned every year around March 20th. He was at the head of a large table loaded with presents and surrounded by his family and a dozen friends. I paused to think that this could be my family moment. It wasn't hard to envision that I was sitting at the head of the table. Tony and I shared the same features—the same pasty-white skin, brown hair, third dimple, and 1-inch-thick glasses. We could almost be mistaken for twins, even though I was a foot taller. My face wouldn't let go of an unrepressible smile, no matter where he was in the room. My mind raced to figure everything out between him and I. It was difficult trying to adjust to our new dynamics. He had a family and I sort of did too. We lived an hour and a half from each other and barely knew one another. His memory of our brief childhood together had faded and was now full of mostly false tales woven by his mother that she had pieced together from Tony's case file.

We had a few picture moments together, and everyone wanted to know all about me. I was asked a hundred questions and was led to believe that I was also a part of their family. Tammie remained ever mindful to answer the more important questions before I could. It was very obvious that she truly didn't want me there. Her eyes stabbed at the back of my head most of the time, and she shot a look of disapproval at me when we made eye contact.

With my presence a focal point of the day, Tammie was forced to repeatedly lie to everyone. She cycled stories about how she had fought to gain custody of me. I heard her tell someone that it was entirely the System's fault that Tony and I couldn't be together. She also lied about her plans to make sure that Tony and I would grow up as close brothers—and it would be a hard lie to break, since Tony heard her say it. So it came to be that "if Louie was there," Tammie had to keep lying. She hated what I made her become to all of her close friends and family. After all, she felt I wasn't worth her integrity; but then again, I was.

I tried to be around my brother as much as I could on that occasion, but he was very distracted by his day and all the excitement surrounding his turning another year older. Like before, I started fading into the background as he would turn to one friend after another and thank them for a gift. We played birthday games and he paired himself with different cousins each time. Tammie, immersed in her facade, intervened at one point and told him to pair with me. By that time, my heart wasn't in it. I felt as though he'd rather be with someone else and I didn't even try to win.

After all my nights of tears, staring out the window and thinking of him, he had still chosen them. I wanted to cry out, to tell him that he meant the world to me, and ask if he felt the same way. But I was too afraid to place my heart on that chopping block. His actions that day had already given me the answer that I had feared every day since we'd been separated— he had a new family and he was happy. He didn't need me anymore. I felt like a third wheel, an obligation to him; not his brother and not his choice.

Once the party was over and night came, Tammie offered to let me sleep over. Reluctant, and suspicious of her motives, I accepted, thinking that maybe I could still prove myself to Tony. I'd make him see that he needed me, and he would want me back. It was a scenario that was to become the sole foundation of our continued relationship through the years. Jackie let me stay, and agreed to pick me up in the morning.

Tony took the time to formally introduce me to Jason. Two years my senior, he was the neighborhood tough guy. He lived across the street from Tony. Jason had become Tony's best friend and like an older brother to him. Tony's adoptive brother, who had embarrassed me over the opened puzzle at Father Matthew's so many years ago, either wasn't living there (Ed's son from a previous marriage), or was unable to attend Tony's party. Jason's father was an ex-marine who had fought in Vietnam. He was a tough older man who was skilled at stringing curse words together in a sentence. Guns, knives, and various flags and medals were displayed on all the walls. Jason handled some of them and showed them to me. Tony was like his puppy; repeating stories to me that he had been told the first time he was introduced to the items.

Our party lasted late into night, as we played "soldiers" in the street. A small group of Tony's friends and cousins also stayed to play military games. Everyone was pairing up and Tony went over and stood next to Jason. He told one of his cousins to be on my team and my stomach felt like a brick had just been thrown in it. Jason, seeing the look of dejection on my face, told Tony, "How about I take your cousin and you and Louie be on the same team?"

Tony protested, "But Andrew sucks! I wanna be on your team!" Tony's complaining was gaining momentum, as he asked why he couldn't be on Jason's team.

Jason reasoned, "It's not cool. We're always on the same team. You should be with your brother. Just show him

how to play and we can be on the same team later. Okay?"
Tony continued the argument but Jason wouldn't allow it,
walking away with his teammate. Tony turned to me and told
me to follow him. Admittedly, I wasn't very enthusiastic in
playing, but I still tried to prove myself to him, and used every
skill my Sensei had taught me about weight manipulation to win
all the hand-to-hand combat challenges in the yards of his
neighbors. Tony had stopped complaining to be on Jason's team
as I continued winning the small bouts, but he wasn't to be
completely satisfied with me, because we were called in before
I had gotten the chance to fight the only battle that would be
important to him—a battle with Jason.

The next morning I woke up in utter denial—denial that
I was again sleeping in the same room with my little brother, in
denial of how the birthday party went, and especially in denial
that Tony had directly chosen to be with his cousins or Jason
rather than teaming with me. Then the worst thing happened: I
wet my bed. I panicked and my heart began drumming out of
my chest. I hurried to ball up my sheets and put them in the
washing machine at the end of the hallway. Tony questioned
why I needed to shower, since we had showered before bed.
Outright lying, I told him that I forgot, and I usually showered
when I got up in the morning. My quickness and lies were good
enough and the subject didn't come up again.

We were scurried off to McDonald's for breakfast with
some of his other friends who had spent the night. Tammie let
us order whatever we wanted, and everyone pigged out. After
eating, Tony and his cousins went to play in the kid's area. I sat
there slowly finishing my breakfast, very obviously stalling.
Tammie sat at my table as her sister went to watch the kids.

"Did you have fun this weekend, Louie?" Not looking
up, I shrugged my shoulders. I could hear Tony laughing in the
background and it stung my heart. My skin flushed and tingled
all over and I grew angry with the woman sitting across from
me. Tony's mom had brought all sorts of pain into my world.
"Did you like the games?" Again, I responded with a shrug.

She knew what was going on, and she wanted to gloat. She wanted to bask in the moment that told her, "Tony has chosen my family over you!"

I grasped her motives and wasn't going to feed them. I kept my mouth full of food and maintained an excuse for my non-verbal responses. She knew she had made her point. One last stab and she'd be satisfied, "Why don't you go play with Tony and his cousins?" I could have spit out the mouthful of food in her face. In retrospect, I probably should have, at least then I would have a good memory of her.

I went over to the kids' area and got on the spinning saucer. I sat in the middle and held on to the poles. Tony's cousins had grabbed the tops of the bars and began spinning me. Faster and faster, it became a challenge between them and I to see if I could handle their cyclone, or would give up. I tensed my body and gripped the poles with all my might. I wasn't going to let these spoiled little brats win, and in some small morbid way, I thought if I had won this competition, Tony would have some respect for me. I knew that I was tougher than these kids. I had survived more than a dozen foster homes including Henry's and Karen's, the dynamics of Father Matthew's, and two years of "Shirley and Jackie." They would not succeed, and I would not give up, even though my stomach felt like it was in my throat. How thankful I was when Tammie's sister finally stepped in and put a stop to the challenge. I got off the saucer slowly. I couldn't walk when I tried, which just made me the laughing stock of the playground. I had lost anyway.

Jackie came to get me and I couldn't bring myself to go up to Tony and give him a hug good-bye. I got in the truck and waved from the road. He turned and waved and yelled thank you for the birthday present. I was very nauseous the whole way home; mostly from my stomach full of McDonalds's combined with the "Saucer of Death," but also from the letdown of my relationship-defining weekend with my brother, whom I considered my only real family.

When my birthday came, I got a letter from Tony with a gift certificate in it. He didn't even take the time to choose a gift for me. I refused to accept that Tony didn't want me, but felt angry and hopelessly responded at the gut level by picking fights with kids at school and by talking back to my teachers. Our 6th grade graduation excursion at my new school was a trip to a local theme park. Looking around at the groups of friends running off together and watching families enjoy their day made me sad and then angry. I roamed the park most of the day alone. When I met back up with the group to leave, a chaperone wanted to see what was in the bag I was carrying. It was full of items from just about every shop throughout the park. I denied everything and physically struggled with a teacher before being sent home. Jackie and I remained silent the whole ride back, knowing full well what roles needed to be played out once I got home.

After my "spankings," the next part of my punishment was to be yanked from karate class and enrolled in Shirley's Institute of Decorum. She went out and got a 300-plus page book on etiquette to teach me how a man should behave, and took every opportunity to correct me any time I came up short of the criteria in my required reading.

My "schooling" stopped when a certain letter came in the mail. Shirley's niece was flying in from Illinois and would be staying with us for the summer. Sheila's arrival was filled with demonstrations of love from Shirley and my summer started off with a long break from any of her lessons. The more Shirley interacted with her niece, the more I began to hope that the love they shared would overflow in my direction. But my hopes were misplaced, and the abuse I suffered over the summer would make every other trauma, from my mother abandoning me to being separated from Tony when I was six, wane by comparison.

Chapter 10 - Judge, Jury, Executioner

**"You people must not afflict any...fatherless boy.
If you should afflict him at all, then if he cries out to me at
all,
I shall unfailingly hear his outcry; and my anger will
indeed blaze..."**

—Exodus 22:22-24

My summer began again with the opportunity to work for Bill, "the rabbit man," again. In gratitude for my work, Bill gave me a rabbit of my own, a black Holland lop with white feet; I named him "Boots." His twenty-something-year-old son was staying with him for the summer and would wrestle me in the pool after I spent the day at the swap meet selling rabbits for them. Sheila invited herself up to the pool and became fond of Bill Jr., evidenced by hand-holding, cuddling and kissing. It seemed that Sheila's presence was enough to restrain Shirley from teaching me how to "be a man" with her usual ferocity. Things were quiet and I was having a great summer playing with the animals and riding trails. Jackie even entered me in a beginner's horse competition, where I rode through an obstacle course.

I was allowed back to karate class and my lessons with Sensei had been going very well. He took the class down to Tijuana for an international martial arts competition. I placed third in the green belt division. I brandished my trophy with pride and thanked Sensei a thousand times for teaching and helping me. He smiled my words of gratitude away.

Our next big event was a trampoline that was sold to Jerry Weintraub's family at his house in Malibu (Jerry Weintraub is a big movie producer for blockbuster films such as *The Karate Kid*). I also spent part of the summer in Denver visiting with "family." Jackie flew me up to Denver for a month upon her sister's request. I was alone on the plane and it felt good to taste freedom, if only for a short while. I spent a couple of weeks that were very uneventful. It seems that if Racine didn't have to outshine Jackie, she wouldn't, and she paid me little mind. After a short visit, I accompanied "Grandpa" Gary and "Grandma" Elaine as they drove back to California to be their little helper if needed. Grandpa had made me feel like a little man, praising me for any help I provided. When our trip was over, he gave me a small pocketknife and my first taste of whiskey.

Everything was going so smoothly and I was having many big, new positive experiences. With all the comfort and joy that seemed to be coming back to my life, as can be expected, I was totally blindsided by the next big event—the next event that would change me profoundly and alter my living arrangements and my sleeping patterns. I doubt that words can truly do justice to my next few weeks, but bound by them, I'm going to try to explain. I was back at the ranch...

I felt a rush of cold as my blankets were yanked back, hearing the snap of a whip at the same time as I felt it sear my skin. All around me there was yelling, screaming, and demands that I get up. Instantly I was cornered and trapped. I began pissing myself, which doubled the sting of the whip. I couldn't understand what she was yelling, only feel the whip lashes blazing against my skin. My eyes couldn't adjust to the light and otherwise prohibited vision through the tears that covered my face. Shirley allowed a small recess in order to pull me by my arm and fling me into the living room. It was somewhere

around three in the morning that horrible summer day that
would change me forever.

Saturated in my own urine, Shirley kept kicking me
across the floor and out the back door. She pushed me down the
first stairway and ran down the steps to hit me and kick me once
I reached the bottom. I caught a glint of light as it hit Shirley's
silver-tip boots as they flew toward my face and then knocked
me over. My nose erupted with blood. Jackie picked me up by
my arm forcefully and was also yelling. The snap of the whip
against the back of my legs forced them to buckle. I lay there,
fast running out of the ability to express pain with tears or cries.
With a powerful determination, I was kicked down the second
flight of stairs and then through the barn. Jackie again grabbed
me by the arm, and with Shirley assisting with the other side;
they brought me to the cows' pen at the far end of the ranch.
Together, they tossed me into the pen and I landed, face first, in
the urine and fecal muck that always filled their stall. Shirley
jumped in next to me and began wiping cow feces in my face
and yelling, "You are sh**! You're a little piece of sh**!"
Jackie had her whip, so she took off her belt and picked up
where she had left off, striking my bare flesh. She lifted me by
my arm and heaved me onto one of the cows. His stiff, bloated
body was foreign to me and I was mute, not understanding its
condition. I wasn't to remain in confusion for long.

"Why did you kill Champ? Why did you kill our cow?!"
demanded Jackie.

"I didn't ki…" then the smack of the belt against my
back.

"Hand me my whip. You better start telling the truth!"
Shirley was in her element and had a sinister tone to her voice.

I rolled off the dead body, onto my back, and looked up
at Jackie. I forced out, "I didn't kill Champ." Shirley pulled
back and let loose. I tried to cover myself with my arms and the
whip tore into them. They absorbed the intense shock and I felt
exacting icy pain right before blood began flowing from the
wounds.

"Stop lying! Tell the truth right now, or else!" roared Shirley as she pulled back for another blow.

"That's enough. Let's finish this inside." Shirley complied with Jackie's orders, knowing that she was going to get more release shortly. Through the chaos, her ominous words, "Let's finish this," rang repeatedly in my head and terrified me to the bone. Shirley snatched me up and threw me over the pen's gate. As Jackie had promised, inside I received more of the same. After several more lashings and yelling, a wide-eyed Sheila came out of her room, screaming at the sight of me.

Sheila yelled, "What's going on? Why are you hitting him like that?"

"He killed our cow!" Shirley answered.

"Admit it! Tell me why you killed the cow. Tell me right now!" Jackie was in a rage and gave Shirley Carte blanche to use any means necessary to extract information. Shirley kicked my legs out from under me and yelled for answers to Jackie's questions. I had none to give. I honestly hadn't a clue why Champ lay dead.

I earnestly cried out, "I dunno."

"Stand up, right here!" Jackie pointed to the carpet in front of her. I got up and stood, hoping for an end. "You'd better tell me why that cow is dead right now. You are the only one who takes care of the animals. You are responsible for them. No one else has even been near the cows. You know they are our food—what we eat for a year!" I had nothing to say and didn't know what would get me out of this. Another blow to the backs of my legs and I fell again, grabbing at them and curling up into a fetal position. Shirley's niece had continued her screams and brought some sense of reality to these horrific events. "You just lie there and think about it. We'll be right back for your answer." Jackie ushered Shirley into her bedroom right after she got in one last kick.

Sheila rushed to my side once they left the room and slowly got me up and to the bathroom. She ran a warm bath and softly asked me to get in. I did and stared as the bathwater quickly turned deep red and then rusty brown. Sheila gently wiped away the cow manure and blood. She cried as she cleaned me up, her hand shaking with every stroke. "I'm so sorry," came out gently. I sat there stunned and wondering about what had just happened. Wondering why these women, who claimed to be caring for me and raising me, would be hitting me so hard. I looked at the stripes on my body and stared into the murky water and was empty. No one loved me. I knew that adults would hurt me whenever they got an opportunity. Maybe the girl cleaning me liked me, maybe she just felt sorry for me; when I found out the true answer, neither was even close. She changed the bathwater out and began wiping me again.

She finished me with antibiotic cream and brought me fresh underwear. She led me to her room and covered me with her huge comforter. She turned and closed the door, locking it. She got in bed beside me and began stroking my hair, hushing my sobbing and pausing to wipe her own tears away. "It's all over now. It'll be okay, you'll see." She laid there consoling me for a short while before Jackie and Shirley emerged from their room.

Shirley started yelling around the house for my whereabouts. Jackie could be heard working herself up, telling Shirley that she should drive around to see if I had run away. "What if the neighbors find him?" was Jackie's concern. Silence for a split moment, and then a knock on Sheila's door.

"Sheila, do you know where Louie is?" After trying the stubborn doorknob Shirley demanded, "Open the door." Her first gentle twist was replaced with a more forceful one. "Sheila. Open the door right now! Is Louie in there? Open this door!" She kicked the door and kept yelling her demands. I had pissed myself again. Sheila approached the door crying, "Leave him alone. He's had enough. Go away, he's bleeding!"

"Open this door right now before I kick it in!" Shirley threatened.

Jackie broke in, "We just want to talk to him; his spanking is over. Open the door."

Sheila adamantly opposed, "I'm not letting you guys touch him! Go away or I'll call the police!" Her threat was a serious one and needed immediate action. Shirley kicked the door in.

Jackie snatched me out of the bed and pulled me into the living room, while Shirley was left in the bedroom, pinning her niece against the wall. She had not made a sound, because Shirley's hand held her throat. Jackie put me on the couch and sat in her chair. We waited for Shirley to come out. I heard two loud snaps of flesh against flesh and the order, "Don't you ever get in the way of us raising our kid!"

As Shirley clodded into the living room, the sight of me sitting enraged her. She grabbed me by the hair and pulled me up. "You stand right here and tell us why you killed Champ."

I still didn't have an answer and my head swam around for possible excuses.

I started going over all the things I had done. "I fed the horses and cows yesterday. I fed the dogs. I watered Boots..."

"I don't care about that," Jackie interrupted. "How did you kill Champ?"

"I....don't...I.....fed....."

Shirley's belt slammed against the back of my legs and my body arched to the impact of the blow. "You better start telling the truth." I couldn't handle these repetitions. I didn't know what to say. I fell to the ground and gave up. She kicked me in the stomach and head but I just curled up. She tried to lift me but I wouldn't straighten my legs out. She kicked, and then punched me, ordering me to stand. I wasn't giving in. Finally, after a few more blows, Jackie told her to stop.

"Pick him up and put him in his room. He'll stay there until he wants to tell us why he killed Champ." Shirley followed orders and tossed me on the ground, slamming the door behind me. I laid there, out of tears, sobbing in a low, shallow whimper. I crawled into the closet and coiled under my dirty laundry. I covered myself with my clothes, my body still shuddering as I cried myself into an exhausted sleep.

The next few days held so much of the same. Every evening I would be ordered to come out and be made to stand until I was beat down, to the order of "Tell me why you killed Champ!" Shirley refused to feed me all day, and when Jackie got home I was brought a small portion of what they were having for dinner. I tried to find hiding places under my desk or in my closet. I stuffed myself under the bed and pulled the trundle bed as far back against me as I could, for any protection it could give me. Every time I heard footsteps, I cringed, hoping that my door wouldn't open. When Shirley came to bring "dinner" in my room and didn't see me right away, she got angry. When she found me, she would kick the chair or roll the trundle bed into me. "Get out of there you little murderer!"

Another week and I was so beaten up that pain was a memory. I had huge bruises covering much of my body, my eyes had to take turns swelling up from her slaps and punches. My legs were covered in stripes that pussed and bled as the long scabs cracked. Sheila did her all to avoid being around; I figured that she realized how powerful Shirley was and gave up on trying to help me. Toward the end of that week I had been presented with evidence of how Champ had died. They hired a vet to do an autopsy and that evening's interrogation began with them giving smug looks since they now knew the answer they thought I was trying to conceal. A handful of small metal clippings were tossed in my face with the threat, "Tell us what you did or else."

I was even more confused; how could a handful of small metal clippings kill a big cow? I got my answer straight away as Shirley accused, "You cut the metal bailing on the hay and fed it to the cow. He bled to death! You're a sick, mean little bastard, aren't you?!" Another blow sent me to the floor. My body had given up telling me of pain and my mind had given up on trying to force movement away from it.

Jackie yelled, "Answer her! Tell us right now why you killed Champ!" I lay there sobbing, without a word. Shirley kicked me a few times more and then threw me back into my room. She threw some of the metal clippings at me and slammed the door.

Had I cut the metal bailing in too many spots? I did kill Champ. I felt bad for the cow, trying to imagine how painful it would have been for him to die from hundreds of cuts inside his body. Dinner didn't come that night and I was far too afraid to report how hungry I was.

For the next few days Shirley followed a routine of coming into my room with her whip and with a few strikes, ordering me to confess. My body and mind had shut down. I barely flinched and she didn't seem to care. I spent those days hiding in my closet, not able to get even an hour's sleep, in terrified expectation of another visit. After the 3rd or 4th day, I had grown so hungry and thirsty that my soul's survival mode kicked in and pushed me to search for food. The token scraps that Jackie offered during the evening interrogation were hardly enough to keep me from hallucinating, and I began to reason that maybe this nightmare would end if during that night's interrogation I admitted to killing Champ.

In my survival push, coupled with some measure of logic, I forced myself to open my bedroom door and look around for Shirley. I bolted across the hallway and into the bathroom. I pushed the door with delicate precision, not shutting it all the way but enough to hide my whereabouts. I turned toward the sink and my mouth tingled at the thought of water. I stopped myself, thinking that she would surely hear the water running and punish me. I turned toward the toilet and gently lifted the lid and lowered my head.

The drink filled my throat and I couldn't get enough. I sucked the water down until my stomach was bloated and sore. I stood and turned toward the door, opening it just a little, putting my eye around its edge. I didn't see Shirley and noticed her door was shut. "Maybe she's sleeping," I thought—or just hoped. I tiptoed down the hallway, leaving five to ten seconds between each step. When I had carefully reached the end of the corridor, I peeked around to find the living room empty. Farther, I tiptoed toward the kitchen without discovering a trace of Shirley.

I made it to the kitchen undetected and opened the pantry cupboard, thinking to grab something for later. I got hold of a package of Mother's Oatmeal Cookies and started to shut the cupboard door. I tiptoed to the refrigerator and just as my hand was in position to pull the door open, the roar of a sliding glass door broke the silence. I darted into the dining room and stood shaking, peeing on myself. She walked to the kitchen and opened the refrigerator, grabbing a beer. I froze solid, in plain view if she had turned. I was petrified and couldn't move. She opened the cupboard, all the while talking to herself. I started toward my room, trying to tiptoe fast. I made it through the living room but as I entered the hallway she had started towards her room and I was caught.

"What the f*** are you doing?!" She wheeled me around by my shoulder and saw the cookies. "You're stealing our food!" She dropped the beer to snatch the package from my hand and then hit me in the face with it. She punched me in the gut and then ordered, "Get your a** back in your room!" I turned toward my door, thinking I had gotten off easy. But I hadn't, she shoved me from behind and as I tried to turn to see her, I crashed into the wall. She paced up to me and kicked me down the hall to my room and slammed the door behind me. My shoulder ached piercingly before becoming an almost unbearable deep throb.

"You wait till I tell Jackie how you tried to steal our food!" She taunted further, "You're never going to eat again!" I crouched and sat with my back to the door. My life was over. I turned and threw up the water I had drunk earlier. I looked down at the small puddle and was sad that it had left my body.

I heard Sheila come in and Shirley giving her a report of my treasonous actions. I hoped for Sheila to come and bring me something to eat. I let out a cry while clutching my shoulder.

"You better shut up in there or I'll shut you up!" Their voices were muffled and in a few minutes they went out the front door. I stayed by the door until the sunlight had stopped filling my room, and then hid in the darkness of my closet. Jackie was next to enter the house and I feared what reaction she might have to the day's events.

My door slowly opened and I got a request to come outside. In an ever-cautious pace I entered the living room. Sheila was sitting next to Shirley, her face red and swollen from crying. "Sit down" Jackie asked. I, of course, refused to sit next to Shirley and didn't accept the offer to sit in Jackie's chair this time.

"Please, sit down Louie." I stood, not knowing what I was being set up for, and remained very suspicious. My legs, tired and worn out, begged for a seat, but my stubbornness and fear wouldn't allow it. "Shirley, why don't you tell him?"

"No, I think Sheila should."

"I..." Sheila began to speak to me. She looked me over, taking a quick inventory of my countless bruises and lashings. She refused to look any longer and looked down, holding her face in her palms and crying.

Shirley ordered, "Look at him and speak!" Shirley pulled her hands away and took Sheila's chin and pushed her face up. Sheila stood, then half-ran to her room, covering her face and crying.

Jackie spoke, "Sheila told us that she killed Champ."

Shirley as a matter of factly added, "Yeah, she was down there with Bill Jr. and was flirting and cutting the metal bailings into small pieces."

I couldn't believe my ears! Not only was I not getting punished for stealing food, but I was also being exonerated of Champ's death! My body's aches gave rest for a couple of moments as I tried to digest this information. My mind was in great conflict. I was so happy to be getting off the hook, happy that Sheila had come forward. But at the same time, I was voraciously angry. So angry, even hateful, at the treatment I had endured these last weeks. With so much going on in my head, I was mostly in shock. I didn't even hear any more details about Sheila or the cow as I searched to understand my new reality. Oblivious to my inattentiveness, Jackie continued telling me how they had been caught having sex in the barn. Shirley jumped in and reported how Sheila got tired of seeing me punished for what she did and finally told the truth. Lastly, she sternly added that my last weeks of punishment were entirely Sheila's fault for being a liar.

Next came the apologies. Jackie took the lead as usual, "I'm sorry we had to punish you for all of this."

"Had to hit me" rolled back and forth in my head like a wrecking ball. I stood expressionless, and the pains in my body had again started reporting.

Shirley added, "We didn't know, and we had to find out. You can see how we would think that it was impossible for his death to be anyone else's fault, right?"

"We were only trying to get the truth."

I didn't know what to do. I did want this to end and I wanted to be back in the fold. I craved to be fed and cared for, or at least given the bare necessities. But most of all, I wanted the pain to stop. I stood in a daze, speechless, and beginning to realize my anger at the injustice. Shirley got up and went to the water heater closet. She came back with the training whip and my legs began shaking, afraid of what was coming.

"Here, take this, I want you to hit me. I deserve it." Shirley tried to force the whip into my hands and I gave way to crying out of pure confusion.

Jackie added, "Take the whip, Louie. It's the least we can do." I wouldn't grab the whip, still thinking that I could be getting set up. Maybe she would let me hit her now, but then what would happen after Jackie went to work? Either way I wasn't taking any chances and I didn't want to wield that whip anyway. Shirley picked up the whip and gave it to Jackie.

"Here Jackie, you take it and hit me for him." Jackie played her game and Shirley bent over in front of me. The scene of this set my head ablaze. Were they serious? Were they now mocking how I'd been "punished" for so long? I couldn't answer and my thoughts subsided with the sound of the first lash to Shirley's butt.

"That's not how you do it. Hit me harder!" A second snap and Shirley didn't even flinch. "I know an old Indian trick to take away pain. It doesn't even hurt." What the hell, she was going to tell me, as I stood there bloodied and bruised, that it didn't hurt, and imply that I was some kind of weakling for crying all those times! I did notice, however, that she had grabbed the training whip, and not its big brother, the bullwhip. Jackie tried again to get me to take the whip and hit Shirley. I wouldn't. She hit her a few more times and Shirley didn't peep or budge; she didn't bleed either.

They both apologized and I refused to make eye contact with either of them. I stood stunned with my arms at my sides as they both gave me a hug and apologized again and again. I tolerated Jackie's hug but pulled away as Shirley tried to hug me. Jackie told Shirley to leave the house for a while, thinking I was only angry with her. I finally sat on the couch with Jackie as she offered first aid. Again, I was sitting there while she took care of the wounds she had allowed. "I'm really sorry that all this happened. If Sheila had only told the truth." I was immediately given full access to the kitchen and Jackie began making foods that she knew I liked. I never gave her a thank you or input as to what to make. I sat and ate until I had literally made myself sick. I would vomit and then eat again, perhaps a little slower. All the while Jackie kept excusing their actions; and her apologies became a drone that I blocked out.

Sheila was kicked out and sent back to Illinois. She avoided me in the weeks leading up to her flight and avoided any eye contact when she was home. When she finally had her bags at the door, Shirley gave her a huge hug and said she'd miss her. Jackie went to her room, as did I. Shirley followed her to try and get her to say goodbye and they could be heard arguing in the room.

Sheila approached my door and knocked. I sat on the other side, blocking it, and didn't respond. In just above a whisper she said, "Good-bye Louie. I'm...I'm sorry." She slipped a letter under the door and walked away.

And so she left—Sheila, the only person who had witnessed firsthand what had happened to me and was appalled by it. The only person who could have truly been there for me to expose the horrid conditions of my foster home. But she didn't. Like every other adult that I had turned to before, there was an immediate knee-jerk reaction to my treatment, and then indifference. But in Sheila's case there was also guilt. How different this story would be if she had swallowed her pride and taken true responsibility for her actions, and then stood up for the person that was punished for them. Instead, Sheila took the responsibility of Champ's death off her conscience, but not my weeks of abuse. In her silence lay another abuse for me; she left me behind to manage my tormentors alone, with a child's intellect.

Chapter 11 - My New Family

"I remember you always had a bruise on your face."

—Tony, years after I left the System,
talking about visiting me at the L'amours

If I had been a little older, maybe I would have run up to the first police officer I saw to expose my lashings and bruises. But my limited understanding of emotional games and the conniving of my "parents" led me to trust in their apologies. Besides which, I was ashamed. My treatment had taken my self-worth as much captive as my dreams. These events were dizzying and I had to place my hope in their promises that I wouldn't be treated like that again, and that they really loved me. After all, my foster-adoptive parents and their promises were all I had.

The next few days were filled with more apologies and even pampering. Jackie stayed home from work and I stayed in bed. I was brought almost anything I asked for, or didn't—from entertainment to takeout. My bed was made for me every morning after the sheets were washed, as I had begun to wet the bed just about every time I closed my eyes. Jackie came in the middle of the night to talk me down softly when I was having a nightmare. When I had complained enough I was finally taken to a doctor. After he examined my shoulder, he offered that my collarbone had been fractured. "Louie fell off his horse." I had long ago learned the lesson that keeping my mouth shut meant I was rewarded with family, or not attacked again. I got a sling

and pain medications. Jackie offered an additional reward for
my silence, informing the both of us that she would be taking
over the discipline. The ride home ended with a discussion
about Shirley going to see a therapist.

In a month or so, I was doing things around the house
again and spent the rest of my time playing the many new
Nintendo games they had bought for me. I wasn't at 100% yet
when it was about school time, and I was enrolled late so that
the points could be driven home that they were sorry, things
would change, and Shirley wouldn't hit me again.

I began the 7th grade at Rancho Canyon Middle School,
where I would learn the hard way about social classes and some
aspects of the law. After my summer, I couldn't tell you which
way was up. The difficultly of emotionally and biologically
dealing with becoming a teenager was intensified ten-fold
because of my life experiences to this point. I had such a hard
time relating to my peers that I eventually gave into just being a
follower so I might gain some type of affection.

My new school was in Anaheim Hills, as we were still
using Jackie's friends' address, and I was a total outsider to this
community of kids that had six and seven figure income
parents. Without thought, the first day I dressed in my blue
jeans and second-hand boots and was mocked and badgered.
For the most part, they all donned Quicksilver and Billabong
surf wear and I stood out like an overturned garbage can. On top
of that, my glasses had made the picture complete for them and
I was ridiculed for being such a "dork," "dufus," or "nerd."
Even though I mostly kept my head down and scurried between
classes, I did try to find a measure of self-worth by attaching
myself to a group of peers. My classmates didn't want anything
to do with me, so I found a couple of outsiders who weren't of
the upper class and spent my lunch in their company. They were
the other "dorks" and our circle included the big-boned kids and
those whose bodies were growing awkwardly. Our group
included a few really rich kids as well, but they were
unacceptable to the others because they were of Oriental or

Middle Eastern descent. My introduction to prejudice was completed when one of my teachers sat me in the back of the class, suspiciously enough, with some of the same faces I had spent my lunches with.

I hung out with the outcasts and got into trouble trying to make them laugh, thinking I would earn a genuine friendship. I never told any of my peers of my abuse because I didn't want to sink to an even lower level of social awkwardness, it wasn't something I felt needed to be shared or could benefit me in any way. And I was trying desperately to find acceptance, a place amongst a group of human friends. Maybe I could earn a phone call at home, or an invitation to an overnighter or a party as a reward for my gestures toward their entertainment. I did many things to try to prove to them that I was normal, to push down my depression and hide my low self esteem so that I could make a real friend. And in their laughs and dares, to me at least, it seemed to be working.

Jackie was forced to drop me off close to two hours before the bell rang so she could make her shift at the hospital on time. I stole porno magazines at the local liquor store and hung the pages around the campus before school began. I pushed in the locking pins on classroom doorknobs and pulled them off, throwing them into the shrubs and laughed with my group as we watched the class wait for the janitor to get there and struggle to open the door. Every week I got bolder; surely "testing" to see if Jackie was truly not going to allow Shirley to be the disciplinarian. I got away with a lot with no one the wiser, but my actions were begging for attention and soon I got it.

At home, Shirley had returned to "normal" and our school year routine was in full progress, the only difference being that she demoralized me verbally instead of physically. We barely saw each other and I spent most of my time outside with the animals. I was able to avoid her on the weekends and Jackie would often take me on excursions that didn't include Shirley.

In school, I began to develop a love that stemmed from experimenting in art class. I had found a medium in pencil and chalk to put pain on paper. My class assignments weren't of the solemn variety that I preferred, so I started carrying a sketchpad that held my true artistic self-expressions. One of our class assignments was to find a magazine photo of a celebrity and graph and enlarge the picture without losing detail. I had chosen Joan Collins, of whom I knew nothing, but the photo was a shot with her displaying a somber expression. My work had conveyed her expression and some of my own. The teacher was taken aback by the piece and submitted it for publication to Artiture Magazine. My female classmates were impressed and started giving me that "the dork is so cute" treatment. The preppy rich boys couldn't stand that I was taking any attention away from them, even if I was being patronized. They stepped up the name calling and bumping into me, which made the girls respond with even more of a "you cute poor thing" treatment. Eventually, their jealous boyfriends redirected their attentions and I sank back into the shadows of the rear of the classroom.

My last art recognition came a few months later, after I entered the annual drug-free poster contest and won second place, receiving a fifty-dollar prize in a school ceremony.

My group of outcasts gave me at least a little respect for my fearless attitude at pulling pranks at the school. My next accepted dare was to begin the chain of events that would lead them to find out everything.

A small strip mall was located downhill from the track and I was dared to throw dirt clods into the opened back doors of the businesses. As the first clods were thrown, the shop owners of these high-priced clothing and jewelry stores ran out, yelling and swearing. Soon the others joined in throwing dirt clods and we all shared menacing laughter at the shop owners' expense. We worked in small numbers and were quick to flee the scene, so we remained undiscovered for a week. However, on Monday morning we were pulled into the office and presented with photos of ourselves throwing dirt clods into the stores. We were suspended and made to pay restitution.

My friends reported that their parents had no big reaction to the mischief and just paid the fines and gave them a warning. Jackie and Shirley could be counted on to make sure I knew, physically, that my actions were deeply erroneous. I didn't return to school for a couple of weeks; but when I did, everything had changed.

Jackie's promise ended up being an empty one as she let Shirley get the whip out of the closet and give me my orders. I looked over to Jackie for some type of protection. "What about all those promises and apologies" I thought. I put my hands on the couch and tensed for the lashings.

They must have discussed a limit to my discipline because Shirley told me I was only getting three hits. Her pending limit on the strikes to give must have caused a lot of frustration because her three hits were very hard. Shirley had great skill with a whip and knew exactly when to pull back for the maximum amount of damage to be done during my three strikes. The skin in that area had almost healed from the rage they endured during the cow episode and her present blows opened them up again.

I curled up on the carpet, denying my pain. I gave out that low growl in opposition to her need for wailing. Jackie wouldn't allow another strike and told Shirley "That's enough." For every surge of pain I grabbed my legs and growled. I squeezed my legs, and with all my strength forced myself not to cry. I wouldn't give in—not in front of Shirley.

I did a lot of work around the yard "paying" for the amount that Jackie had to give to the shop owners. As my punishment ended (meaning I looked presentable enough to return to school) Jackie started cajoling again, preparing me to go back out in public. She complimented me on the jobs I had performed and then arranged for the two of us to swim in Bill's pool. I watched the sun set as we walked in complete silence to his house. I wanted to ask her why she let Shirley hit me but I knew better. I was just going to be a "man" and take my medicine and move on. We got there and jumped in the water without a word to each other. She swam a few laps and then got out and sat in a lawn chair. Bill came down to offer cold drinks and to make an apology for his son's part in having Champ die.

Jackie brushed away his apologies, "Don't worry, its no big deal. We have another and we'll just get a second earlier than usual." No big deal! I don't even need to write what was going through my brain at this point. I'm sure you have a pretty good idea.

Bill asked, "Hey Louie, you wanna come over here and have a soda?"

"Yes, sir." I got out of the water and walked over to them. He opened a soda and handed it to me. "Thank you sir." I stood at the edge of the pool, drinking and listening to their conversation.

"Louie, what is that running down your legs?" The aqua blue light from the pool reflected against my lashes that had reopened in the water and it looked like black oil was trailing down my legs. I looked at the blood and then at Jackie. My heart was in my stomach.

Jackie tried to play stupid. "Yeah Louie, what is that?"

Bill pulled me to him and touched one of the trails. He gasped as he realized it was blood. "Who the hell did this to you?!"

Jackie kept up her part, "Who did this to you, Louie?"

I would play her game and took it as an opportunity to let someone in on our "Family Secret." "Shirley did it."

"How?" Bill inquired.

Jackie sat silent and so I answered honestly, "With a whip."

Bill swiftly spun in his chair, "Jackie, do you know about this?"

"No, of course not."

"I'm going to call the police."

Abruptly she cautioned, "Wait, ... (inaudible)... we should talk to Shirley first."

Bill directed me to go wait in the house with his wife and I grabbed a towel and complied. Her nurse aid tended to my wounds and dressed them. Bill and Jackie went down to the house and talked. I don't know what had happened, but I would have loved to have been a fly on the wall during what was surely uncomfortable at the least. Bill came back up with Jackie and he stated, "You won't have to ever worry about her again." I had thought that before, only to find false hope. I just nodded my head in agreement and didn't put too much faith in his words. After all, he didn't even know the real Shirley. Bill told me to let him know if anything else ever happened. I thanked him and he gave me a big hug.

An hour or so later we were on our way back to the house. Jackie was dreadfully quiet and I was very afraid of what might happen to me once we got back in the house. I asked if I could go see Otay but she refused to allow me and said I needed to put some clothes on, as I was still in my swim trunks. When she opened the door, my eyes began to water in terrified expectation of what would take place next. But to my suspicion; a whip-wielding Shirley didn't greet me.

I went straight to my room, tensing as I passed every corner. A ball of nerves, I made it to my room unscathed and grabbed some clothes out of the drawer. I put on my pants while facing the door; just waiting for the moment that Shirley would burst in and start hitting. I sat on my bed afraid to move.

Jackie called out, "Louie, if you're dressed then come out and have dinner."

"I'm not hungry." There was no way on earth that I was going to voluntarily come out and make myself an open target.

"Come out and eat, now." I knew what the consequences of not following her directions might bring, so I complied. I walked out and tried to hug the walls as I made my way to the living room. I sat in the chair in the corner so I could at least see her when Shirley came at me for revenge.

We ate freezer pizza in silence. The pressure was killing me and I finally broke down and asked, "Is Shirley going to have dinner with us?"

"Shirley isn't going to live here anymore." She replied flatly.

Trying to sound concerned I asked, "Where is she going to stay?"

"With a friend. Hurry up and eat your dinner."

My wildest dreams and wishes had come true! Did Bill really do it for me? Was this the last I would see Shirley? My mind raced back and forth relishing in my newfound hopes. I finished my dinner in absolute disbelief, with my brain going from optimism to denial.

As the evening came to a close, Jackie's silence was evidence that she was upset at the events that had taken place. I played Nintendo for a while and went to bed after her. I couldn't manage to keep my eyes closed so I got up and walked around the house aimlessly, somewhat looking for Shirley. I walked up to her door and stood there in curiosity and anxiety. Was she inside? Did she really go, or was this some sick game they were playing on me? Although I had never had so much fear, and my hands and legs never shook so much, I built the courage to find out, and pushed the door open.

The room was bare. I opened the drawers, looking for a sign of Shirley. Maybe if I found something then they would both jump out and yell "Surprise!" I didn't know what to expect, and the fact that the house was dark turned my stomach inside out. I searched everything—the closet, dressers, and under the bed. Although her scent remained, I was unable find a trace of my tormentor having ever lived there. I went to bed, going back and forth between happiness and thoughts of freedom, to being terrorized at the thought of her keeping her threats if I had ever told anyone. My brain in overdrive, I went to sleep, but awakened every twenty to forty minutes in absolute terror of her coming back to wreak revenge on me.

Bill's promise proved to be true and Shirley never lived with us again. I got to stay home alone and had the run of the house while Jackie was at work. My life changed so significantly. The air filled my lungs in a different way now. I was able to do what I wanted, when I wanted. I coveted my time in the house, as normally I had been outside trying to avoid Shirley. I went through all the drawers again and again, and in a few days, started doing things to her room to see if she'd notice and come after me. I left eggs in her bed, pissed in her bed, and even wiped snot on her pillow. All went unnoticed. Fears started to subside and I began to do similar things around the rest of the house. I smashed eggs on the wall behind the couch and wiped snot on Jackie's chair. And there were no repercussions.

The biggest test of all came when I built up the courage to open the water heater closet. I stared at "it" resting against the tank. My mind flashed back to the hundreds of times it had been used against me. Its partner, the bullwhip, was rolled tightly and on the other side of the tank. I glanced back and forth between them and thought I heard footsteps behind me. I shut the door quickly and ran down to the end of the hall and balled myself up in the corner, shielding my head with my arms. I huddled in expectation of Shirley. Overwhelmed with emotion, I began to cry and I felt like throwing up. For some reason, I still thought I could hear footsteps, but after fifteen to twenty minutes of tension I got up and explored the house to find that no one was there. I went through the house and locked all the doors and windows.

Then I went back to the closet and grabbed the whips. I put them in a garbage bag and got on my mountain bike, heading for the state park. I peddled as fast as I could until I couldn't even feel my legs anymore. Up and around I sped through the winding trails until I hit a large rock and fell off my bike. I gathered myself and grabbed the bag. I ran about 200 feet off the trail and chose a spot. I clawed into the earth and used my knife to dig until I had a hole big enough for my bag. I shoved it in and covered it over. I grabbed tumbleweeds and placed them over my pain's shallow grave. I walked around my spot first at ten feet, then twenty, then thirty to see if it was obvious that I had placed something there. Satisfied, I returned to my bike and rode home.

When I returned, I ran around with the dogs and laughed as I told them what I did. They were all excited and jumped around me playfully. I went to see Otay and was so excited I got on her bareback and clung to her mane as she ran around the pasture. It was one of the most exhilarating hours of my life.

I was so jubilant when I got back to school that I even reached out towards recreational and extracurricular activities. Eventually my athleticism again garnered me some acceptance. We had a cross-country team and a flag football team, both of which I was encouraged to join, once my PE teacher saw my raw ability. Although I wasn't ever accepted by the "in-crowd" of athletes and rich kids, I was mostly left alone once I had proven myself physically.

Jackie had let me go back to karate class with a minimal explanation to Sensei. He put his hand over my shoulder and replied, "That's too bad." With that unemotional response, I didn't get the feeling like he really cared, but then again, he responded to everything in a steady, unemotional way. Maybe he didn't want to make me relive one moment of the tortures I had endured, even mentally. I should offer that in reality the "issue" was relatively over and he most likely felt powerless. But he wasn't—he could have been more than an instructor to me, for that was how I felt about him, and opened the door to let me talk about what had happened.

I was so happy to be back in his class, and I focused on soaking in every move. My determination was clear and Sensei voiced approval over my progress in class. He let me know that I was close to earning my green belt, and to say that I was excited would be a gross understatement. Sensei had explained that in the old way, advancement in skill wasn't marked by a new belt, but rather by one belt you kept your whole life that changed "color" as it got progressively dirtier from use. He gave out four belts: white, green, brown and black. And moving toward another "level" was a serious challenge.

Time spent in his home became rare and eventually ceased. I found out years later that he was having marital problems and eventually divorced his wife. At the time, though, I thought I was entirely to blame. I had gotten in a fight at school when some rich kid was making his friends laugh at my expense and wanted to take matters further. He pushed and I pulled; he fell to the ground and I locked him up. A teacher stopped the fight and although I wasn't suspended, it was reported that I had used some type of martial arts moves to handle the boy. Sensei was upset that I hadn't walked away from the fight, and held back my test for green belt, seeing that I was developing a spirit for retaliation. He gave me grueling workouts and made me spend entire class sessions meditating to learn to control my emotions and lengthen my fuse.

Jackie was distancing herself as far as possible from Shirley's actions and it seemed that things were going to take a permanent, positive change. Every night for a week she came home and reiterated how Shirley had persuaded her to let her "spank" me. She worked for hours on end on exonerating herself, telling me stories about Shirley being sick from her years of abuse by her own father. Jackie shared intimate details about her own past, sharing how she was hit when she was little and how some boys had raped her in high school. She lamented about how we were going to start over and redefine our family—a new family. She crafted her words well and led me down the path of my childhood dream. I would be her one priority, her son and best friend. I would have a say in what chores we would share. She even came in one day and told me we were going on a river-rafting trip in Northern California. She showed me a brochure and had me pick one of the dates listed, reporting that we needed a vacation from the house. Over and over she expounded on details of how we were going to truly be a nonviolent family of love. She promised that I could trust her;

and she solemnly swore that Shirley would never hit me again. When she tucked me in, she finished our all-night dialogues with how Tony was going to be welcome over anytime.

Jackie was a very intelligent woman, and although I had been through similar circumstances, I was totally unsuspecting about the visit that occurred soon after. A DPSS worker showed and asked about any inappropriate touching or hitting. And although I knew, when she arrived, that a setup had taken place, I chose to believe Jackie's "new family" speech and put all the blame on Shirley. I remembered being told that I wouldn't get another chance at foster placement if this one failed. I wanted to blame Shirley; I wanted this placement to work. I intensely desired to be part of the "new" family Jackie described and not trapped in an orphanage until I was old enough to be kicked out. I would do whatever it took to stay here, with my animal friends and another opportunity to be with my brother. The social worker talked about everything in Jackie's presence and I followed my mom's lead in relaying what had happened.

Before the social worker left, we spoke outside, alone, and she asked me a few questions that I could give a quick 'yes' to without having to be too convincing. "Do you feel safe here?"

"Yeah."

"Will you tell me if there is any inappropriate hitting or touching?"

"Yeah." She never asked to see any wounds or scars and never asked any real leading questions to find out what had gone on. She handed me her business card and I promised to give her a call if I needed to. It was a short visit and she left me in Jackie's care.

When I went back to school in Anaheim, my group of outcast friends greeted me warmly. They had continued pulling some pranks at school and told me about how they were calling in fake reservations to the airlines. I joined in and, wanting to test if Jackie would continue to be a gentler disciplinarian, I dared to be bolder. It did start off as a stupid prank; making reservations for people who would never show, mostly our teachers and administrators. But I pushed the envelope, hoping to get a bigger laugh, and called in a bomb threat. I snickered, thinking that maybe they would stop a plane or two and hold up a bunch of people. Everyone in our circle seemed to think it was funny as I covered my mouth with my sweater, made some dumb comments, and hung up.

But one of the girls took our prank seriously and told the principal. I was called in and questioned. I didn't really think anything of it and admitted to my crime. It was, after all, just a phone call, right? No, actually it was a federal offense and this would be the first time I was to be arrested. While waiting for the police to show up, the principal relayed the information that he had heard from his informant about our morning rituals of vandalism. I refused to speak, anxious over my impending arrest. What would my Sensei think? What would Jackie do? It wasn't hard for the principal to lay blame on me for the other morning pranks. He put two and two together after Jackie had been called and he learned that she always dropped me off two hours before the bell.

The police came and took me into custody. I sat in an observation room watching the clock on the wall count off three hours while waiting for Jackie to get off work and make it to the police station. I guess they couldn't really question me without my legal guardian there. I killed time with a pocket chess set. After a little while I searched the room and found a rubber band and a bolt. I stretched the rubber band between my two fingers and tried to sling the bolt across the room. It didn't go anywhere but got caught up and swung into my knuckles. The bolt hit the ground and I rubbed my stinging hand. I gave up on trying to eradicate boredom and just sat, waiting for news of my fate.

Two detectives entered the room, informing me that they had a recording of my call and that the operator had known it was some dumb kid and no action was taken. They informed me how serious my actions were and started mentioning huge fines and jail time. They intended to scare and intimidate me and it was working. Then they commented on me hitting myself in the hand with the bolt. "It's not easy to fly a bolt with a rubber band is it?" and they both laughed. They started in on me again, asking why I pulled such a brainless prank, and reiterating that I could be punished severely.

"I was trying to make my friends laugh." I said with a bowed head.

"Why don't you just join a chess club? I'm sure you could make friends there. And you wouldn't have to be here right now." They were letting me know again that they had been watching the entire time; they smiled at each other in recognition of having awakened my paranoia.

"I don't really know how to play chess. And besides, the rich kids there won't play with me."

"Well either way, the kids you're hanging around with now aren't your friends anyway. If they really were your friends, then they wouldn't tell you to do things that will get you into trouble and then laugh about it. Right?"

"Yeah."

"You're going to have to find friends that are going to like you for you. And not because you'll do something bad so they can laugh at you." He sounded sincere; and after my affirming head nod, Jackie came in and they went out. She had been listening to the whole thing and had already been talking with the cops for a while. She put her hand on my back and told me to get up.

"Let's go home," she said soothingly. We got into the car and began the long, two-hour drive home. Her silence was killing me. What was she going to do to punish me this time? Surely an arrest required stiff discipline. My legs began to shake nervously and I was biting my fingernails.

"You've been expelled," broke the silence, an hour into our drive. "Why didn't you tell me about these rich kids getting you to do their dirty work?"

"I dunno." But I did know—I just knew you wouldn't listen. If I had admitted to stealing pornos and gluing them to the school windows or any of the other things I did, my consequences would have been far more severe than the punishments Shirley had handed me over the dirt clods.

Maybe she had been empathizing, as she had had horrendous acne as a teen and was also an outsider in school. The long silence before she spoke was probably filled with her memories of what she had gone through as a little girl. She offered, "It's not your fault. I don't want you to worry. You're not getting a spanking, okay?"

Heck yeah okay! Trying to not sound like I was getting away with something I let out a sincere, "Thank you." I didn't get any punishment and spent my extra time at home riding my horse and playing alone on the ranch. It was a great week. If it wasn't enough that I wasn't going to get any punishment for my expulsion, Jackie's next news would be, by far, the sweetest piece of news that had EVER fallen on my ears.

Chapter 12 - The Price of Pride

When Jackie came home, she wore a constant smile and took me out to dinner. She explained how she had talked with Tony's mom and had arranged for me to go to Chemawa Middle School, a mere couple blocks from their house. I was going to stay with them after school and wait for her to pick me up. My heart soared! I was going to get to spend time with my brother again! She went on to explain how she told them Shirley was kicked out and wouldn't return.

Jackie was still distancing herself as far as possible from Shirley's actions, and it seemed that things were really going to take a permanent, positive change. In the evenings leading up to the day this new arrangement would take effect, Jackie came home and reiterated how Shirley was totally at fault for what had happened to me. I guess she wanted to be sure that my story wouldn't falter if Tammie scrutinized her story.

I started going to school at Chemawa Middle School and could hardly contain my excitement. I couldn't sit still in class, in expectation of seeing Tony afterward. When the final school bell rang, I ran the whole way to his house. Rushing inside, I bolted into his empty room. I walked to the back of the house and asked Tammie for his whereabouts. To my surprise, Tammie was still in her nightgown and barely nudged at my presence. She informed, "He's at baseball practice. Go have a seat in the living room. He'll be home anytime now."

I went and sat down and watched TV for a while, but got up every fifteen to twenty minutes for the first hour to ask when he'd be home. Tammie joined me eventually, even grabbing us both a snack. I waited and waited, fidgeting impatiently.

When Tony got home he went right into the kitchen and then to his room. Tammie called for him to come out, but he said he needed to finish changing his clothes. When he finally appeared, he sat down in a rocking chair across the room. Tammie said, "Louis has been waiting for you for a while. Why don't you two go play?"

We had a quick awkward exchange of glances, both looking at one another as if to say "Now what?" I had had such high hopes for what I thought would be a dramatic reunion, but now I thought maybe my expectations had been too high. Remembering the time at the lake when Tony had wondered why I would want to go away with him forever, I resolved to not throw myself out in front of that train again, just to have my heart run over once more.

Tony acted coy and reserved, like it was merely OK that I was there. I tailored my reaction to mimic his and we shared many uncomfortable silences. Our few conversations that first day included him showing me his room and his toys. Eventually we settled on his bedroom floor playing video games. We played until Jackie came a couple of hours later. She checked that everything had gone well and we left for home. The whole two-hour ride I tried to calculate where I might be able to gain some ground with my little brother. But no answers came.

This pattern repeated daily. Every day I would rush home to find that he was at a cousin's house or baseball practice. Tammie and I would have our "coffee chat" about various talk shows and then he'd finally get home. I couldn't stand being next to her, and many things about her reminded me of the first foster mother I could recall—Karen—except Tammie had blonde hair, not black. She had the same weight problem and seemingly the same mood swings. I did my all to be a non-factor in her afternoon while I waited for Tony to get home.

Sometimes Tony and I played video games and other days we went to Jason's house to see his ninja stars and throwing knives. Every now and again I went to one of his baseball practices or games. To see the support his mom and dad gave him was confusing for me. I was rooting for him, too, and I could understand that, but at the same time I was jealous that he had truly found loving parents. I wanted to protest the limited time in which I got to see him one-on-one or participate in activities with him, but I knew that I was fortunate to even be seeing my brother again. I took advantage of every second we were together and didn't complain to him.

Again I was having trouble fitting in at my new school. Since the first day the teacher called out my name for attendance, I had to put up with the "real" Mexicans making fun of me.

"Your name can't be Martinez, white boy!"

"Look at those goggles homz!"

"His mom must be a white whore in TJ!" Some of these comments I had no problem brushing aside, but a few of them hit just the right button and I would close my eyes, trying fiercely to stay in control. I wasn't going to blow my chance to be with my little brother again.

In history class, I made friends with a Mexican gang member. Aldo was always drawing elaborate pictures of cars and girls covered in gang signs. I showed him my sketchpad and he asked how I did this or that and I would show him. I mimicked some of his drawings and showed him shading and light direction to add 3D qualities to his work. He never smiled any other time I saw him, except in our history/drawing class.

History was the last class of the day and we would walk off campus together before parting. One time one of his friends jumped on his back and said, laughing, "What's up Esse?"

"Nada. This is Louis Martinez. We got history together." Aldo pulled my sketchbook from my hand and opened it to his friend, "Mira Esse."

"This is yours?" his friend asked.

"No, Louis did this."

"Serio?"

"Serio." Aldo put his hand on my shoulder with acceptance. The boy's girlfriend walked up and saw the drawing.

"Aldo, that's really good!" She kissed her boyfriend before Aldo started to deny credit.

"What! You let this white boy draw this?!" She voiced a few profanities along with the reason I should have never draw their signs, then took the pad and threw it to the ground. Her boyfriend supported her and shook his head and walked away. Without a word, Aldo turned and walked away, never speaking to me again. From that time on, he ignored me in history class.

I was upset about the whole thing, but not angry. I didn't get why it mattered so much how I looked. No matter that I was one of the fastest and best, I would never get picked by the in-crowd of Mexicans (mostly gang members) for soccer at lunch or in PE. Along with the actual Mexican kids that barely spoke any English, they would taunt us and bully us. They constantly made comments about my skin when I scored, and pushed or fouled me when I got the ball. I eventually just stopped playing and spent most of my time drawing. After all, my main goal there was to get close with my brother again, and having friends at school would just be icing.

Tony and I played hard during the time we spent together. He even went with me to karate class a few times. He wasn't very interested, and I was disheartened when he said it was a waste of time. Truly hurt, I did my all to shake off his comments and kept trying to find some way to win him over.

While having a snack and waiting for Tony to get home one day, Tammie struck up a curious conversation. "I heard Shirley got in trouble for hitting you."

"Yeah."

"You gave a report to the social workers?"

"Uh huh"

Smugly she commented, "If Tony ever reported on us that we hit him, he would get twice that after they left." I felt stung with shock and rage and could feel the tip of my ears aflame.

I snapped back, "Yeah, and then they'd send you away too!"

"What! I can do whatever I want to him because he's my kid!"

"But he's my brother."

"That means that we are family Louie. And you can't talk to me any way you like!" At that she came around and grabbed me by the wrist and started to pull me toward the living room. Anyone who has taken a week of Judo knows how easy it is to break such a hold and I did, falling backward onto the floor. She grabbed me with both hands then and dragged me into the living room. "Stand up!" She faced me in the corner and ordered, "Don't you ever talk back to me! Stay right there!" She walked away and I could hear her shuffling through things in her room.

I was convinced she was getting something to hit me with so she could make her point and began to think of my options. She had stood me next to a grandfather clock and every second ticked away in my ear. On impulse, I turned and walked straight out the front door. I ran down the street and crossed the intersection, nearly being smacked by a small pickup truck. As soon as I got to the other side, I ducked behind some bushes that decoratively fenced a yard. I peered through a small opening to see if the blonde-haired blob, still in her nightgown at four in the afternoon, had the guts to give chase. She probably just smiled and ate something, because she never appeared.

I waited, crouched behind those bushes for hours, watching for Tony to come home or for Jackie's car. After the sun had set, I finally caught sight of what I thought was Jackie's Mitsubishi Mirage. I stood up and she flashed her bright headlights at me. I darted across the intersection, this time looking both ways first. I opened the door and shot into the front seat.

"What happened?! Tammie is very mad. She told me how you fought with her and ran away for no reason."

"I didn't fight with her! She said she would hit Tony twice as hard as Shirley hit me. She was getting something to hit me with. So I ran."

She burst out, "You don't get to run away because you are going to be disciplined!" She gathered herself and continued on calmly, "Either way, she doesn't want you back at her house." The whole trip home I sat in silence and Jackie didn't inquire further about what happened. She found a family to watch me before and after school so I wouldn't have to transfer schools again. This house was just another two blocks past Tammie and Ed's, and as I walked back from school it killed me to be that close and not be able to see Tony. I wasn't worried about Tony's safety; I knew that Tammie wouldn't risk alienating him with a beating. We had been locking horns, her and I, for so long and she was far more cunning than I in our battle over Tony. He would be fine, but I craved to really know that he was okay.

Daily I hid around the corner and waited for Tony to get home. I didn't have a plan to do or say anything; I thought that maybe just the sight of him would be able to put me at ease. Day after day I waited and watched as he played in his yard with Jason, his cousins, or his twin brother and sister, Nathan and Naomi. I wanted so badly to go over and get Tony to come play with me. I just looked on, crouched behind a shrub, crying on the inside at the realization that he was very happy without me there.

Jackie had made a show that she was going to be the mother I always wanted. The only problem was, she had to be either at work or in transit eighty percent of the week. I found some joy clinging to my animal family. They had been loyal to me, they were always happy when I arrived. Lobo had become my best of friends. He was smart and strong; he commanded respect from all the other animals and gave it all over to me. I rode Otay and played with her and the dogs by the lake. I sat and stared at the rope that had once supported my brother's weight. I felt like that rope—like a thing just dangling in the air waiting for someone to come along and play with me. After clearing my tears away, I talked to my animal friends, who had gotten so used to my voice that they knew to gather around me and listen. Lucky was the cuddler and would always crawl onto my lap. I stroked her long black hair and when I was done venting, got a group hug from the dogs, and then one from Otay, right before we went home.

These were weeks of deep sadness and frustration. I had once again lost contact with Tony, and had been forced to go with Jackie to visit Shirley in her new home. Her new living situation was almost identical to the one she had at Jackie's. She stayed on a ranch in Norco and lived with a friend rent-free while she took care of the horses. We barely spoke. She had to prove that she could still tell me what to do and gave me orders to go get this or that. Jackie would give her authority and support her orders by repeating them. I kept my distance and did what was asked; there were whips on this ranch too.

Emotionally reeling from this further traumatic separation from my little brother, I spent that Thanksgiving with my head down in depression and in some amount of shame over having been expelled from one school and fumbling my current arrangement. Jackie's mom had made a point to be verbally cutting to me in an effort to coerce me into not making my mother's life so hard. Grandpa stayed silent but I could see the disappointment in his eyes.

With Shirley in daily contact with Jackie again, her teaching methods got transferred back. When Jackie got an inadequate response to a question she asked me, she punched me in the stomach, knocking the wind out of me. Hitting and kicking were gaining momentum in her house again and I just wasn't going to be a punching bag all over. The night she brandished another whip was the night I took my stand.

Because of a sudden heart attack, we had flown out to
Colorado for a week to bury Jackie's father. Gary had always
been kind to me the few times I got to see him. He had given
me a 4-inch pocketknife and a sharpening stone after our
driving trip from Denver. He showed me how to shoot pool, and
my first head rush from a shot of whiskey came during his deep,
crackled laughter. He once towed me behind his moped around
the trailer park on a skateboard Racine got me. He always
showed me respect, and on that long drive back from Colorado,
he let me have the wheel a few times. He had been a prideful
old man, but fair to me. I shed tears over his grave as I clutched
the knife in my pocket.

Once we got back, Jackie made a daily habit of going to
see Shirley. She would send me outside to brush Shirley's
friend's horses while she was being consoled over her father's
passing. At home I couldn't do anything right in her eyes. She
would yell at me and it often led to punching. I didn't
understand. And not knowing the real reason for her bursts of
anger, I grew confused at her actions and frustrated with trying
to please her or just stay out of her way.

Jackie held the whip out and ordered me to grab the
couch for talking back to her. Expressing my opinions had
always been forbidden while Shirley lived with us, but the rule
had grown lax since her departure. When I finally said
something that she didn't have a comeback for, the rule had to
be put back in place.

I stood facing her, in defiance to the demand. She
repeated it and I stood, legs shaking. Pure fight or flight—it was
just her and me. If I gave in to this treatment now, then it would
again be a norm in this house. I had been there almost three
years and had shot up from a little boy to a stronger-than-
average pre-teen. I had a few years of hard labor and, matched
with my martial arts training, I thought that this would be my
chance to assert my pride as a human. I wasn't a small
frightened child anymore; we were eye level with each other

now. I'd be damned if I'd let her start this all over again. I stood there with this determination.

She pulled back and swung, catching the front of my leg. I didn't budge as the strike lacked heart and power. She pulled back for a second strike and I stepped toward her. As she leaned into her attack, I sidestepped and grabbed the offending wrist that held the whip. I pulled and used her momentum to fling her against the wall. I grabbed at both ends of the whip and pushed it into her.

Complete shock was all over her face and she stood there, frozen. In a second, I had taken back power from her—but I didn't know what to do with it. My hands trembled and I backed away, pulling the whip from her hands. I dropped it to the ground and held eye contact, in anticipation of what her next move would be. She took a step forward and in a cold, steady, low tone said, "That's it."

She stepped past me and went over to the phone. "You're going back to the group home." She started dialing numbers and I became terrified. She was still holding the ace. I saw Lobo through the sliding glass door and refused to lose my best friends.

I grabbed her leg, crying, "Please don't send me back! I'm so sorry, I'll never do that again." I went and grabbed the whip and brought it back to her. She threw it down and kicked me away. I could tell she was talking to the police. I next went to the kitchen and grabbed a 12" butcher knife. She screamed at the sight of it and reported my activity to the operator.

"Please don't send me away! I'm sorry, I'm sorry!" I turned the blade toward the ceiling and motioned to cut my wrist.

"Put the knife down!" she yelled.

I continued my pleas, "I'll be good! Don't make me go!"

"If you put the knife down, I'll talk to you." I complied and came out of the kitchen. She put the phone down and punched me in the gut. She opened the sliding glass door and shoved me outside. I looked up, watching her lock the door and then picking the up the phone again.

I pressed my face to the glass. Crying, "No, please, mom!" She hung the phone up and turned to me.

"The police are on their way. They are coming to take you!" I looked around and found a broom. I held it with both hands and swung it toward the glass, stopping it just before contact.

Jackie jumped back and I repeated the motion this time with the demand, "Let me back in. I'll be a good son!" I repeated two more times but the door wasn't opened.

"I'm calling the police again!"

"I'm going to tell them you hit me, and about the whip!"

She slowly came over to the door. Her hand reached over and unlocked it. She motioned for me to sit down. The silence was broken when she began to bargain.

"I won't send you back, if you promise to get some help. You can't swing a knife around and threaten me." Although she was angling, I had her on the run and I knew it. I agreed to her terms and let her do all the talking when the cops showed so I could stay in her home and not be arrested or taken to another orphanage. She told the cops about the knife incident and reported that she had to punch me in self-defense. She said that everything was okay now and put them at ease by telling them I was going to see a psychiatrist friend of hers at the hospital. They told me not to give her any more trouble and that I had to go see the doctor. I wholeheartedly agreed to the arrangement. They left and she kept her word.

We drove all the way out to UCI that evening and stayed late into the night. The psychiatrist asked me what had happened and I described the entire incident. When asked to see the place she hit me with the whip I complied, and dropped my pants. There wasn't any evidence of my current allegations. Jackie was called in to explain and told how she was trying to regain control in the house because I was swinging the knife around. When he pressed about the thin whip scars, Jackie explained about Shirley, and how she was removed from her home. After hearing the unemotional telling of my horrendous abuse, he suggested that I may truly be suicidal, that's why I grabbed the knife. He wrote a bunch of stuff and talked a little more with Jackie, alone.

He sent us home in the early hours of the next morning and I went right to sleep after taking the medications he prescribed. I thought for sure everything had been worked out and told myself that next time I would just be a man and take whatever hits she dealt. She didn't get me up for school the next day and gained my confidence by saying that we both needed a rest. I got to go for a little ride with Otay and the dogs. I didn't know it was to be my last.

When I got back, Jackie said that I had to go with her to talk to some people to clear up what had happened the night before. She prepped me the whole way there; telling me how it wouldn't take long and asking what I wanted for dinner. We arrived at Charter Hospital, Corona, in about an hour and I hadn't a clue what was in store for me. I was interviewed and then shown a room. Jackie followed me in and the nurse left us.

"They said you have to stay here a while. It's the only way to clear up this mess. It'll just be a few days and I'll be back to get you. Okay?"

"I don't want to stay here. I want to go home."

"Well, I'm afraid that that isn't an option right now. Just stay here and everything will be okay in a couple of days." My eyes started to burn and my hands shake.

"I'm not f****** staying here!" She didn't respond and started backing out of the room.

A large female nurse filled the doorway and scolded, "We don't talk like that in here young man! If you can't control yourself, than we will."

"I got to go, Louie. Just a couple of days, okay?" She walked to the door and the nurse let her pass. I walked up to the door and the nurse blocked it again. I turned and looked out the large pane window at the far side of the room. Should I believe

her? Did I have a choice? I had already played my cards with
the doctor from UCI and nothing happened. I was stuck and
doubly trapped in the lockdown facility by some huge nurse. I
picked up the chair at the desk and flung it at the window in a
desperate bid for freedom. It bounced back, hitting me in the
face. I fell to the ground holding a bloody nose.

The nurse and some assistants rushed the room and
picked me up and carried me to a small room with a bed bolted
down in the middle of it. They stretched me out and strapped
my arms and legs to the bed frame. It was so cold in there. The
air was stale with the stench of plastic and urine. I could see a
small mounted camera in the upper corner of the room and I
gave it the finger. I yelled out profanities and pulled at my
restraints. I lasted maybe five minutes before realizing how
futile my actions were and gave up. Every so often, an assistant
would come in and check the restraints and ask if I was okay.
My eyelids were stiff from dried tears, the taste of my own
blood remained on my tongue, and my arms sore from pulling
so hard on the restraints. I was freezing, hungry, and terrified of
this place. Was I okay?

I stayed at Charter Hospital for about three weeks and
didn't have another incident. I worked my way up their level
system in record speed and was actually getting comfortable
with the hospital's predictability. Jackie had sent flowers as a
showpiece to the hospital that it was I who needed the help.
That hospital couldn't give me the help I needed nor could any
institution, for that matter. There was no help from abusive
adults who took advantage of children stuck in the System
without anyone to speak out on their behalf; no help from the
sickos and power mongers that tortured and abused children to
feed their power agendas or twisted mental dysfunctions.

When the time had come for me to go, I was informed
that I wouldn't be returning to Jackie's, but to a group home.
"Father Matthew's?" I asked.

They didn't know of such a place and told me of a group
home in Rialto. It was a small three-bedroom home that I would

go to until Jackie was ready to take me back. I guess the UCI psychiatrist had done something after all. He had recommended that we needed some time apart and ordered her to take more parenting classes.

I said good-bye to my three-week friends and went off to live in my new home that was, at the very least, away from medication, leather straps, and locked doors.

Chapter 13 - The Empowerment of Louis -
A New Path Isn't Always a Better Path

Another long car ride, staring at the back of some stranger's head. On the freeway to a brand new reality. Barely able to comprehend what was left behind, unable to see or direct what lay ahead. Here I go again. Bouncing around the System, hoping that the next place I land would be softer than the last—it usually wasn't.

After riding for some thirty minutes, I recognized the landmarks that were near Father Matthew's. Childhood memory sent a quick panic through me until we had passed the old freeway off-ramp I remembered. The staff person who drove me was a dark black man with a thick African accent. Struggling to understand what he was saying only added to my air of anxiety. From polite conversation and some of my new home's expectation review, I learned that he was from Nigeria. His demeanor reminded me a lot of Sensei's. He was affable and kind enough to stop at a fast food restaurant for us before we arrived at the place I would next call home, somewhere deep in the back streets of Rialto.

For me, moving to Rialto was like moving to an island, complete with its own culture and customs. To say that my next experience was unique and defining is like saying that the sun is merely bright. As alone and targeted as I had been up to this point, I had never before had my eyes opened so wide to how cruel the world could be. How can you hate someone because of the pigment of his skin? It was a question I really never had to

answer before. But now I was forced to understand the adult
world of hate and teaching social hate, including blaming others
for what someone else had done to your relatives or ancestors.
My island's anthem was gangster rap, and contention filled
most of my days. I felt totally alienated, and far too intimidated
to say anything.

Things only got worse for me at my new home. When
we arrived at the three-bedroom house, I was shown my room
and found that no one was back from school yet. The staff
inventoried my bag of clothes and sat me down to talk about the
rules. When my new housemates showed up, they walked right
by me without a word. Two boys started snickering from the
couch and one covered his mouth and sarcastically called,
"Honnn- Keeey." I timidly left to go to my room.

The two boys followed me and stood in my doorway to
announce their disapproval. Devin said, "Aw, hell no. Not a
white boy." Devin professed to be a black power enthusiast. He
wore a huge leather medallion with the shape of Africa in the
middle, Malcolm X T-shirts, and posters of the Black Panthers
Flag were taped to his walls. He was tall and lanky, but had so
much attitude that everyone thought he was invincible. This was
true even though, once he took off his three layers of clothes
and all-red Chicago Bulls jacket, you could hardly find a muscle
on his body.

Clarence, my new roommate, just nodded his head and
said, "What up."

"Hey," is all that came out and I started toward my bags.
We all turned our heads as staff yelled out, "Group!" I followed
the boys to the TV room where everyone sat and began going
over their day. When they stopped to introduce me, only one of
my peers offered a head nod, while the others smacked their lips
or looked away. I was in a very cautious mode and didn't know
what to make of my new home. Everyone, including staff, was
black. This was not Father Matthew's, but I feared my new
placement no less. Admittedly, all the dark eyes sizing me up
intimidated me. I knew institutional life, and I knew I had a

choice to make: Leader or Follower. I chose to stare at the floor.

Foster Parent/Guardian Rule No. 6: *Be Approachable*

Don't expect gratitude. You are very often the only family that a System youth has. Put yourself in his shoes and think what it would be like if you felt like your parents hated you. Always have the door open and watch your body language.

Things went very quietly the first few weeks as I got a handle on all the rules and dynamics. I stayed quiet and, as if I had a contagious disease, was left alone by the boys. It is very disturbing to open your eyes one morning and not be where you expect to be. I was in limbo for a while because no one would even acknowledge my presence. I ended up settling into an old part: I did my chores, faded into the background, ignored snide or racist comments, and hid in my room. Out of curiosity, or perhaps seeing I wasn't a threat or contagious anymore, my roommate finally decided to say something to me.

After lights out, Clarence asked a few questions and told a few war stories in an effort to either impress me or scare me. I gave him a few of my own, including the one about my trophy from the martial arts tournament in TJ. Big mistake. He went and told everyone that I thought I was some kind of white Bruce Lee. Devin quickly chose to call himself the ghetto Mike Tyson—who was knocking out opponents in 15 seconds or less. Within days of beginning their ridicule, "Mike Tyson" challenged me to a fight.

Devin held the place at the top of the heap, and my report of physical prowess challenged that. He found me alone shooting pool on a warped table in the garage. "So what's up pa'tner? You think you're hard blood? Why don't you try some of that Ching chong chow sh** on a ghetto boy and see what happens?" In the back of my mind was a warning from Sensei

that a good street fighter had some advantage over a trained
fighter, and I didn't want to find out.

Forcing my voice steady, "No. I don't want to fight."

"I didn't ask what you wanted, Ghostface. You ain't no
contender, I'm gonna knock you out in two seconds, chump."
He lunged forward and I dodged, grabbing his shoulder and
pushing him with his momentum against the garage door. *It was
on.* He turned, pushed off, and swung madly. I blocked some,
but one wild blow landed hard on the side of my head. I fell
back onto the pool table and raised my legs to kick him off. He
landed on some stacked boxes and I stood with my hands up
ready for his next attack.

The garage and staff office shared a wall

and within moments staff were in there and ordered us
to break it up. Two of Devin's boys were jumping behind the
staff trying to get a look at the action and Devin decided to put
on a show. He took another swing, and I was ready. I ducked
and caught him in the mid section with an uppercut. Staff
pinned me to the pool table, holding me down while Devin was
left to catch his breath.

"What happened?" the staff demanded. Devin didn't say
a word and I understood the look he gave me. I kept my mouth
shut and we both were assigned "early beds" and a week of
house restriction. When Clarence asked for a recap that night I
wouldn't oblige. I didn't want to talk about it and unwittingly
incite another altercation. He kept up with the questions and
then began drawing his own conclusions.

"I bet you beat his a** huh? Yeah, that's why he hasn't
said anything isn't it? Bruce Lee beats Mike Tyson." I turned in
my bed and remained silent—but smiled. The next day Devin
and I didn't talk to each other or about what had happened. But
his challenge wasn't going to end that easily.

School was worse. Almost everyone there was Black or
Hispanic and I stood out like a sore thumb. In my new school, I
was immediately seen as "that white kid," who probably has
everything they didn't. People thought I had a perfect life

because I had pale skin. I was constantly addressed as "Cracker," "Peckerwood," "White bread," among many others. Added to the climate of unreasonable hate was insecure bullying, emotional and physical projection in the form of verbal abuse, and then violent outbursts from those who were perpetuating a cycle of destruction. I spent a couple months with my head down, ignoring taunts and stayed immersed in my sketchpad. I did my all to try to fade into the background. When I had to walk somewhere, it was like I was tucked under an umbrella, observing only a couple feet in front of me, and peeking out every now and again to make sure that I didn't run into anything.

Every day there was a fight between gang members or a lover's quarrel. To survive I knew that I needed to lay low and not draw attention to myself, but it was lonely path. There were days that I was pushed to the suicidal edge after the name calling and getting pushed or slapped on the head. I felt like everyone hated me, the whole island. I desperately needed some type of acceptance or camaraderie. Again, it was history class that yielded a friend for me.

We were studying about the Holocaust and the teacher had even arranged for us to meet a couple of concentration camp survivors. I was spellbound and full of sincere questions. I felt I could relate to the experiences as they were told— abandonment, cruelty, injustice, and suicidal thoughts brought on by questioning one's lot in life. I hung on every word— looking for answers as to how they got through it. My teacher was impressed not only by my interest, but also the following heartfelt mid-term essay. Without studying, I aced the mid-term exam, even though I hadn't been there for the whole semester. It was the A on the test that caught the eye of the classmate sitting next to me.

Rodney had a menacing disposition and the size to back it up. He was at least three times my size and carved out of stone. When he walked, he swung his arms purposefully, like he was ready to end any stride with a punch. HGC was tattooed across his fingers on one hand, and his other had a giant four-finger gold ring on it. Three oversized gold rope chains hung around his neck with large gold medallions on them. He always dressed in black or khaki dickies, white T-shirt, Raiders hat and a black Raiders jacket. He pulled up on me after class and I thought I was in for a severe white-boy beat-down.

I flinched at his words, "Yo, hold up." I clenched my eyes shut, waiting for impact. "What's your name cuz?"

I opened my eyes, turned and responded cautiously, "Louie."

"Louie?" I sensed the note of sarcasm and had started to get used to that reaction to my name from the boys at the group home. "My uncle's name is Louis. I live with him and my aunt." The speed in which he gave me all this info showed nervousness and I began to let my guard down, interested to hear what he wanted. "I saw you drawing something. Let me see." I opened my pad and he saw sketches of Otay, Lobo, and of a little boy staring out a window. "Damn, that s***'s good." He handed me back my pad and then got to the point. "So you got an A on the test, huh?"

"Yeah."

"Maybe you could help me with my homework? I don't wanna get held back again, ya know? I'll break you off a little some-im'-some-im'. Cool?"

"Yeah, alright." I was desperate for any type of interaction and was willing to play helper nerd to him. So everyday during first break we'd meet by the gym and I shared my answers with him and tried to explain, as best I could, the main points so he could pass the tests. We'd walk towards his first class and it felt cool to have someone to walk with. Once we got there, he'd "break me off" (or give me five dollars) after every lesson. At first I would turn down the money, but he would insist. I had the best lunches because of those five dollars. I walked right past all the other group home boys in the free lunch line and right over to the hamburger and chili cheese French-fry line. I sat with a box of food and a large cherry coke and felt like I owned the world. It didn't matter to me that I sat alone; it just mattered that I had a good lunch.

Basketball was nearly the only sport played, and I was horrible. My roommate Clarence was on a league team and showed me some basics for a little cut on my lunch money. He helped me practice dribbling and shooting free throws. I was fast but lacked finesse and shooting skill, so I focused on defense. This got me into my first fight at Frisbee Junior High.

"Damn, that white boy just took the ball from you!" Others joined in instigating the fight by taunting the boy, "Are you gonna let that honky punk you for the ball like that?"

"Damn," from one kid.

"Damn," from another.

"He made you his b****!"

"Damn."

"I made his momma my b****. Just give me the ball!" The boy headed straight for me and threw an elbow into my nose. I fell on my back and he stood over me. "Who's the b**** now, m***** f*****!" I stood up, thinking it was over, but the kid put his fists up, thinking I was looking to get some respect. I had tolerated enough, and I accepted the challenge. Though terrified inside, with false cockiness I waved him toward me.

He threw the first punch and I grabbed his arm and pulled with one hand while pushing against the back of his shoulder with the other. I brought him to the ground and held him there, twisting his wrist and arm. One of his friends punched the upper side of my head and I lost my balance and fell backwards, then caught myself. Then Rodney stepped in and pulled out a large knife. The other boy reached down and grabbed his friend and they backed away.

Rodney quickly shoved the blade into his jacket before security approached. Everyone turned and walked away and security didn't know who to stop. "You got some moves, huh?" Rodney said with a big smile. After looking around he offered me the knife. "Don't worry about those dudes, they're some mark-a** fools. They don't wanna see me." I gladly accepted the gift and walked away with the feeling that I had a measure of protection from my new friend.

I didn't know it then, but the real reason for their lack of retaliation was the fact that Rodney was one of the biggest drug dealers in the school. I found out when weeks later he asked me to hold a paper bag for him until after school and gave me fifty bucks for doing it. He had begun to introduce me to all his homeboys and schooled me on how to be tough. Even though I knew I wasn't really part of his group, I heartily accepted any measure of acceptance.

I also must admit that I idolized Rodney because of the power he wielded over other people. I wanted to be strong like him. Surely I would never be on the receiving end of abuse if I could emulate his attitude, right? It would be some time before I would find out that cruel answer. My new group of associates were the first "friends" that didn't ask me to do something stupid to be cool with them. They rarely heckled me about my glasses and skin color. More importantly, they verbally jumped to my aid if anyone else did. When my first clothing purchase order from the State came, I went to the Colton Swap Meet and bought the same clothes that they all had—which also happened to be the only type of clothes that the Colton Swap Meet sold. Black and khaki dickies, white T-shirts, and a long black trench coat. I moved around the school a little easier and was starting to feel like I had finally found a niche on this island that would allow me to survive.

Rodney had a small idea of what types of hits I had taken from Shirley, and to be "hard" meant that you could stand up and keep coming. Besides my confessions and scars, I had proven my strength after a few more fights. I was quickly learning that to get respect on this island meant you never backed down. Rodney told his boys that I was born in LA and had grown up in foster homes. This was a fact that was not looked on as disgraceful by this crowd; rather, it gave you more respect. By the time the school year ended, I had made the transformation from a timid, eye-dodging young boy to a glaring roughneck who required respect and was willing to take it if needed.

I spent most of that summer competing with the other boys. Whether it was playing Nintendo, behavior points, or basketball, I was gaining on all fronts and had Devin trying to find something to beat me at. He was always better than me at shooting pool, but his biggest embarrassment came when he challenged everyone, including me, to a weightlifting competition. If he curled fifteen pounds, I curled twenty-five. If he benched 150, I benched 180. He tried to dead lift 200lbs and failed to gain 6 inches. As I lifted the same weight, the boys started chanting "Bruce Lee, Bruce Lee" and Devin couldn't take it anymore. He punched me in the face as I had the weight over my shoulders and I fell backwards, dropping the bar in front of me. He hovered over me and I gave him a swift kick to the groin. Staff jumped in and separated us.

I did everything I could to stay away from Devin for the rest of the summer, but in brief moments of eye contact, he knew I wasn't afraid of him. The majority of our summer activities consisted of going to play basketball at the school up the street, where I practiced relentlessly. Before the summer ended we were all signed up for a summer basketball league. I soaked up the finer points of the game and our coach gave me a little extra time because of my willingness to learn and apply myself. I found camaraderie among my teammates until the six-game season ended. It was one of the better experiences of my life.

I continued to try and train myself and practiced shadowboxing and judo moves alone in my room. I used these times to think back to Sensei. I wondered if he knew what had happened; I doubted he got an accurate account of events. I didn't want to lose honor in his eyes because he was the only adult whose opinion I cared about. My brother's face was fading from memory and Jackie didn't really want me—not as a son and real family member anyway. With the pendulum quickly swinging the other way, Sensei's opinion of me is what kept me from losing myself in street ethics and committing any heinous violent crime.

After school started up again, one of my housemates had been accepted back into his home and his bed was filled with another white kid. He didn't adapt as quickly as I had and was fast becoming a daily target for Devin and his cronies. While one of them was trying to punk him, I stepped in and told him to back off.

Devin stepped up. "What did you say whiteboy? You must be crazy, I know you ain't talking to me, fool!" Devin pushed Todd, the new boy, to the ground and came at me. He punched; I blocked and then connected one to the side of his face. His boys stepped in and jumped me. They pushed and kicked me down the hall until the staff started coming.

"What's going on out there?" Everyone ran back to their rooms and Devin could be heard attacking his new roommate. The staff approached as I picked myself up off the floor.

"There's a fight in Devin's room." The staff went down the hall and pulled Todd out and sat him at the dining room table. They had a little discussion and then decided to let Todd go back to his room after Devin halfheartedly shook his hand. Todd looked terrified and was visibly shaking. I offered to take him as a roommate and was ignored.

Louder, I repeated, "You can put Todd in my room!" They gave me a raised eyebrow expression as to say, "How dare you raise your voice."

Devin agreed with the proposal, saying, "Yeah, I don't want that …uh hum… boy in my room anyway." Upon Devin's response, they acted and allowed the room change. Devin had been angling to get Clarence to be his roommate ever since I got there and had finally gotten his wish.

Todd moved his stuff and gave me a heartfelt, "Thanks."

"No problem." I was already the house outsider and accepted that the new kid would probably be my only chance at a cordial roommate. At least both house targets would be in one room, and hopefully we could stick together. During the house meeting that followed, no consequences were given to Devin's pack because the staff didn't actually see anything. I was pissed and let them know it, but they didn't care.

That night, as I was having my usual nightmare of Shirley, I awoke to a new one. Devin and Clarence were telling me to wake up and turn over. I grabbed my pocketknife, kept under my pillow, and squeezed its handle. They were both standing there with erections. I could make out two silhouettes over Todd's bed, holding him down.

"Suck it b****." Devin ordered just above a whisper. Clarence grabbed my head and pushed it toward his penis.

"F*** you," and I swung the knife out at them. Devin dropped back but I caught Clarence on his arm.

"He cut me!" They scurried out the room. I jumped out of bed and started towards the boys holding Todd. They were trying to force his mouth open and didn't expect a kick from behind.

With no regard to the hour I yelled, "Get out!" They pressed themselves against the wall and squeezed out. "Todd, are you okay?" He didn't answer and began crying. I went down the hallway and woke up the "awake" night staff. I gave a report and our housemother came to check on Todd. He wouldn't speak to her either and she started walking away. "Aren't you going to do anything?"

"I didn't see nothin'. He ain't speakin'. So what choo wan me to do?"

"I just told you what happened. Ask the rest of the boys!" She shuffled her feet down the hallway and turned on all of the lights.

"Get up! Get up! Everyone to the livin' room." They all faked like they had been sleeping and sat down on the couches like a pack of sloths. Everyone denied seeing anything and stuck together that they had all been sleeping.

Devin spoke out, "That wannabe crab is just trying to get us in trouble. We didn't do nothin'!" Everyone backed him up, and our housemother either didn't want to deal with it and have to document anything, or just didn't care what happened to the white kids in the house and wanted to protect her own. Remembering all of Devin's racial slurs and his group's privileged status, I was prompted to choose the second choice.

Standing and looking dead in her eyes, I shouted, "You're a racist! You're always sticking up for the black boys!" At this, Devin charged me and it was going to be a big mistake for him. As he approached, I didn't wait for the first swing, like I had trained so many years to do; I just locked my arm in place and threw my body into my punch, which landed right between his nose and mouth. He fell down and wasn't getting up. Immediately, the other boys started to rush me and I swung frantically before I was overtaken and stomped.

Our housemother started yelling for them to stop but they ignored her. I rolled on the ground trying to get far enough away to stand again. I quickly found myself in the kitchen, then grabbed a chair and stood. Everyone was waiting for someone else to make the first move but it didn't happen. The housemother stepped in the middle and directed the boys to go to bed.

Once they left the room, she slapped me across the face and said, "You better start actin' right, you stupid little white boy."

"Don't ever touch me again...racist." She saw how very serious I was and just smacked her lips and rolled her eyes before walking away. She turned and wiped Todd's and my levels off the dry-erase board and continued down the hallway.

"What the hell! Why is our level being dropped? They were jackin' with us!"

"It's for lying."

"What?! Hell no!" Just then Devin came around the corner and hit me with the telephone. Dazed, I fell back into the dining room chairs and pushed them in front of me. Our housemother looked on. I glared at her, "Ain't you going to do something?"

"Devin. That's enough, honey. Just go to bed. Don't worry, I'll take care of everything in the morning." She cut her eyes at me and walked away with Devin. I went to my room and grabbed some clothes and shoved them in my school bag. I got my stash of cash from under the box spring and showed Todd.

"Come on Todd, let's get the f*** outta here." He grabbed some of his things and followed me out the door.

"Where do you think ya'll goin'?" she sneered.

"The hell away from your racist a**!" I snapped. I pushed past her and went right out the front door. The boys opened their windows and were ridiculing us, giving loud sarcastic, fake laughs. We got halfway down the block and Todd got scared.

He stopped walking and told me, "I'm going back. I'll tell my mom and dad and they'll get me out of here tomorrow."

"It's up to you. You better sleep with the light on." I envied his convictions, his trust in his parents to help him if needed. Throughout the years I have often thought of how he had said that with such confidence. He went back but I wasn't going to give in. I walked around the city; it was somewhere around midnight when I saw Rodney with two of his boys hanging out in the parking lot of Churches Chicken.

"What's up Loc?"

"My staff is trippin'. She hates white people and just lets the other boys do whatever they want."

"Sh**, I hate white people too!" The group erupted with laughter. "Just playin'. Just check they chin. They'll treat you right."

"I did. But there's four of them and one of me. I can handle a couple, but I need a gun to handle four."

"We can fix that." Rodney lifted his shirt to reveal a chromed 9mm. He pulled it out and handed it to me. It was the first time I had handled a handgun and I was dumbfounded.

"I can't go out like that. I ain't goin' to jail for them." I held out the gun for him to grab and he did.

"Suit yourself. Forget all that drama. You want to go to a party with us?"

"Hell yeah." My first party. I had heard them talking about these all the time at school and I had to turn them down because I couldn't get away from the group home. The thought alone conjured up images of girls, loud music and something to talk about at school on Monday. But most of all, acceptance.

We got in Rodney's car and headed for his friend's house. When he got behind the wheel I wondered if he had a license. He did look old enough to have a car and I guess his confidence deterred him from getting pulled over.

When we got to a house overflowing with people we stopped. Everyone knew Rodney and I just stuck by his side. As we entered, the bass from the speakers pounded my chest even though the lyrics could barely be heard. Thick cigarette and marijuana smoke filled the air and burned my eyes. People were standing everywhere and their faces were hard to make out due to the low lighting. He introduced me around and caught some flack from an older teenager playing dominoes. "Why'd you bring in that dumb a** looking white boy? Look at those glasses, they look like, like coke bottles!" He laughed at his own joke, and the rest of his group at the table soon followed.

Rodney came to my defense while draping his arm over me, "This is my boy right here. This little n**** is crazy."

"What's that little a** white boy gonna do?"

"He'll take you out fool." I had a comfortable look on until that popped out.

One of my friends from school added, "That crazy m****** f***** knows some Kung Fu type s***." I didn't know how I should feel. My friends were giving me props, but at the same time, I knew that boy was being disrespected and would probably want to fight.

"I know some of that dragon fu stuff too. What's up fool, come on." He waved his arms up and down and yelled, "Whatta!" He stepped to me and swung haphazardly. I blocked and sidestepped, pushing him onto a couch. He played it off and said,"You're lucky I just drank two forties or I'd put that chop suey on your a**!" Everyone laughed it off and I walked away with Rodney. After that, I wanted to take in everything and enjoy myself, but I was hyper-paranoid, realizing that I was a bull's-eye.

We hovered for a while and Rodney's girlfriend, who looked about twice his age, grabbed him to dance to a slow jam. He came back in a few minutes and brought a girl for me. Leticia looked about 17 and had every curve in the right place. She sat really close to me, throwing her arm over my shoulder. I fidgeted nervously as she rubbed my inner thigh. Rodney came over and slipped me a condom, "The bedroom's empty. Go handle your business."

I accepted the condom and was glad that the room was dark so no one saw how red my face was. "I can't," and shook my head, not knowing if he could hear my quiet response over the music. One of the older boys heard and broke in.

"Sh**, I can." He grabbed the condom from me and took Leticia by the hand and into the bedroom. I realized then that Leticia was a hood rat or party sex toy and wasn't sitting by me because she thought I was cute or cool. During the course of that night I watched her go in the room with two other guys, and I held my shock on the inside. I felt pity for her lot in life, to see such a young beautiful girl sleeping around like that. I was somehow drawn to what she was going through and felt bonded with her by how I had been used by some of my foster parents for their violent and sometimes sexual pleasures.

I declined every time a joint was passed my way. But they didn't give up that easy. "Come on. I thought you was some kinda Baby G? Take a puff off this. This is what a real gangsta smokes."

I shook my head and stood up.

"Awe, go on then little punk a** white boy!" I turned my back on their taunts and walked away, making my way over to some of the boys I knew shooting craps. They all let me in

the game quickly, surely thinking that I would give up
everything I had easily.

When everyone started to leave, Rodney asked where I
was going to go and I shrugged my shoulders. "You come
spend the night at my house, alright."

"Cool, thanks man." He put me in the top bunk in his
room and I fell asleep wondering where I was truly headed.

The next morning I woke to the smell of bacon. I put on
my glasses and looked around the room to see turntables, a huge
stack of records, and a bunch of model cars. I got up and peered
out the doorway. Rodney was sitting at the table with his uncle.
He saw me and waved me over.

"Uncle, this is Louie. My friend from school."

"Louis," I corrected him. I knew his uncle's name and
was trying to sound more mature and maybe even connect with
this family on some small level. I looked over to his uncle and
extended my hand, "Nice to meet you, sir."

He grabbed it and said warmly, "Good to meet you too.
Have a seat boy. You hungry?" He called out, "Hey momma,
bring Louis a plate." When Rodney's aunt made her way to the
table to present the plate I stood and took it from her, "Thank
you, ma'am."

She gave me a warm smile. "You're welcome, Louis."
After breakfast, Rodney showed me all his albums. We
basically spent the rest of the morning with him giving me a
formal introduction to rap music. While he was showing me
how his turntables worked, I caught sight of a picture of a little
black boy with thick glasses.

"Who's that?"

He somberly replied, "That's my cousin Ben. He got
sick and died last year."

"Sorry." I had slept in his bed and sat in his chair at
breakfast. He shrugged me off but his pain was obvious. It
wasn't hard to put two and two together to figure out why he
had warmed to me so quickly now. After the records, we went
outside and he started to mow the lawn. I asked him to let me do

it but he told me to relax. After a few exchanges he agreed to let me rake the yard after he was done clipping the grass.

I sat on the porch with his uncle, waiting for my turn to help. "Rodney says you're a smart boy. He says you've been helping him with his schoolwork. That's real good. He's been held back twice now and we don't know what to do." I thought "Twice?" that would make him old enough to be in the tenth grade.

I answered, "It's no problem. He looks out for me a lot."

"You don't let him get you into any trouble. You seem like a nice boy."

"No, he wouldn't do that, sir." I was trying to defend him.

He chuckled, "You mustn't know Rodney very well. He was expelled from his last school for stabbing a kid. Trouble seems to find him." He gave a serious look my direction. "You be careful, son."

Was he still talking to me or the child he had recently lost? I didn't know, but gave him the only response that was in me. "Yes, sir." It seemed strange that this man showed any concern for me. I knew what kind of trouble Rodney was, but I didn't care. He was the first person to take me into his family without receiving a check from the state. Thick glasses, white skin and yet he was willing to look beyond all that. And even though we started out on a business relationship, we had soon become inseparable.

We finished the yard together and then walked to the corner liquor store. He flashed his fake ID and got a pack of cigarettes. He offered me one but I declined. He got a little pushy trying to get me to smoke and I showed him the burn mark on the inside my left elbow. I told him how it was a gift from my real mother and her boyfriends before they took me and my little brother away. He backed off about the cigarettes and wanted to know about Tony. I gave him a few pieces, knowing if I talked about it too much, I wouldn't be able to hold back the tears.

He responded, "That's really f***** up."

All I could do was agree with him.

That night we went to a small gathering at one of his homeboys' houses. The party was the same scene: people getting drunk, smoking weed, having sex in the bedrooms. But with fewer people and music at a level that was easy to speak over, the pressure was on to talk about something. Everyone had something to share and I kept quiet. I sat in my awkward seat and focused on the table game we were playing. I was still an outsider. Rodney's girlfriend didn't show, so we just played table games and drank.

"Let's get out of here." I was nervous amongst these strangers and readily accepted his offer to escape. My glasses and skin had usually made me a target, and I didn't want to have to be part of any fight. Rodney grabbed one of his boys and we got in his car and left.

We got about a mile from the party when we heard the single tone of a police siren and saw police lights flashing. Rodney pulled over and we sat completely still. Scared out of my wits, I tried to keep my legs from shaking.

"Put your hands out of the vehicle." The cops shined their flashlights in our faces while pointing their guns. "Where are you boys going tonight?" Before there could be an answer came, "Slowly step out of the vehicle." We followed orders and next they had us face down on the sidewalk. They wrote down our names and I gave them my group home address with the numbers in reverse. They started searching my pockets and found the $200 I had in my coat. It looked like a lot because it was mostly ones, fives and a few twenties. "Where did you get all this money from?" I was scared and couldn't find any words so I said nothing. I didn't get the opportunity to, either, as the cop took the glasses off my face and showed his partner. "Whoa, look at these things!" He gave a chuckle and then put them down next to my head. They found another cash roll on Rodney's other friend and asked him the same question.

"My momma gave it to me for my birthday."

"Yeah right." The cop said and pushed his head back down to the pavement.

The other officer called out for his partner's attention. He had found Rodney's stash, which was just as fat as mine, but was all hundreds, fifties and only a few small bills. He showed his partner and pointed his flashlight at me as I tried to get a look. "Keep your head down boy."

They then directed us to get up and walk around the side of a building, and ordered us to put our hands on the wall, then asked more questions about the money. They told us to take off our jackets and shoes and toss them over and hold the up the wall. As fast as a cheetah, Rodney's friend bolted down the street as we were handing over our jackets. One of the cops flinched like he was going to give chase but then stopped and grabbed a hold of Rodney, pushing him to the ground. The other cop did the same to me.

The officer holding Rodney said, "I'm starting to get tired of dealing with these little punks." He punched Rodney in the back and put his foot on the back of his neck. The other officer rested his knee on my spine, and, aiming his gun, gave me the order to stay still. They started searching our stuff again and found Rodney's real stash. "What do we have here? We got ourselves a little drug dealer, huh? I hate drug dealers!" The officer started kicking Rodney. I jerked with all my strength towards my friend, in a futile impulse to help him, but the officer hovering over me pushed a blunt object into the base of my skull and commanded me to not move. When the cop was satisfied, his partner kicked me in the gut twice. He cursed a few more times about teaching us a lesson and then walked away and left us in the alley. They took the money and drugs and wanted nothing else. They threw our shoes and jackets in a trashcan to humiliate us further.

Rodney and I made our way slowly back to his car. They had definitely given him the brunt of the beating and one of his eyes was starting to close. He broke the silence first, "I hate those f****** pigs." I didn't know what to say and chose to keep my eyes fixed on the pavement. Rodney got in the car and grabbed his gun out from under his seat. "I'm going to take those m***** f***** out." He had rage in his voice and I knew he was serious. I stood there on the driver's side with the telling look of fear. He wanted to cross a line I was unwilling to. He understood what the look on my face meant. He pulled away without a word.

I walked into a public bathroom at some park. It seemed like the whole world was out to get me. Was I ever going to enjoy a day in my life? I just kept landing in one bed of hot coals after another. I washed my face off and looked in the dimly lit mirror. What the hell should I do? Should I go to Uncle Louis' house and tell them what happened? It wouldn't help and would probably end my friendship with Rodney. I knew the snitch code and wasn't going to risk being one, especially to Rodney's last-chance home. Although the last thing in the world I wanted to do was go back to the group home, I was frustrated with my options. For a split second I thought to call Jackie. But the thought passed quickly, as I knew that there wasn't any hope in that. My only choice was to face the music at the group home. In the back of my mind I felt defeated by the streets, like I wasn't ready for them. With a small amount of conscious humility, I started back towards the group home.

Chapter 14 - The Light Getting Brighter

I didn't want to go back to my placement, but felt like I had no other alternative. I was a little sore from our police encounter, but their hits were nothing compared to Shirley's. I got within a block of the house and laid down on a bus bench. Maybe this and maybe that exchanged places in my mind. As I was trying to find a good reason not to return to the group home, it started to rain. I leaned against a tree and stared at the group home. A little more water and I gave in and looked for a way to get into the house.

I finally sneaked in the back door and hid in the office. I slept behind the staff desk undetected until morning. Our housemother found me and seemed very nervous at my presence. She told me to get in the bathroom and get cleaned up. Then she called Jackie and gave me the phone while I sat in a hot bath.

"What happened, Louie?"

"My name is Louis."

"What?"

"My name is Louis."

"That's what I said. What happened? Why did you run away?"

"The staff here are a bunch of racists. Two of the boys tried to make me suck their d**** and the staff didn't do anything about it. So I ran away."

"What?!" her voiced bellowed. "Let me talk to the staff."

I handed the phone to the housemother and shut the bathroom door. I heard some high pitched "I'm innocent" talk as she pinned everything on the boys and said they took control. She knocked on the bathroom door before handing me back the phone. "Get your stuff ready, I'm coming to get you right now."

I was shocked. In my eight months there, she had seen me only a few times and now she was concerned? Her parents were both very much racists and I remember arguing with them over calling all the football players the "n" word. Was she upset that these black people had treated me this way. Or was it deeper? Was she jealously guarding her right to be my sole abuser and trying to fill her psuedo-role as protector once more? Either way, I was glad to get out of that house.

When my bath was finished, I went to pack my stuff to find that it had already been done for me. There was a 72-hour rule where they could fill your bed with someone else if you didn't return. I could see that Todd had gone as well, and hoped that his last night wasn't a horrible one. I came to find out that Devin had been removed and the other boys had all been placed on house arrest.

Jackie showed in a few hours and took me back to the ranch. There was little talk of what happened. She had grown annoyed at the transformation that I had made during the last year, and I'm sure she felt that just by gracing me with her presence, she was fulfilling her role as good cop.

When we got home, it was obvious that Jackie was irritated with my presence. She hadn't entirely won our battle over her hitting me, but wouldn't give me the satisfaction of letting me know to what extent either a social worker or a psychiatrist had counseled her about physical discipline. What I did know was that once I was home, we had to go to family counseling.

Our sessions were a mockery of manipulation and justification. I was taken to a therapist that had been seeing Jackie while I was in Rialto. No matter what I said, "our" therapist already knew why I was having trouble. Jackie had him thoroughly convinced that I was merely rebelling from the "spankings" that I received from Shirley. She couldn't avoid the details of what happened with Champ, but she did everything to minimize and explain that it was a one-time, unique incident. For my part, I argued at first, but then realized that the more I talked, the more I would have to cope with my feelings about what had happened, which bolstered Jackie's case. I would break down and cry and/or clam up and remain defiant at his prodding. Why should I trust this doctor that Jackie had brought me to? I didn't want to share and feel vulnerable. Having just finished a year at the "School of Hard Knocks" in Rialto, I wanted to remain in some type of self-assumed position of power and control. Eventually, our therapy sessions settled on weekly events and not on what any clinician would surely have diagnosed, my suffering from Post Traumatic Stress Disorder.

Jackie now reasoned that if she couldn't hit me, then she would send me to a school that would; and I was enrolled at a Christian school that utilized physical discipline. I was among many kids who had been pushed to learn and did so without fighting it. Everyone seemed smarter than me. They all had broad bases of knowledge and spoke like adults. Complicated phrases and conversations filled the classrooms and I was very intimidated. Corky Pigeon, from the TV show Silver Spoons, attended and basically ran the school. Everyone followed him around, looking for his acceptance. He had his own car and whatever fad was sweeping the school was usually started because of him. This made it very hard for me to find a friend, due to my lack of "good" looks or wealth.

While I had trouble fitting in, I enjoyed the challenge of my classes. My assignments were very difficult and required real thought. I fed off them and was getting good grades. I remained guarded over my emotions, but I put away my "tough guy" exterior, because it wasn't needed here. There were no fights and students were trained to regard one another respectfully. In quick fashion, I assimilated to my new surroundings and began getting along with the other students. I even made a friend that reminded me of Chris Peterson from Father Matthew's. We both hung out together after school waiting for our respective parents to pick us up.

Shirley had obviously been taking care of the animals while I was away and was noticeably upset at my return, when she had to leave again. She would come over on the weekends and be used as a babysitter for days that I was off school. She had a job delivering gourmet meat and I was told to help her accomplish various tasks. When I complained to our family therapist, all he said was that I needed to learn about forgiveness. I was infuriated to have her in my life; I hated every minute, especially anytime she brushed against me or touched me. She verbally scolded and demeaned me, but I think that she may have actually thought twice about raising a hand to me, as not only was I bigger and stronger, but also I wasn't a wide-eyed bewildered child any longer, I had the calculating eyes of a rebellious teen.

Screaming for attention and certain change in living dynamics, I looked for opportunities for rebellion at school. My private school was also a working ranch that had pigs, chickens, and sheep. Animal husbandry was part of the curriculum and we learned to raise and slaughter farm animals. The smaller of these animals were often the targets of childhood pranks. We'd move a pig into a classroom during recess or chase the geese. My battle of rebellion began when I took part in riding the rams.

During lunch we would all sit at the top of sheets of aluminum siding that leaned against the fence and "play" with the sheep. Food and small amounts of money were offered to the brave soul that would run into the pasture, mount a ram, grab a ride, and then run back up the siding before you got caught with a horn. Naturally I volunteered, having helped break horses and having always been the one to try and prove myself. I thought, "What can a little animal like that do that a horse hasn't already done?" I was in for quite a lesson.

Round 1. Upon being offered a Pepsi, a Brownie, and $4, I gladly accepted the challenge. I rushed the field and then slowed to sneak up behind one of the rams. Once close enough, I grabbed into its wool and threw my leg over. My first attempt went horribly. I had shifted too much weight into my mount and rolled of onto the other side, eating some dirt. The kids laughed and the ram must have thought I was just some idiot and scurried away.

Round 2. I sneaked up behind him again, this time very slowly, and got as close as I could. I dug my hands in and jumped on. He started running and my legs wrapped around him, and I held on for life. He reached his top speed and then slammed on the brakes, bowing his head and digging his hooves into the ground. I flew forward and my face plowed into the ground. My glasses went flying, and as soon as I realized what had happened and started to look for my glasses, he let me know that I really was an idiot. He rammed his horns into my back and practically lifted me up from my kneeling position. I stood up and raced away back up the siding.

I knew I had to get my glasses, and no one was willing to go—not that they even heard my request through all their laughter. I slid down the siding and walked over to where I had been tossed. The herd had moved to the far side of the pasture and I had a few minutes to look. Once I found them, wiped them off, and put them back on, my ears began working again and I could hear their laughter still.

Round 3. I sneaked up, jumped on, and rode him all around the pen. He tried to throw me, but I hung on with every muscle, leaning back and bracing for his sudden stops. Finally, when he had run near the siding, I jumped off and started for home base. He tried to chase me up the wall of aluminum but slid back down after the first foot or two. I sat at the top in victory. My comrades gave me praise and the food. I was feeling like a million bucks and then I heard the principal's voice.

"Louis, get over here right now!" My stomach flinched.
"Yes sir."

"You know better than to mistreat the animals. We've been over this before. Go up to the office and wait for me there." He turned his attention to my friends. "You guys get to class, and I don't want to see any of you down here again! This area is off limits!"

I got to the principal's office a good ten minutes before he did. Mr. Monroe was a very large, obese man, and the sheep's area was at the bottom of the hill the school was built on. He came in out of breath and paused at the door. "Now Louis, I've warned you about the animals before. So this being your second warning, I am forced to teach you a lesson." An enormous 2-foot long wooden paddle with two rows of holes in it hung by the door. A little sign above it read,"Spare the Rod, Spoil the Child." He retrieved the "rod," then turned to me and offered, "I'm sorry it had to come to this, but you've left me with no choice. Turn around and put your hands on the desk."

I couldn't believe this—another wooden paddle! Inside I trembled, but I chose not to show my fear. I turned and grabbed the desk and braced for my spanking. Three swats later I was done and hadn't turned in a single a tear. I was very angry but wasn't going to give him the satisfaction of any emotion. Later that day I put a chicken in his classroom.

The next day I refused to adhere to my "lesson" and went for another ride. Unlike the others, I hadn't been groomed to respect authority, and I didn't care about the consequences. Since everyone knew the sheep's area was a hot spot, the dares and bets were triple the amount they had been the day before. I rode the ram with relative ease, now an "experienced" rider. He ran to try and throw me, but I clenched my legs and dug my hands in and was immovable. I jumped and ran up the siding and could hear the cheers of my friends from the playground. Then Mr. Monroe's voice boomed out at me. "Louis, get out of there right now! Get over here!" He was seriously angry this time. The sharp, deep tone of his voice warned me about his blazing agitation, which was soon to be alleviated in his office.

I went up there in understanding of what was to take place. I wasn't afraid, although a little nervous. It wasn't going to be difficult I thought, three taps and I'd be done. But this time was different. He slammed the door behind him as he entered the office. I had managed to infuriate a very large man who took my actions very personally. "You put the hen in my room yesterday, didn't you?" I didn't answer. "You shouldn't have gone back down there after your lesson yesterday." Mr. Monroe's voice cracked as he tried to hold back his rage. I began to get frightened now, unsure of what to expect. He grabbed the paddle and gave me the order.

One, two, three. Every fierce swat coursed through my body, letting me know that there was a serious lesson to be learned. I gave way to tears but wouldn't let out a whimper or cry. In a rage I turned and screamed something to the effect of, "F*** you, you fat m-f*****! That didn't hurt, I hope you die!" He reached for my arm but I crouched by him and darted out the door. I ran to the edge of the campus and sat on the road. Some of the teachers came up and tried to talk me back to school. Mr. Monroe came out and demanded that I go back to his office. I turned and yelled out more profanities, sitting there until school ended and Jackie came to pick me up. As she arrived, the principal's secretary emerged from behind me to flag her down.

Jackie got out of the car and walked straight to the office. They were in there for thirty to forty-five minutes and came back out, sharing a fake, nervous laughter. I watched them say their goodbyes and as she turned to me, I turned my back to her. I could hear the gravel crunching under her feet as she got closer and waited for her first words. Flatly she ordered, "Get in the car."

On the way home she lamented about the money she had wasted putting me there. She continued to ask all the "why's" and began to swear at me. She told me what a failure I was for being expelled from another school. Her questions renewed themselves and I sat looking out the window, thinking how I knew that I didn't really mean to swear at the principal. I knew I was in the wrong and actually liked him. He was in charge of the animals and had given me a position in their care. I surely defied him, believing he wasn't the type of man to really hurt me. I had to be kicked out because a good Christian school couldn't tolerate that kind of outright disobedience and profanity. I knew it was personal because I had embarrassed him in front of the school and he had to make an example of me. I actually received a letter of recommendation from my English teacher when she found out I was gone. It stated that I should be tested for a gifted program and that I had great potential.

I knew I was going to miss that school, and I knew I was wrong. I just craved to retaliate at an adult who was hitting me, and the principal proved to be the first available target. If I had turned and professed strength to Shirley during one of her episodes, it might have been me whom she thought needed to be put down for biting its master.

As I stared, lost in these thoughts, Jackie backhanded me in the mouth. My lip flared and then bled. "You're not even listening! Answer me!" She was right; I wasn't listening and had no response. She struck at me again but her hand was blocked this time. "You know what? Who cares? I'll just put you in whatever school will take you and you'll have to deal with it!" She swallowed a chunk of air, let it out slowly and was done with me, for now.

Because our therapist had basically told me to "forgive and forget," Jackie thought that that also meant that her order by social services to not allow me to be in the "care" of Shirley was also rescinded. I spent all of my time with Shirley making deliveries while waiting to go to another school.

I was enrolled the elementary/middle school that I had started out in so many years before. I had either failed to succeed or been forced to move through seven schools during my 6th-8th grade levels, then returned to where I started. Some of the kids recognized me immediately; how many people do you know wear fishbowls on their face every day? My old group of friends reached out to me but I refused to receive them. I found that I had some anger and jealousy that they had been growing up together while I was shuffled and abused.

Having dealt with so many types of people, I wasn't comfortable with these kids as before. Like they were stuck in a time warp, they acted pretty much the same as when I first went there. They were in their own world, focused on their own things, and seemingly oblivious to any world around them. The worst thing happening was what girlfriend or boyfriend dumped whom. Other tragedies concerned clothing and fashion or not getting invited for a sleepover. My perception had been forever changed due to all my experiences, especially in Rialto. I was a completely different person.

It was at this time in my life that I began to stop looking for the acceptance of my immediate peers. I joined the band, not to be a part of any crowd, but because I had been pressured to learn an instrument. I could only choose between the flute and trombone—I chose the trombone. I did my part, but avoided the gatherings of the band members, who treated me as an outsider anyway. I had just been myself around Rodney and he accepted me. He took me in, as it were, and taught me how to be a little stronger. I stayed with that and wanted no part of my "home" school's environment. From now on, people would have to accept me for me; otherwise they weren't wanted in my life. This view empowered me to be an individual. I could be selective, and I could stand on my own. I began to choose as to how I would be perceived. In other words, from this point on, I would refuse to conform. I had moved in and out of so many homes and schools, and with the evidence of how various people were in so many places, I inadvertently gained some self-esteem. After more than three years of an extremely abusive existence, I was still standing. Walking away, standing up for myself, arguing, fighting, and running away; I knew I was different if just for that, and had something in me that set me apart. I had life experience and some wisdom. I wasn't

going to give in anymore, and was ready to begin standing my
ground.

Jackie was still working at the hospital in Irvine and I
didn't see her much. I again had the run of the place. I didn't
feel the need to trash the house like before, and was content to
tend to the horses and play with my dogs. Lucky had a litter of
pups by Lobo and I was enjoying double duty keeping up with
everyone. The puppies helped me to remember that I only had
to be tough and standoffish in the appropriate environment; and
that I could let my guard down when I was around them. A
small event reinforced this just before the school year ended.

I was riding my bike to school in an effort to avoid the
bus. Not only did I want to isolate myself from these kids and
their shallow dialogue, but also I needed a way to vent my
anger. I had much to think about and a lot to be angry over, and
the exhausting five-mile bike ride up and over many hills was
my sedative. As I approached the school, I started to put on my
"disposition"—my "you little punks couldn't understand me
and I don't need your acceptance anyway" disposition. I turned
down the street the school was on and could hear a bus groaning
towards our collective destination. It flew by me and I looked
up as it passed to see a squirrel run out in front of it. The bus
tire crushed its head. I raced up to it seeing movement and
thought it may still be alive. The movement was from the
nerves in its body playing out their last command until there
wasn't energy left. Another boy on a bike rode up and came
over to see what I was looking at. He laughed at its final
movements, then rolled back, and as I was staring at the
creature in sympathy, he rode over its flailing body.

I yelled profanities at him and wanted to give chase, but
he sped off. I returned to the squirrel and knew what I had to do.
I had felt a small bond with this animal and wanted to give him
a little respect. Like me, he had just been trying to live his life
and got smashed without warning. I loved animals and saw
them as the only honest beings on the planet. I wasn't going to
leave him in the middle of the road to be run over time and time

again. I picked him up and laid him on the street's edge. I dug a small grave for him with my hands and placed him inside. Staring at him, I couldn't really understand why I was crying; I had just been caring for animals for so long that I had gained a true respect for their qualities. I wiped my face and went to school, looking for the boy on the bike.

The main reason I mention this relatively small incident, is because I feel like that day was a starting point for me in connecting with another living thing's suffering, and it prompted me to act on its behalf in whatever way I could. I had acted on behalf of Tony and other kids for their safety, but it was possible to receive gratitude from them. This time however, my actions had no physical reward—it was a wholly unselfish act. My reward didn't come from a point system or a handshake; it was peace of mind. As time progressed, you'll see what I mean, and maybe you'll think back to the time I buried a squirrel that had been hit by a bus.

I am very excited to tell you about this next summer. This would be that "One Great Summer" for me where things changed and I would begin my own path towards becoming a man. I could feel that Jackie probably wanted to be done with me, but I took care of all the house responsibilities and, I guess, even I was a better roommate than Shirley.

Jackie put me in a summer YMCA program. She dropped me off at Shirley's house at five a.m. and then she would take me to the program around 8. I never slept when I was in Shirley's presence and some in the program joked that I was a stoner because I always looked tired. I was reluctant to invest in any relationships, but I did enjoy some of the activities. On the weekends, the three of us would work around the ranch to make repairs. As it became more of me working that anyone else, I decided to say so.

I had started making an effort to stand up to Shirley. I refused to jump to her snapping. When I began to raise my voice to her, Jackie quickly came in the room to calm us down.

Shirley and I continued into a big argument over who was doing the most chores.

Shirley was furious that I didn't take her orders, "You think you're the boss?"

"I know you're not!"

"You think you can disobey me?"

"I'm sick of doing all this work while you sit in the air conditioning!"

"You have it so easy and all you do is whine!"

"If it's so easy, then why don't you take care of everything?"

"Oh. That's right. We treat you like a slave, don't we?"

Jackie had finally stepped in and separated us. I was sent to my room. My body was trembling as I paced back and forth. I swung as hard as I could and put my fist through the wall. Jackie came in to see the damage. After getting a glimpse of what was in my eyes, she didn't say a word and closed the door again.

I sat on my bed stewing for an hour before I was called to a meeting at the dining table. Shirley began, "So, you think we treat you like a slave, huh? You don't know what hard work is boy." I smacked my lips.

Jackie chimed in, "You don't have to work the ranch if you don't want to, but you will pay for that hole in the wall."

Shirley offered a solution, "I'm going to get you a real job." She went on to order me to keep my mouth shut and threatened, "And you better do a good job or you'll end up in another mental hospital."

After I fed the animals, we took a short twenty-minute ride, stopping at the edge of a large field. Standing around were many Mexicans and a few Orientals. Shirley walked up to a darkly tanned, pudgy, greasy looking older man in a tattered cowboy hat. He handed her something and she returned to me to present it. "Take these and fill this up." They were big metal shears and a burlap sack. She directed me to a long row in the field and then pulled an onion out of the ground.

I spent the next several weeks on my knees pulling onions from the earth and clipping the tops and bottoms off of them in the blazing California desert sun. The others in the field with me were illegal alien families trying to make a living. I used some of the Spanish I had learned to try to say "hello," but wasn't acknowledged. My hands burned as the blisters busted open and bled. I couldn't stop; I saw children in the field with their parents and thought maybe I didn't have it so bad. It was a while later that I reasoned that yes they were struggling, but they were together and had each other. After meeting many illegal aliens, I realize that they weren't there in despair, but in hope, trying to build a new life in a new place. Don't get me wrong; I don't by any means think that these families had it easy. I'm simply stating that they had each other to lean on and I yearned for that more than anything else. The main reason I bring them up is because the sight of them was a turning point for me. I started to see that others had hard lives too, and began to grasp suffering on a larger scale, rather than focusing on just my own pain.

I used the sight of them to make me push on and to really begin appreciating anything I could. They taught me, just by their hard work ethic and family commitment, that it is possible to struggle and be happy. It was evidenced by them sharing lunch together in the middle of those sweltering days, and seeing the smile on their children's faces when they left to go home. I found hope in watching them working together to build something for themselves. As I rubbed my sore hands, I would let my mind wander back to the night at Tom and Donna's. I pondered the night when Tony had been pleading with me to go and I couldn't answer basic survival questions. I relished the thought, "What if I had found these people and we worked with them and lived like they do? Surely we could have made it then?" I fantasized about how much better my life could have been. But I knew better. Sadly, I was unable to prevent my mind from going through the details. I knew that if we had approached that fat greasy man when we were so little, that he would have turned us away, probably laughing at the prospective amount of work we would be able to do for him. But this lesson of knowing that it is possible to start from nothing was one that I would lean on throughout my life.

I passed the time thinking about Tony and trying to think of ways I could get back at Shirley. I knew I was powerless to do anything to her, but thoughts of revenge passed the time. And there was a lot of it to pass. When the field was clear, my lesson was over. I thought of the families I had worked beside and wondered where they would go next, daydreaming about going with them. Clearly this wasn't possible, and I went back to weeding and taking care of the L'amour Ranch.

I refused to accept that it was okay for me to have spent my summer picking onions and continued to complain about Shirley. I should have known that my grievances couldn't be made in confidence.

This proved itself one of the times Jackie took me with her to visit Shirley. Shirley had been kicked out of her previous living arrangement and, of course, according to her, it was the other lady's fault. She now lived in Riverside, almost within yelling distance of where my brother's house was. I met her new roommate as we got together to help her move. She was a Native American and she said that she could sense that I had suffered a lot of pain. Her apparent ability to "see into my soul" intrigued me and we talked for a little while. Our session was cut short as Shirley asked me to go with her and get more boxes from her old house. We got in her filthy, worn-out, early 1980's Buick Skylark. Jackie stayed back to get to know Shirley's new roommate and reasoned that we wouldn't be able to pack as much stuff in the car if she came along.

We didn't speak the whole way there, and to be honest, I was still very much terrified of her. I had been having nightmares about her beating me for over two years now, and constantly woke up covered in cold sweat and urine. I couldn't stop the nerves from rattling my legs and I pushed down on them with my hands, hoping she wouldn't notice. I pressed myself as far as possible against the door and felt pretty sure I was out of striking distance of her in her huge automotive boat. We loaded the car in silence, and when she finally did speak on the way back, I flinched.

She baited me, "I heard you've been giving your mom an earful about me."

Pressing hard against the door, I sneered, "She's not my mom." Shirley slammed on the brakes and pulled over. She grabbed me by my T-shirt and pinned me between her arms and lap.

"Still a disrespectful little sh**, aren't you?" I tried to squirm, but she used the steering wheel for leverage and I was trapped. She pulled the cigarette lighter out and waved it around my face. I could see the intense red circles aglow and tried to bite her arm in a last ditch effort. "You think you're tough, don't you? You're not a man yet. You're still just a little punk!" She pressed the lighter into my palm and branded me. I remember so clearly wondering why it didn't hurt at first; in fact, it almost felt cold. Then the burning came. I yelled and started shaking so violently she couldn't hold me any longer. As I sat up, she pushed on me with her free arm to pin me against the door. Her second attempt to use the lighter caught the back of my hand, and as I flinched she dropped it. I sat trying to curl up in my seat while holding my burns.

She punched at me, yelling incoherently. When she was finally content, she put the car back in gear and sped off. The little boy she had terrorized came rushing back to the surface and I instinctively retreated into my fearful shell. I stared at the road outside and then the door handle. For one moment I stopped caring what the result might be and opened the door. She taunted, "Jump. Go ahead, make everyone's life easier." I looked at her smile and shut the door in defiance. Maybe people would think that I had committed suicide because I was a messed up orphan, and never learn of these events. I couldn't let her win that easily. I knew that I was going to be able to twist a legal knife when we got back, so I waited.

When we got back, she slowly got out of the car like nothing had happened. I searched the house and found Jackie in the Indian lady's bedroom, talking. I rushed up and showed her my burns and tried to explain what happened. She wasn't going to take my word for it and met Shirley at the door and began asking her what happened.

"He was being disrespectful again and then tried to bite me."

"What about the burns?"

"He was acting all crazy so it was the only thing I could do to control him."

Jackie was buying; nodding her head while intently listening to Shirley. It was the new roommate who had the common sense to denounce her actions. She asked, "You burned him because he just started 'acting crazy'? That doesn't sound right at all." They went back and forth a few times and Shirley was getting upset that she was being questioned. She began raising her voice and yelling over her roommate's every rebuttal.

"You don't know this boy! He has a lot of serious problems. I'm the only one that knows how to control him!"

I thought it was safe to jump in. I thought that this new witness to Shirley's disciplines would be vigilant on my behalf. "She's the crazy one!" was my input. Shirley grabbed me by the arm and gripped into it hard. She swung me around and grabbed my plastic picture case out of my back pocket. She opened it and then pulled the picture of my sister out of it. It was my flowerpot picture, the only picture I had of her. I had always cherished it and always carried it. She knew it would be there and began ripping it to pieces.

Like her actions had somehow made her point she antagonized, "Who's the crazy one now?" With Jackie holding me, I cried and twisted in a tantrum at first and then it set in. She had finally crossed the line that gave me the courage not to care what would happen. I broke Jackie's hold and lunged at her. She tried to pry me off and began slapping the top of my head. I punched at her midsection, trying to break a rib. Jackie and the roommate pulled us apart and Jackie took me outside. I was crying and shaking. I wanted to kill Shirley, and for some reason blanked out the fact that I had a knife in my front pocket. We went to stand by the car and more yelling could be heard from inside the house.

"I told you he was crazy!"

"You're crazy!"

In a minute or two Shirley emerged with tears in her eyes and started her fast pace towards us. I knew, all too well, the meaning of that walk, and began to tense for her first hit. Just before she got to me, Jackie stepped between us and commanded, "Go away and leave him alone."

Were my ears working correctly? Shirley shared my shock and chose to act like it hadn't been said. She motioned toward me again and this time Jackie pushed her.

"That's enough; leave him alone." Shirley paused and then pushed Jackie into the car. She was stepping toward Jackie like she was going to punch her and I saw my opportunity. I took one step forward and then jumped. I extended my leg and held my hands in fighting position. My jump kick landed against her chest and knocked her to the ground. I landed right by her head and I started kicking. I couldn't feel my foot, or the rest of my body for that matter. I began to cry uncontrollably as I kicked her and kicked her.

I saw my target getting out of my reach and didn't immediately realize that Jackie was pulling me back. She opened the door and put me in the car. Jackie got in without a word to Shirley, who was starting to get up, and sped out the driveway. Shirley managed one last kick to the fender before we got away. I'll never forget the look on her face as our eyes met. Blood was running down her face this time and she wore disbelief like a veil.

We drove home in complete silence. I had forgotten about my burns and had the vision of her tearing up my picture replaying in my head. I wanted to go back and retrieve the pieces, but I didn't know where I stood with Jackie. Did she think that I was trying to protect her? Or, did her silence express disapproval of my fight with her closest friend? She never gave me a direct answer, but the lack of a 'thank you' meant to me that the latter must be true.

That night I couldn't sleep at all, thinking that Shirley was going to bust into my room and exact her revenge. I couldn't lie in my bed and ended up falling asleep in my closet, clutching my knife. It was like that for me weeks after the altercation.

When Jackie did address the issue a few days later, it was to cover her butt. She promised me that I would never have to see Shirley again. So high on the defeat of one of the biggest monsters in my life during daylight, and yet so terrified of the same monster at night, I didn't realize she was trying to make sure she was again disassociating herself from Shirley's actions in case anything legal came of it. I was pretty confident that she was telling the truth and bought into her promise, again. I remained fearful of being kicked out of her home for good and so I played my part. For once she was being honest, and I never dealt with the team of Jackie and Shirley again.

In my mind, the book on one of the world's most horrendous monsters was closed and I desperately wanted to move on. I did my all to try and block her from my memory. I tried to avoid touching my burns or other scars that hadn't yet healed so as to not be forced to give a thought to her. I began trying to minimize what she had put me through in an effort to gain a night's rest. I would even try to remember every detail of how I had finally taken physical control back, to encourage a dream about the fight. This would usually backfire and I would still wake up with my legs shaking as they remembered four years of torment.

Did it stick in Jackie's mind that she had made a choice? Undoubtedly it did. She knew that she had, at the very least, committed to me being there to take care of the ranch while she was at work. In my hopes, I thought that maybe she was committing to me finally being the number one in her life, someone she would respect and not hit, and someone who would be her son.

My hopes seemed to becoming true as she hired someone to take care of the animals and we took off to see the Grand Canyon and visited Yosemite National Park. We took a lot of pictures and by the end of my trip I had let my guard down some. The only negative outcome that came from my overpowering Shirley was that I was wholly unprepared for it. No one wanted to talk about the incident, and the pendulum started to swing in the wrong direction. I decided, based on that experience, that I would never appear weak again.

I told Jackie that I wouldn't go to high school without getting fitted for contacts. She argued, but when I demanded to talk to my social worker, I got a check sent out and that was that. My prescription was so strong that I could only wear gas-permeable hard lenses. I stood in the mirror staring at myself. It was strange to be able to actually see what my whole face looked like. My contacts gave me an enormous self-esteem boost. I could walk around in public without noticing people staring at the thickness of my glasses. I started making eye contact with everyone, especially girls.

My "Great" summer ended with a lot of alone time. No school, no friends, and no Shirley. I played with my animal friends, but as a young teenager with raging hormones I craved human interaction. TV had shown me a dream world of people getting along and friends and family working things out. With what I had observed at my last school, I thought that maybe such a world just might exist. TV programs were starting to carry more realistic programming that included teen pregnancy, drug use, and domestic violence. And so many talk shows popped up that ran from the ridiculous to the very serious. In shows like Oprah and Montell, I observed that tragedy was everywhere and there were answers to be had. I could always count that at the end of the hour, every problem was resolved, even legally. I recommenced reading anything, mostly nonfiction, that I could get my hands on. These included *National Geographic* and *TIME*, but seemingly the most powerful was *Life* magazine.

I found a real world inside these pages—one telling of real people's actions around the globe. The images and stories were often gripping and sometimes comical. I connected with these people and looked at them as filling my need for human interaction. Lacking physical attention was something I had to deal with, but there was no reason I couldn't feed my mind. Truths about poverty, history, love, sufferings of today and yesterday, and the human experience filled my afternoons. I wasn't the only one in turmoil, and to grasp the fact that pain and suffering resided everywhere on the planet, and knew no color or class, inspired me, like many in the stories I read, to search for an inner strength to press forward towards positive goals in life.

To fill my final summer days, Jackie sent me to Catalina Island with the YMCA. I didn't make any friends whose names I can remember, but I did flirt heavily with one of the youth staff. Her name was Kathy Borowski; she was 18 and drop-dead gorgeous. At the close of the trip, she and I exchanged information. Our little interactions helped pass the time and would prove a mental respite for me some years into the future.

Chapter 15 - A Felon at Fifteen

When it was time to begin school I was informed that I had to go to what I'd like to call Hellhole High School—the most notorious in the region, known for gangs, drive-by's, and drugs. Half of the kids from my last school had been sent here, while the other half were sent to Suburbanite High across town, depending on your physical address.

My new school was very familiar to me. The heavy smell of cheap perfume and hair-sprayed girls filled the halls, just like at Frisbee. Gang signs were thrown and profanity was the only language spoken. Before the first bell rang there was a fight. I quickly donned the "hat" that Rodney had given me, knowing that I needed to navigate the halls with a constant projected anger. I walked between classes as if I was on my way to a fight. My eyes were taking in everything purposefully, while I knew better than to make prolonged eye contact with anyone.

My first class was English and the teacher was an older black woman dressed in traditional African clothing. I remembered the nice African man who had brought me from the hospital. I didn't try to hide the small smile that jumped to my face. We stood and introduced ourselves after she gave us the class rules. After I gave my name, Connie, from our previous junior high, asked aloud if I had gone to her school. She didn't recognize me at first, but then began telling everyone how I used to have really thick glasses. No one seemed interested and she lapsed into embarrassed silence.

At lunch, I passed a table full of the privileged country kids sitting together and she again pointed me out, but this time got her desired laugh. They made glasses with their fingers and put them over their eyes and pointed. I paid them little mind, knowing what was in store for them. Their superior attitude and "special people table" was like a piece of white lint on a black velvet blanket. It wasn't going to be tolerated by anyone for long.

I sat down by the basketball courts everyday to have my lunch. At first I was given the same assumption-of-social-status treatment as when I was enrolled at Frisbee. I had come to love the game of basketball since my training and summer league a couple of years ago. I practiced at every opportunity and my game was pretty decent. But eventually, my khakis and white t-shirt got the attention of a gangbanger sitting with his pregnant girlfriend nearby. "Ray Ray," as he was called, sat in the back of my math class and we never had a reason to talk to one another. I had started shooting around on the court and practicing with a couple of classmates when he approached. I was startled when he began walking in my direction, looking right at me. He stood six foot two and was built like a track star.

He approached, "Where you from homie?"

"Nowhere."

"Why ya rollin' like a gangster then, cuz?" I shot the ball and tried to avoid the question. I retrieved the ball but he still stood there.

"I just moved here, this is how I dress."

I guess he had seen me play and I was surprised when he changed the subject. "I see you can ball a little. Wanna come run over here?" It took a second before I answered—I can't say I ever noticed him playing before. I thought that he might just be looking for an opportunity to embarrass me. After all, I was just a pale-skinned freshman. I took a chance, thinking that maybe if he was trying to use me for some joke, I'd get to prove who I was.

"Yeah, alright." I joined him and his three buddies and waited to take on the winners. They had obviously played together for some time, and I didn't want to interfere with their rhythm. I ran my butt off stealing and passing, taking maybe two shots a game. We ran the courts for the whole lunch break and collected some money from the losers. Drug dealers and betting always seemed to go hand in hand, because they wanted to brag that they had money and use the money to brag how they could do something better than others. I played my part on the team well enough and Ray gave me a twenty for my hustle. The next day in math class he asked me if I was coming out to the court and if I wanted to run again. I had done it; I had proven myself. "Yeah, alright," was my answer.

And so it went—my training and experiences with Rodney had proved to be the key to an extended family. No matter where I went, I knew the code and had what it took to prove and maintain my status. I had found my stronghold in society, a family that (to me at the time) accepted me. Sure, at times I was called a wannabe or a cracker and I would have to step up. These times just reinforced my place at the table, so to speak. The kids that had teased and ridiculed me from junior high didn't understand these dynamics and soon became objects of ridicule at this school. I didn't take part, but I didn't step in to help them either.

On the way to and from the courts or math class, I shared little pieces of my past with Ray and he shared how his family had broken apart and he lived with his grandparents. Even though we never discussed life strategy or solutions, my conversations with Ray were far more beneficial to me than going to see our family therapist.

On the other side of the equation, I had made friends in most of my classes. Many of my teachers called on me because I paid attention, even though I refused to turn in any homework. My tough exterior was the epitome of "cool," as it would have been in any high school era. I ended up having two groups of friends, my gangster-type friends and my classmates. Although it was obvious, I didn't really grasp that I only got into fights because of the former.

Seeing that I was choosing to become a fireball, Jackie reverted to old tactics and took me to another martial arts instructor, to train in Aikido. I didn't get a reason why I wasn't allowed to go back and see Leonard, but after what my street training had done to my attitude, I didn't know if I could face him anyway. My new instructor was loud and very full of himself; and I hated being among another group of strange people. I trained for a few weeks and asked to be dismissed. I didn't want to be around people very much anyway, as I had just lost my best friend. Jackie told me to be "good" at school and I wouldn't have to go anymore.

Yes, I lost my best friend. Having been my confidante and most zealous protector, Lobo had become old and was having hip problems. When the vet checked him, he said that letting him live any longer would be cruel due to his suffering state. Jackie gave him permission to put him down. I watched in disbelief as he got a needle ready and turned toward Lobo. I stood between them, with my heart overwrought with pain and dismay. I wasn't going to allow this man to take my best friend because his step wasn't what it once was. How serious was hip dysplasia anyway? I swore at the man and pulled my knife out and told him if he stuck Lobo, that I'd stick him. He backed, put down the syringe, and walked toward Jackie. I stood crying and refusing to budge. Lobo growled in support of my actions and I put the knife down and started rubbing him and talking to him.

Jackie came and took the knife away and asked the doctor if he wanted to press charges. The doctor declined and said it was okay and he understood. He told her that they should leave and give me time to say good-bye. I accepted his offer without a look to him and embraced Lobo. I thought of the times he had proven to be like a father to me, protecting his son. I thought of our trail rides together and playing fetch with whatever was around. He had always been there when I needed him and although I understood the whys, I still felt like I was letting him down. I put my head down on his shoulder and cried for the friend I was going to miss. He just laid there calmly with a sedative already in him and licked my hand.

The vet came back in and said it was time. Jackie started to pull me away and I shrugged off her grasp. A tearful yet very serious, "I'm not moving," was enough to get her to back up. The doctor said it was okay and let me hold my friend. His injection went unnoticed by me as I was holding Lobo. When I caught him moving out of the corner of my eye, I thought he was approaching, but quickly realized that he had already finished. I let out a wail for my friend and felt him slip away.

I loved Lobo. I would have to say that he was the first living being that I had love for. I loved Tony, but realized that we really didn't have a loving bond. The last time we were truly brothers had been almost a decade ago at Tom and Donna's. Lobo had protected me and gave me affection. He played with me and wanted me around. He had taught me what it meant to care for someone or something else and now he was gone. I rested my head on his still warm body and began jumping back and forth from angered denial to utter grief. Finally, I took his collar in my hand and wept silently.

After his death, I rarely played with his puppies, or the rest of the animals for that matter. I gave into grief and isolated myself in the house. At school, I got into an argument with the music instructor and was thrown out of class. I was a ticking bomb waiting for someone to vent on. I didn't have to wait long at Hellhole High, where fights were as common as the school bell ringing.

During lunchtime, a gang fight had broken out between Ray's gang and some Mexicans. There were at least sixty kids fighting it out and security couldn't be found. They probably had gone to call the police. I saw Ray being held by two Esses and getting wailed on by a third. I jumped into the brawl and kicked the legs out of one of the boys holding him and caught the other on the chin. Once Ray was loose, he made quick work of the boy who had lost his easy target. I let out my pent up emotion on the two boys until they stopped trying to get back up. I felt someone jump on my back and I flung him over to the ground and started punching. In a rush, Ray grabbed me and led me, running, to the basketball courts.

"Thanks, cuz." he said out of breath. He offered a handshake that I accepted.

By the time the police arrived, the bell had rung and we were on our way to class. Everyone understood that there was nothing worse than to be a snitch and no one had any fear of being arrested. I had vented considerably and had gotten even more respect from Ray and his boys. Not only had I stepped in for him, but also he took it as I stood in for his gang. "We're going to have to jump this little n**** in." I was being offered member status and I did my all to hide my excitement. Someone wanted me. My party was set for that weekend and I took all their knocks without a peep. They hit hard and even leveled me, but again, punching doesn't measure up to the tear of a bullwhip.

I got home stammering drunk and chose to sleep in the barn to avoid confrontation. It didn't help, as Jackie came out to feed the animals at four in the morning, thinking I had run away. She found me as a puddle only an hour or so after I had gotten back. I woke to the thud of her foot against my back.

"Get up!" My eyes refused to adjust to the bright fluorescent barn lights. Another kick and I remained motionless in defiance to her wake up call. One last kick and she just smacked her lips and walked away. We avoided each other all weekend and found no reason to speak.

At school, my gang was like a warm blanket of security. Knowing that a large group of young men who just didn't care about consequences would take my back whenever the occasion called gave me a false sense of security. Why false? First and foremost, I was now a new target of enemies that I didn't even know about. And second, most of them had access to guns. I would have to say that there were probably as many weapons on campus as students. Every now and again someone would get caught during a random search and expelled, but our gang rarely had to worry about that. The security guards were predominantly black and had almost all been gangsters or hustlers before. As long as we gave them token inclusion to our tales of fights and girls, they left us alone for the sake of nostalgia.

Over the next few months we got into a dozen fights over pride and "honor," but for the most part, we just sat together and laughed, busting jokes on each other and especially on passersby. I jumped to protect my homeboys and they would do the same for me. It's what being "jumped in" was—the total commitment to each other. You were sought out to join if you proved that you were tough, crazy, or just didn't consider consequences or personal safety. And that was me—a stick of dynamite waiting for anyone to light the fuse, hoping that I would get to vent all my pent-up emotions from my dismal life circumstances and horrific abuses. I was the perfect candidate. Ready to fight, ready to put my hands on whomever stepped in my way. I don't mean to sound like I was invincible; in truth I was a monster—an emotional monster created by the System, primed and ready to deal out some of what I had been given— the cycle of abuse coming full circle.

Being part of a gang isn't fantastic nor do I want to glorify it in any way. A gang is not like getting a job at McDonald's—when you get sick of it, you can't just quit. I felt alone in this world and a gang seemed like a real family to turn to. To have people who were actually concerned about your personal safety and were willing to fight for you was an irresistible prospect for this orphan. Ray knew I had no one and that I had lost my little brother. Even the name he gave me reflected an inner desire, as I was called "Brother." But in those motives, you can clearly see that it was an act of desperation. I was willing to jump in with whomever offered me a real or figurative "home" first—and it turned out to be a gang. To feel that you have no choice but to surround yourself with a family of violence couldn't be called anything but desperate. But trust me, only the young and naïve wanted to "bang for life." Anyone who has done some time usually realizes that this is a destructive path and eventually chooses more than death row or a life sentence as their life course. Only the fools in the music business want to be associated in "the life," and only to sell records at a safe distance from the reality of being a gang member. If you were willing to really dig, you'd never find much of any real gang connection with 98% of those jumping around on stage telling everyone about how "hard" they are. They project a marketable image, but you'll rarely hear about them committing murders against enemies. They don't drug deal and do drive-by's; they are millionaires far removed from the lifestyle they may have witnessed while growing up and perfecting their flows. Being part of a gang is not glamorous, but at times it felt comfortable, as an orphan, to finally be accepted by a group. But admittedly, even if I could put that all together at the time, I probably would have still accepted Ray's offer and gotten jumped in.

Everyone knew that I was a foster kid and I was literally prompted to call my gang my family. I allowed myself to laugh and I watched over my own shoulder a lot less. But I silently refused to share explicit details and let anyone into my secret world of personal trauma. With at least shame or embarrassment holding me back, I was able to stay on the outside of most of the "work" that was done. I showed them respect and managed to not be around when they were planning something really vicious. But being part of a gang was my focus for a relatively short while, for a Christmastime field trip helped to eventually put my priorities right.

My English teacher was collecting donations of canned food and clothing for the homeless served by the LA mission. I filled a large black plastic lawn bag full of clothes that I had grown up with (always afraid to throw anything away), and donated them. The teacher, impressed by the size of my donation, offered me one of the six spots to go and deliver the donation. I accepted, thinking I would be getting out of a day of school and not expecting to have my eyes opened.

We packed into her huge old Ford Econoline surrounded by bags of clothes and boxes of food. We arrived after a very long uncomfortable ride and joked about how maybe we should have stayed at school. In the middle of downtown Los Angeles, immense buildings all around dwarfed us. Homeless people and businessmen filled the streets and the contrast couldn't have been more definitive.

The bags were opened immediately as we entered and the worn volunteers began sorting and handing items out before we could even stand up straight. The volunteers thanked us repeatedly, but few of the recipients made even a small gesture. The line was full of men, women, and varying combinations that often included babies and small children. Some were very obviously drug addicts, to whom I gave a prejudiced look, as if I knew what had really put them in that line. My surprise came when I saw gang tats (tattoos) on some of the hands and arms of the men and women. It didn't dawn on me until I was standing there serving these struggling individuals that they had made choices in their lives that got them here and that it directly applied to me. I *had* choices. Upon sight of those tats, I thought about older gangsters—or the lack thereof. Gang life had few paths and none of them were legally successful.

I didn't make a decision to change my path completely, but after my visit to the LA mission, I started carrying around my *Life* and *National Geographic* magazines again as a reminder that an immense world was out there, and if I played my hand right, I might get to see some of it. When asked about the magazines, I would say I was using a photo to draw an animal or person. An artistic gang member, whether through poetry or drawings, was given a measure of extra respect, as reflection and thought were considered signs of maturity and were embraced. I would draw out animals or designs for tattoos and my share of cars and girls, which also kept anyone off my case.

Jackie had arranged a gift exchange session with Tony during the next week we had off school. I harbored strong feelings for him still, but this time I would try not to bare my all, knowing my heart would probably just be kicked around anyway. But it couldn't be helped, and when he arrived I was unable to hold back my desire for my brother's affection. The first thing I told him about was my fight and victory with Shirley. He seemed disinterested, as if I was speaking about a taboo subject. He directed his attention to the gift in my hand. I had gotten him a couple of CD's and he seemed a little impressed. He gave me a card with a gift certificate. I started to walk him toward the house, but Tammie interjected that they had to go. My mind screamed, "What?!" She described a Christmas party at home with cousins and that they had to get right back. I was assured I would get a phone call later, to set up a weekend visit, but I never received one. The small crack of a genuine smile on Tony's face when he opened his gift clued me in on a part of Tony that I had not been mature enough to notice before (or chose not to): Tony's affections were for sale.

I waited out the rest of the school break, digging into books on history, religion, and philosophy. The library was fast becoming my home away from home. The more time I spent there, the less I had to spend getting into mischief. Reading about Frederick Douglas, Anne Frank, and others kept my mind on the big picture. I still hung around my boys but pretty much just lurked in the shadows and kept myself uninvolved.

Within two weeks of returning back to school, I was thrust back into the heart of my gang. While walking between classes, I heard a gun go off and Ray fell down at my side. I knelt down to see where he'd been shot, but couldn't find anything at first through his thick black jacket. He didn't wail or even tear up, he just kept trying to get to his feet, and couldn't. The shooter ran by us like a lightning bolt and aimed his gun in my direction. Before he could fire again, he hit a security guard like a hummingbird flying into a window at full speed and went down. They moved towards him, but were halted by the threat of gunfire. He got back up and bolted off campus.

I helped Ray up and started toward the nurses' office. Security intervened and helped by carrying him. He was in no danger of dying, because the bullet had only nicked his body— in and out, and now he had a good scar to show everybody. Ray gave me credit for shielding him from further attack and for helping him to the office. I was almost as big a hero as he was for taking the bullet. In the following days, we made plans to get the boy back, but they would be in vain. The school knew who the boy was and assured Ray that he had been caught and would be charged with attempted murder and sent to CYA (California Youth Authority or young people's prison). He wasn't from any gang, just some kid that wanted revenge for a beating and knew no other way to satisfy his vengeance.

Even though I was a freshman (I always lied and said I was a sophomore and was large enough to look the part) and one of the newest of the homeboys, I had gained the respect of an older member, Ray, and it carried a lot of weight. We played ball together and fought together. I had even won him a little money in a couple of brawls at a party. Everyone always felt like superman with some booze and weed in their system, and at a house party where more than one gang was represented, it was common to have the toughest boys fight, often with some big money on the table. If it wasn't people fighting, than it would be dogs and I wouldn't hang around to watch. These were sanctuaries where an invisible truce was in place so the OG's (gang leaders) could conduct business concerning drugs and guns. It was a dynamic known as "getting along with" this or that gang. Even though we weren't in the same gang, there could be a measure of protection expected if you saw someone from a gang you "got along with" in a fight. You were also allowed to relax around gangs about which the OG's said, "We get along with."

While putting in work for the gang was often just a good release for the torments that plagued my days and especially my dreams, I was growing uncomfortable at the random attacks made on those not in a gang. In time this would be my downfall, as I couldn't stand to watch some kid being used as a soccer ball just for looking at one of our more angry brothers.

In gym we were to change without any supervision and this is where most of the drug and gun deals went down. Plenty of corners and locked containers made this an obvious choice for such actions. It also made it a perfect place for fights.

Most kids carried out exactly what business they had in the locker room without a look to the right or left; but a curious few had to be taught the rules. Once a "glare" or "look" was caught, it was at the discretion of the sentry to dole out the necessary "lesson." Some felt it their duty, while others their privilege. So once, while one of the homeboys was punishing an onlooker, I stepped in to stop it. He had been hitting the kid for a good full minute without any struggle and had no end in sight. The boy had long stopped crying and movement was only slight.

"What the f***, cuz! I'm not finished with this punk."

"That's enough—coach is coming." One look up and he knew I was bluffing.

"F*** you trying to give me orders?"

"I ain't trying to do nothin'. Lets get outta here." Coach had really started coming and everyone dispersed. Later that afternoon we had all been anonymously pointed out by some of the other kids and were forced to meet with the police in the office. They tried to pressure us to snitch on the one responsible for bloodying the boy, but they already had the answer and were just looking for corroboration.

"We know you were there. We know you pulled the other boy off. So tell us who it was and we won't lock you up too. Aggravated assault could get you a couple of years in CYA. Do you know what they do to little white boys in CYA? You're going to be someone's girlfriend." I didn't care what they threatened; I wasn't going to rat out my homeboy, even if I didn't agree with his actions. That's how it is and I knew (or thought) he'd do the same for me. Some of our boys had taken raps for crimes they didn't even commit rather than confess; it was our code and one of the main laws that governed our society. "Snitches get stitches."

They questioned me 15 minutes at a time and held us half the day. They finally let the bulk of us go but kept the one responsible. He was arrested and hauled off. Outside we theorized about how they had known what happened, because we weren't aware of any witnesses. "You didn't say anything, right?"

"Hell no, I ain't no snitch." I knew the question's implication would be echoed and I fiercely defended my integrity at the park that night. "If anyone thinks I'm a punk, then why don't they come prove me a punk?" Everyone had seen me fight and none wanted a piece of the offer. Although Ray stepped to my defense, whispers about me remained for my stay at Hellhole High and I was avoided.

At home, my rare interactions with Jackie included discipline. She smacked me for my school fights and for phone calls about me ditching class. She was furious to see that my first report card had nearly all F's. But she didn't hit very hard and by this time my attitude wouldn't let me show any weakness. I acted like it didn't hurt at all. I had proven myself tough at school and got respect; maybe I would gain respect at home as well if I took these hits? I knew better, and I just honed the skills to hide my feelings and protect my heart—skills that would make me less vulnerable but would also keep everyone at a distance.

I knew that Jackie was in contact with Shirley again and I was sick of it. I vowed that that wasn't going down again. With my criminal activities at school the basis for my thoughts, I decided to make plans against them both. Admittedly, these plans included wicked acts that could impact every aspect of my life.

Tony's birthday was coming around and I received an invitation to his party. I wanted the opportunity to prove my theory about the monetary value of Tony's affections. My brother still held a sacred place in my heart; a spot reserved for him by the six-and-a-half-year-old child inside me that yearned for the return of a dream. I was still desperate for a sense of real family, regardless of the uncomfortable fact that he had already chosen time and time again his new family and friends over me. I set out in search of the perfect gift, one that would make him stop and take notice and maybe choose me again. I decided on a new video game modeled after the new Tom Cruise movie. The game was very expensive and the lack of my interactions with the drug and gun dealings in the locker room had stressed my pockets. But I had come upon a possible source of income not too long before that might make my effort to gain ground in the battle for Tony successful. Unconcerned with the repercussions, I set out to activate a part of the plans I had been fantasizing about.

Having thoroughly rummaged through the entire property, I had found many articles of interest and curiosity over the years, from guns and knives to strange special tools and a safe. Yes, a safe—a large metal safe with a dial combination and key lock concealed at the bottom of Jackie's closet. With a thorough search of her room, I found the small paper containing the combination located in a jewelry box, and across the room, I found the key found lodged at the bottom of a makeup kit. I had often dreamt of opening the safe and taking the spoils, and using what was sure to be a significant amount to run away. After some of my hits and nightmares, I had even incorporated the murder of Jackie and Shirley into the fantasy.

But I knew what crime was and knew the kind of trouble that would come from committing such acts. I had come dreadfully close many times, even to fetching the shotgun and shells and standing at her door with vengeance on my brain. I thought of smearing the blood of both women on the walls and taking the loot and making a new life for myself. Then logic would always set in and detail the consequences to me. A life on the run, unable to contact Tony, or worse still: life in prison.

After a long time resisting temptation to rob and possibly commit murder, Tony's birthday would be my excuse for exploring the safe's contents. I gathered the necessary items and sat in front of the safe trying to open it. It took a few tries but then I did everything in just the right order and opened it. At first I thought that it might be empty, as the darkness inside revealed nothing. I reached inside and felt a small block of something in the upper far left corner. Just as I had expected, the safe yielded treasure. The block, measuring about 4 inches by 4 inches, was a thick wad of cash. I unwound the thick single rubber band and separated the four smaller rubber band groups of cash. I held the money gingerly, mindful that my intention wasn't going to be to take it all. I counted off hundred after hundred with groups of twenties and fifties bundled in between. My mind raced fancifully down paths of what-ifs and maybes. After an afternoon of deliberation and returning to open the safe fifteen to twenty times, I decided to take a hundred dollar bill and see what would happen.

I rode a bus after school to a mall in Riverside and bought the video game for Tony. I still had about fifty dollars and I spent it frivolously. I sat down to a smorgasbord of fast food that I couldn't finish, and spent the rest in the video arcade. On the way home I tucked the game down in my backpack and ran over paranoid thoughts of possible consequences. I got home before Jackie and scurried to my bedroom to hide Tony's present in my closet. Jackie finally came home to me lying on the couch reading a magazine. We exchanged short pleasantries and I informed her that I had already microwaved a can of soup for dinner. We watched some TV together without a word.

The next few days I said nothing unnecessary and stayed away from the safe. That weekend I gave the gift to Tony and got the response I had expected. Tony was excited and bathed in praise from his friends over such a coveted present. I was his hero that day; I had been bumped a couple of notches up the ladder of priority.

Although I understood that the gift was tainted, I cared little and just reveled in the psuedo-affection I received. The following week I was called and invited over to play the game with him. Tammie was forced to buckle under his pressure and give me another chance in their home. She did so begrudgingly and refused to make eye contact or speak to me. She did stumble upon a key to pushing my buttons, however, as she still called me "Louie" and I refused to acknowledge this "old" name. She said it a half dozen times an hour just to get a rise out of me. I did my all to ignore her game and was just happy that I was getting to spend time with my brother without the priority of sharing him with Jason or his cousins.

Time continued to pass and Jackie continued, oblivious of my actions. I got brave and having many hours alone in the house, I couldn't resist the urge to make more small withdrawals. I took $100-$150 at a time, spending the money on collectable baseball cards, somewhat planning a getaway. Having that kind of money was nothing to raise an eye over amongst my friends at school and spending it on them helped to smooth over the recent disregard I had been enduring. I ditched school to take my "true friends" to the mall and play big shot, buying them all new Nike Air Jordans. When I paid with one hundred dollar bills, Ray decided to ask what was up.

"You win the lottery or somethin' Brother?"

"No, I just saved some money and wanted to get ya'll somethin'. These shoes are tight!" He allowed me to change the subject and let my excuse stand. A couple more weeks and $1,000 more went by the boards and Jackie still hadn't made comment about her diminishing chunk. I began to let the "what ifs" take over. I started to imagine that maybe I could get away from this house and live content and free somewhere else.

Waking up from my nightmares of Shirley beating me over Champ, I had gotten even more inclined to kill Jackie and run away. I started ditching school entirely and staying home, letting plots and plans fester in my head. I would kill Jackie and then find Shirley. I wanted nothing more than total revenge: to avenge the childhood that had been filled with pain and enforced work. My fantasies soon became my torments and I argued with myself over having spent the day with such terrible thoughts. I reasoned that she had deserved death over the pain that had been my life for the last four years, some of which she had inflicted and most that she had just allowed. I rationalized that all the money was owed to me for all the years of work I had done around the house. Jackie had put up a barn, landscaped the entire property with trees, walls, sprinklers, grass, had me remove every rock one by one, hurling them to the fence in a half-acre portion so she could lay sand for a training and barrel running arena. I had weeded huge sections either to plant ice plant, fruit trees or dig posts for an electric fence. For years I had busted my back around their home to threats of a whip if I didn't complete my tasks fast enough. I hated her and I hated Shirley. I would do something... but could I murder? As often as I had awakened from a nightmare soaked in sweat and urine, legs shaking uncontrollably, I thought maybe I could. And I started making preparations. I hid the shotgun under my bed in the trundle bed. I loaded it and waited for her to go to sleep. I would fall asleep dreaming of what I would do that night, but I never had the resolve. I never once thought that the consequences would be worth the result.

But plots like these were plaguing my brain and I knew that I was reaching a breaking point. These imaginings began to dominate my every thought, and the availability of the shotgun, the money and the possibility of escape grappled with my conscience. After enduring another physical lesson from Jackie for ditching school, I became determined to run, to take "my" money and see how far I could make it. I packed my backpack full of clothes, with the intention of making it to Rialto. I would seek out the person who had befriended me and had shown me that I had power and had choices in life—Rodney.

I wandered the streets aimlessly, looking for landmarks I remembered so I could find Rodney's home. I gave in to asking people on the street where this or that was and eventually I found myself on their doorstep at about midnight. I didn't want to wake them up, so I slept on the front porch and waited for morning to announce my arrival. I was scared and anxious, but even so, that swinging bench was the most comfortable bed I had ever had.

Morning came and I woke to familiar sounds of cooking and the smell of bacon. I roused myself and knocked on the front door. Uncle Louis answered and was puzzled to see me. "Can I help you?" he offered inquisitively.

"It's me, Louis. Rodney's friend." I realized my contacts had made a drastic change in my appearance and then informed, "I got contacts now, no glasses." The mention of glasses was key and he warmed to me immediately.

"Louis!" He invited me in the house and sat me down at the chair I had occupied not so long ago. After commenting on how I had grown and how different I looked, he began to tell me about my friend. "Rodney doesn't live here anymore. He went back to stay with his momma." I ate breakfast and told them I was still doing well in school and just came by to visit. By the opening information I was given, it was obvious that Rodney didn't go through with his threats to shoot the police. In fact, he must have started doing well because those were the conditions for his return home.

After breakfast, they gave me Rodney's phone number and I called. Rodney wasn't home but his mom said it would be okay if I came to visit. She relayed that Rodney had mentioned me as the guy who made him see his choices. She said I was welcome in their home. After I thanked them for breakfast, big hugs were exchanged and my heart was at peace that morning. I hadn't received a deep hug like those in a long time. I relished the thought of the embraces as I got on a bus and headed for downtown LA.

It took a while to connect to the right buses and night fell before I had made it to one of the main bus depots. I looked for my bus route and talked to various bus drivers, who all seemed to give me different directions. Frustration was setting in and so was fear. The bus station was dark and filled with vagrants. I had put on a baggy sweatshirt and pulled the sleeves over my hands to conceal the knife that was lodged in my watchband. My eyes jumped from face to face, searching for a threat. I put my back against a wall and waited for a bus that would bring me to my friend.

I finally made it to the general area around USC and started asking gas station attendants for directions. Everyone had a different take on the best way, and I allowed the corners of my mouth to turn up as they scolded each other over who was right. When I had finally gotten an answer they all had agreed upon, I was even more confused and walked down to the next gas station. I pulled one attendant to the side and offered him twenty dollars for directions to my friend's house. He gave me directions but refused the money. Upon my insistence he took it and reiterated exactly how to get where I was going in a relatively short walk.

Finally, around 11 o'clock, I made my destination and knocked on their door. "Who is it?" a stern male voice required.

"It's Louis." Rodney came to the door and didn't hesitate to welcome me warmly; introducing me to his mom and sister. Smiles filled the room as if they had known me my whole life, and hugs and kisses were exchanged. I answered all the standard questions and waited for time alone to let Rodney know the real reason for my visit.

"You robbed her?" he said with a half smile on his face.

"I couldn't stay there anymore." I knew I didn't have to justify to him but felt an excuse was courtesy. I explained that I wasn't really running away from my home as much as I was running away from murder. He knew I was serious. It was the first time I heard him step back from encouraging criminal behavior and offer me support in taking my option to run. I took it as a sign of true friendship, that he'd rather see me on his doorstep than hear about me in the news getting a life sentence in prison for murder.

"She's going to call the pigs and you're going to get
locked up. What are you gonna to do?" I just shrugged my
shoulders, knowing that there wasn't an easy answer or one that
even made any sense. "If you get caught, you should tell your
lawyer about how she hit you. They might let you off easy."
This statement puzzled me at first. I didn't really understand
until long after that Rodney was basically letting me know that I
would eventually get caught. Everyone usually does, and he was
already trying to think of a loophole for me.

I shared some money with his family and tried to help
around the house in any way I could. His mother knew from
Rodney that I had been beaten by my foster parents and wasn't
shocked at the report. She told me I could stay as long as I
wanted. I had immediately been accepted as part of their family
unit and they made no distinction between Rodney and I. His
mom scolded me verbally the same way she did her own son
and I nearly found it comical. During the day, I stayed in
Rodney's room and watched TV or cleaned the house while
waiting for him to get back from school. At night, Rodney
would take me around to his friends and introduce me as his
adopted brother. I was someone's brother again.

I was getting comfortable with my new life very
quickly. A little too comfortable, as my guard from being on the
run had receded and my eyes rested only on my immediate
scenery and were not on the lookout for the police. It would be
at a small gathering that I would be forced to end my vacation
from reality and be thrust back into the System life my
biological parents had left me to live.

I suppose a neighbor had made a complaint and three or
four police cruisers showed up. The officers immediately started
asking for ID's. The cops discovered people doing drugs and
underage drinking and started making arrests. Those who had
been outside when they started pulling out handcuffs jumped
fences and got away. I wished I had been outside. I gave the
name of a kid at school that I didn't like and we were hauled to
Central Juvenile Hall. The intake officer asked a steady stream

of questions that I mostly lied to. I was stripped, searched, and given a mat to sleep on.

A couple of hours later I was pulled back up to the intake desk and told that my answers didn't match. In his rush to get everyone processed he had overlooked my answers, but somehow they had been itching the back of his head and he wanted to talk to me again. He somehow figured out I was lying throughout the interrogation, and then requested that my prints be run immediately. He was probably thinking I was running from a large crime, like a murder.

I got a cell to myself and the officer told me sarcastically not to worry, they would find out the truth. I was wet behind the ears and didn't know to what extent he had been bluffing. As he turned to walk away, I asked for another chance to tell the truth and he gladly gave it to me. I didn't mention the money but I did mention the beatings and running away and who my legal guardian was. He shook his head and let out a deep sigh that showed tired frustration from listening to kids tell him horror stories of abuse. He took down Jackie's number and sent me back to my locked room. As cold as the room was, I couldn't feel it because of the heat that my distraught brain was exuding. In panic and paranoia, I kept asking myself, "What's going to happen, what's going to happen?"

In the morning, Jackie came to pick me up. Not a word was mentioned of the money and her silence conveyed that she still hadn't discovered my crime. She was told about my reports and she was very nervous over the possible impact they might have. Over the next few days, she pretended that nothing had happened. She stayed home from work and made sure I went to school. The next subject we discussed was my birthday. She offered to have Tony over for the day and asked me what I'd like to do with him. I didn't really know what to say and stayed in a state of expectation of legal punishment. Either she was playing a game with me, or she was trying to butter me up for any inquiry by the Social Services Dept..

When April 17, 1991 came around, Tony, still reeling from the video game I had given him a month earlier, greeted me warmly. He made no mention of my AWOL and I didn't know if it was in my best interest to let him know that I had basically given up on any real brotherly relationship with him and tried to make a break for it. But that day was different—he had stopped asking the normal "What are you going to do to entertain me?" questions and had asked me what I wanted to do. Had an expensive present changed the way Tony would interact with me? Could it have had such an impact? Regardless of the reason, I sensed a sincerity that had been missing for years. I was taken aback by its return, and was fully absorbed in our day together. Again, just as my guard had been let completely down, Jackie summoned me to her room.

Her voice challenged more than questioned. "Have you ever opened this safe?"

"What safe?" I replied in the most oblivious voice I could muster.

"There was a lot of money in here and now it is gone. Four thousand dollars!"

"I didn't even know you had a safe."

"Well, let's go to the movie and we'll figure this out later." All throughout the movie, I squirmed and wondered if my story was going to hold up. And this was just as I thought I had sensed genuine emotion from Tony for the first time since he had asked me to run away with him nine years earlier, or since the time he had stuck up for me with Clyde Peabody, kicking him in the shin in an effort to protect me eight years earlier. Had I possibly given up too soon? Maybe he was starting to remember. Maybe it was just going to take an expensive gift to force him to give deep thought to his one-time brother he had left behind.

We dropped Tony off at home and were stopped at a gas station before the matter was brought up again. "You can tell me the truth. Are you sure you didn't take the money?" I wanted to get out of it at first. I wanted more opportunity to explore these new feelings that Tony had displayed. She pressed and pressed and my mind was pushed into the whys of my actions. The work, the beatings, my vengeance.

"Just tell me the truth, nothing's going to happen, I just need to know. I have to find out who robbed me." I didn't believe her, but thought that I had a bargaining chip in my confession at Central Juvie. Besides which, my blood was starting to boil, and I began craving to see the look on her face when I told her how I had violated her possessions and she deserved it.

"I took the money." Those words hung there for everlasting seconds and her mouth hung agape in shock. She repeatedly punched the steering wheel and took a few more moments before her mouth allowed words again.

"Why?"

"I didn't want to live with you anymore. I don't want to be hit anymore. I hate you. I hate Shirley. I took the money because you owed it to me and I wasn't coming back." My words ran together in one fast hurried sentence, but a weight was lifted as I got them out. It was a few minutes into the drive towards her house before she responded.

In anger and frustration, she repeated, "Why?" I didn't dignify her question with further response. She knew why. She had been at the center; she had been the source. She had not been my "mother," my protector and provider. She had been my owner; I had decided that it was over.

If she had only known how I had planned to kill her then maybe she would have let me go right then. I was smarter than to confess those fantasies; maybe it would get me sent back to the mental hospital. Her question remained in the air and she didn't ask again. We rode in silence and she ordered me to my room once we reached the house. I complied, if only in agreement that I didn't want to share space with her.

I heard her get on the phone to her mother and begin reporting my crime. I figured she was just going to vent and knew that she wasn't going to call the cops. I would sing to them about my tortures there and they would be taking her into custody. She didn't call the cops, but called everyone else she knew. I lay in bed hearing her mumbling with an occasional rise in tone for hours. Her drone eventually lulled me to sleep.

The next day she stayed home from work again and sent me off to school with the notion that we were going to work things out ourselves. Racine had been robbed by her nephew for a few thousand dollars and had worked it out with him without bringing the law into it. After telling me this, Jackie made a similar promise to me. On the bus to school I thought of Tony and the animals, and of my new persona in her eyes—one that showed a lack of fear for consequences from her. I thought I'd agree with her terms, if only for these small things. Maybe the dynamics in the home would change now that she had to deal with Louis the Young man who had grown taller and stronger than her, vs. Louie the boy who was unable to protect or defend himself.

I arrived at school thinking that I had the upper hand. I ditched every class to hang around my friends and tell them of my exploits. I played basketball and hung around the courts most of the day. Near the end of the school day, I heard my name being called over the PA system. I wasn't going to heed to their call, but a friend of mine came and told me that the office staff had been looking for me all day and needed me right away. I followed her to the office and entered.

Chapter 16 - Betrayed by My "Parents"

As I went inside, the receptionist looked up and gave me a half smile. Then she averted her eyes to the side and I turned to see what she seemed to be warning me about. The door was forced closed and two police officers were standing there with their guns drawn. The first officer paced to me, aiming his gun at me, as the other flanked me and grabbed my arms and pulled them behind my back, as he barked orders to get on the ground. I complied, knowing the drill. They searched me and then went through my bag. It was only a few seconds before they came upon my knife. The discovery elevated the level of tension, giving them a reason to be forceful. They rhetorically flung out questions. "Why do you need a knife at school? You think you're going to stab somebody?" My Miranda rights were recited as they pulled me up and directed me out the door.

They hadn't been able to complete the arrest and search before the final bell rang. As we made our way to the parking lot, chaos ensued. Many of my friends saw me and began to throw gang signs and yell my name. As a large group approached, the cops and security guards told them to step back. They sneered and heckled, but didn't break the security line.

I was transported to an adult lockup. I sat and paced in my own cell for hours while awaiting transport to Riverside Juvenile Hall. I knew that Jackie had sold me out. She had struck the first blow, but I was sure that I would prevail. I would tell a judge everything about her and Shirley. That thought left a smile on my face, where anxiety should have had me in knots.

I got to Juvenile Hall in the middle of the night and was taken to my unit where again, I was given standard issue clothing and put in a single 8' x 10' cell. I was provided a two-inch thick mattress and a thin white sheet. A small frosted glass window was aglow from the moonlight. I stood steady in front of it, staring as if I could see out, and thought about my plan for legal retaliation. The room was freezing, as spring had just begun, and I didn't get any sleep. I alternately stood by the window and paced the room, thinking and planning. I vowed she wasn't going to get away with this.

The whole next day I was kept in my cell. I did push-ups and other exercises between meals, purely focusing on my situation. I knew the odds of a foster child, but remained hopeful that someone would listen, once I got my chance to speak. I stewed hour after hour; my only human interaction coming from a guard shackling me to take me to the bathroom.

Another night and then next day I was given a bunk in the main dorm with maybe eighty others. I followed a mammoth-sized female guard and frantically took in every inch of my new home. The color scheme of windows with lima bean green and baby blue painted panes remarked that his place had, at the very least, been redecorated in the 1960's. The cracked cinderblocks and peeling paint revealed that this was a place no one cared about. The walls were stained with old urine-colored dirt, the kind that if you wiped for hours would still be there. Not that I think anyone had tried to clean anything around here since that last redecoration in the 60's, anyway. It was a home that was built to keep your spirits down, to depress you and make you think. It worked.

Next I had to take in my new family. I had walked into a dead silent room. All eighty or so inmates welcomed me lockup style, staring me down. We sat on a long concrete bench except for the "top eight" and were expected to hold a stoic, posture-perfect pose for as long as the guards determined. While sitting like juvenile gargoyles for thirty minutes to an hour at a time, one guard in particular decided it was his job to put us in our place. He would come by and verbally demoralize the "fresh fish" like myself. He let everyone know the charge you were brought in on and then found some way to humiliate you over it, a sort of exchange that was meant to take the "cool" or "toughness" out of your actions and add emphasis to the power the guards already had.

"You robbed your mommy because you didn't get the toy you wanted for Christmas, huh, punk?!" "You held up a store because your homeboy's wanted to laugh at you!" "You brought a gun to school because the boys were f****** you in the shower room, right?!" He went down the list and some with too much heart and something to prove would retort, which would get them "suitcased" and thrown back into solitary. "Suitcased" meant that you would be taken just slightly out of view, often stripped, and then handcuffed on both wrists and ankles. The cuffs were pulled together to make you a human suitcase. Next you would be put in a room to wait until you weren't considered "dangerous" any longer. Like the many who knew better than to talk back to anybody with keys, I kept my mouth shut when it was my turn for belittlement.

Once arrested and detained, it was mandatory for the Justice System to put you in front of a judge within 72 business-day hours. I was brought in Wednesday evening and my 72 hours didn't start till Thursday morning. It ended up being an angst-filled five days before I would get an opportunity for justice. Finally, Monday morning, I was on a short white van with thick metal grating covering the windows. Our destination was the courthouse—a short, bumpy ride away. Shackled, handcuffed, and connected to each other with a waist chain, we were pulled along to the back of the courthouse. Once inside, the shackles that had been digging into our Achilles tendons were removed and we were put in one large holding cell. We sat and listened to each other's war stories and especially to the experienced ones as they told of loopholes that could get us freed. Hearing all this, I was sure that there had to be something in the law for my case, a loophole that would absolve me of the responsibility of my crime and focus the arm of justice back onto Jackie. Although sitting on the floor of a cramped cell, I allowed a tiny smile to creep across my face as I pondered the thought.

My public defender's office was cramped by a homeless person's standard. Stacks of manila folders filled the corners and a paper mound on his desk threatened to fall over at any second. He had several degrees on the wall behind him that were obscured by post-its and thumb-tacked notes to himself. But even amid the chaos that was his job, the older gentleman smiled over what was surely my manila folder. "Grand theft" was uttered before introductions. "Louis Martinez; robbed your foster parent." Those words were stated rhetorically and then he gave me another look to begin introductions. He mumbled his name and then offered a handshake that I cautiously took. "So how do you plead?"

"Well, I'm not sure. I want to have a chance to tell the judge about other factors. Innocent, I guess."

"But you did steal the money?"

I didn't know how I should answer this question, as pleading the fifth wasn't in my knowledge yet. "No one saw me take it." He read between the lines without a look in my direction and started scribbling on his legal pad.

"So "guilty" is what we'll plead."

"But I want to tell the judge why I took the money, that I was beat in that home for years and I was trying to run away." I was almost begging him and my frustrations were starting to turn to tears. I was losing the ace I thought I held.

"If your mother hits you, that is no reason to steal from her. If you have a trial and then admit to stealing the money, the judge will be very upset and throw the book at you. You could get fifteen to twenty years in prison for grand theft and perjury." My heart sank to the floor at the sound of such sentencing. A brief pause, some note writing, and then he continued, "If you plead guilty, the most you will probably get is a few years of probation. My advice is that you don't commit perjury and accept responsibility for your actions. It will be your word against hers, and who's going to believe a kid that just robbed his mom?" What could I say? How could I argue with his logic? I had no legal knowledge to the contrary and the effort to use my harsh treatment as a get-out-of-jail-free card seemed to make my public defender hostile.

"She's not my mother" was priority with me. I thought, then said carefully, "Isn't there any way I can tell the judge why I did it? I want him to know about my foster parent." I didn't want to tell this lawyer to what extent I had been beaten. He was fast becoming my adversary; playing devil's advocate to my legal efforts. Maybe Jackie had already talked to him, or even paid him? More likely he just wanted a quick case and that's what he got.

Years later I found out about an Affirmative Defense. All in juvenile court have the option to request this special defense, but most pessimistic public defenders don't want to put forth the effort it would take to verify any facts and have a court battle over hearsay, your word against the adults. Another angle would be to bring up my case history and show that my theft and subsequent runaway was a logical reaction from a child that had been neglected and abused for years in the System. But there was the huge issue of confidentiality barring anyone from using those social service facts to help the judge reach a fair verdict about my criminal case. There wasn't going to be any way that my lawyer would be able to share with the court any of the severe past abuses in the System from this last foster home or any other placement. The family court and juvenile justice systems aren't permitted to share information with each other, and the grand term for this rule of silence is confidentiality. It is possible that my attorney knew that in a case like mine his hands were pretty much tied. Lastly, public defenders are especially deterred because they have a limit to the amount of hours they can bill the court per case, unlike private lawyers for kids with affluent families. This meant that if my defender wanted to really defend me, any extra effort would be practically volunteer work.

So, to my plea to tell the judge of some of these events, all I got was a "maybe." I had been beaten, starved and almost killed by two conniving women for years, and all he could say was "maybe." He sent me back to the holding tank for the next couple hours until I was called into the courtroom. I was unsure how anything would go. If push came to shove, perhaps I would just rip my clothes and show the judge my scars and tell him about Jackie and Shirley. So lost in my own thoughts, I barely recognized my own name when I was called for court.

I sat in a partitioned back corner behind the judge's bench so that we could hear verdicts and processes, but couldn't be seen. About six others were crammed back there with me, and all wore a silent dread on their face. Once my name was called, the bailiff took off my handcuffs and shackles before leading me to sit at a table next to my defender.

The lawyer and judge exchanged a half dozen monotone sentences and I heard the word guilty. I raised my brow to the judge who had begun asking me a half dozen monotone questions that I was to answer yes or no to. I answered "Yes, sir" to everything, just like my defender had coached. In a sweep of events I made out the word probation and then the sound of the gavel. I turned to my lawyer and asked if it was my turn to speak and he acted as if he couldn't hear me at first.

I repeated myself and he flatly said, "It's over boy."

Rage surged through me as the bailiff prompted me to get out of my chair. I turned and saw Jackie standing in the back of the room. I let loose, "I wanted to say something! I wanted to tell him about how I was hit!" Pulling back my paper-thin orange lock-up shirt, I tried to reveal a whip mark on my shoulder. Pointing I shouted, "She hit me! She whipped me!" My cries went without reaction from anyone except the bailiff, who was now yanking the "crazed criminal" out of the courtroom. Looking at the bench, I saw the top of the judge's bald head and nothing more. The thought of justice that had given me strength for the last few nights was nowhere to be found.

I stayed in the holding cell for hours, as we were all rotated to court and back again, and didn't have the heart to complain about what had happened. Not that anyone would have cared in that room anyway, and I knew I had to remain tough in front of my peers. I wanted to yell, I wanted to tell somebody; but who was there for me? All I could do was squeeze the bars as hard as I could and get lost in my frustrations. Barely more than a boy, 15 years old, I had no mother, no father, nor any other adult who would fight for me. I knew that Tony's family wouldn't help. I didn't care about the probation, but my entire soul yelled to have something happen, to show that the blame was mine in one sense, but entirely my foster parents' in what I thought was another.

A week passed with me rotting from the inside at Juvenile hall. I had internalized my anger and blamed myself for what had happened in court. I thought I should've pleaded innocent and taken the fifteen to twenty years, if it meant that the world would get to hear what type of monster I had lived with. Then it struck me that maybe Jackie had set me up. I thought I was clever in finding the combination and key, but Jackie had proven to be far smarter than that. I didn't dupe her; she duped me! Jackie and I both knew that our relationship was reaching a boiling point. Surely she knew that convincing me to remain silent about my abuse was going to be more difficult as I got older. I overflowed with rage, imagining her looking into her safe to check if I had stolen anything yet, or how much. I thought of her noticing that I hadn't put the paper with the combination on it back exactly right, and smiling to herself, and berated myself—what an idiot I am!!

I struggled with blame and regret as I sat in the cell, waiting for I didn't know what. Long days turned into weeks, as I repeatedly stared at the scars on my arms, chest and shoulders. I retraced them and thought back to this day or that, and wove in and out of frustration, anger, and depression. I wondered what Tony had been told about what happened, or if he even had been told at all.

While I sat on the bench as a sitting statue for the guards, so much was running through my head that I didn't pay attention to how sore my tailbone had become from holding such an unnatural position. Ironically, my sitting there writhing on the inside with hatred got me "points" for holding my position so well. I was rewarded with a move up the good behavior system, and given a choice of candy rewards. After a few weeks, I was finally awakened extra early with the boys who had a court date and thought maybe I was going to get a second chance. Instead I was about to be humiliated further.

After we dropped off the boys at the back of the courthouse, I was taken to a small square building that was, in my estimation, very close to the courthouse. I was put in a meeting room with a large steel table and a huge one-way mirror. I sat and waited for about twenty minutes before two men entered the room in plain street clothing. They introduced themselves as probation officers and started talking to me about the terms of my probation. I listened to the procession of requirements and heard nothing that was to be of any consequence. After we jointly signed all the documents, one of the probation officers left the room and immediately returned with the last person in the world I had expected to see.

She had on her courtroom best; she was all made up with earrings and the one thing I didn't even know she owned, a dress. She sat at the far end with the probation officer and he started, "Your foster mother has agreed to take you back if you follow the terms of your probation and start making restitution. You'll have to work off what you owe her and get a job to pay her back." My face flushed with angry heat as the P.O. finished his statement; I glared at Jackie, who was trying her best to keep a straight face.

It was in this brief moment that I found an immeasurable period of time within which to weigh my options. My conclusion was all too easy to come to, and yet not made hastily. If what my experiences up to this day were what a "real" family was like, then I didn't want one. From Henry and Karen to Jackie and Shirley, I had found nothing but severe pain in an adoptive family home. I remembered the threat that I wouldn't get another chance with a family if this one didn't work out. I didn't care anymore. No matter what orphanage or group home they sent me to, I would just deal with whatever dynamics existed. Maybe in the back of my mind, I thought I would run to the streets again once I got the chance. Whatever my destiny; I would not be a part of another foster home situation again.

"No," was my reply.

"What do you mean 'No'?" the P.O. volleyed.

"I won't go back to live with her." I responded flatly. My eyes wouldn't shift from Jackie. "I don't owe her anything."

The P.O. reeled and his voice bellowed, "What! You don't owe her?! You stole from this woman who took you into her home and took care of you! You thank this kind woman by stealing her life savings?!" He lunged out, pushed me back in my chair and then onto the floor. He was furious and spit drooled from his bottom lip, as he continued. He repeated the same statements, and I began to wonder how far he would take this; after all, I was still in handcuffs. After a few more heavy words laced with profanity, his partner pulled him off and sat him down. I was lifted up and into a new chair. Tears were streaming down Jackie's face in mock pain over what I had said. Her eyes told the truth, though, along with her steady demeanor and calm body language, which all confirmed the game she was playing with my life once more. Again she had me on the ropes; again she had outsmarted me. I was perfectly alone in that room full of enemies—just the type of odds she was so good at manipulating.

But I wasn't "scared straight" by the yelling officer and continued steadfast in my decision to not live with Jackie again. The P.O. ordered me back to the Hall, full of disgust.

As I was pulled up and pushed out the door, I got one final look at the room. I took in everything—the chair on the floor, the papers I had just signed, the P.O.'s faces, but mostly, Jackie turning and watching me being hauled away, marked as a criminal who had just taken from the one person who had shown him love and gave him a home. My eyes looked through her and my mind went back to my fantasy with a shotgun.

When I got back to the unit, a note that was obviously written by the outraged P.O. got me suitcased by the one guard who was always all too happy to punish a street punk. My face rested on the cold concrete floor and I couldn't hold back the tears any longer. I had faced thorough defeat, and my current physical position was the perfect metaphor for my entire life. The guards "forgot" about me for dinner and left me in solitary until the night crew came in. When the cuffs were taken off, my arms and legs flopped to the ground and refused to move. They tingled at first, responding to the blood flow slowly, my limbs suffering from throbbing and soreness, which remained through the next day.

In Juvey, everyone clearly understood the code of conduct and none moved outside its laws unless given a certain measure of "juice," or favor. The gang that flourished would be the one with the most juice with the head guard. And that usually corresponded with the gang with the most members in at the same time. We got three meager squares, or meals, a day and an evening snack. We had a common area that was maybe thirty feet by thirty feet where we spent most our "free" time. We went to a school program in a mobile trailer for a few hours a day and got a one-hour fresh air break for P.E. No one made eye contact unless you knew the person intimately, or there was to be a fight.

The only exception to this was the harassment that the gang kids with the most juice were allowed to dish out. They would taunt during our shower time and sometimes brush up against a naked new fish just to frighten the hell out of them so they could punk them for whatever food, snacks, or other items they wanted. During bedtime, whispered heckling could be heard as one of them threatened to sexually assault a new fish lying in a bunk above or close to their own.

Some of the kids who didn't belong to a gang or clique talked amongst themselves and moved quickly when a gang member pushed into their spot. I had heard some of the kids talking about my lashings and pointing the scars out to one another, while waiting in line to take a shower. I guess that is why no one ever really gave me a hard time. I was also smart enough to keep my head down and my mouth shut. I stared at nothing as I thought of my brother, Rodney, my gang, and ending my life. My new home was cold and often violent; but it was mostly predictable. Violence happened for a specific reason and it was easy to stay out of the way if you really tried. It was a dreary existence but one that I embraced in futility—a home with consistency and a mitigated harshness that I could find a certain peace in.

But in a short while my comfortable quiet place was going to get a little shaken up with the arrival of an inmate: one of my own homeboys.

James had been pulled in on a drug possession charge and although we hadn't spoke much when we were free, our current environment was known to make best friends out of little more than strangers. He had stayed only a day before his parents picked him up, but it was long enough to let everyone know where I was from. I started making sure I knew what the colors of the person standing behind me were, and sleeping as light as I could. My nightmares of Shirley waking me with a whip and my shaking legs were almost welcome, as they woke me up when I would doze off.

The average stay at Juvie was less than a week. But I spent months locked up for a crime that to me seemed justifiable out of self-defense or self-preservation. Every week was the exact same routine. We had to ask to use the bathroom or to walk from one part of our main area to another. When we walked between buildings, we formed a perfect line one behind

another, our fingers interlocked behind our backs, our eyes
locked on the back of the head in front of us. Our food was
always plain, lukewarm to cold, sometimes burnt, and always
government-issued. I hated every minute, every second. I only
dreamed of freedom, of turning into one of the birds I watched
flying over and away from this prison. Where was I going to
go? Who would pick me up? I faced the fact that I had no one
with trepidation. My time was starting to wear on me and
claustrophobia was setting in. Every Monday a dozen inmates
were released to their parents and the rest of the week they
consistently trickled out. I was never told of any plan to move
me and I began to believe the System had forgot about me, and
I would stay here until I was 18.

During a PE softball game, one of my new
acquaintances pointed out a spot in the fence he claimed his
homeboy had escaped from a week earlier. So when the guards
were busy deliberating a call, I made a break for it. Sprinting as
fast as I could, the adrenaline seemed to give me wings. I
jumped onto the fence and had started up it before I heard yells
and then a campus siren. My hand got caught on the sagging
barbed wire at the top of the fence, as I tried to negotiate it. It
cut into my hand, and as I flinched to cradle my torn flesh I lost
my footing and fell off the fence. Before I could stand, guards
were all over me, pinning me under their legs and pulling my
arms behind my back to slap on cuffs. With a guard on each
arm, they dragged me to a high security wing that had 23-hour
isolation. After passing a series of corridors of inmates cheering
at me, I was dropped in front of a cell, un-cuffed, strip-searched,
and re-cuffed as they asked a few questions about my plans and
if anyone else was involved. I refused to comment and they
shoved me into a cell and bolted the door.

I lay there cuffed and naked on the floor once again, but
at least with the comforting thought that I had tried. Possibilities
for escaping filled my head and I promised myself that next
time I would do it right. I stayed in maximum security nine days
before I got a visit that would make my escape plans

unnecessary. It seems that my attempted breakout put some pressure on my probation officer to find me a new placement. I knew that I wasn't going to be adopted or go to live in a foster family setting, and that was okay. I just wanted to get out from behind these bars.

Chapter 17 - Still in Shackles

Spending hour after hour in a cell contemplating hate and escape was in no way beneficial to my heart. As you can expect, by the time a guard pulled me from my cell to visit with someone, I was ready to explode. Maybe Tony's mom would come visit and threaten me to stay away from Tony, since I was officially a criminal. Or maybe a social worker would appear to offer me a new foster home, or it was a probation officer to check on my status. I had a list of things to say to whomever I was about to meet with. I flexed my body and pulled against my handcuffs as I waited for the guard to unlock the door that concealed my visitor's identity. Maybe I would just yell or jump on the person, I didn't know or care—it wasn't like I could be punished any further for venting my emotions.

When I walked into the visiting room, I didn't find a probation officer, Tony's mom, or heaven forbid, Jackie; I found a gentle looking older man who stood when I entered the room. He smiled and offered his hand. When I offered to haphazardly shake it, Mr. Lowen leaned in and made sure that we had a proper handshake. As we sat down at the table, I remained tense and glared at him. What was this guy selling? Although I thought I knew what to expect, my next placement of less than a year would be, by far, the most surprising and eventful of my life.

Foster Parent/Guardian Rule No. 7: *Don't Be Intimidated or Frustrated by Defensive "Walls."*

Whether you are meeting, working with, or permanently caring for a System youth, respect their right to have Walls. Grasp how hard it is for them to appear vulnerable, whether amongst their peers in placement or living with strangers, AND be everything you want and hope them to be. With time and trust, these walls will come down.

Mr. Lowen sat across from me at another cold, long metal table. He began to cautiously interview me, weighing all of my answers, to see if he would accept me for his group home— Revelations Christian Home for Boys. He was a stout, middle-aged black man with a gentle, calm voice. In my initial observation of him, I instantly found things that we had in common. His hands were calloused and his shoulders hunched from many days of hands-on, strenuous labor. His eyes reminded me of my sensei's, kind and purposeful, telling me he wasn't egotistical or proud, and the confidence in his voice relayed that he was a capable man. Every now and again during his questions he gave me an enormous smile that the little gray room couldn't contain. I began to relax a little. After about twenty minutes he informed me that I had passed his test and was accepted for placement. I accepted his offer instantly; anything would be better than my current home of decaying buildings. Within a few days I was released to his custody.

On our way to Moreno Valley, Mr. Lowen told me how he had been a knucklehead during his youth, and then explained the philosophy of the house members to all work together. We stopped at a Kmart, where he let me pick out a few pants and some shirts. Coming from the Hall, I had only the clothes on my back from my arrest at school. His eyebrow raised in a knowing expression when I grabbed two pairs of dickies, slacks and a package of white t-shirts. After adding socks and boxers to my order, it was time to find out where my new home was going to be. When we arrived, the entire staff greeted me after the conclusion of a weekly staff meeting. The house sat on the back pocket in a cul-de-sac in the fairly new suburban community of

Moreno Valley. Three bedrooms lined the hallway on one side, and the bathroom and staff office were on the other. Two living rooms and a backyard, that held both a swimming pool and a small basketball court, made up one of the roomiest groups homes I'd seen.

The boys came back from school and I remained in Juvey mode while meeting them—eyes cold and direct, making known that I wasn't going to be a punk and that I was ready to prove myself. I was first introduced to Robin. He was a lanky pale-faced boy whose name must have been chosen after his birth, due to his beak-like nose and elongated neck. Tommy, a short, obese 12-year-old, raced up and started asking intrusive questions. And then Lamont—he walked in casually with a gangster lean and an attitude. The puppy yipping questions was mute while we exchanged glares. Lamont had on full gang attire, but no visible telltale color. We exchanged head nods as he walked by me and went straight to his room. I had been given a room to myself while Tommy shared with Lamont and Robin had a kid that wasn't back from a special school yet.

Things were quiet at first as we felt each other out. The staff had arranged for us to attend a summer work experience program coordinated by the school district and major offices of the city government. While we were getting assignments, Mr. Lowen told Lamont and I that the money we made would be sent to our P.O.'s for restitution we owed. This proved to be an icebreaker for Lamont and me, as we exchanged the "what did you do's."

The Department of Transportation in city hall was to be my assignment. Making a record of every sign in the city, and its exact location, was my first job. My adult supervisor, Kevin, and I rode around town as I marked down what I was told to. He was candid with me about his job, including expectations, necessary skills, and salary. He showed me the ropes and was courteous. He paid no mind to my clothing and wasn't invasive as to who I was. I gave him the minimum about myself, knowing that being without a family and living in a group home was a shameful thing. I was glad he didn't press for more information.

After we got a few pages of data down, it would be time to go to the office and input it into the computer. In a simple software program, I entered the street, location, and type of sign. After days of input, I was given a day to goof off in the office. I got to know everyone and they gave me small gifts like a replica traffic sign and a name badge.

The secretary showed me how to type a document, and edited it for me, as I went to work on a statement to my probation officer. It included a summation of the abuse I had endured and physical things that were left behind that were of value that exceeded the value of my restitution debt: a horse and saddle, trombone, jewelry, electronic equipment, and a $400 voucher from a trip to Denver in which I had volunteered to wait for the next flight. My report also detailed the work around the house that I had performed and the lack of compensation, and this was backed by the dollar amount Jackie had received every month from the government for my care. I noted this to make sure the idea that I was "doing my part to stay in the house" didn't emerge. I made sure to point out that in nearly five years, Jackie had continued to dance around adoption, so she could keep receiving her monthly tax-free stipend. I reported the new truck, van and horse trailer that my monthly stipend helped finance. I detailed the barn that was put up, the barrel arena and fencing, all the landscaping and sprinkler systems I had labored on. And I reported that Jackie had paid for all this in cash, even though she had a mortgage on a 5-acre ranch and her job only paid $20 an hour. I wrote how we had sold some trampolines, but not that many—I knew because I took most of the calls. I lastly noted the lack of affection and the employer/employee relationship that had prevailed while I was in her home; this just to make doubly sure that they understood that my labor wasn't something that she deserved or should be expected. All this shook up the secretary, and while I was inputting street sign data, she came up after editing it, with tears in her eyes.

Touching me lightly on the shoulder, in sincerity she said, "I'm sorry." I turned and saw her face and my eyes began to well up. I turned again and tried to focus on my computer screen, which was a blur through what my brain was telling my heart was okay to do. She put the papers beside the monitor and walked away in a gesture that was meant to give me dignity and privacy.

At the house, our first paychecks came in the mail and were sent to the probation department. I told the Lowens about the document and a meeting was arranged with my P.O. at the home. He was not the same one that had been part of the fiasco in the probation building months before. He introduced himself as Alex and his body language wasn't at all confrontational. I was hopeful that this visit would go well.

I gave him the 6-page document and he began to review it carefully. As he read, I started in on telling him about the incident that had occurred when I signed my probation papers. Then he got defensive. "I read your file. You stole your foster mother's life savings after she took you in. I doubt that anything a P.O. said or did would match what you did to her."

I stared at the ground, I didn't have remorse for robbing her, but I had remorse for the way I went about trying to get away from that home. I needed to be smart, play Jackie's game better than her. Solemnly I offered, "She beat me. Her roommate beat me with a whip and got taken out of the house."

"I've heard that one before. How can you say things like that about someone that took you in? You said yourself that she was crying when you refused to go live with her."

"She was faking! She wanted to get rid of me."

"Why?"

"Because she was afraid. I was getting too strong for her."

"What do you mean? Did you threaten to attack her?" Alex was good. I wasn't going to win this line of questioning so I changed the subject.

"If she loved me so much, then why haven't I heard from her? She hasn't tried to talk me into coming back. She never even called me 'Son.'"

"And that's her job, is it?"

"Why did she send a box full of clothes that I wore in 6th grade? Do you wanna see the box she sent?" He took me up on my offer, surely thinking that I would be proven to be an exaggerator and a liar. We examined together dozens of items that he admitted were far too small for me to wear. "She hates me, Alex. She twisted everything around me so things would go her way." I took off my shirt and showed him my back. He sat on my bed, next to my old clothes, and asked for some time to finish the document. I left the room and started pressing weights in the back yard.

Alex came out during my third set and sat down on a lawn chair. "You must be a very bright boy. None of my other kids would take the time to write something this encompassing." He then gave me a "Don't waste your potential" talk and said he'd look into the paper's allegations. I don't know to what extent he pursued my paper's quest, but my next and final paycheck was given to me.

I had finally won some battle, no matter how small. I found a small pleasure in having some money of my own—to finally be paid for long hours of work was a new and empowering feeling. But the couple hundred dollars that I made was not enough to overshadow my daily reality: I was alone. I had made the decision not go to another foster placement, and therefore had given up any chance to have a family of my own. I contended with this harsh reality, to wake up every morning to a houseful of boys and be ruled over by various staff with dozens of rules and expectations. I knew I had already missed my chance to understand a little child's security in having his or her parents in the next room, or to go to school with lifelong friends from your "own" neighborhood. Family gatherings and holidays were never going to be a part of my childhood memories. And as I looked to the future, I knew that there was only to be more of the same. I would never know what it felt like to be encouraged by my mother, or ride on the shoulders of my father. In my anger, I took a sour grapes attitude toward these realities, but honestly, I feared having to admit how much I truly wished I could turn back time and get another chance to be a child.

At the end of the summer, my old friend Melancholy visited me all over again. The group went to a park where maybe 100 other families were and watched fireworks. They all sat together with smiles and shared their amazement. Brothers and sisters ran around and played together, yelling and smiling. Parents hugged their children and each other. My heart ached for my little brother, and I wondered what he thought of his sibling who had now been convicted of a crime. What story was he told, how did he see me, what did he think of me? All these questions pounded in my head as I tried to hide my tears from the other boys watching the show.

Night after night at the group home, I stood in front of the bedroom window with the lights off and cried to the moon. I was completely alone, I belonged to no one, and I belonged nowhere. On the outside I was tough, I could handle myself, but just below the surface I was insecure and afraid. I longed for family, security, peace, but most of all, love. I fantasized that maybe my brother would be able to give me these things if we were together. Maybe we could be a family and share a loving bond once again. I just needed an opportunity to see him, to get him away from his mother, and I could prove myself to him.

I excelled at hiding my feelings, both from others and from myself. I would do my best to get wrapped up in any activity that was offered. I soaked in my free time that was mostly spent at an elementary school up the street, playing basketball with the neighborhood kids. We often played the whole day, bringing our lunch with us and staying until the sun ordered that there be a last game. Lamont loved basketball as much as I did, and together we ran the kids in the neighborhood. On fantasy courts, we perfected ally oops in games that humiliated the kids with the steady homes that we shared contempt for. When school started, Robin and I went to Valley View High in its inaugural year and Lamont went to a lockdown school. Robin had tried his best to imitate the dress and demeanor of Lamont and myself in an effort to get in on what was fast becoming a good friendship and a house sub-clique. Having been made my roommate for fighting with Tommy, Robin copied the way I ironed and creased my t-shirts. He would borrow my clothes without asking, which would get us into fights and then consequences. He even tried to ball with us but had no skills; his lanky body wouldn't cooperate due to his lack of rhythm and coordination.

I would have taught him if he had at least tried to act humble, but he was the exact opposite. He was cocky and arrogant and thought that if he listened to the same music and wore similar clothes that he was down. At school, he made the mistake of telling everyone that he was from LA and started claiming Lamont's gang. When Lamont was mainstreamed (sent to public school), and found this out, he duly punished Robin physically and kept him from our circle permanently. For me, having Lamont at school was like having a brother there. Suburban middle to upper-middle class kids filled the halls and only a few of the gangster-type kids were there. At another school, the gangs would have taken over immediately, but the parents of the more affluent kids had pushed for tight rules regarding dress, colors, and strict suspension and expulsion rules for fighting. The few gangbangers there stuck to themselves and silently sold drugs to the "normal" kids.

If I was to maintain my image, then I couldn't show intelligence and did very little class work. Remaining unapproachable and ready to fight, I became exactly what I had hoped, seen as a shark among guppies. I sat and stared, "people watching," as it were, seeing what made these kids normal.

Why certain boys had girlfriends and smiles on their faces all the time and what I needed to do to find their normalcy. I watched, but knew I didn't have the necessary prerequisites: a family, home, and a huge group of friends they had grown up with that gave them popularity. As my jealousy boiled over, I waited for an excuse to put one of them on their back, to prove that they weren't any more a man than I was. Just the projection of this attitude was enough and I rarely was called out to fight, and not by the pretty boys I wanted to jack up. "Momma" jokes were pretty much the only ones we told, and my gift of putting together descriptions to invoke an immediate visual had earned me acclaim and pissed off some really big kids. I had so much pent up anger in my heart for my life and for Jackie and Shirley. I craved an opportunity to prove that I wasn't all talk and shortly my mouth put me in that position.

While walking between classes, one of my verbal victims pushed me from behind and wanted to settle the matter of his pride physically. I welcomed the opportunity and put up my hands, but a girl cut my game short. It was Monika from my science class, a sophomore with beautiful curves and long golden brown hair a shade lighter than her skin. I secretly watched her in class, peeking over to catch her gentle smile and emerald-green eyes. She stepped between us and commanded, "Leave him alone!" I was swept with an instant rush of calm as she backed into me and wrapped her arm around my back. The boy left and I thanked Monika, who was soon to become one of my only friends at school.

I ditched class often and broke into the school's lockers with a bent hanger. I stole many things, from pull-out car stereos to expensive comic books and portable CD players. I started selling the makeshift lock picks to kids for twenty bucks each. When security would see me, I would duck and run to the nurse's office to fake a headache and gain sanctuary. The nurses were becoming fond of me and through a small file, had found out that I lived in a group home and I shared that I had never met my parents. They gave me notes to get back to class so that it wouldn't be known why I had been missing. I tried to edge my way in on the drug money by buying weed from some of the gangbangers who respected me, then selling it to the rich kids in my class. I earned a few dollars, but not near as much as my small robberies were yielding.

My small stash was growing and I was planning to run again, to seek freedom from house rules and the coldness of parental figures that were only there on shifts. But depression was getting the better of me as I tried to figure out where I could run to, and I started giving into thoughts of suicide. With nothing to live for, no one that cared if I ditched class or got an A on a test that I hadn't studied for, it seemed my best option. The fact that the boys were getting home passes and leaving me to my solitude only made me feel the weight more. There were many nights that my emotions were almost the end of me.

A stolen syringe from the doctor's office lay on the bed in front of me. I thought to pump a tube full of air into my artery, having read somewhere that this would cause a heart attack and sudden death. I stared at the needle, my eyes bloodshot and sore from rubbing my tears away. I prayed for God to forgive me for what was to be my action. I pushed the needle into the vein that regularly protruded on my left forearm. I cried to Him, "I can't handle the life that you gave me." I tried to convince Him and myself that I needed to end my suffering. Knowing that suicide was a grave sin, I asked again and again if He'd understand and let me pass into heaven. But thinking of my current actions at school, I didn't think my request was reasonable. Although I thought it was unfair that I had been placed on this path that was my life, I didn't think I stood on grounds to ask God for a favor. And this was key: for I had come to look forward to the fact that maybe God would be my family and I would find the peace and bliss in his house of angels that I hadn't found on earth. My waves of depression subsided slowly as I reasoned with myself. I pulled the needle out and tucked it under my mattress. I lay down and began praying incessantly, eventually crying myself to sleep.

    In my thinking then, God seemed to be listening to my broken heart, and sent me the one person who had never hurt me. Coming home from school one day, the sight of a new staff member, also known to me as my old instructor, sent me reeling into disbelief. "Sensei?" I rushed up to him, just to see if he was real.

    "Hey, son! How are you doing?" He put his long hand on my shoulder and turned to Mr. Lowen, "I knew this boy when he was only this tall!" motioning with his hand around his knees. My heart soared as he gave me a huge warm smile and offered a small jab to see if I would block it. I did and his face beamed almost as much as mine.

    My world changed quickly in the next few weeks. Leonard had a class he taught on the weekends at a type of country club, and he invited me to assist him. It felt as though I almost had a father. I led the class often and would demonstrate judo falls when asked. He gave me my test and I passed, earning a long awaited green belt. At this victory, everything else faded away and only pride emanated from me. Leonard took me under his wing and brought me back into his home to visit his daughters and wife. It was like a family reunion, complete with tears of joy and hugs all around. I felt whole again in those days, and when the boys went on home pass it felt to me as though I had a home pass, a place to go, as well. I stopped stealing at school and began doing most of my class assignments. I tried to stop "people watching" and stayed focused on making sure that Sensei wouldn't find cause for shame in me. Life was finding a pace that was a normal as could be for someone with my circumstances, and I was feeling a little peace.

    In our house social dynamics, Tommy had become a huge snitch. Being three years younger than the rest of us, he was only accepted to play in coerced group home functions and watch TV with us. The fact that he was there for hitting his single mother, who visited him regularly and brought him gifts, only fueled our (especially mine and Lamont's) anger and annoyance with him. He had to pay, and the more he snitched over our entering the kitchen or being outside without permission, the more retaliation was heaped upon him. Many of the staff, including Sensei, had begun to ignore his tattling, and Leonard asked him once if he had mental problems.

"You must have mental retardation to keep tattling on these boys." Sensei shared our annoyance with him and even gave him a nickname—"helmethead." That meant that he needed to be in a mental ward with a helmet strapped on to prevent him from doing serious damage to himself. I harbored a mean and retaliatory spirit, and it took little encouragement or apathy for me to really dig into being cruel to Tommy. The lessons I had learned, suffered and honed since before I could remember just played out in an automated cycle, now with me being the aggressor. Tommy couldn't recognize what was happening and had no clue how far institutionalized kids could take things. He wasn't deterred in the slightest and continued to act like a spoiled little brat, thinking the world was his oyster and no one could really touch him. He was right, and we didn't risk violating probation to teach him the physical lesson his father obviously hadn't and that his mother was unwilling to.

But there are many ways to get at someone who is in need of a lesson. I took the syringe that was to be my implement for death, and turned it into my "teaching" tool. I pissed in a cup and in the middle of the night and shot the urine across the room at him. Not being able to contain my laughter, I sought refuge in the bathroom and stored the evidence in the far corner under the sink cupboard. The next day Mrs. Lowen smelled the urine, and although unable to find its origin, assumed that little Tommy was having trouble controlling his bladder at night. On nights when I awoke and found myself soaked in urine from a nightmare about Shirley, I would wipe myself down in the bathroom and grab my tools. I shot his clothes with urine and waited until he was showering in an effort to conceal what he thought was his error, and switched his mattress and bedding with mine. This catapulted him into consequences of no liquids after dinner, and with the night staff waking him three or four times a night to make him use the toilet. He was even started on medication for his infirmity. I shared my sordid deeds with the other boys and we laughed so hard we would cry and have abdominal cramping.

But Tommy was still snitching as much as ever in retaliation to our teasing about his bedwetting. His whining, "They're teasing me!" or "They're provoking me!" got him little attention from the staff, who was tired of his complaints, and gave us more reason to get him in trouble. We managed to get the house locked down for the weekend by our feud and he missed his home pass. He still looked for reasons to get us in trouble, and we looked for ways to get back at him. And while he was yet again on his way down the hall to tell on us for teasing him at dinner, he failed to consider the ramifications of leaving his bowl of chili unattended. Completely oblivious of what boys could do to other boys. Tommy, who had a sheltered life and was spoiled by his mother, didn't think that something might happen if he went to tell on us and left his food behind. He was going to learn that day.

The second he turned the corner, I stood and told Lamont to watch the hall. I unzipped and relieved myself in his bowl. Before I could finish, Lamont rushed over, loudly whispering, "Staff, staff!" Unsuccessfully, I tried to sit and zip at the same time and urinated on the table, Tommy's chair, and ultimately in my pants. Tommy's napkin was soaked in urine and I grabbed the pile of napkins in the middle of the table and frantically tried to clean up some portion of the mess before we were discovered. Robin only had time to stir Tommy's chili two or three times before they emerged, then he walked in front of me to block their view as I finished wiping the chair and myself. Staff Dennis gave us the typical, "Leave Tommy alone or everyone is going to get early beds," and we all agreed with grins on our faces. Tommy sat down and gave notice that his chili was very watery. We all waited in ravenous anticipation to see if he was going to eat, or if he was to figure out that something was wrong. We sat motionless as he began to stir his chili, possibly thinking that the grease and oil had risen to the top. And then he finally ate. The room roared to a deep, out of breath laughter, and we hit the ground in pain, unable to control ourselves. Dennis came out to see if everything was okay and Lamont reported that we were just telling jokes, so he left again. As Tommy took bite after bite, we continued to roar with laughter and Tommy paused, not knowing what was so funny. In annoyance, he asked "What the hell are you idiots laughing at?" Robin couldn't resist and let him in on our prank. Tommy started crying and headed back to the staff office.

Dennis came back out and demanded to know what was going on. We all stuck together and called him a liar and said that he was making up crap to get us in trouble, and Dennis bought in. Whether he didn't want to deal with the headache of all the paperwork or truly believed us was inconsequential. We had gotten away with it and Tommy had learned a lesson. He dramatically decreased his tattling and we stopped pulling pranks. It wasn't an end to our war but it did make for a recess. He would never leave his food again and would look around the room, making eye contact, each time he was about to eat.

A new boy named Jason joined the house and was as wet behind the ears as Robin. He talked a lot, most of it being lies to hype his past—but boys like him were always the easiest to spot. It was the ones who isolated themselves and didn't say much whom you really had to look out for. Jason was in a couple of my classes at school and sometimes I ditched class to get in his weight-training course. He pointed out a girl that he liked and reported how all the boys said she was easy. She was sprawled across a leg press bench with many boys and girls around her gossiping together. Her baggy black clothes couldn't hide her weight problem, and the colors she wore said she was protected. I informed Jason about the inaccessibility of this girl to him and told him that he should look elsewhere. He remained smitten and ended up pressed into a corner by her boyfriend for giving her "looks."

"What the F*** you looking at white boy?" The boy towered a full head and shoulders over Jason. I stepped up for Jason and told the guy to back off, reaching to the inside of my trench coat and gripping a 12" miniature baseball bat. "What?" the boy turned and looked, understood my hand gesture, then stepped away.

I pulled my hand out of my coat, "He was looking at the lifting records on the wall, not your girl. Everything's cool, right?"

Reluctantly the boy accepted my attempt at peace, "Yeah, everything's cool." Before he turned away, he gave one last hard look at Jason to mark his territory, and walked away. I walked Jason outside and gave him very specific instructions, and he thanked me a dozen times for stepping in. I made sure he understood about giving looks and what challenge would be implied, and once he understood I went to the nurse's office for a pass to go to class.

I mention this story because it is imperative in my mental development. Although I would continue to project a tough image, this event triggered a new awakening for me. I registered that it felt better to play a type of hero, such as when I was helping someone, than to be consistently looked at as a threat. I began to understand that my tough guy exterior was just that—a front. It wasn't really who I was inside. I relished Jason's thanks at the group home, and how Leonard told me that he was proud I stuck up for my house brother. I was a hero for a day. These feelings were similar to those I had had when I went to feed the homeless, took care of the animals, or the first instants after I let out Lobo to protect my little brother. However, while there would be a time soon when I would really try to put my hard image away, for now it was too useful.

Three new staff had been hired at Revelations Christian Home for Boys and they were to all have influence in my development. A new therapist, Roger, was an obese older man who played chess with us and claimed to have won tournaments when he was young. In an effort to break the therapeutic ice, he offered fifty dollars to anyone who could defeat him. After watching and listening intently, I won the fifty dollars within a few weeks. He was very impressed and told me that I had the potential to do anything I wanted. Although I was still the avid pessimist, it was nice to hear those words.

Rhonda was another new staff whose gentle way and encouragements would make anyone want to try just a little harder to earn her praise or a back-scratch with her long fake nails. She often took the time to say a nice word to me, taught me to sing "Amazing Grace," and encouraged me, saying that "one day" I was going to make a good husband.

Finally, there was Ernest, who had to be the goofiest, dumbest, most naive staff ever hired into a group home. We called him "RoboStaff" due to his rigid rule applications. But because of his taking us to his church to feed the homeless, he had helped remind me about humanity. On top of that, I had met a girl there who gave me butterflies to the point that I let my guard down enough to flirt.

Janet sang in the church choir and always seemed to find a spot next to me in the serving line. She was sweet and kind and had a voice like an angel. Lamont teased me for "going out" with a sista' but he was happy for me. Her parents didn't like the sight of us holding hands or her lying on my stomach under a tree, and made sure that there was an end to this. Before I had even had a chance to kiss her, I was blocked from going to the church any more. I was furious, as Janet was keeping me from the depression that usually surrounded the holiday season, and I thought that just maybe I was feeling romantic love for the first time. But as often as I voiced outrage over the situation, a new chapter was about to unfold that distracted me from my abrupt first chance at romance.

Leonard was quitting. He gave two weeks notice and told me he wouldn't be able to take me to class anymore. He later confided that he was getting a divorce and was moving out of his home. Utter shock filled my heart. How could any of this be true? Was he just going to leave me abruptly and not see me again until our next chance meeting? Two weeks more and he would be gone. Those two weeks ended up being filled with a tremendous whirlwind of events. Lamont and I helped him move out and into his new apartment. I remained quiet, in shock and disbelief, trying to fool myself into believing that something would change and Sensei would tell me he could stay. I knew I was fooling myself, but I needed to believe in something. Then my surreal atmosphere was quadrupled, as we finished the last few days at school before Christmas break.

The nurses at Valley View had tried to ease my holiday suffering in small ways with talks, and they even chipped in together to get me a Christmas gift. The ribbed college-type white sweater from Millers Outpost was like nothing I had ever worn, but I think that was the point. They gave me hugs and kisses, and tried to give me encouragement that I would make it through the holidays okay. They said they'd be praying for me and would see me in three weeks. The sincerity in their words and the gesture in their gift was more than my hard shell could handle, and my eyes watered with every hug. They left me my pride and said that there must be something in my eyes and told me to go lie down before returning to class. I lay there with my heart thankful for the love that I received from those ladies, and a blanket of calm covered me. Just as I was cleaned up enough to go back to class, the PA system called out a request that a girl, Terry Martinez, come to the office.

I couldn't believe my ears! Could this be my sister, Terry, with whom I had spent a day five years earlier? I told the nurses about the possible connection and they gave me access to their files to look up the name. I found the birth certificate copy and quickly everything was confirmed. The names in the places for mother and father were the same as on mine. I handed the documents to the nurses, who were in almost as much shock as I was.

"What do you want to do, Louis?"
"Can you call her in for me?"

"Of course!" They pushed the little red button on the wall and spoke, "Terry Martinez, will you please come to the Nurses' office? Terry Martinez. Will you please come to the Nurses' office? Thank you."

My stomach was in knots and I began a hustled pace back and forth. Who was on their way to me? Should I be excited or will I be disappointed? My normal gangster-type exterior withered away to reveal a young man terrified and fretful, about to face what might be his second chance to have a real family. I couldn't bear it and went into the bathroom and threw up. Then I rinsed my mouth out and the nurses gave me some mouthwash. I sat on the thickly padded cots in the sickroom and waited, my hands and legs shaking, my mind racing between possibilities, my stomach thoroughly knotted and coated in an almost unbearable anxiety.

The moment of truth came, but I didn't hear the door open. She stood before me at the entrance to the "sick room." I looked up and was doubly shocked at what my eyes saw—it was the girl Jason had been gawking at in weight training! She was looking at me with a question mark in her eyes. I stood as bravely as I could and stepped toward her. "Do you have a brother named Louis Martinez?"

"Louis Martinez? Yes. Why?"

"I am Louis Martinez." I held out our birth certificates. She received them gingerly and took only half a minute to confirm what I was reporting.

"I don't believe it. My brother?" She rushed me with a hug and embraced me like a mother would her child that was taken from her. I put my arms around her and rubbed her back, to comfort her crying. She pushed me back to see my face again and pulled me into her once more. I was in shock and overjoyed—maybe too much so. My eyes couldn't shed a tear, even though my heart was pounding out of my chest in rapture. I had hoped that she wasn't taking it personally; I doubt she noticed, so overwhelmed was she by her own emotions. We sat side by side holding hands and began our who's and what's.

"How long have you been going here? Where is our other brother, Tony? Where are you living? How old are you?" She fired questions at me with a blazing pace, and I did my best to give her answers to everything I could.

We stayed in that room for two periods until lunch, catching up and giving out pieces of the orphan's puzzle to each other. She told how she had stayed with our maternal grandparents when Tony and I had been removed, and she had seen our mother only a few times while growing up. Her words came out slow and pressured. In my mind I could see her heart breaking over and over as our mom came to see her and left. Eventually, she too was thrust into the foster care system. She told me of another sibling of ours who had died a short time after birth, a crack baby. She carried a picture of the infant lying in an open casket and as I looked into the baby's face, I was able to produce tears again. She put her arm over me and gave me the last few scraps of knowledge she had about our mother.

Then she offered me a picture of my father. It was the picture of a pale man with black greased-back hair sitting in a beat-up brown recliner, with a joint hanging from his lips. The picture made me sick. This "man" she carried in her purse that she knew to be our father was no more than a street punk. It was instantly obvious why I had never heard from him over the years, or why I should never expect to hear from him. The picture made me want to deny where I came from. Surely my father had to be more of a man than this. I shook my head as I handed back the picture, subconsciously denying that I shared the same genes with the person pictured. She had no comment about the picture and I took it to mean that she shared my disgust and was holding onto it for mere biological historic value.

After the brief silence, she told me that she was still in contact with our mother and would be seeing her for Christmas. "You talk to our mother? Our real mother? Do you think I could see her?" Without my even considering any of the factors, or the possible result, the request had pushed its way out and was on the table.

"Yes, of course! She is going to be so happy I found you!" We stood, as the nurse informed us that the lunch bell had rung. I gave both of them a deep hug and thanked them again and again. They had tears in their eyes and hushed me out the door before they started really crying. Terry showed me off to all her friends and, of course, to her boyfriend whom I had threatened not so long ago. Her girlfriends were all over me, asking all the same questions I had just answered for Terry, and my shell came back up. I wasn't going to expose myself to these strangers and didn't need to, as Terry was happy to field the questions for me. I ditched my classes and went to hers and told her about some of the harder things I had been through. She cried a dozen times that day. And after the bell announced our day's end, we exchanged phone numbers, and promised to call each other.

I got back to the house and couldn't wait until phone hours. The clock seemed to stand still, and then I found out that Tommy had signed up on the phone list before me. I had never received or made a phone call, so I didn't even think about the protocol required to get in the paper phone line. Lamont kept Tommy busy while I squeezed my way in front of him and dialed the numbers.

"Hello?" Terry's foster mother answered.

"This is Lou-"

"Ohh!! I get her right away!" Within seconds I was on the phone speaking with my sister again. We talked the time away, giving more details to each other and telling each other how much we missed and needed one another. Phone time was only 15 minutes each, but I managed to weasel over an hour. We said our goodbyes and promised to meet at school the next day.

When I got to school next day, I jumped out of the group home van and rushed around the school campus with wide eyes, looking for my sister. When we met again, it was almost as if five more years had passed, and our long hug was imbued with the same emotions that we had felt the previous day. We wiped our faces and she told me about talking with our mother after getting off the phone with me. "Mom is so anxious to meet you! She has been looking for you for a long time."

"Really? When do you think I can meet her?"

"Maybe we can get together for Christmas, if your group home will let you." The mere thought of meeting my mother sent me into a plethora of mixed emotions. Why had she left me? Why were there all types of burn marks and scars on my body that, as I was told, had been inflicted while in her care? Why were there drugs in my system when DPSS had taken me from her? Why had she kept Terry, yet allowed Tony and I to go to an orphanage to eventually be separated? Why hadn't she found me sooner? What were her intentions and motives for meeting me? I had hundreds of questions and although I knew that a lot of the answers might be painful, I needed them answered. Regardless if I was to go live with her again or just find out that she needed to ease her guilt; I desperately needed closure.

Terry and I palled around school that day and it felt surreal to have one of her friends ask me if I had seen Terry, or better yet, "Where is your sister?" I knew the answer for the first time in my life, and I had felt the impulse to not give the answer away in an effort to keep her to myself. I visited the nurses again. I had drawn them each a card to thank them for bending the rules for me and giving me the gift of a family back. At the end of the school day, Terry and I exchanged hugs and kisses again and I rode on clouds all the way back to the group home.

After giving Mr. and Mrs. Lowen all the information, I made the request to get a pass to meet my mother and spend the day with my sister, in her foster home. With little deliberation, I was granted my request and given a day pass for Christmas to be with my family for the first time. As if this wasn't enough, it seemed that God was going to give me yet another gift—not as momentous as a family, but rather one to solidify the empowerment and resolve over adults that I was starting to develop.

Ernest had arranged for us to go watch a play put on by a local community college. Everyone moaned and groaned over being forced to watch ballet, but the evening at "The Nutcracker" ended up having dramatic and ironic connotations. We arrived in our best clothes of ironed rayon shirts and baggy overalls or dickies. We were instructed to try and lose our gang walk and act "civilized" for the evening. Mumbling under our breath, we complied, as Ernest "RoboStaff" was the type to overreact and lock the house down over the smallest issue.

And there she was, pulling apart tickets in a traditional theatre usher suit—the one who tormented me in my sleep and had left marks on my body and severely scarred my mind. The lady who had so many times overpowered me and beaten me in her twisted efforts to enforce her style of discipline: Shirley.

I asked Earnest if I could go to the bathroom and said that I would meet them inside. Being on the highest level possible in our point system, it was not an unusual request. Ernest gave me the nod and I left. I went into one of the stalls and pressed myself against the back of the door. My heart kept pounding harder and harder and I couldn't seem to catch my breath. An opportunity was here—to get back at her, to humiliate her in a way that would allow me to take back the piece of my pride that she had kept when Jackie was able to successfully maneuver our legal battle. I could put action where there had been a dearth of response to my verbal outcries. What would I do? I hadn't the usual weapons that I carried to school—no knife, bat, nothing. I would have to face her with my bare hands. But still, I had no clue as to what I should do. I felt some apprehension at the thought of facing her. A little for what she might do, and a lot for what I *could* do. I couldn't just walk up and start to beat the crap out of her, could I? I would surely have my probation violated and miss my opportunity to meet my real family. Without a plan, I splashed my face with water and dried it. I closely examined some of the scars on my face. I stared into the mirror and convinced myself that no matter what happened, I would be ready.

I stood in her line, and as I got closer, my mind retraced the steps I had been forced to walk through all the years with her in my life. My "lessons" and "discipline." How she had tried to drown me for getting a drink of water. How she had beat and starved me for weeks under a false charge of killing an animal. Her bending over, taking a few lashings from Jackie in a perverse form of apology. The onion fields, and the countless hours of weeding. Working alongside the Mexicans to landscape their ranch property, and digging at least a three hundred holes two feet deep or more for fruit trees and fencing, electric and otherwise. Hurling rock after rock to clear an area for an arena at the sound of Shirley's whip snaps if I was showing signs of "laziness." The hundreds of nights I awoke from the nightmares of her and her "way of showing that she cared."

Then a smile peeked through my scowl as I thought of how Lobo had attacked her for whipping me while I lay naked, wet, and bloody by the horse stalls. How, in response to her hitting Tony, I opened Lobo's pen up, to send her running to the house like the coward she truly was. My face was beaming as I made the final transformation to extreme pleasure, as my mind took me back to the details of our last visit—how I jump-kicked her and pummeled her with continuous kicks, right before I was pulled into a car and rushed away.

My shoulders now back and chest full, I hadn't realized that I was standing in front of her already. She took my ticket and made the brief eye contact that forced her jaw to drop. I thought right then, that second, what if I just punch her in the mouth? That moment was my chance to throw her to the ground and start beating her. But I didn't; I waited for her to make the first move, as I had been trained to do.

"Louie!! How are you?" She said with half amazement and half concern. I was no longer the sixty to eighty-pound little boy that she had so easily battered. I stood almost six feet high and weighed the very lean, muscular 160 pounds of a trained fighter. Schooled both professionally and by the streets, my body language conveyed that there was not an ounce of physical fear left in me. My eyes leveled her and there was an uncomfortable silence that couldn't have been cut with a broadsword. She was not the monster that had lived in my mind anymore. I could really measure her up this time; I was not afraid. She was over fifty and her body was well aged from years of working horses. Her skin was leathery and her back slightly hunched and withered from work and natural frailty. Her eyes could not hold my glare and she looked away, her brain calculating her only two options: run, or discard her former pride. She chose the latter.

In a gesture to cede the power she once (and to some extent still) had; she motioned toward me as to give me a hug. Dumbfounded, I stood, and with my hands at my side, I allowed it. She began to cry and make excuses, blaming Jackie, and turned her gesture back into a way of rescuing her own dignity. I pulled my arms up and broke her hold with enough force to knock her off balance and send her onto her back. I spit at her feet and gave release to my anger, coldly ordering, "Don't you ever touch me again."

The people in line rushed to her side and I turned my back on her. Someone had grabbed my arm, but I easily jerked free and walked away. I could hear her tell them that it was okay and it was a family issue. My heart burned and my fists desired to go prove otherwise, but I continued walking away and found the boys. I knew that I had gotten about all I could exact without being arrested. I sat, my hands and legs shaking. Tears had made their way to my eyes and I resisted the urge to wipe them away until they were rolling down my face. I sat in oblivion to the ballet and continued to think about the consequences that might occur because of my actions. She might call the police, but it was unlikely. The Shirley I knew was more likely to come up behind me and stick me with a knife. That thought made me uneasy in my seat, but it was an action I hoped she had the guts for. My ears were tuned to every minute sound, and my eyes constantly scanned the room. If she would retaliate, I would be ready, and welcomed the opportunity to really prove my dominance.

But my paranoia was in vain, as not only had she not come for me, but she had left her post as usher altogether. I made doubly sure by asking one of the other ushers where she was, and he informed me that she had gone home sick.

Was forgiveness an option for me? Was it possible to just let it go and tell her it was okay? I don't think everyone deserves to be forgiven by his or her victims, and in my personal belief in an existing God, I knew that there were actions that were right and wrong. It was mostly due to this belief that I didn't snap her neck or take the bus down to Quail Valley and give Jackie what I thought she deserved. I had applied what resolve to the matter I could, and it made my nights easier. I had confronted my abuser, held her accountable, and moved on. I walked out of the theater with a huge portion of my pride restored, and with the monster under my bed slain.

When we got back to the house, I called Terry right away and told her what had happened. She lent verbal support and said she wished she had been there to help. We passed "what ifs" back and forth and then I asked if there had been progress on visiting with my mother on Christmas. "Everything is set. My foster mother knows a newspaper writer who wants to do an article about our family reunion on Christmas day. Would that be okay with you?"

Her genuine consideration for my feelings was something new to me, and although uncomfortable with the idea, I agreed. The days leading up to my meeting with my mother were the longest in the world. With my documented allowance, I shopped to get perfect gifts for my family—a first. My elation was written all over my interactions with my house members, and nothing could be done or said to knock me off my wave of excitement.

December 25, 1991—a day that was to be mine. I did not sleep a wink the night before, pacing the house and talking to the night staff to expend my limitless adrenaline. All the other boys had left days before, but being the last one to go didn't matter—for the first time in my life, I was going to go! The knock came and I went to my room to hide. Fifteen and a proven roughneck, and still I sought refuge, terrified by the moment when I would face my mother again.

I checked the mirror one last time and made my way down the hallway. I peeked my head around the corner, and was frustrated because Mr. Lowen was blocking my view. I couldn't take it anymore and stepped around the corner and behind Mr. Lowen. I hid behind him just like a 3-year-old would to grab the leg of his parent in the presence of a stranger.

Terry burst into the room to hug me again like it was our first. And as we released our embrace, I looked into the eyes of my mother for the first time. Frozen, I took in everything carefully. She had defeated, worn eyes. Her frame was surrounded by a shell of long, straight, wiry brown hair frosted with grays and whites. She stood about five foot two and couldn't have weighed more than ninety pounds. I reached out to my mother and hugged her, her tiny frame engulfed by my own. We exchanged tears and shared cries of a deep, baritone somberness. We both refused to let go and couldn't be interrupted by our onlookers. She stroked my back and hair with her tiny hand and whispered, "It's okay, son. I'm here, I'm here." I wouldn't let her go—I wasn't going to risk losing her again. We held onto our moment and, without need for paperwork, knew we were mother and son again.

I thanked Mr. Lowen and turned to spend the day with my family with a little hope and a lot of anxiety. When we reached Terry's foster home, the newspaper writer greeted us and took photos. I don't know if it was by chance or it was planned, but the stereo began belting out "Reunited" by Peaches and Herb. "*Reunited and it feels so good.*" The room filled with tears and a group hug for my family was in order. We exchanged long hugs and held hands on the couch. I didn't want to let go of my mother and did my all to stay in physical contact with her. I remained silent most of the time, wanting to absorb every sound and touch. I tripped over my tongue when I timidly spoke. I knew questions needed to be asked, but I thought that I should wait and just enjoy my day. I didn't want guilt or blame to have a place on that day and thought I should wait. After all, I had my mother now and I had all the time in the world to slowly ask the tough questions that had troubled my peace for so long.

Her voice soft and cautious, she asked about Tony. "Do you know where Tony is?" My pause conveyed that I hadn't a definite answer. I shared a photo of him that I carried and reported that I heard Tammie had moved her family to Oregon months ago and deliberately hadn't left a forwarding address. I told my mom, Abbie, that Tony had been adopted and I rarely saw him. I remembered the last phone number I was given, and agreed to try it. I went with Terry into her room in an effort to call without fear of expressing the disappointment that would surely be the result.

The phone rang only twice and I heard his voice again. His excitement from what was surely a fantastic morning in his house filled my receiver. "Hello?"

"Tony, is that you?"

"Yeah. Who is this?"

"It's Louis, your brother."

Like he had just seen me yesterday he responded, "Oh, Louie! Merry Christmas."

"Tony, I found our sister and our mother. They want to talk to you." Tony turned to say something to one of his parents and informed them I was on the phone. Tammie erupted on the line with bewilderment and fury.

"Louie!?" Frantically she started to demand, "Where are you calling from? Why are you calling here?" I didn't know until years later that her attempt to move Tony away from me had ended abruptly with the failure of their private plumbing business. She had changed the phone number and moved residences countless times over the years and now, right after they moved back into the same house they had failed to sell when they left, she was on the phone with me because she had forgot to have the number changed.

"I have found Terry and Abbie, our mother and sister. They want to say hi to him and meet him."

She played her roles of Jekyll and Hyde to the T and calmly excused Tony from the phone to finish opening presents. Then her rage exploded as she got back on the phone in the privacy of her bedroom. "No way! Tony is not ready for a step like that yet. Don't call here again without my permission!" She slammed the phone in my ear just as my sister had grown unable to contain her anxiety and pulled it away from me.

"Why did you hang up? I thought you were going to let me talk to my brother too?"

"His adopted mother hung up on me. She was very mad that I called." The tears welling up in my eyes remarked on my truthfulness.

"Well hell, no! She can't stop me from talking to my brother!" Terry picked up the phone and hit redial. The frustration on her face informed me long before she did that there was no answer. And there wouldn't be, either, as she tried fifteen to twenty times throughout the day to call the number. I talked to our mother about what happened and she was a little upset, but not outraged like Terry.

"Maybe she will let us talk to him soon. Let's try to be patient." She tried to calm her daughter. The rest of the day we spent sitting on the couch in constant physical contact with one another. We watched a movie and opened presents. My day was only marred by my inability to control my emotions. I broke down crying in front of my mother and fell into her small embrace.

"You don't know how hard it's been. I've been all alone." She hushed my sobbing and assured me that everything was going to be different.

"You have me now son. We're together again." We talked of becoming a family and living together. She asked, with a wall ready for disappointment, if I wanted to live with her again. When I told her "yes," Hoover dam wouldn't have been able to control the flow of emotions.

I reluctantly went back to my group home, wanting to suggest that I go with her now, that we all loose ourselves from current attachments right then and be a family. I didn't want to wait for anything, but, judging from her appearance, and knowing that she couldn't be more than in her early thirties, I realized that she was probably still on drugs and placement with her would be near impossible. I hugged her at the door and wept on her shoulder, not wanting to release my mother to the world. When I had to let go, my body immediately ached for her as if my mother's embrace was the oxygen I had been missing all those years. I desperately wanted to be rid of my "orphan" status and have my family back. I didn't care or want to consider the costs, thinking for sure I could find happiness with my real family.

I went to bed clutching the bottle of cologne and wearing the gray sweatshirt she gave me. I could really feel the hole that had always been in my heart. It flared and grew, reintroducing the pain of being abandoned. I hugged my pillow and wailed internally; my eyes had again filled with tears, somehow knowing that this was all a fantasy—somehow realizing that Desperation and Loneliness had been my parents for too long, and they surely weren't going to give me up so easily. In this subconscious realization, I cried myself to sleep.

Chapter 18 - I Met My Family Just Once

In the following days, my world was again flipped upside down far more than I would have thought possible. The kaleidoscope of events that was to take place made the preceding weeks wane by comparison. The day after Christmas, Mr. Lowen received a phone call from the probations department. They were questioning him about a newspaper reporter who was trying to get permission to use my name in his article. This led to more inquiries over my visit and, according to Mr. Lowen, the termination of any and all contact with my mother. The petty grounds given were her lack of valid identification. Mr. Lowen tried to put a positive spin on things and remind me that I had gotten to spend the day with my mother, albeit illegally. This was no comforting thought at the time.

My rage grew and the excuse they gave me seemed to truly be legally far-fetched. No call from a social worker or probation officer confirmed any of Mr. Lowen's excuses. Neither could any such worker be counted on to make a call to comfort me, if any of this was true. My real family, the System, had no time for human consideration and I was left stunned and guessing. But the result was absolute, and I never saw my mother again.

A week later and I was back in school talking to my sister. I informed her that I wasn't allowed to call, since our visit, and repeated the lame excuse I was given. We worked out our plan for her to call and pretend to be my girlfriend, an obvious loophole but one that could only be challenged by a seriously cold-hearted staff. I actually went to all my classes knowing that staff would be closely watching me. How twisted was it that the only way to raise any concern over school attendance was their effort to prevent me from talking to the only family I had.

When Terry called that night, she confirmed what my gut had been telling me. Abbie was still on drugs and even prostituting herself. She had done nothing with her life and had only cleaned up enough to spend Christmas with us. Her promises of taking me home sank in my stomach, forcing nausea. Just as Terry was in the middle of relaying these hard facts, Ernest told me it was time to get off the phone. My time was up and I needed to say good-bye to my girlfriend. I pleaded for more time but he was steadfast that I follow house rules. I blew him off and continued my conversation, trying to get every last piece of information I could. Ernest pushed the button on the phone that ended my call. I yelled at him, threatened him, and made motions to force his flinching. I was maddened by both the phone call and then by this staff that saw my plight as a "case" and afforded me no humane compassion.

Did he try to find out what I was so angry about? Or search for a reason why a client on level 4 (the highest) would suddenly fly off the handle? Not "RoboStaff" Ernest, he just dropped my level and tacked on a slew of consequences that included no phone time. Injustice, Intolerable, Inhumane—all with capital "I's." I paced my room for thirty minutes, thinking of how to get back at RoboStaff. The more pressing matter of my mother finally distracted me and I found the solitude I needed in my closet. I curled into a ball and sobbed, thinking how I'd be trapped forever in these group home and foster placements. I would never escape the clutches of loneliness and despair.

In school, my sister and I had less and less to say to one another. The excitement of finding each other started wearing off, and neither of us had experience in maintaining a family relationship. What do teen brothers and sisters talk about? My role became more of a protective one and I saw Terry less and less between classes. We passed in the hallways and hugged or she would wave if she was in the arms of her boyfriend.

That weekend, I was confined to the house to meditate on my deluge of life events. My mind swam as I tried to make sense of the madness of the weeks past. Leonard had stayed an extra week while waiting for the final acceptance response from his new job, and the thought of him also leaving only filled me with more feelings of abandonment. Lamont tried to be a friend to me, being an ear and doing his best to offer distraction with cards or basketball.

He got me to laugh again amidst my anxiety and depression. We practiced dunking on the eight-foot rim in the back of the house. For these small times I forced my troubles aside for the sake of our slam-dunk competitions. Between sticking by me at school and aligning with me at the home, I felt I had found a best friend in Lamont, a brother. We laughed and played hard, enjoying a sort of sibling competition. Every now and again the ball hit the back of the rim and went flying in the opposite direction, sometimes flying over a nearby fence and into the neighbor's yard. We took turns retrieving the ball and it was while I was waiting for Lamont to come back over the fence that circumstance offered an opportunity for rebellion.

Lamont had taken so long to come over the fence that I hopped over to see what was up. He stood by a sliding glass door, peering inside. He turned sharply when my movement caught his attention. He looked back through the door and hushed, "No one's home." He started pointing out what was clearly visible and seduced me with how easy it would be to take what we wanted. Agreeing with him, we went back to the house and grabbed gloves, a screwdriver, and slid the window to my room (which was the closest to the house) open.

In a matter of minutes we were creeping through our neighbor's house. We checked the whole place first to make sure no one was home. Next, we divided up the bedrooms and began our search for valuables. The house was decked out with ornaments, expensive dolls, large framed paintings, and large crystal vases and figurines housed in cherry wood glass cabinets. Expensive electronic components, big screen TV, a then-expensive CD player, and huge speakers completed the living room. We rummaged through drawers and started over the fence with the stuff we wanted. Nothing was difficult—there was no alarm, no dog, and no one coming home while we were shopping. It was broad daylight and no one had a clue what was going on. We took our time and unplugged the CD player I wanted without making a mess. We pulled one of the speakers apart in the living room, taking only the actual speaker, and replaced the grill to make it look like nothing was wrong. Shuffling through valuables, we took selected jewelry, coins, and cash, leaving behind traceable credit cards and larger collectibles.

When we finished closing up everything, we returned to the group home to sort our loot. We traded items with each other the way children do baseball cards. When we finished trading and chuckling, we hid our treasures in our respective rooms. I pulled apart an old receiver I had bought at a pawnshop with my City Hall money and hid most of the jewelry in it. In the box spring of my bed were CD's, more jewelry and other small collectibles; next I searched for a place to hide the enormous CD player.

Hours went by and our telltale hearts forced us to ask one another over and over if we thought anyone was the wiser. We nervously watched TV and jumped at every sound. It was hours later, right when we started to relax, that there was a knock on the door. Dennis answered and greeted two police officers. My resolve grew and I knew I had to be steadfast in front of them. I wasn't very fond of law enforcement at this point in my life, to say the least, and had had nothing but injustice dealt me by them. From their lack of action way back at Henry's home, to Jackie's manipulations, not to mention my encounter in an alley, I must say that I quite loathed anyone in a police uniform. And my personal reasons were compounded by what the consequences would be if they found that Lamont and I were burglars.

The officers entered and began questioning each of us. Tommy and Robin were honestly dumbfounded. I looked on as they were questioned and thought that maybe their sincere responses would deter the cops from asking all the same questions over again. I was right, and by the time they got to Lamont and me, there were only questions of our whereabouts and if we heard anything. I answered the first part honestly: playing basketball. The second part I didn't directly answer but gave more of an answer to the first question, "I was playing basketball out back. We were having a slam dunk contest and bagging on each other and it was very loud." They bought it, hook, line, and sinker. Lamont followed my story but when the cops asked him a couple of extra questions, he slipped up. He changed his story to say he thought he might have heard a window breaking—and it was all over. They asked permission to search the premises and Dennis agreed. They searched Robin's room first and came up empty. My room was next and I stood in the doorway nervously as they tossed my drawers and dumped out my closet, but again they found nothing. Finally, Lamont's room. Everything was going well until they bumped his receiver and an 18" herringbone gold chain slid out. Lamont swore that the chain was a gift from his mother. Refusing to make eye contact, the officers shrugged off his excuses. They thoroughly searched his closet and found some costume jewelry. "Is this a gift from your mother too?"

Lamont sat in handcuffs on the couch. A list that the neighbor gave the policemen prohibited them from concluding the matter, because it was missing all of the more expensive items taken. They questioned me a second time, and I stuck to my previous story and played dumb, keeping my mouth shut to the incriminating inquiries. The neighbor was now in our house and looking over his possessions spread over our kitchen table. Lamont still protested about the herringbone chain and the man argued, giving a story of how a kink had come to be next to the clasp. His argument unnecessary, he asked about the CD player and got no response from Lamont. Detailing what it looked like to the police, his frustrations mounted as they reported not seeing anything like that in our house. They even offered that maybe a schoolmate had helped Lamont and it was probably on the way to a pawnshop. The neighbor started describing other things and drew even more blank looks from the cops. Lastly he spoke of a special speaker that had a silver center dome for acoustic sound reproduction. One of the cops gave him a knowing look then. He had passed it over in my sock drawer; covered and looking beat up, the officer had thought it was just a piece of junk. He went into my room and retrieved it and the man's face glowed in expectation of finding everything else. As the cop turned to me and asked where I had obtained the speaker, Lamont spoke out, "I gave it to him." I looked at Lamont and them back at the cop, "Yeah, he let me use it." I couldn't believe the loyalty and respect Lamont had shown in not revealing me. I knew right then that I had a brother in him, someone as equally protective of me as I was of him. Although this is the very definition of street rules of the criminal code, it was all I had. Apparently frustrated, the cops asked whether they could do a second search. Thinking I might give away the position of something, they wanted me present for the search. They tossed everything and still came up empty. They searched the bathroom and hallway closet, thinking I might have stashed it somewhere else. Nothing.

I sat next to Lamont on the couch and listened as they read him his rights. I wanted to say something, to take the heat with my best friend but I knew that his gesture, his offered sacrifice, would be in vain if I did. When they finished, they began to grill us as if they had read me my rights as well. They tried to find answers about the man's stuff by threatening, and then by a guilt trip. "Do you know that this man is a pastor of his own church? He was giving Sunday service while you were robbing him."

Although the thought of robbing a "man of God" was wearing on my conscience, the fact that he was pushing for charges and yelling and cursing made it subside. I thought of how his house was so expensively filled while seemingly hidden in a low-key, middle-income neighborhood. I remembered the pastor at the church we were sometimes asked to go to spending a great deal of time working up to and explaining to his congregation to not be upset or jealous that he had just bought a new Lexus (one of the first years they had come out), saying, "God blessed my family" with the car. Hypocrisy had been the norm for God's servants. Too many people had used Him as a way to manipulate their emotions and responsibility. I always wanted to believe that there was a God, but honestly, as an orphan, it was hard for me to truly believe that a loving God existed. If there was one, then why would He allow an infant to be tortured, or a child to be severely beaten for years—or any amount of time for that matter? Why wouldn't he just give me a family? Why was my life a continual torment? My mind turned back to my immediate situation. But their pushing this fact in my face had no effect.

Then Sensei walked in. Our eyes met the second he came through the front door. He held his inquisitive look and slightly shook his head. Only then did my actions weigh on me; I felt like scum. I knew what disappointment my actions would bring to the only adult that had been like a father to me; I had a genuine fear of displeasing him. I knew that no matter the outcome, our relationship would take a sharp turn.

Dennis asked to speak to me for a minute, either seeing the window of my defenselessness or just coincidentally having good timing. He shut the door behind us in my bedroom and in just above a whisper said, "Lamont told me you have the stuff. I'm not going to report you, but we need the CD player to get them out of the house. Just give it over and I'll say I found it."

Dennis. He had been there since my first day and he was one of those staff that seemed to have his own rules. Some things he didn't care about, which made him seem kind of cool, but then other things he overreacted to, yelling and swearing at one of us. We had been walking around the block with another staff once when we thought for sure we saw him running with a shopping cart full of meat away from security guards out of a supermarket parking lot. He was a very short man. His thin, straight, dusty brown hair draped over his shoulders. He wore John Lennon type prescription sunglasses that were the only thing visible on his face other than his ZZ top-like beard and old military green hat. An unmistakably unique look, coupled with his stories of drug running and prostitute chasing "back in the old days" made him a rare staff indeed, and most likely the one we saw stealing the meat. Although I knew Lamont hadn't rolled on me, I wanted to help him if I could, and maybe have something to redeem myself in a small way to Sensei. I pulled the player out of a large box of clothes and handed it to Dennis.

The second he opened the door the police came in. I glared at Dennis and mumbled, "Snitch." The officers put on the handcuffs and sat me next to Lamont once again, now reading me my rights. I saw the utter disappointment on Leonard's face and I couldn't directly watch as he turned and walked out of the house. Mr. Lowen had arrived and had the explanations necessary to get the police to release us into his custody until our court date.

Once we'd been released, Mr. Lowen had nothing to say to us and sent us directly to bed. We could hear him chewing out Dennis for not watching us and spelling out the time required to pull off the task we had. Dennis was suspended for a week. Once he was done with him, Mr. Lowen came into each of our rooms and ordered that we write an apology letter to the pastor. He shut the door and demanded that the oncoming night staff stay awake (for real) and keep up 15-minute checks.

I lay there trying to imagine the consequences that a judge might throw at us for robbing a pastor. Both of us were already on probation, and I thought for sure we would get time in CYA. Next, like a lightning bolt through my mind, I thought of Terry, of how I might get moved and never see her again. Of how Tony might get word of this and be even more convinced by his mother that I was a waste of any of his energy. I lay there contemplating options—running away or suicide? I didn't have an answer and thought I would just wait and see what happened. I had made a dumb decision and I should pay the price, what difference did it make anyway? I was still not allowed to have a family—what difference did it make where I was?

My mind racing, I couldn't force sleep. Every decision, every impacted part of my life called out in my head, seeking priority. And especially begging for thought was the jewelry that I was still lying on top of, as well as the collectibles hidden in the receiver. With the return of his prized CD player, the man had had the cops help him lug the table full of goods back to his house. Everything else that we had taken, to him, was unimportant, and he carried the CD machine like it had more value than any Bible. I had a great number of items left, and the next morning I put all of them in my backpack and got them out of the house. I gave Lamont his choice of what was left and thanked him repeatedly for not giving me up and for trying to take all responsibility. He just gave me a big Lamont smile.

I had no problem selling the stolen items to the rich kids at school and made over two hundred dollars doing so. Lamont had fewer connections and only made about fifty bucks, so I suggested we pool the money and divide it 50/50. It's not that I had the better merchandise; I just had a way of convincing the person of the urgency of such a good deal. When I told my sister what I had done, and the possible consequences, she was very concerned. I bought her lunch a few times, but before I knew it, something happened that made me feel that I had called down my own punishment by the Almighty himself.

Out of the blue I had gone to school one day and Terry wasn't there. Some of her friends asked me for her whereabouts and I was clueless. She had vanished and not said a word to me. One of her girlfriends told me at lunch that Terry had run away to live with her boyfriend, that she might be pregnant and was not going to let the System take her baby away from her. I was sickened by the implications: Terry had left me, knowing that she was the only family I had. She had left me without a word of warning. Didn't she think that maybe I wanted to run too? I was lost again. I had no connection to any of my family. The brief contact I had had with my brother on Christmas would surely not be repeated due to Tammie's fears of me coming, cloaked in the middle of the night, to steal him away. A quick, deep depression swept over me and thoughts of suicide again rushed to the forefront of my options.

Lamont and I spent a lot of out time doing extra chores to work off the debt for the theft. I spent hours scrubbing walls and floors and got lost in my thoughts countless times. The rest of the house functioned in oblivion to our work. And then Leonard finally left, again without a word. My mind tried to convince me that my only option was the black blanket of suicide. But my heart yearned to be loved and the battle raged inside between the great silence and the hope that I, someday, would find an enduring love. I had had a taste of its power, and the love that I got from Terry in the first days, and the comfort that Abbie had tried to impart, left me wanting, desperately. Maybe a chance happening would be repeated and I would have them back in my life. Although this never happened, the thought of its possibility pushed me through some of the really hard days.

A month later, Lamont and I went to court over the burglary. I had been bouncing back and forth between the hard shell I projected around people and my scared inner child, when the door was shut. I didn't allow myself to talk about anything seriously, especially not to the staff—but they didn't ask anyway. Dennis had been trying to get back in our good graces since he had become a house outcast (a disrespected, lied-to and loathed staff), and offered advice on how to gain the judge's sympathy. "Just pinch your nuts and let out a tear; then the judge will go easy on you."

Neither of us replied or made eye contact at the suggestion. I sat in juvenile court and waited with Lamont and another staff for them to call my name. I sat with my headphones on and kept listening to "Ghetto Bastard" by Naughty by Nature. The words in the rap song fit my life so perfectly. Born without a family, left to fend for myself. I wanted to take back power and felt the anger in the heart of the song. This was a song for me. By the time I was called for court I knew that it didn't matter what they decided to do to me—just like the song said:

> "I've been through more sh** in
> the last week,
> than a fly flowin' in doodoo on
> the concrete.
> I've been a deadbeat, dead to the
> world and dead wrong.
> Since I was born that's my life,
> oh you don't know the song?
> So don't say jack, and please
> don't say you understand.
> All that man to man talk can
> walk, damn."

I walked into court still not wanting to be sent to California Youth Authority, but then again, how much worse could it be than the rest of my life? At this point I just didn't care. My short appearance in court was a similar trial to the one before. There was a rushed, quick reading of a few papers, some repetitive statements that were reiterated by both prosecution and defense, and then the gavel. Quick justice for a quick crime. I was asked the same questions as before and gave the same head nods. "Do you understand—? Are you entering a guilty plea of your own free—?" and so forth. Within minutes I was returned to Mr. Lowen and had no clue as to what my legal situation was. I didn't really care anyway, because I knew they weren't sending me to CYA.

Lamont and I pressured the others to be disrespectful to Dennis and tried to incite mutiny on his shift as much as possible. His fuse getting shorter every day and he eventually struck out at the smallest one in the home, Tommy. He pulled him into the bedroom, alone, and backhanded him across his face. Tommy came out with a bloody nose and Dennis went to the staff office, most likely to write some bogus report. We decided to back off of Dennis, but it was too late; we had pushed him too far. He made up new rules on his shifts and docked us for breaking them. Every house privilege was suspended when he came on duty, and after a week of this, our resolve to do something mounted.

I drafted a letter while at school, a 10-page, front and back, handwritten letter itemizing incidents and house conditions that might be of interest to the social service department. The list went on and on: staff hitting kids, abusive speech, corporal punishment, cockroaches and ants in the food, the lack of supervision and inconsistency in the rules. When I finished, I had at least one detailed incident per kid and after having everyone read it, they each signed the last page. I taped the grievances to the bottom of my dresser drawer and waited for our first outside visitor: Robin's social worker, who was due in a few days. Although everyone made a pact not to say anything about our plans, Tommy couldn't resist the urge to taunt Dennis while he was being verbally harassed. "We're going to get this place shut down! You'll see! Then you won't even have a job! You're probably going to jail!"

Dennis took these words seriously and went back into the office to call the Lowens. Lamont socked Tommy in the arm for the breach of our pact and he went to his room to pout. "What are we going to do?" asked Robin.

"We'll wait. And if anyone asks, we'll say Tommy is a liar." Everyone agreed with my plan and we went to bed. The next day Mrs. Lowen pulled each one of us aside and inquired about the validity of the information that Tommy had given her. She knew about the letter and asked around. The air in the house was thick with stress as many of us thought that we were probably going to get kicked out or arrested. We all took turns urinating in a plastic sports bottle and Robin defecated in it. The next morning while Tommy was doing his chores, I pulled back the covers on his bed and poured out the mixture between his sheets. The smell was horrendous, and immediately covering it with the blankets provided little release from its stench.

Mrs. Lowen had made me stay home from school for a "doctor's appointment." Passing the night staff in the door, she entered the house without eye contact towards me and immediately reacted to the smell in the house, contorting her face. "What's that god-awful smell?!"

"I dunno." She walked through the hallway and into each room quickly like a bloodhound, looking for its origin. Without any indecision, she settled on mine and Tommy's room, pulling his sheets back. Her hand snapped to her mouth to cover it, dry heaving, and then falling back slightly, as if the smell had a physical component. As the smell made its way to the doorframe where I stood, I shared her disgust and started to dry heave, eyes watering from the horrendous fumes.

Reeling, she exclaimed, "What in the hell?!" and made her way out the room. She went and grabbed a dishcloth and garbage bag before reentering. Covering her face as if to avoid teargas, she pulled his bedding back and piled them into the bag. She threw the bag outside and turned to notify me, "I know there is no way Tommy did that in his bed." I didn't respond and followed her direction to get in the van to leave.

As we got on the freeway, it was obvious that we weren't going to the usual doctor's office only two blocks from the home. She pulled out my signed grievance list and placed it between us. "So I hear you've been on the soap box lately? Everyone told me how you got them to sign this letter and are trying to get the home shut down." I sat stunned as I stared at the document. I knew everything was accurate about her statement except for Lamont; he would never roll over on me. The others, however, would report their parents to the Nazi

German government if it meant they would incur some favor. She went on about how they are going to make some changes around the house and that Dennis was going to be let go, but that the trouble I had almost raised was too much for them to accept. They were not going to permit me to live in their house any longer. I sat quietly as she drove me to Riverside Juvenile Hall and dropped me off right after she tore my paper to pieces. I knew I was stuck; that I had no say in the matter. I tried anyway and told my P.O. (now my fourth) who saw me a few days later about the paper and all the kids' signatures. Her face seemed unmoved, as if Mrs. Lowen had been smart enough to cover that trail with a story or two. My excuses and questions were brushed to the side and I was told that I had violated my probation for failing to meet house expectations.

I served four months this time—far too much time to spend shackled and treated as subhuman while falsely imprisoned. It was hard to believe how easy it was for the Lowens to get me put away for complaining about them. "Failing to meet house expectations." More like failing to lie down and be treated however Dennis saw fit. Those 120 days were long and filled with varying measures of anger and depression. If it wasn't bad enough that I was going through life without a family, I had to take into account that I was also making life even harder on myself by committing crimes. I needed to stop and realize that I was only hurting myself. Caught in a youthful rage, yet on the verge of gaining a measure of adult maturity, I was beginning to really see my place, understand who I was, in the System.

Every day I ran into kids I had seen before and also had to deal with some of the same staff. Remaining quiet, I knew that I had to play this game right or end up in solitary or worse yet, suitcased. The judge that saw me didn't even call me by the right name while reading the necessary documents to his court. When he was corrected, he offered no apology or embarrassed smile, like this mistake was familiar. He just agreed with the prosecutor to have me sent to a facility. I thought this meant

California Youth Authority at first and my face stiffened as if to say "So what." The prosecutor explained I would be sent to a behavior treatment center. I didn't know exactly what she had in mind, but I knew that behavior treatment didn't include CYA.

Chapter 19 - David's Horizon

"The heart of locking somebody up is the deprivation of love and touch. The way you disempower people is to strip away all human contact."

—Denise Johnston, Director of the Center for Children of Incarcerated Parents

At this time I struggle with how to really put you in my teenage shoes. No friends, no parties, and especially no looking to the future with hope and preparing for a good life. I didn't deal with the usual teenager angst towards Mom and Dad, or feel the butterflies going on a first date. I wasn't going to "the dance," "the game," or getting a driver's license. I was by all means and in all ways alienated from the golden teenage experiences I witnessed at school or on TV. But more than all of that, I had never been able to put my faith in any adult; they had always let me down. No matter how things had started, I had always been lied to, abused and ultimately abandoned.

I want to offer a little exercise if you would permit, even if you participate only mentally. Find a dark, cool room without carpet and take off your shirt. Making sure there are no outside distractions, just meditate and stand there. I want you to focus on feeling a little vulnerable, and a little more vulnerable. Someone could walk into the room and see you topless, they could laugh, or they could attack. I want you to remember a

time when your mother or father was there for you; maybe for
support or maybe for reassurance. Do you remember how your
family offered you the world? Can you remember a time when
your family told you that nothing was impossible? Think hard;
remember a single kiss or an embrace that made you feel safe. If
you have this thought, this feeling in your heart and a tiny smile
on your face, you are ready. Lie on the floor, with your shirt off.
Soak in the cold as it shocks your skin. As your mind fights to
tell you to get off the floor, you have lost your precious thought.
Something has taken your most precious moments and left you
with emptiness. The cold is all you feel. How can you fight to
regain your moment? Who will listen? Each and every hug or
kiss that you received as an innocent child is being taken away.
Cold, empty, you lie on the floor, powerless, vulnerable. Take
in a deep breath, let it out—nothing has changed. If you have
really put your mind and heart into this exercise, then you may
have a small inkling of what it was like in my shoes every day,
every hour, and every minute. Remember this feeling as you
read on.

        After a long locked-up four months of waiting in the
paper line for a spot to open up, I was placed at Guadalupe
Home for Boys. It was a semi lock-down sixty or seventy-bed
therapeutic-based treatment facility. Low-level gang members
and wayward kids without (documented) violent behavior were
sent there to try and figure what went wrong, and to start
making the choices that would help them be successful. Most of
the youths in there were on probation from various places in
Southern California.
        Brother John, a Catholic priest, greeted newcomers and
made sure they had an understanding of their placement and any
necessary toiletry or clothing items. His smile was kind and he
seemed sincere—an unsettling welcome for entrance into such a
rigid program. I followed closely as he showed me where I was
supposed to live for the next six months to a year. My arms
were full of towels, clothing and topped by a bar of soap and a

toothbrush. With my head stiffly straight ahead, my eyes took in everything slowly—this was now my home.

Four of the dorms or "cottages" were arranged on a small campus that was mostly all-encompassing. There was an enormous dining hall, sprawling basketball courts and field, art therapy building and then the main office building, which a final dorm was attached to. The air was clinical, and other than Brother John's initial welcome, a smile was hard to find.

After being given another more specific grand tour that included interpretations of various rules by a campus leader and fellow inmate, I was shown to my dorm and my room. The building, cold as the bricks it was constructed with, was an example of perfect space management. The rooms lined the far wall and the TV/group room faced the staff office. I unpacked in silence, as everyone was at school, and afterward was directed to the kitchen for lunch. I sat in my room alone for the hours before everyone returned. I thought of Terry, my mother, Abbie, and especially, Tony. I wondered where they were and if they thought of me. I knew I was alone, and the thoughts of my various family members, who were only concerned with their own agendas, left me empty inside. I had no one any longer and it hurt, deeply.

The door to my room swung open and Ruben burst in, leaving me barely enough time to wipe my tears away. My new roommate was 13 and an American Indian. He was as hyper as any thirteen-year-old I had ever met, but also twice as big. He greeted me with a flurry of questions and a huge smile. We very quickly became friends, sharing what little we had with one another. Ruben's father was a very abusive drunk, and the scars on Ruben's face attested to his rage. Ruben shared his experiences with me and I in turn with him. He was the first person I had ever talked to about Jackie and Shirley, and it felt good to have an ear that could relate. We spent many nights awake till 2 or 3 am, exchanging horror stories and small triumphs with each other.

Foster Parent/Guardian Rule No. 8: *Listen Up!*

There are few things more helpful than having someone who will be a good listening friend for you. If you ever have the privilege of a child offering you their personal story, insights, or perspectives, then, with all due respect, close your mouth, don't assume, and don't be pushy.

The doorframe to our room was the outside perimeter for any interracial camaraderie in our dorm. Everyone was divided into small groups based on skin color, gang affiliation, and even music. Black, white, yellow, brown, and then Ruben. I stayed out of the cliques and spent most of my time around Ruben. The entire campus of Guadalupe was bused to our own staffed private school, where the small segregated groups tripled and quadrupled. The busy schedule and harsh penalties kept fighting to a minimum. Our "counselors" acted more as our jailers, looking to quell any trouble before it started. It was hard to find a staff that was there because they really wanted to help troubled teens. Most just wanted a steady paycheck, not wanting to invest themselves in their job, and this was obvious. These staff even formed their own cliques as they monitored their prisoners—our "role models".

At our private school, five teachers rotated groups of students by age levels in core subjects. Our P.E. teacher was a serious bodybuilder and offered many training techniques, rewarding outstanding efforts with sugary treats. He'd finish the week with a cross-country run contest, offering a six-pack of soda to the fastest time among each class, and another for the fastest in the school. This proved to be my first opportunity to display my physical prowess, and after turning in a time that had edged the rest of the campus scores, I was given a note of celebrity. When asked, I didn't hesitate to tell coach my secret of focusing on something that had brought a lot of pain in my life and once in "the zone," I didn't feel my legs. He offered a compassionate look along with two six-packs, once I finished telling him everything. In comparative real world value, each six-pack was worth about twenty dollars in our placement currency. And all of a sudden I had friends I never knew before. I blew them off and shared what I had with Ruben.

Every day after school we had a large therapeutic group meeting where everyone was given the chance to talk about their life, their day and any feelings associated with either or both. In order to advance up the level system, you had to show that you were willing to put yourself out there. Many participated to brag and look tough, but most only shared anything in mock sincerity; they just wanted a higher level and more privileges. Everyone knew that our groups were the most important part of the game of being locked up here. What we said went in our files and hence, to our probation officer. Some peers didn't care about any of this or about doing their program and getting out, and remained destructive and sometimes aggressive during our groups. The staff interfered only slightly with these dynamics when things were starting to get out of control. We had an information board that hung in the group room that had short bios on everyone and negative peers often used it against us. All of your information—what city you were from, your age, your probation officer, everything—was used to play the game of trying to disrespect one another and set somebody off. Groups became a way of finding out information that you could use to piss an enemy off, to push their buttons when you needed or just wanted to. We spent a lot of time talking about anger management in group; but with so many short fuses in one room and only small networks of friends, it rarely did any good.

A weekly one-to-one session with a psychiatrist was also part of the program, and to my utter shock, Dr. Sandler, who had been the house psychiatrist at Father Matthew's, was the provider. After all these years, I was face to face with the man who had been key to having Tony and I separated. I didn't hold back the second I saw him.

He looked at me in disbelief as I started in before he could make an introduction. "You're the doctor that had me and

my brother separated! A long time ago, when I was six, at
Father Matthew's!" The question in his eyes quickly
disappeared as a smile came over his face and he nodded his
head.

"I remember Father Matthew's. That was a long time
ago." He turned a few pages in my file. After finding a clue he
offered, "You're that Louis Martinez? I remember, Louie and
Tony, right?'

"Louis."

"I didn't agree with what they decided and my
arguments with that home over many issues forced me to quit."

"You didn't help them? But you took me out to Bob's
Big Boy, you got me away so they could take him." I was still
standing.

"It was the only way there could be a smooth transition
for your brother...we didn't want you to go off." Dr. Sandler
could tell I wasn't satisfied. "Besides, they said that they were
taking you with them after he adjusted. I guess they didn't?"

"No. They didn't. His new mom has done everything to
keep us apart. Moving, changing phone numbers; she hates me
or something."

"She is probably just threatened that your brother will
choose you over them." Finally, he had put into words what I
had been feeling all along. I gave Dr. Sandler the benefit of the
doubt, and in my position, I really couldn't afford to have
enemies anyway. I told him a few things about by brother, the
rest of my family and some of my experiences. It was almost as
if he was my student—he'd hang on every word and ask lots of
questions about programs and the System in general. Always, at
the end of a session, he offered everyone a choice of candy from
a large chest. He offered me double, and for some reason I took
it as a show of respect for what I had been through. A sort of
peace offering for the years of torment I had endured. At least
that's how I took it.

As program months passed, I had made my way up the
level system and earned a position on a paycrew. A paycrew

was a privilege for only the top 10-15 kids among all dorms. We were paid a dollar an hour and given in excess whatever our job offered. Therefore, as a kitchen worker, I got double portions and sometimes got to take food back to the dorm—which was otherwise forbidden. The more "juice" I got, the more I could bargain with other boys (and sometimes even staff) to get the items I couldn't get without a home pass. But right as I was starting to get a little comfortable, Ruben was discharged. To add insult to injury, I was forced to room with Eric, an overly muscled white supremist.

Now I, who had been endeared by the acceptance of black and brown people and the one constantly abused by those of lighter skin, was going to be put to this test by the staff. They saw my dress and took note of whom I was inclined to talk to and pushed the issue. We stayed on opposite sides of the room and never spoke at first. We argued when he would play his heavy metal crap and he would complain about my rap and R&B. But over time, our grudges wouldn't hold, as we would laugh while making fun of each other's music. "Kill your momma, drink goat's blood, dah dah dah dah!" Shaking my head and playing the air guitar. He would retort with, "Do a drive by and kill some little kids, boom boom." We both had points, but chose to see the flaws in our petty music-based prejudices and forged a friendship. In the world of orphans and foster kids, and sometimes single-parent families, racism was commonly an excuse to vent or a façade to gain acceptance. After getting to know one another and letting our shields down, we began to see each other and not each other's social training. He agreed to listen to the Naughty By Nature and Cypress Hill and I agreed to give Metallica and Guns and Roses a trial. Having spent the last months with Ruben, my mind was already open to finding out about the other cultures of my dorm "brothers." To my shock, I actually liked some of the music; like Metallica's "One," Guns and Roses ballads of "November Rain" and "Don't Cry." Eric caved on many Cypress Hill songs, and through our willingness to laugh at ourselves and try something new, we had broadened our horizons.

Once we had let our guard down, we found that we had many similar issues. Eric had been abandoned by his father when he was little, and had to live with his neglectful white supremist uncle in a racist part of a community in Hemet, California. After a couple of years, his mother came back to get him. He was a ball of racial hatred that she couldn't handle, and eventually, his actions got him put in this program. We had many heated talks over his use of the "N" word. But finally, when we were venting about our pasts and he was trying to defend his racist views, I attacked his logic and he gave in.

"All those dirty Mexicans are invading my country and stealing our jobs!"

After relaying my onion field experience, he admitted that he wasn't looking for that kind of job. Then I went on, "I've driven from Colorado to California and there is so much open, unused country out there. The countryside looks just as open as Hemet for hundreds and hundreds of miles. I don't think we are going to run out of space anytime soon." With the consummate nerd always hiding inside me, I went on to give him a little history lesson on manifest destiny and he received a lot of the information without much objection. Although he didn't put away his façade while out in our lock-up community, he stopped using racial slurs when we were in our room.

The main dynamics of placement were that either you remained who you were, "fronted" your program, in effect faking it or "doing time," and usually got kicked out—or you actually started to make changes and altered your thoughts and perceptions to better yourself. The amount of boys and staff at a large placement like this home made these decisions obvious. No one was able to sit on the fence, because it was being pushed on so hard by both sides—the ones who realized they needed to change—and those who refused.

The boy who took Ruben's bed, Michael, was a gangbanger from LA County. He was extremely arrogant, and once he found during a group session that I had been involved in gangs, it wasn't long before he found out which color. The fact that I had befriended a white supremist was totally unacceptable to him and he branded me with the name "Buster" (a chump). I knew that I had to respond or face having to wear the punk label until the day I left—and who knew how long that would be? I got mad immediately. Who was he to call me anything? He didn't know a thing about me, other than that I had a white roommate that I was cool with.

For this he challenged me, openly trying to punk me in front of everyone and calling me a sellout. I refused to stop talking to Eric and give in to his harassment. I wanted to beat the crap out of this guy, but I knew that my level would get dropped and I would lose what little privileges I had worked for. My privileges were everything to me, as I never went on a home pass or ever received any phone calls. I had NOTHING to lose other than my level. I tried my best to not give up my privileges just to prove myself. He took it as though I was afraid of him, and because he was six feet tall and a trim 140 lbs., it wasn't hard to convince the others. Our two resident devil worshippers (literally), Robert and Jaime, loved to instigate anything, and did their best to encourage a fight. I held on for a week and that was it.

During a group session, Michael taunted whenever I spoke, whispering, "Buster," 'Mark," and "Punk." And finally I responded. My eyes deliberate, I said, "Say it one more time and we'll see who's the buster."

Cocky smile and all, he did say it, and I stood and darted over to him. As I got close, he lifted his feet to kick at me but I slid between them and began punching. I let off as many as I could; with a week's worth of vengeance powering my shoulders, he became my punching bag. I could feel staff pulling at my mid-section and I put him in a headlock, forcing him to the ground with me. I shoved his head into the linoleum-covered concrete floor before staff was able to separate us. I was lifted and thrown to the couch. The second I hit the seat I

purposefully remained completely still. With only one staff
blocking me with his leg, I resolved not to move. I just enjoyed
the show of Michael getting slammed repeatedly by multiple
staff as he tried again and again to get up and come for me.
When he was finally worn out, he submitted to being pinned on
the floor. But not before one of his flailing arms had caught a
female staff in the mouth and busted her lip. Charges were
automatically pressed, and Michael was gone. But before the
sheriff came to pick him up, he had to listen to everyone taunt
him, "Who's a buster?" and "Who's the punk now?"

My level was dropped, but because of the circumstances
of him riding me all week, I was only dropped one level and got
to keep my paycrew. On top of that, I was elevated to superstar
status around campus for the way I handled the fight. The part
about sitting down calmly afterward to watch staff take him
down repeatedly was a keynote. Robert and Jaime, who had
done so much to instigate the fight, were vociferous in their
attempt to play down the altercation. They had something of a
hold on the dorm, because some were afraid of the devil
worshipping antics that went on in their room. Many new kids
were scared at the pentagrams they drew on the floor and the
chicken bones they kept. They both even grew out their nails
and sharpened them to fine points, when they could get away
with it. With their big mouths, they threatened anyone who tried
to push them off their power pedestal. I had always paid them
little mind, they were obvious attention seekers to me. But with
my new status as a physical leader, they felt challenged and
came after me to earn their spot back.

While playing a basketball game of 21, an every-man-
for-himself game, they teamed to score, even passing the ball to
each other. They fouled and added points to their scores to try to
beat me and I wasn't able to contain my frustration. Instead of
walking away, knowing their motives, I took everything too
personally because of my love of basketball. I tripped Jaime and
grabbed Robert by the throat and spun him around into a
headlock. As the staff started to notice, one of the other boys

said "staff" and I dropped Robert to the ground. As the staff approached, everyone tried acting like we were playing ball without conflict.

"What's going on over here?"

The collective, "Nothing" meant to dissuade intervention was useless. We were called to the group room and forced to settle an issue we kept insisting didn't exist. The staff were adamant and we finally offered that we were horseplaying, an offense that carried a level drop, but not possible expulsion from the program. Everyone in the group supported our story and offered level drops to the staff, but they weren't satisfied. They knew what they saw, and though they couldn't get the support of the group, they still had options to punish us.

"Critical" was the sentence. This sub-level meant the revocation of all privileges and less than introductory (or first week) privilege level. To Robert and Jaime, it was a momentary setback, but I took it much harder. My level and its privileges were all I had, and knowing that the staff decision was final, I made sure that they knew how deeply their consequence cut me. I stood and tossed a chair through a large plate glass window. I next turned over the pool table and picked up a pool stick looking for something to break. Everyone, including staff, scattered. The staff closed themselves in the office and the kids all ran to their rooms or to the emergency exit. I threw a chair at the TV and then went to my room and packed a few things in my backpack.

I barged out of the dorm and was met by multiple staff, ready to attack. Marcus, one of the few staff whom I trusted with personal information, asked them if they would back off as he tried to reason with me while I walked off campus. He tried to tell me that no matter what, everything would work itself out. I explained what happened, and how it seemed that everyone wanted to make sure I didn't get ahead. How I didn't want to work hard for my level to just have to deal with my dorm brothers jealously trying to make me lose it. I pleaded with him for an answer. What was the point of my existence? To live in these homes and always live by all these rules? I had to live by a strict code of conduct 24 hours a day, seven days a week, or there were to be consequences. I was never allowed to just have a bad day. And even if it was a staff that came in with a bad attitude and found fault in any small action, there would never be any fairness, it would be my fault no matter what. When was I ever going to be able to act like a teenager? Where was the slack for me to deal with raging hormones and elevated emotions in such a rigid, confined setting as placement? As always, there was no answer to give, I was just expected to be able to deal with everything, including being an orphan, by some innate skill.

After a while, Marcus turned and informed me that he would have to call the Sheriff. "Go do what you gotta do then!" I didn't want to be harsh with him even at this point, but I needed to push him as far away as possible. I walked the streets and late into the night I made it to a gas station. I didn't want to go any farther and I knew what was in store for me. I would be looking over my shoulder for the police and then get double the sentence by some frustrated judge tired of dealing with troublemakers like me. I decided to be proactive and accept the inevitable. I called the police and told them where I was and that I was ready to go to Juvenile Hall. They came and picked me up, instead driving me back to Guadalupe.

"Where are we going?" I asked.

"To get the authority to send you to the Hall." The officer must have had some database or been told something about the runaway from Guadalupe. "It must be hard to not have any family? You must get very angry and lonely."

What did he know? Words can't, and never will, be able to relay how hard it is day in and day out, knowing that you have no one. He further offered, "Sometimes you just need to blow up to get everything off your chest, huh?"

I let out a mumbled, "Yeah." He was right, and the mention of my lack of family rubbed in another fact—no one would care that I had gotten in trouble or run away. When I got back, they said that they'd have to wait until Monday to process the paperwork and discharge me. Even then I had a sneaking suspicion that they were lying, but it wasn't confirmed until Monday. My staff, after getting the full story, kept me on critical but made a deal to speed up the level earning process in light of the new information, and only restricted me from paycrew for a week. The fight and then the outburst had made my name soar through the dorms as some kind of bada**.

But none of this notoriety was of any real value to me. I spent many weekend hours alone in the bathroom, holding my head in my hands, mourning a family I almost had and the brother I had lost, standing on the toilet, peering through my tiny window and watching in agony as the other boys went on home pass and ran to the open arms of their respective families. My right hand laid over my left so that I could pretend someone was trying to comfort me. I felt like I should have never been born. I was so out of place, and didn't belong on this planet.

Music was invaluable in helping me cry deeply enough so that my levels of depression could fluctuate. When we went on outings in the community, I caught myself family-watching, looking on at something I was convinced I'd never have. I sank deep into my thoughts, and was totally alone. I know I projected a hard shell. But that's all it was, a shell. I was like any other kid. I craved the same things. I just wanted to be loved and accepted. I could be a nice kid, I could put away my tough exterior; but I never got the chance. I drew whenever I could, and read anything I could get my hands on. I had made deals with kids for access to kitchen goods if they brought me back novels by Robert Ludlum and Clive Cussler. I did my all to lose myself in their stories.

There were a few sunny program days. I wrote a letter to Kathy Borowski (YMCA Catalina trip) and she sent a letter and a picture of herself. While I never wrote her again, it was nice to have a picture of someone who cared a little that I existed. Eric, having told his sister of my situation, had come back from pass with a letter for me and the option to have a pen pal. I took him

up on it, and the couple of responses I got at first gave me a
little hope, but then I was forced to admit to myself that our
writing situation wasn't normal. I stopped writing because I
didn't want to have someone writing me because of pity. When
the school year ended, I was given numerous certificates of
merit at a small ceremony held for Guadalupe. Good grades
weren't hard for me to get, as I had nothing else to keep me
busy. My paycrew leader, Phil, was proud of my
accomplishment and because of my hard work ethic he started
extending extra privileges. He matched my earnings and I got
two dollars an hour, making me the envy of all the other crew.
He would brush off their jealous comments with, "You show
me a bunch of A's and some effort around here and I'll give you
a raise too." None of them followed through and knowing that
my pay was a direct result of behavior, they stopped harassing
me... mostly.

Diana, our dorm supervisor, had also allowed me extra
privileges because of my little successes. No one was allowed to
have a boom box, but after the awards, she took me down and
let me buy whatever radio I wanted with my paycrew savings.
On top of that, she would randomly place a bag of goodies on
my bed just for maintaining status (level). Her interest and
gestures to make me feel like my efforts weren't in vain helped
me to not focus on the negative so much and try to remain the
big brother of the dorm.

Many kids came up to me from all dorms and asked how
I had gotten this or earned that. And when a kid was upset, I
was often first to speak to him to de-escalate him and keep him
out of trouble. In group, this had pros and cons. I was sought
out as a peer leader and respected by the staff, but then again, I
was used as an example to struggling youths, often with the
reasoning, "Louis doesn't have any family, he can't even earn a
home pass, and he's doing good." Sometimes I was even asked
painful direct questions by staff, such as, "Why do you choose
to help everyone else?" or "Why didn't you give up?"

I had no conscious insight to give at that age and usually replied, "It just feels good to help others." These interactions made clear why I often went into the bathroom to be alone and cry. I never voiced the fact that I actually felt I was only building psuedo-relationships. I felt that I was the one being fake by acting like I was deeply invested in helping others when, on the inside, I resented them, mistrusted them, and was jealous of them. I knew that it was only a matter of time before *they* went home. It hurt that I didn't have anyone to share my accomplishments with. If another kid got an A on his report card or earned a level, his parents would shower him with affection and gifts at the miracle. However, if I received all A's, earned countless awards and maintained the highest level, I had no one to turn to for even a congratulatory parental hug or kiss, and it stung like hell.

I started seriously contemplating suicide again. Every day in group I listened to someone talk about their family—their brother, sister, mother or father. Every day I felt left out and worthless. Thinking about the last time I saw my mother broke my heart all over again. Watching every other boy work on a Mother's Day project or one of the many other special day projects in our art therapy building was more icing on the same cake.

I would ask myself why I had this "gift" called life. I would never have a family, and love was never going to be mine. Becoming transfixed on these thoughts, I found a way to get a knife in trade from a kid on pass. Although I was excelling in the program, the cumulative stress from my life had balled up and pushed at me for a response. I went into the bathroom, and night after night, I would sit on the toilet and do whatever I could to convince myself I needed to live. On the outside, program-wise, I was every other boy's envy. I had every privilege and the staff really listened to me and took my side. But on the inside, I hid the blackness, the emptiness and cries that craved to be silenced. I wanted death and release from the life that seemed too much for my struggling heart to bear.

Praying long and hard for answers, I tried to ask God for direction and forgiveness. I would try to make deals with Him. If He would only give me a family, I would live on only to praise Him. I prayed fervently and often emotionally. Maybe I prayed wrong, maybe there really wasn't a God. Without an answer to my prayers, I thought it was inevitable that I should take my life. But then an answer came.

In the middle of one night, not long after I had cried myself to sleep, I was awakened by my bed leaping off the ground. The room rolled and shook, objects and furniture were jerked around, and I thought the building was going to come down on me. My roommate started yelling in fear and I called out, "Earthquake!"

After a few long moments, the room stopped vibrating and I tentatively put my foot on the ground. It was terrifying to think that death wasn't going to wait, but had come for me. It seemed as though I had lost control of any option regarding life and death and God was telling me that I was playing a serious game. Through the earthquake, He literally shook me awake, physically and mentally.

In the following weeks, the dorms pulled together to help clean up the mess the earthquake had made. We talked to one another about the possibility of death, and many boys confided in our group sessions that they had often thought about suicide. But now, having had their lives seriously threatened, they knew they wanted to live, and we all talked of plans for the future. Everyone reached out for aspirations to work as a professional or in a family business, to be a part of their babies' lives growing up, and to be a positive part of their families again. It seemed that God had shaken the very foundation of all these wayward kids and they took their lives seriously again— even if, for some, it was only for a few weeks. The earthquake ended up being one of the largest in California history, a 7.3, and Guadalupe, sandwiched between three fault lines, took a heavy hit from it. Some of the buildings had major damage—

but the main effect on Guadalupe was the impact it had on the boys.

I listened to the boys and their plans for the future and began to look for something I might reach for. My mind settled on a 5th grade photo of my brother. I reached back to the center of my heart and thought, "Maybe I could become successful and then Tony might come live with me." From that point on, I would worked every day to build a life that my brother might want to be a part of. I could find him again and have a family—my family. This wind of reinvigoration filled my sails on this sea of hope. I had the answer to my prayers, and a first step towards dealing with my past—I had a goal.

My suicidal thoughts subsided and I doubled my efforts around the dorm. I still dealt with some of my peers, mostly newer ones, playing games with me, trying to start a fight or get me to say something that might make me lose my privileges or level. But now I knew better, and I wouldn't give in. Constantly repeating to myself that they weren't worth it, I put up with their games and focused on what was really important to me—graduating my program and looking toward the future, a future that I was making serious plans for. And this is the one great credit that I give to my stay at this program: that I got to develop and put into practice how to make daily choices, mostly about dealing with my anger or peers, that would have a positive impact on my future, or toward my goals.

After a seven-month stay, I was given a certificate of completion from Guadalupe and sent to an emancipation house in Fontana. My program graduation ceremony was enormous. All the teachers came and I had my paycrew supervisor, Phil, give the traditional farewell speech for me. Everyone gave me hugs and a few kisses (female staff only) and I felt important, if just for a day. Feeling like I had people who were sincerely concerned that I had made it through the program, I almost didn't want to go. I basked in the room's affections, which, by far dwarfed any affectionate gestures I had experienced throughout my entire life combined. I got a huge ten-foot banner, filled with the signatures of everyone I knew, staff and youth, and comments of praise and of support for my future. I was not able to prevent my eyes from tearing up, and for the first time in my life, I felt like I really counted, like I had the option to do something with my life, and my dream to make a life for Tony and me wasn't so far-fetched. I got in the van to go to my new placement with a sense of purpose and accomplishment that I had not known before, coupled with the training and resolve to follow it through.

Chapter 20 - Final Interlude with Juvenile Justice

At least the System legally recognizes now that being an orphan or ward of the court means that you have been tossed into a hole without resources. Over the years up to today, this statement has been constantly reclarified, as newer and more comprehensive programs pop up to help young adults "age out" of the System. "Age-out" is the term meaning that on your 18th birthday, the System remands you to your own custody and you must now take on the world with whatever is in your suitcase—both physically and mentally.

In the mid-90's, when I was aging out, these programs were like candy stores for some. The piggy bank was easy to raid because no one really knew how to define what was important to teach a child that was aging out. So by definition, my new placement was supposed to prepare me to emancipate—to get ready to move out and live on my own. At minimum, I was supposed to learn the concepts and real-world math of how to function as an adult and handle the living expenses and responsibilities that my parents, the state, had been shouldering my whole life.

My new placement in Fontana had no such program available.

"Mom," as everyone was expected to call her, ran a four-bed house with little help from her son, a 27-year-old ex-Dallas Cowboy. Our life skills training included house chores and microwaving foods. We did have a few nice dinners that Mom prepared, but she never taught any of us how she made them. Mom would also take us to her church and have us volunteer to clean around the large buildings. She was a small, middle-aged woman who was very obviously running a cash crop house. She didn't get involved or inquire about any of our school issues or living needs. She often locked herself in her room or headed out alone to be with her friends.

Foster Parent/Guardian Rule No. 9: *Be a Positive Role Model!*

Every action and response will be observed, measured and often emulated. System kids already know the general rules or ideal of the System; instead, share the little things in life. Be a great communicator, for the curt response, "Because I said so," is either for violent adult inmates of prisons or someone else whose views you don't feel deserve to be recognized.

The up-side to this was that she allowed us the freedom to roam the streets, as long as we didn't break curfew and got her house chores done. The first time I walked out of that house with Allen, my roommate, I couldn't help but take in a deep breath and smell the heady air of freedom around me. I walked the streets and would look in one direction or another and smile at the thought, "I can go down that street if I want to."

Phil, my paycrew supervisor from Guadalupe, came out to visit me a couple of times to make sure I was okay. He encouraged me to do well in school and talked about how to go about getting a job. He truly acted as an uncle to me, showing me how to fill out job applications and talking with me about the importance of saving money. And once, when my jacket got stolen at school (and "Mom" wouldn't do anything but blame me), he took me down to Miller's Outpost and bought me the jacket of my choice—a jacket I have kept to this day. But "Mom" didn't like being upstaged and accused Phil of harboring sexual agendas in visiting me—after that, he was no longer allowed to visit.

The next visitor who was to be cut from my life was my new Social Worker. She had bought me art supplies and a silk shirt for Christmas and taken me to see her husband's airplane, all in the short couple of weeks I knew her. Again, "Mom" implied that something was going on more than just social work. Before I knew it, I had no visitors, as I waited for a new social worker to be assigned.

I was enrolled at Fontana High, an extremely tough urban school. I immediately felt comfortable in the classrooms filled with attitudes similar to those I had been locked up with. I knew to be guarded and I knew when someone was offering friendship. I felt normal here. I flirted with the girls in my class and reached out to join one of the athletic programs. I tried out for the basketball team and was suspiciously told to play a tryout game with some obvious rejects. I kept looking around for approval when I stole or passed, but coach didn't even look in my direction. As a junior (by age), I was not even close to six foot six. Although disappointed, I accepted the inevitable, not even bothering to look at the cut list.

Then I tried out for the wrestling team and my judo and jujitsu skills made for a perfect match. One of the assistant coaches there rode me just a little harder than everyone else. I did my best to ignore him and focused on trying to make the 152-weight class. All the spots were filled, and I was a reserve due to all the other wrestlers grandfathering-in. At our first tournament I was benched, as well as the second. The third, however, was a Varsity match that the junior varsity was supposed to watch and learn from. The assistant coach who disliked me thought he could embarrass me by allowing me to compete for the first time. "Don't expect to win anything, but if you want to, you can wrestle the 152's for us." I invite you to take a look at the size and abilities that fill the 152-weight class at any high school, and I'm sure you'll see why coach was confident he was going to teach me some lesson.

He was wrong. He had no idea how thoroughly I had soaked in every lesson and technique taught in practice, or how hard I trained. He didn't really pay attention to me and was put off by my ability to grasp advanced techniques, though I was a first-year wrestler. Even though I dislocated my shoulder in one of the final matches and couldn't continue, I placed third in the 8-school tournament. Coach gave me a little respect after that.

As I walked between school, jobsites, and home, I took the time to contemplate my place in the world. Often fighting bouts of depression, recovering from bad dreams or haunting thoughts, I could feel that I was different from everyone around me. Taking in another group of peers at school (now my 18th), I finally understood what answer I had been seeking during all those years of "people watching." Where everyone was, or where they were going, had a lot to do with where they were from. So I took time to sit and really answer these questions for myself: Where was I from; and where did I plan on going? With some soul-searching, I was able to articulate the answers in a journal. I embarked on this maturing process because I was apprehensive about aging out of the System and I didn't want to feel as lost as I felt walking home from school alone, with unsettling thoughts about my personal worth. Here is a rough draft from my journal entries:

> This is my legacy, where I am from. I have been abandoned, abused, and neglected in the System. I have been raised by cruel foster parents and rigid staff. But mostly, I have been influenced by, and soaked in the values of, hundreds of destructive, aggressive, authority-defying juveniles.

> This is where I want to go. I want to be normal and have a good life. I need to defy my training. I must reject System values, like proving

> myself physically, stealing, revenge, hatred of the police, and others, that were handed to me and laughed about. These values could keep me in the System by leading to adult incarceration. I need to be a leader. I have to be smart. I have to be nice. I can get a job and save some money. I can live near Tony and we can raise our families together.

Every day I carried my journal and added countless notes to it—some to do with my current situations, and many to do with my future. The folder was also where I kept my job applications and homework assignments. I felt that as long as I held onto my journal, I physically held onto the hope that I could be normal, and have a good life. Attending Fontana High made this a daily proposition, because there was so much negativity in the student body. I refused to be influenced by these kids, who probably were on their way to Guadalupe or something similar very soon. It had been hard to maintain focus at home, as well, because my emancipation housemates had not made any preparations or come to any conclusions about what they planned to do when they aged out of the System. Most of them had some family member who was ready to take them in once they left. And finally, "Mom" couldn't be counted on to offer any guidance—she just wanted a check. I felt alone in my quest, but I knew that I wouldn't be alone if I accomplished my goals.

Then the "Curse" of System life struck again. Allen and Billy had been snooping around "Mom's" room and found her 22mm handgun and a stash of pornographic movies. When I came through the door, they were watching the videos and Allen jumped to show me the gun. "Now we know why she locks herself in the room!" I was briefly shocked and intrigued by their discoveries, but then wanted no part.

These two became bosom buddies and their actions snowballed. They were shoplifting and getting into fights at school. I kept my head down and avoided them whenever possible.

In a matter of months, my plan was bearing fruit—I was accomplishing tasks at school and getting second interviews for jobs. But suddenly my placement came to an abrupt finale. Coming home one day from school and job-hunting, I passed "Mom's" room to hear people having sex on the other side of the door. I thought for sure that the forty-five-or-so-year-old woman couldn't be responsible for the noises, and it was probably her ex-pro football player son, who had brought many girls home for dinner, who was making the sounds. Admittedly, I was curious to see what was going on and I cracked the door open. To my complete shock, Allen and "Mom" were in the bed together. My jaw hit the floor. The sound from the door's hinges or my shadow caused Allen to turn and see me, as I tried to leave.

They got up and "Mom" came to my doorway in a pink robe. She stared a hole in me as I tried to pretend not to see her and ruffled through my homework. She didn't say a word. Allen slept on the couch that night (most likely to avoid having to look into my eyes). I knew that a fuse had been lit, and I was going to be the one who was blown up. Anyone who has been on probation knows how easy it is to have you violated without any evidence. I knew I would get the boot and I panicked. I wasn't going back to Juvie; I wasn't going to let someone else, with just a few strokes of a pen, determine how my life was going to go.

I stuffed a duffle bag and stole as much food as I could the next morning. "Mom" usually went to visit a friend after breakfast and that is when I planned to make a break for it. But to my own folly, I had waited too long. Right as I was zipping my bag, two officers entered my room. With just a sigh, I assumed the position I was so used to taking—knees bent on a chair until shackled and hands folded behind my back until handcuffed. I knew that any argument would be futile and that these officers wouldn't do anything to help me. I had been beaten and cried out and no one had responded; I had tried to complain about how a group home was being run, and no one cared. Telling these two officers that the reason I was being violated was because our housemother was having sex with one of the 17-year-old boys was surely going to be useless. In fact, because I sat so quietly on the way to Juvie, one of the officers commented, "You seem like a decent boy, wonder why you're being violated." It was probably unusual that someone in my position wasn't giving excuses, but they weren't really interested, they just wanted a possibly amusing story to pass the time.

In one fell swoop; one person had shot down my every effort at normalcy with no more than a few words over the phone. At first, I accepted this as the hard facts of the System, but when they put me in solitary because I was a runaway risk, I went into a rage over how unjust virtually everything in the System had been for my entire life. I was shackled and handcuffed whenever I was out of my cell, and the guards barked orders, waiting for a chance to "prove" that they were in control. How much of this could anyone take? I promised myself then that I would never see the inside of a jail cell again. My anger grew hot, and when yet another probation officer saw me, he took my accusations of the sexual escapade as a far-fetched effort at retaliation.

Angrily I asked, "Then why was I violated? What did I do to get kicked out?"

"You weren't complying with the rules by not getting along with the house mother."

"What?! Check out my grades, ask the other boys! I never got in any trouble and I hardly talked with "Mom." I was just about to get a job!" He didn't care, and the tone of my voice, in his mind, only confirmed what he thought.

Again before the judge in a courtroom who had no time for talk or excuses, at least the judge got my name right this time. Violating probation right after release from placement didn't look good, and the judge ordered me to another placement—one that I had no chance of leaving until I was 18.

When I got back to the Hall, I was assigned a unit, this time with the oldest kids. Jailhouse rules applied doubly in this new house and the guards were twice as tough. I kept quiet, although I was seething inside. I met up with a number of kids I had practically grown up with in the System, kids from various high schools, placements, and from previous admissions to juvenile hall. Most surprisingly, Eric, my roommate from Guadalupe, was there. I felt a note of familiarity, knowing that I had many acquaintances in all racial categories. The only inmates I had to worry about were the gangbangers. There wasn't a dominant one and they were in the middle of a struggle for power when I arrived. People were getting jumped in the bunk area and during hall clean-up. Weapons were everywhere, from sharpened toothbrushes to pencils smuggled in from school. Our unit was on a constant state of lockdown and tensions were very high. I remained quiet and looked at my surroundings in disbelief.

How did I end up here? Didn't I serve my time? How could they resentence me to another placement without having committed another crime?

As I was getting lost in my thoughts, one of the Esse gangbangers took the thoughtful expression on my face as a sign of weakness.

As they were handing out evening snacks, I had refused mine—not entirely uncommon—but the Esse sitting next to me ordered, "Get your food homz; I want it." There was no question as to the implication of this exchange. If I got it, then I would be marked a punk and everyone would take a turns getting what they could. It was a threat that had to be answered, lest I wanted to wait in the paper line for placement every day in fear.

"F*** *** Esse." I mumbled under my breath.

"Get it or I'm going to f*** you up white boy."

I clenched my fists, and uttered a little deeper and louder, "I could kick your a** with one arm behind my back. Shut the f*** up." My voice carried and a guard turned and demanded to know who was speaking.

"This dude right here. He said he could kick my a** with one arm behind his back homz."

"Ratta." I lastly mumbled. The guard, "T-bone," as he was known, didn't like all the racial tension so he was going to make an example out of the white man. (I'm sure much of his response had a lot to do with the Rodney King beating and trial that was all over the news at the time). He waved one finger and motioned me toward the back solitary rooms. After pushing me to the ground and telling me how I wasn't s***, he locked me away for the final weeks of my stay. I knew that unintentionally he had done me a favor. I would surely have been jumped or stabbed if I was back in general population to face the gangbanger I threatened. I sat in my cage, rotting from the inside out and waiting for what would happen next. I knew that I was powerless in my life and in this System—a fact that was crushingly made clear every second I waited in my cell.

Part II

THE HAVEN OF DREAMS

Chapter 21 – Until I'm 18

"Give a little love to a child, and you get a great deal back."

—John Ruskin

My head bobbed as the van tumbled down the freeway to Chino. I was on my way to Boy's Republic, a placement well known throughout those locked in Juvie. Anger dominated me as the sun beat on my face through the window. I fumed at the thought of having to deal with another program, again. And this program was known to be far harder than Guadalupe, and to have twice as many inmates. Once more I would have to contend with a set of rules and expectations laid out for me by those who had never walked in an orphan's shoes.

My mind wove back and forth between thoughts of self-destruction and any possible future. Everything had been taken away with a phone call, and before I had set foot on the program's grounds, I had it in my mind that I was DONE. The System had failed me, horribly at times. I would not cooperate, I would not be a victim again, and I would not believe anything they said. My mind raced to bitterly review the many directions and paths I had already been down. I was mad that I'd have to prove myself all over again to my peers. Then I thought about what would happen if I tried to fight back. I wanted this to be the last place I would have to live before being freed. No matter how terrible it might be, I had grown weary and exhausted of the many homes and situations I had faced and desired closure. I wanted the nausea from my life's colossal roller coaster to end. I was going to be 17 in a couple of months and stress tied me in knots as I tried to work out what I would do, and where I would go, when I turned 18.

I met with my cottage supervisor, Dan Kennan, to do the initial welcome and rules once over. Even then I couldn't contain myself and had to ask, "Why am I here? I already graduated placement and I didn't commit another crime."

He flipped through my folder and replied, "Um, here, it says, Grand Theft. You stole a car, right?"

"I've never stolen a car! Grand theft is the crime I got probation for two years ago! I graduated placement for that already! I didn't commit any crime to be here." I saw a ray of light for a split second, thinking that now they would realize that they had made a mistake and reassess my placement. That light was quickly extinguished.

"Well, if you violate your probation, they can send you here. Better just make the best of it."

Better make the best of it? He must be crazy! Didn't he hear me? I said I didn't commit any crime and yet I had been sent to one of the largest behavioral placements in the country! After a little infuriated thought, I realized he was right—I better make the best of it, or face a judge upset at seeing my record of multiple placements and decide I needed CYA. And if I got placed there, they said they could hold me until I was 25. What could I do, anyway? They held all the keys and had the ability to write whatever they wanted in my file. I finally accepted that the System owned me and anyone it employed was my immediate owner. They could place me anywhere and no one would care, except me. What could I do? I already knew the answer: Absolutely nothing, so I decided to try and keep my head down and deal with my placement day by day. I just wanted to lay low for a year and get out.

There was nothing else to argue and once we finished our intake, we left the office and walked up to Fowler Cottage.

My "System suitcase"- an overstuffed black plastic trash bag- in tow, I was dwarfed by my surroundings. Everything was so big. I was awestricken at the beauty of the landscaping—it looked like a college campus in the movies, with rolling grass-covered hills, huge, full trees, and large twenty-five to -thirty bed dormitories. The tour of the campus included a swimming pool and recreation center donated by a former BR resident, movie superstar Steve McQueen. There was a farm area with cows and a slaughterhouse, a full-sized indoor basketball gym, and a private school on campus with vocational printing, woodworking, and auto workshops. There was even an auditorium with a movie screen inside. At lunch, there were more choices and better tasting food than I had eaten in any System home. Although there were subtle telltale signs of who was from what gang, everyone ate and joked together with smiles on their faces. Yes, there were squabbles between gangs, drug dealing and fighting, but mostly from newcomers who hadn't bought into the program yet.

And what a buy-in it was. Every young man who came there was offered a chance for reform and the whole buy-in came in how the campus was run. A student government maintained much of the order on campus and in each separate cottage. Where Guadalupe left off, Boy's Republic had just begun. Boys were offered a chance to become men and develop leadership. Here we were more than just encouraged to mentor fellow struggling peers, 1:1 peer mentoring was mandatory if you wanted to achieve and maintain your citizenship. Citizenship meant that you were an active part of the community and a part of the student government. We had general elections for Mayor and Major pro tem. Each cottage voted in their own councilman, and had the power to endorse a candidate for one of the many commissioner positions. And only those who had bought in, who had earned their citizenship, could vote or be nominated.

The size and complexity of the place bewildered me at first. Nothing shoved this in my face more than standing in the two-person shower hall. Letting the water drum on the back of my neck, I stared intently at the pale blue tiles all around. How many different showers had I been in? The fact that I was naked seemed a perfect metaphor, if the shower represented the System. With the new shower room representing another move, I vigorously washed off my last placement and considered what lay ahead. I would not be moved again, but I was filled with trepidation as to how I could move forward. I didn't want to learn a new program and didn't feel I needed to be here. I should have been moved to another emancipation house where I was allowed to walk the streets, free, and join the school's extracurricular teams if I desired. But mostly as a teenager, I should be allowed to look at, and possibly interact with, GIRLS! I got so frustrated that I punched the blue tile wall. But just like trying to strike back at the System, I had no effect. I was still here, naked, powerless, and not given the dignity of choice or information.

I continued in my resolve to strike back for the first few weeks of my placement, refusing to buy in. The councilman at my cottage was also the drug dealer who had supplied me at Valley View High. He recognized me, and telling everyone I wasn't a punk, he helped me to avoid having to prove myself physically. After a couple weeks of attending classes, I was called in to see Lisa Recendez, our school guidance counselor, she informed me that I had less than fifty high school credits—I was still classified as a high school freshman. How could I move forward?

"What?! I know I earned some credits in the Hall and at Guadalupe. I can't still be a freshman, I'm almost seventeen!"

"I don't know what to tell you. I can look into the possibility of missing credits, but I doubt it'll turn up very much. The good news is that at this school you can work at your own pace and possibly earn a high school diploma faster than at a public high school. Or maybe, considering your credits, you could start preparing for a G.E.D." She went on to explain the difference and temper the bad news with school and vocational options that could follow either decision. But her words offered me little hope as they replayed in my mind throughout the day. I was nearly four years behind and I knew that I had only myself to blame. Although sidetracked by the years of abuse from Jackie and Shirley, and the training I received from the streets, I chose which lessons to keep and apply. I ditched class, I thought it was cool to not turn in homework, and I refused to take tests. I was a rebel and didn't want to be labeled a schoolboy, right? But now I deeply regretted it. How am I going to make a life for myself without at least a high school diploma? Not even the military will take high school dropouts anymore. The vision of me going to night school into my twenties to finish off my four years of high school bore down on me like an anvil. Why even try? I wasn't going to have a good job, and even if I found where my brother was, he wouldn't want anything to do with me. I couldn't move forward.

Foster Parent/Guardian Rule No. 10: *Never forget your first interview*

Remember why you started on the path towards being involved in the System. I know that at some point the question was raised, "Why do you want to work with children?" And the only answer that could have allowed you to take a step forward was "Because I want to help children..." Your interactions will never be forgotten, and any lessons, good or bad, will stay with them.

I gave up mentally first, then struck out physically. My new staff treated me like a number and I acted like I didn't care. I was hostile and surly, certain that no one was to be trusted. I got lost in the crowds of BR, seen as another punk who had pushed the rules of society too far and needed to be taught a lesson. I fought behind closed doors and projected a menacing disposition. In response to my behavior, I was told during group, by staff and kids alike, that there were no locks on the doors, and if I refused to do my program I should leave. I was tossed in the turbulent crosscurrents of turmoil as I took in how my life had gone and the dismal future that lie ahead. Screw it. In the middle of the night I sneaked down the fire escape and headed for AWOL Road. I sat on the long, red and white painted pole fence at the edge of the 200-acre campus, contemplating my life and my options.

Here I am, with no one to turn to, and no one that cares. This is the reality of "aging out" of the System: No one ever chose me. No one wanted me to be their son. I wasn't good enough to be in anyone's family. It's my own fault—I'm ugly, and I'm stupid. I'm just taking up space. Why am I here? What is the point of my life?

Then I turned to anger. This is everyone else's fault: my Fontana "mom" that searched for a sexual partner in a group home, Jackie, Shirley, Clyde and all the other staff at Father Matthew's, the System that took my brother from me, Donna for trying to kill herself, Henry and Karen, my parents, and my real family, whomever they are. So what if it is all their fault? So what. So what! So now what? What am I going to do?

I went through all the options running through my mind. At first my plans were emotional. I could jump out in the middle of the road the next time a car came by and end it— maybe the easiest of all the options. Or I could run back to LA and see if Rodney would take me in. But I understood the concept of imposing. Maybe I'll rob Jackie again—and maybe I'll spend the next twenty years in prison.

I didn't know what I should do. Then my brain kicked in. The core choices at hand were to give up or push on. All I owned in the world was packed tightly in a large duffle bag given to me by my roommate who said he never heard of a more messed-up life. I was an orphan and knew I had nothing to look forward to. A mental list of pro's and con's quickly surfaced. I had so many reasons to quit. Yet it ate at me that if I did, I would end up being the failure that my parents had been. The easy way out would have been to give up before I tried, blaming all those in my past for my failure. Would anyone blame *me*? Would God?

With that, I knew that taking my own life was probably what those in my past wanted—that I just lie down and give up. Maybe I could use this mental antagonism as motivation to push on? Could I make this a battle to prove my parents, my many tormentors and abusers wrong about my own worth? I had been pushed on and I had pushed back—I didn't want this cycle to continue forever. How can I stop it?

I accepted that I had no one in this world, and digging deep, it finally hit me that I had myself. My accomplishments would be for me.

I thought of Boys Republic and how for-real everything seemed to be. It was obvious that this was a placement where people were really concerned about results. I decided to see if Lisa was on the up and up and I could make up my credits fast. I reasoned that if things didn't work out, I could check out of this world anytime; but I was only going to get one chance at this "accelerated" program. I refused to be the failure so many assumed I would be.

I would have to say that this instance was the first time I actually sought to make real detailed decisions about how I would be the leader of my life. I decided that I was important, and I could build a future for myself. Sure this would prove painful and I would slide back and forth between happiness and depression. But I was not a different type of human—I could live a normal fulfilling life, as did others. I made a mental note of the things that truly seemed to make others content—family, friends, a secure job, a place to call home, helping others. Then I thought about how I would come to those phases or create those opportunities for myself. And not just as guesses and wishes, but how I would once and for all put away my System upbringing and do my all to remain positive.

On my walk back, I thought of Tony. I wondered what he was doing right then. I looked up at the full moon and thought; "Maybe we're sharing the same night scene right now.

Does he still care that he has a brother?" So many years had gone by—an entire childhood—and I could count on my hands the number of times I had seen my little brother. I wondered where my older sister Terry was. I know about gang life, and living on the streets left few options: drugs, prostitution and death. Sure, there was the fantasy that her boyfriend had married her and would provide for their new child, but it was too remote in the real world for it to have happened that way. My mother, I felt sure, was dead from drugs and living too hard. I started to convince myself that night that she had either had a drug overdose or contracted HIV. I didn't need anyone, I had myself—I could make it completely on my own. I held on to only a flicker of hope, fueled by a spark of determination. Keeping my life plan simple, I got back to the dorm willing to put my best foot forward on every step needed to accomplish my goals.

Within the next month I earned the approval of my dorm mates and I earned my citizenship. I focused intently on my schoolwork. The books we worked out of were standard high school criteria, and this was an accredited high school in the Chino Unified School District. My teachers, seeing my efforts and straight A's, allowed me to take books up to the cottages—normally prohibited. I participated in the program reservedly, using the small goals of finishing this chapter or that assignment to keep me distracted from the typical negative games that were played by my peers. I stayed out of fights and avoided the underground (hidden, against the rules and often illegal, activity) whenever I could. As I made more and more progress schoolwise, my rays of hope started to expand and brighten and my determination to achieve my goals solidified.

In the following months, I made solid plans that I would later make into small checklists to reach any particular goal. I called it "preparing to be 18 and a day." This may sound like a simple thing to do—to sit down and plot your life—but for me it was a daunting task, and one that I had in no way been prepared to do. To me, seeing specific goals in writing made them more real. (I guess this was because the only thing that made me a real person to my caregivers was my unwieldy System case file.)

One of the night staff, Darryl Wingate, allowed me to stay up well into the early morning, working from the light in the hallway as I lay in my doorframe. Many times he would nudge me awake to get to bed, as I had fallen asleep there. On nights that I was unable to curb my depression in order to focus on my schoolwork, he would lend me an ear as I vented and confided about my life. Never assuming, and always allowing me to share at a comfortable pace, Darryl became my best friend and a father figure I looked up to. And I had to look up to him, since he stood about six foot six. He took time to lend me a hand on my chores, and when my 17th birthday came around, and I felt lost in a canyon of depression, he surprised me with a trip to a park on his day off and taught me the most unusual thing: how to fly a kite. He was my one connection to normal humanity. He did his job, but in a way that was similar to how a parent would watch over their children or an uncle his nephews. He showed me what a normal balanced concern was, versus the typical overreaction by the staff when a small rule was bent or broken. His modeling helped me to put my institutional upbringing into perspective with real world expectations, lifestyle and attitudes.

I don't mean to give the impression that this one staff was enough to turn me into an angel or put my institutional guard down. I remained on alert and dealt with Darryl only when he worked his two or three nights a week. His was a face I saw seldom in comparison to all the other staff. I did start to bond with one "day staff," but then he quit and my acute sense of abandonment kicked in and I decided to relate only to Darryl. When my friend wasn't there, I didn't turn to anyone to talk about my daily pains. And I still dealt with a lot of them.

I remember waking up in the middle of many frigid winter and spring nights, freezing and trying to wrap myself in my program-provided thin blanket in a futile attempt to stay warm enough to sleep. I remember how cold my tears were while looking over at my roommates, who had an extra blanket or comforter that their parents had sent for them. I dealt with the pain of hearing the boys share letters from their family and thumbtacking photos that were sent on the wall. I did my best to avoid the hallways after dinner, when everyone would be fighting to be next on the phone to call their mother, father, friend or girlfriend. But mostly, I endured the crushing feeling during our groups, when peer after peer asked the cottage if they had earned a home pass. At BR we all had to vote yes or no and were obligated to bring up reasons why we thought the boy may or may not deserve to go home that weekend. But usually the vote just went around the group and everyone voted yes. I sat and listened to peer after peer tell the group what they would do on pass to prove to their family that they had changed and were worthy to be reunited.

"I'm going to help my mom with my baby sister and clean the garage with my dad this weekend."

"I'm going to spend the weekend at my cousin's birthday party and stay away from drugs."

"I'm going to show my baby's momma that I can be a good father and help change diapers and feed my son."

All these goals were things that most parents expect from their children and things I would be all too happy to do, if I had a family. But as common sense as these goals were, these boys had to prove they could do them. They had to prove they would follow through in being a productive part of their own family; something that I would have given my right arm for a chance at. It was only during Darryl's shift that I found a small amount of peace. In him, I had a friend who would often just give a compassionate look or encourage me to keep trying hard in school. Although meager, these rations of sincerity got me by.

By accepting his support, and with my determination, at the close of our traditional school year I had earned enough credits to catapult me into the 11th grade. I had become truly focused to blaze through my assignments. When I got tired or was working on a boring subject, I would play a simple mental game with myself, where I would challenge myself to "just finish this one assignment." And before I knew it, my game had earned me a hundred high school credits.

I was, however, slightly sidetracked by one of my dorm mates. Spencer was one of the quietest kids you would ever meet in your life, but he was also one of the most talented. After a mutual letting-down-of-the-walls, we exchanged horror stories. It was cathartic to share some of my innermost pains, but the real reward came when this quiet inner-city youth looked to me for some answers that I was capable of offering. Helping Spencer helped me. It helped me again see that I was useful and wanted, important and worth some dignity. After our interchanges, I was open to relating to many other youths and began cherishing the role of big brother or positive peer. In my small successes, I inevitably became something of a dorm leader. I accepted my position and became a mentor. Besides helping with program-specific details, I did my utmost to relay that the secret in my success was understanding that I wasn't a kid anymore, and I was focused on facing an adult life. Doing what I could to help my dorm mates plan their futures and make choices to reach their goals. I leaned on my many years of experience of abuse, neglect, racism, gang life, and the System in general, to relate to the boys and share my hope and determination.

And they seemed to respond to me quickly. Regardless of color or background, I became a big brother to many and I felt like I was in a house full of relatives. I had finally found a place I was starting to think of as home, with other youths that I began seeing as family. Instead of resenting my System placement, I found that it was a real place I could succeed and build myself up.

The diversity in our cottage provided a sink-or-swim atmosphere unparalleled by any place I had been before. You either got over your prejudices, including gang affiliations, or

you ended up getting kicked out or taking the walk down
AWOL Road. If a kid came in and refused to reach for
citizenship and just tried to cruise, he would be thrown out. If
someone was proved to be fronting their program (or faking that
they had bought in) they were thrown out. Although sometimes
rigid, it was just the kind of stern direction many of these
fatherless boys needed. This system was often the first time that
they had been given a black and white set of rules to succeed or
fail by. And far more often than not, we all thrived because of
it.

At the conclusion of the school year, we were notified of
an annual scholastic achievement award ceremony. Lots of
secrecy shrouded the candidates for awards, and the possibility
of recognition and praise from this parent figure that was BR
was something all the citizens looked forward to. I had gone to
the office countless times to turn in pink "course completed"
credit slips with an A on them. I dared to think that I had a
chance to win at least one award. Although I had been in the
school for only four months, I thought it was possible. My
existence down to that day had been made possible by fostering
such hopes of success and acceptance. The avalanche that
followed not only took me by surprise, but also everyone else in
the auditorium.

Five trophies sat on the stage. After the first speech
about her winner's efforts and achievements in class by our
English teacher, Mrs. Padgeant, my name was called. I sat still,
not believing my ears. My roommate, Lim Leang, nudged me
out of my seat and I took the walk down the aisle and onto the
stage to be greeted by Mrs. Padgeant. When the 300 plus people
had stopped applauding, I thanked her, my staff, and my cottage
for their help and support. My teacher could barely hold back
tears as she hugged me and said in my ear, "Good Job. You
earned this Louis."

I nervously took my seat with trophy in hand and hardly
heard as our Math teacher, Mr. Dalton and his Teaching
Assistant, Mrs. Russell, finished their speech—and called my

name again! As I got on stage, Max Scott, who at the time I didn't realize was the executive director of BR, stopped me on my way and with a warm smile said, "Are you going to take my job next?" I shrugged my shoulders; after all, he could have been the janitor, right? (Just kidding, Max.) Unbelievably, three more times I was called up to the stage to receive college scholarships and a certificate of merit for winning a writing contest. My brain couldn't even begin to deal with all the praise I was receiving. I knew that many of the citizens were my friends and were looking on in sincere congratulations, which made all the difference in the world. This proved itself as we made our way back to the cottage at the ceremonies conclusion, when student after student came up to pat me on the back and staff after staff told me I had done a good job.

At the cottage was more of the same, with me receiving more support from my cottage mates. I'm sure it helped that in our government cottage merit system, the equivalent of fifty dollars in "upgrades" were given to a cottage for each award a student received. This meant I had single handedly made Fowler "Cottage of the Week" and earned the pizza party that goes with it. I rode on a cloud of optimism for some time after that. I earned a position on the student government as a commissioner and was looked to as an example of the BR motto, "Nothing Without Labor." I became well received by all staff in the cottages, and although still very guarded over my emotions, allowed myself to bask in their praise. When school's summer session had started, I worked even harder than before. And after a total of just six months of hard work, I had made up almost four years of high school and was graduating a year ahead of my traditional class.

I wanted all of my teachers to speak at my graduation ceremony, especially Mrs. Padgeant and Mr. Dalton. Dan Dickson, my elective class teacher and paycrew supervisor, was my other choice, having given me the much-needed jokes and encouragements that had gotten me through some rough and dreary days. Dan also brought his five-year-old son to work

some days, and it was key for me as I got to relive what it was
like to be an older brother with him. I also got to choose a staff
to speak at my graduation and I knew it had to be Darryl. Still
remaining ever mindful of my feelings, he had become the only
person I had ever completely trusted. It was because of his
support, both mentally and emotionally, that I was graduating,
and I wanted to share this moment with him. He stood at the
podium in his nightman Nike jumpsuit, leaning down to speak
into the microphone, and told everyone of the long hours he had
watched me pour into achieving this day. I was able to hold
back the tears only until I saw the rip on the elbow of his
windbreaker. My mind returned to the night when we had had
an abrupt 3 a.m. wrestling session and he had caught his elbow
on the light switch, creating the tear. That night a small amount
of horseplay had made the client/staff line vanish for me and I
didn't feel so alone. My eyes began to water and I rushed to
wipe my face; I was sitting in a room of criminals and gang
members and still had to maintain some insecure male pride
preservation, right?

　　Although mostly elated, I still contended with feelings
of want surrounding my graduation. I wasn't going to a prom. I
wasn't expecting some type of graduation present or party. But
mostly, I wasn't going to get a parent's deep embrace, filled
with love and satisfaction, for the hurdle I had just leaped. Most
people are determined to achieve certain goals so that they can
get their parents' approval—I didn't even know my parents. I
could hope for more, but I had dealt with want my entire life. I
was all too familiar with this shortfall, and so for now, I was
just going to hold my diploma and be glad for myself.
　　My graduation posed a unique situation for BR. I was
out of the school system, but I wasn't 18. They had arranged for
me to be enrolled at Mt. San Antonio College and I was moved
out of the cottage and into their then budding on-campus
Independent Living Skill (ILS) program (a true emancipation
program). Everyone on campus had the impression that this

program was a cakewalk and a way to manipulate the strict rules of BR, and like all before and after me, I pushed on the staff to see what I could get away with. We were given the leeway to learn how to manage our house as though we were on the outside, and we were all roommates. We budgeted our house money for shopping, and cooked and kept our house clean. We paid "rent," which was put into a savings account for us when we left. Along with her staff, Lori Kezos, our program director, thought up many activities to help teach us various skills.

One of these activities was to be dropped in the middle of a city and complete a checklist of to-do's to simulate a new move or aging out of the System. We had to get three job applications, water, phone, and electric company numbers, and find an apartment based on the salary of our prospective job. Without knowing I had a connection, they had dropped us off in Moreno Valley, where I had worked at the City Hall for a summer. While all the other boys ran around trying to complete a near-impossible list, I went straight to City Hall and found my old friends. I called everyone on my list and had all the documents faxed to the office. I spent the rest of the time catching up with my old workmates and letting them know that I was going to make it. They were pleased with my visit and had a small office pizza party for me. At the end of the day we exchanged hugs and wished each other well.

Of all our ILS activities, I truly enjoyed all the opportunities that BR provided for us to volunteer to help others or fix a problem. Between mentoring struggling peers and doing graffiti removal in the community, I really learned how rewarding and heart-developing helping others could be. With these experiences to add to my inventory, I was starting to become a productive, thoughtful adult and member of society. I was learning that I could make a difference and that my life had value.

BR had become the haven of dreams for me. I had been able to touch the stars and was given the resources to make my dreams come true. I returned to my BR cottage countless times to reach out to other youths and mentor those who were struggling. Various staff would ask me to speak to their cottage if they needed a boost to remember how to stay on track. I felt truly useful and wanted, two things I had never experienced together on such a grand scale.

Another awards ceremony was coming up and these were for program achievements and college or vocational school scholarships. Again I received confirmation that my efforts weren't going unnoticed and that my new family was going to do their all to support me. Having won thousands of dollars in college scholarship awards and my picture in the newspaper, I got a much-needed boost to my self-esteem as the holiday season was once again approaching. I got on a special paycrew picking cedars for the BR charity wreath program, supervised by John Lemieux. We had driven through most of Riverside visiting properties we had permission to pick cedars from, and one day ended up a block away from my brother's old house. At lunch break, I asked John to let me go for a few minutes and take a look. The last I had heard they had again moved to Oregon, and the house I now stared at looked vacant. I went across the street and knocked on Tony's friend, Jason's, door. When he emerged, I asked if he had any idea where Tony lived. He looked dumbfounded by the question, pointing across the street and reporting that he was still living there. I asked about Oregon and he remained bewildered and said that they had only gone to visit for a few weeks a while ago. I practically skipped back to the truck and let everyone know that I had found my brother again.

Although I would have to wait to contact him, I at least knew that it was definitely in my future. I had been waiting over three years already, and I wasn't going to throw away all my small successes at BR to run away, just to be arrested if I tried force myself into his life. When the holidays came, I had less anxiety than years before. I had hope, direction, and the support to begin to understand what it would take to make me happy.

When Christmas came, I was the only boy left in the ILS house. In fact, I was practically the only kid left on campus. Lori offered to have me spend the night at her house on campus, with her son, Greg. And although previous attempts to have me spend a holiday with a staff had turned out miserably, this time was different. Lori wasn't pushy or invasive. She allowed me my space, and on Christmas Day there was a pile of presents of things that I liked. Not the usual one-size-fits-all gifts that had been my normal lot. Rather, there were presents that showed that she had been paying attention to my likes and which showed sincere thought for me. I had the strong urge, from that day forward, to address her as Mom—the first time I had ever chosen to do so. I found the word hard to push through my lips, and only managed to force it out about one=tenth the number of times my heart actually desired.

In the next months BR helped to get me a car, a 1966 Ford Mustang, capital letters C-A-R! They matched the $1,200 dollars I had saved and took me car hunting. My disbelief mounted, as my car sat in the BR parking lot, waiting for me to drive it. I would sneak out of the house late at night to go sit in it, play with the radio, or pretend to be taking a drive. My eyes took in every inch of the interior. "This is my space!" I had so much pride for my own little space. It needed a little work and BR's mechanic, Dan Brae, took me under his wing and showed me the ins and outs of vehicle maintenance. Lori helped me to get a driver's license.

My next step was to get a job. Darryl worked at a restaurant and helped me to get work there. Within a month I was driving to work, going to college, and feeling like I could conquer the world. This taste of life that I was getting was addicting and I wanted nothing more than to be out of the System. And even though my stay at BR was going so well, I craved independence and was having trouble containing myself from taking the extra looong way home from school or work each day. Just having the ability to drive here or there was overwhelming, and I would try to get lost on back roads.

My big day had finally arrived—on April 17, 1994, I would be 18. After some thirty placements, 19 schools, and 6 arrests, I was getting out of the System's pinball machine. My minimum wage busboy/prep cook job at Darryl's restaurant didn't pay me enough money to live on after I was on my own, but Lori and Max weren't going to throw me out on the streets as I had envisioned for so many years. Rather, they gave meticulous attention to helping my transition to the big bad world go smoothly. They worked to get me a job at BR in the kitchen.

I wasn't sure what I'd do about reuniting with Tony, or if that was even going to be possible. I had a roof over my head and I had been training to take things slow and get my ducks in order before I made a move. This would be imperative, especially when it came to dealing with Tammie.

In a little over a year, Boys Republic had been a proving ground for me to see that taking responsibility for myself—controlling my anger and staying focused on my goals—would lead to success. I had an independent spirit now, one that was optimistic toward facing the challenges ahead of me in the real world. I wasn't looking to have some program or foster home take care of me or tell me how to live from day to day.

I decided to no longer carry the name of my biological father, a man I had never met. I realized that my life, and anything I accomplished, would be solely mine. After much deliberation, I chose David—mostly because of the David and Goliath story in the Bible, but also because of how ordinary and common the name was. I knew that I was normal and could have a normal life. I understood what was required of me now and BR had provided an opportunity for me to examine how I could make a life in the "real world." After all my years of living with an orphan's desperation inside the System, I had finally found keys to deal with it and maintain hope. I now knew that my birth had meant something, and I could make an impact with my existence. I was going to make it—I would get my first apartment, my first set of bills, my first trip to the grocery and clothing stores; I was going to get everything like a normal person, like someone who has a place in the world, like someone that has real worth. My life has value. Even though I was intimidated by all that I was going to be responsible for; I wanted to face a life—my life—after the System.

I would like to take one moment to thank Boys Republic and its truly caring administrators and staff. If I had aged out from any facility other than BR, there is a great chance that I would have ended my life or become a serious criminal. After thirty years of first growing up in the System and then becoming a counselor, BR is the only program I have ever come across that truly invests in the youths they take in. Even today, I call back to check in and my calls are warmly received. To emphasize this point, I went through the experience of having a youth I was working with pass away suddenly and, in essence, I then had no job. After a consoling phone call, Max Scott and BR sent out a check to cover all my bills until I got back on my feet—and this was seven years after I had left the program. Their commitment to their graduates is complete and lasting.

Chapter 22 - A Letter to My Brothers and Sisters— Youths of the System and Victims of Abuse

How can you learn what's never been shown to you?

After I Aged Out:

I stand at the large wooden fence that encloses my new paid-for space—my first apartment. I let out a deep sigh and watch as a small cloud of my warm breath disappears into the darkness. I am on my way—but it's not enough. I still have no one, and I am still rushed with moments of depression that crave for death. I don't want to feel anymore. I want to have silence.

I have not been anywhere near a perfect man, and I'm scared—but I don't want to wait for whatever consequence God wants to give to me. Does he care that I exist, has he ever? I've been so alone, so heartbroken. For as long as I can remember, I stood alone in the shadows. Self inflicted or imposed, I felt that no one wanted me.

End my torture. End my life. Take my breath away while I sleep. Take my heart, my soul—I don't care anymore.

Aging out isn't easy. Everywhere I looked, I saw that everyone else had long-time friends or extended family. Everyone else had at least one person that cared what they were doing with their life. I had no one—and it hurt tremendously. I kept telling myself that I was working to achieve goals that would bring me happiness, but the wait was excruciating. I just keep telling myself, "Press on. Press on."

Thank you for reading my book and taking the time to read this letter. Having been raised by the System, I remember what it was like to have no choice but to wait for the time when a family would choose me or I would age out. No matter what comes first for you, I hope that your road will lead to peace and happiness.

I want you to read this book and *not* feel like there needs to exist the competition of "My story is more tragic than yours." There is no comparison; it is a lot harder to grow up today than five, ten, or even twenty years ago. I don't claim to be tougher than any one of you. Nor do I claim to have all the answers to fix your lives. Instead, I want you to know that I have deep concern for your needs. The reason I wanted to share my life with you was so that you could get to know me a little, hopefully relating with me. I've included this letter because I wanted to talk directly to you. And I wrote this book to make changes in the System to make your lives better. I have nothing but sincerity, and I hope that you'll open your minds and hearts for just a moment, to let me be a big brother to you. I have so many things I want to say to you, I hope that you'll give me a chance.

Without trying to minimize my life or yours, I want to say that in short, I dealt with a lot of junk. From how I was born into this world to the various living arrangements that I dealt with, I've had a lot of reasons to blame everyone, fight everything and altogether quit. But I didn't quit, and I've overcome being orphaned, child abuses—physical, sexual, and emotional—suicidal tendencies, enduring many injustices from the System, gang ideology, the juvenile justice system, trying to become a "regular" adult, conquering the cycle of abuse, grappling with anger and depression, and learning to build a family and love them. I pushed on day by day and here is what I have to offer:

About the System:

I remember not understanding what was going on with me more than half the time. But after working in the System for a number of years, it became clear. Facing the System is exactly the same as entering the adult world. Unlike children who are allowed to make mistakes, express their emotions or rebel against authority, with only the consequence of the redirection of a concerned parent, being in the System means that you are subject to all the federal, state, and local laws the same way and with the same severity that a thirty-year-old man is. Our adjustment to this dynamic is, of course, burdensome, because often we are dropped into this adult System as a baby, or grade-school aged child. Facing this world with those limited skills and insights can only breed anxiety, contempt, and rebellion. But this is where my first piece of advice comes into play:

I found out that it is most beneficial to explain that the reason that most foster parents, staff, therapists and social workers can't get anything done on your behalf—at least not right away—is because the smallest request is usually surrounded by as much red tape as getting a driver's license, starting a business, or paying taxes. And as unfamiliar as those processes may be to you, getting you an opportunity to see your separated sibling, or to go to the mall for the day without a guardian is equally challenging for the workers in the System. What is the solution?

I ask that you do your best to be just like an adult standing in line at the Department of Motor Vehicles or Internal Revenue Service, and be patient, but don't get out of line and give up. Usually, right when you approach an adult they think, "What is this kid gonna want?" So I say, don't beat around the bush—just tell them every time. Never let the issue rest—stay in line! Every day, tell every System adult what you need, until they do it. And when they say, "I'm working on it," ask for details, and write them down. Just remember to continue in your adult mindset and watch how you say things, be patient, and try not to be loud or violent. I guarantee that if you make it a point to tell everyone you see, every day, what you need and want, that eventually they will accommodate you. After all, in essence, System employees are YOUR employees. And just like in the adult world, if you are not a good boss, they will run all over you, or quit and desert you.

For Foster Children:

You have to go into a home with your own expectations. It is your Right to have a say in how you are cared for and treated—so say something. And if things take a turn for the worse, do whatever you can to tell everyone. Never believe that only you can make things better, or that any of what happens is your fault. That's a mistake I repeatedly made. If you tell someone, a *lot* of someones, then if things can be fixed, they will help. You shouldn't try to shoulder that great task by yourself. If you have the advantage of having a social worker, probation officer, or teacher involved, then as hard as it may be, share with them and hold your abusers accountable. I know this may result in you being moved, but in all honesty, isn't it for the best?

You have been faced with one of the toughest lives possible and you must emerge with your chest full and your head raised. One of the biggest obstacles may be controlling your anger. I can't stress enough how I know that this is no small task—and likewise, one of the most important. Please realize that retaliation gets you nowhere. To release anger and frustration might seem to feel good, but your anger will never be satisfied. Every time you strike out, you add to the pain of being in the System. You add to the cycle of abuse. And what are the results? You'll get locked up or retaliated against by staff and peers. And what purpose will that ever serve? The System will take away your choices and freedoms.

We have a lot of anger, but we must learn to find constructive outlets. Do your best to understand your pain and frustrations, and how and why they are triggered, and you will find yourself with less anger and more patience. My request is that you find a qualified person to help you explore your soul and develop ways to vent. And I don't mean a friend to talk to. I mean that you need to connect with a mentor who is trained to listen to what you have to say (without thinking about themselves) and be capable of offering you real options to handle your feelings. It is a solid way to resolve deep-rooted matters.

Children in the System are not a different type of human. You deserve love and you should be treated no worse than any other person on the planet. As you know, these things don't always happen. We are often treated like a cold statistic, another "so and so" type of kid. No one seems to care about us, so we refuse to care about them. This can turn us into something we will regret: a self-serving and ungrateful person. After a number of years in the System, many youths start to show a mark of entitlement. They begin to see that the world isn't fair and then feel like the world owes them. I too have felt that the adults around me should try to understand me better and then compensate or help me in some way because I had been alone for so long and beaten so badly, so many times. We feel like we are set apart from everyone else. In a small way we are, but this thinking can become destructive to your personal growth. People don't want to build a friendship with someone who thinks everyone else owes them. You can't punish everyone in your future for what happened in your past. The world isn't a plus-and-minus system in which you are marked special because of what you have been through. Rather, it just keeps coming at you full speed.

It is no exaggeration to say that everyone has dealt with tragedy. There are those who that have dealt with the loss of a loved one because of disease, murder, drugs, an accident or act of nature. These people are as much entitled to compassion and understanding as we are, even though compassion or empathy may be hard to find. Being abused and/or orphaned doesn't automatically make you extra special; what will make you special is your ability to show love and care for others.

This is such a hard fact to swallow because we often look at everyone else and convince ourselves that they all have it better. But do they? With an honest look around it is easy to see the harsh reality. There is no such thing as a perfect life. However, there are those who may try to convince you that you are owed, and "one day" God is going to bless you, that everything happens for a reason, or everything always balances itself out. If that were true, then everyone who has aged out of the System would be a millionaire with a huge family. How many times have you heard someone offer you hope by saying that your circumstances are part of God's special plan for you? (*I know that I heard it many times*) In movies and books we commonly see stories of orphans or foster kids getting some special treatment or miraculous gift like it is some kind of birthright. In the productions of Aladdin, Cinderella, Harry Potter, Spiderman, Oliver Twist, Angels in the Outfield, and Like Mike, we have been stuffed with tales of special talents or wishes given to mythical System kids. The list goes on for miles of stories in which a character's worst fears are realized—they lose all of their family—but then it is replaced with some miraculous happy ending. These make for entertaining stories, but the harsh reality is that you will never get a magic lamp or become a super hero because Fate or God feels like He "owes you one." To hand you a hard truth, I offer that whatever you get in life will have to be earned, with lots of hard work. This is a concept that many of you are already familiar with, and a quality that will be an inspiration to all the people around you.

To Victims of Abuse:

You must keep your spirit alive. Remember to keep your chin up and never believe anyone who tells you "you can't." Just because someone has mistreated you *doesn't mean that they have limited your opportunities for happiness in the future.* Don't ever let anyone make you feel like you have no value. You are very important, and as you explore the offers of life you will find this to become truer. The second you start to believe "them" and give up by remaining silent, acting out, rebelling, committing crimes, or seriously attempting suicide, you are giving them the ultimate victory over you. You give them the power to destroy your hope. You cannot let ANYONE have that power over you, ever.

Stay away from negative people. They see our anger, frustration, desperation, and loneliness and want to exploit it by using us for sex, violence or as a garbage can for their problems. Don't walk into a trap of thinking that they really care about you.

If You Age-Out:

This next part of my letter is for the older ones out there who are close to becoming adults or who have already aged out of the System. I want to share exactly how I fixed my brain and heart, as it were. My "success" came after a five-step process (and each of these are explained further, below): (1) Understanding, acknowledging and accepting my past, by (2) choosing who to forgive, and whom I *survived*; (3) setting goals; and then availing myself of the personal nurturance of (4) hope and (5) determination. Now I want to pass these keys on to you.

First, I want you to seize every day. Trust that it is important to acknowledge what you went through and discuss it with a qualified individual. We each have a unique story, and it is ours alone—don't be ashamed of it. Then, realize that you can't change yesterday but you can prepare for tomorrow. When I finally began to understand this, I started to see the possibility of a happy future.

Second, for each person and incident in your life, choose to forgive, or to be a survivor. Deal with every person and incident in your life and make a choice that will set your heart free. Write down all of these people and incidents and the decisions you came to, and why. This can be helpful in allowing you to reflect on your decisions in the years to come.

I hope you will discover that, most times, forgiveness is in order—for a young mother who made the mistake of leaving us in the care of the System, and maybe for family members who became addicted to drugs or alcohol. These are things that if you put yourself in their shoes, do some research and be reasonable, you might see that they made a grave mistake—but it was not a personal attack against you. I know forgiveness is a word too often thrown around and not explained, so I'll offer what it means to this orphan. To forgive is not to forget; rather, it is to pardon, or to no longer hold someone accountable for any action or deed that may affect you in any way. To forgive is to say that you are ready to "pardon" them and continue on with that person in your daily life. This is most often no quick process or by any means easy. But when appropriate, it is what you have to do so that the event(s) don't build up inside you to the point that they dominate your life or make you explode.

Something that was key in helping me to understand the concept of forgiveness was what a staff kitchen worker once shared with me. It was his view of lending money to a friend. He would lend out, say, $100, in his friend's time of need and instantly forgive the debt, not expecting it back. As he explained, the friendship was worth more than the money, and if he had it to lend (or in his view, give away), then why should he allow it to come between them? Right after he told me this I hit him up!—but as he reached for his wallet, I decided to keep his lesson instead.

To forgive someone an emotional debt has similar components. You are saying that you value your own peace and a possible lifelong relationship *more* than a mistake that happened in the past. My only addition to the above moral tale is that with an emotional debt, you may find that it would be nice to receive a verbal request for forgiveness, or an apology.

If the person is in your life, then allow them to show gratitude for your forgiveness by their actions. But, if you will have no opportunity to talk to them, perhaps ever, then forgiveness has the powerful capacity to release you personally from any anger. For example, forgiving my mother for not fighting to take me out of the System means that I realize that she was in the grip of powerful drugs and I acknowledge that any human could have been in a similar position and made the same mistake—it wasn't a personal attack on her part. I forgave her and now I don't feel like she is accountable to me for what she didn't do on my behalf. I would accept her back into my daily life if that were possible. To forgive will help your heart move on toward your goals in life without animosity or blame.

On the other hand, for those who have severely abused you in any way, targeted you for some sick game or to play out some psychotic cycle, I don't think that forgiveness is the word that needs to be used. It would be unfair of me to ask you to forgive or pardon a heinous act repeatedly perpetrated and often premeditated against you. To me, that would be like asking a mother impregnated by a rapist to allow the offender back into her life to raise the child. What I *can* ask is that you choose a route to set you free from an anger that is otherwise bound to consume you, and move forward towards positive goals in your life. In this instance, I offer that you choose to consider yourself a "Survivor."

To live through the experiences of a severe abuser in your life can be like having to survive a serious illness like tuberculosis, malaria, or even cancer. Although it is more than unfortunate that the disease crossed your life's journey, you would have to continue on. The day that you were cured of your disease would be like the day you no longer had to live with the abuser in your life. For a person to say that they escaped the clutches of cancer or severe child abuse holds the same weight in my eyes. And with the "disease" gone you could start anew with possibly a greater appreciation for what your future can hold. It is possible to move on and take back any mental power the disease held over you.

As a step to explore healing, I suggest that you say to yourself that you will avoid the person but be able look back, to look into the face of the disease, without holding a grudge of hatred and anger against them, just as you can't hold a grudge against cancer. Again, finding someone to talk to is crucial. Understanding that your abuser(s) are very often severely psychologically disturbed can provide a direction for you to begin finding resolution. Consider the fact that enduring serious abuse or malaria are equally random events—**don't take any "sickness" personal.** (If some other child had been placed in the home with Shirley, it is very likely that they would have suffered the "disease.")

One of the best healing steps I can offer to being a survivor is to take all of the feelings of suffering and use them to be an advocate so that someone else might not suffer in the same way. Share your story, let people know the problem exists, and let them hear your voice so that they can't ignore it. If you can find a voice by helping a charity or being a mentor, then you can add your name to the fight against the disease of child abuse (might I suggest you contact your local Heart Gallery).

You must find a way to make the transition from a victim to someone who has control in their life. I must stress however, that this needs to stay in check, be balanced; otherwise you are likely to become the abuser you detest in the same or a different form. The only way to beat your former "condition" is to take control, make your own choices and not just react or follow the example of what has been done to you. You will make your heart calm and gain needed maturity if you try to find your place in life and press forward to achieve your goals, short and long term.

Please believe in yourself. Please know that one day very soon you will have happiness and a loving family. That's why it is so important that you look for something to place your hope in, to strive for—in other words, goals. There has to be something on this planet that appeals to you. Take time to better yourself, do your schoolwork, and develop any skills you have—sports, art, reading, crafts, anything. Learn how to care for something like plants, fish, birds, cats or dogs, or whatever you can. Keep track of your small and large goals, and always remind yourself that you are preparing for your future. I promise that you will find a peace in these activities; and that *your personal success will be your tormentor's greatest defeat.* Remember that.

On top of the hope that you will develop in whatever avenues or goals you choose, you will have to build and maintain determination. To start with, we can look at the literal definition of the word. The *Merriam-Webster Collegiate Dictionary* in part defines determination as "the power or habit of deciding definitely and firmly." Think of any famous athlete or musician. You can rest assured that not one of them got where they are by just sitting around and waiting for someone to knock on their door and offer them the opportunity of a lifetime. Often they are heard saying, "If you work hard enough, you can do (be) whatever you want." I often shrugged comments like that off, while thinking, "Yeah, right. If I was born with your abilities or family I could be like you, too." But truly, you have to consider how many hours athletes put into perfecting their skills, or that musicians put in so they can create a unique or beautiful sound. It all took a huge amount of effort and determination for them to decide that they were definitely going to take their life in that direction and then make it happen.

And about talent that was born to them? Think of Ray Charles, Stevie Wonder or even Ludwig Von Beethoven; how much determination did it take for Ray and Stevie to learn to play the piano and write incredible songs while literally blind, or for Beethoven to compose his masterpieces while deaf? Even Michael Jordan had trouble making his high school basketball team. Then he became determined, focused, and the rest is history. These are a just a few examples of pure determination that should be looked at when you may doubt yourself. Some other really good examples are the life stories of Lance Armstrong, Helen Keller, Baron Davis, Sirr Parker, and whatever you do, don't miss Kyle Maynard's, *No Excuses*.

I need to finish this point by saying that becoming a great musician, artist, or athlete shouldn't be done with the expectation of being world-renowned. There are many great singers and basketball players who are great, even magnificent, but unheard of. When pursuing your goals, make sure that you are doing them for *you*, because it is where your heart is, and not just for public recognition or money. I'm sure everyone would agree that there is just as much honor and pride in teaching your child to play a game or an instrument, as in getting paid a lot of money or being idolized. Fame is no real or reliable substitute for the love and attention you didn't receive as a kid in the System; it is most often fleeting and attained at the whim of a finicky, fickle mass audience who often "loves" you one day and forgets you next week. But those who do achieve public fame and keep their heads on straight realize they are doing their art or music because they love to create that art form, and they look to give and receive love through family and other fulfilling long-term relationships. Looking at those who struggled, emerged from obscurity, and then achieved their goals is intended to inspire you, because, "If you put your mind to it, you can do whatever you want."

And it is no different for any of us. To hone the determination to accomplish your goals, you have to remain focused and create a habit of deciding firmly not to be swayed from whatever your goals may be. For me, it was to one day have a family of my own and find the inner peace to interact and grow with them without ever becoming an abusive husband or father. Now, this is not done with a simple statement like, "I will never hit my kids the way I was hit." It takes so much more; it took focusing on a lot of little goals that would lead up to my main goal. I had to remain determined in every aspect of maturing into the type of man who had dealt with his past and learned all the ways of dealing with everything from small life issues to large frustrations in a way that didn't include violence. I wanted to build a solid home for my family financially, so I became determined to do well in school and get the training necessary to get an adequate job for my goal. This is no spectacular feat in the eyes of many, but *to me it is*, and likewise to my family.

For you, too, it will be the same. Remaining determined to find your happiness, in whatever way that may be, is not useless wishful thinking, but rather it is a skill that can only bring you what you desire. No matter how stacked the deck is against youths in the System, we all have an opportunity at happiness if we remember to nurture our hopes and develop a strong sense of determination. You *can* deal with the life you have been forced to endure. It won't be easy, but if you do your all to take responsibility for yourself and your actions, then you will emerge as an adult two steps ahead of everyone else. In this you will find that you can be powerful and you can succeed. Never doubt your worth and never fall into the snare of thinking that you will never be happy. You may have to be patient and work hard, but I guarantee that it will be worth it and you will be able to define love in a way that few are able, and find your inner peace.

You have great potential to accomplish all of your goals. With the sort of strength training you and I have been forced into there is raw power. Sometimes this gets used for negative thoughts and actions, but it is far more useful when you use this energy to create a solid life for yourself. And for those times when you are struggling with negativity, I have a couple of suggestions that may put you back on the right track.

When my life became overwhelming, it was always helpful for me to take in the big picture. Look outside yourself to what is going on in the world around you. You might do some research about orphans in other countries. You will often find that they are in the same boat as us but have near zero options awaiting them when or if they become adults. How do you think they would react if they were taken out of their own country and placed in America's social service system? Do you think they would appreciate being placed in our system? I know I wouldn't have wanted to grow up in theirs. With little searching, it is too easy to find heartbreaking stories of real children who are starving to death or who are forced to work as slaves in labor camps. I don't use this to imply that you have no reason to complain about your own life. Your personal perspective is crucial and your trials are important. Rather, I want to push you to think of others. I know you'll find a great benefit if you try to turn that inner spotlight that at times can push us to the brink of suicide towards others' needs and even think of possible ways that you could help. Volunteering at a homeless shelter, being a positive peer, and helping those around you are ways that I got started. Maybe you'll find that helping someone else is just as rewarding for them as it is for yourself.

Another key is to be grateful for anything you have. Remind yourself of what is positive in your life. Be grateful if you are a talented swimmer or artist. Find outlets that will distract you when you have to deal with boredom and loneliness. But most of all, whenever possible, talk to someone, anyone who will listen and bridge you to a new day. Using any or all of these suggestions can help you to avoid making one of the biggest mistakes ever—taking all the offers of life for granted. That is a mistake that is fatal for your heart and soul.

Finally, I want to touch on a quality that, if you focus on it, will make adult life an absolute success. When you have worked on your mind and heart, your anger and love, then you'll be ready for this biggest step: to be a leader. Once you take an honest inventory of who you are inside, you can use this to begin charting a life course. Being accountable to yourself and others for every one of your actions and life choices is the definition of adult maturity. As an adult, it is always your fault, your choice, and your success. *You must not go through life being a victim.* You have a choice. At some point you need to begin the life that *you* have chosen for yourself. How? (1) Not looking back to find blame for your actions today. Use your skills and strengths to make a place for yourself, a home both inside you heart and under your own roof. And (2) by not buying into what is supposed to be ideal, as defined by the media: materialism, beauty, popularity—but rather, finding what your needs are, setting goals and working toward them.

There is nothing that we can do to stop our lives from changing—we grow older and face new obstacles every day. You can either think for yourself, or, as many people allow, you can fall into letting your past or the world around you dictate your actions and desires. This is a path that will surely have you struggling to the bitter end, chasing "their" mirage of happiness or repeating harmful cycles. Please never allow yourself to think that if you make that "one" special purchase, you will be happy. "Happiness" and "Contentment" are not sold at any store; they are things that only you can personally measure. If you choose to be a leader, no longer a victim of your past, and refuse to be turned into something you are not, you will find satisfaction, inner peace, and happiness.

I know that you can remain strong and have the courage to put this letter to use. That is proven by the initiative you took taking the time to read this. I know how long winded I can be. I just didn't want to miss anything "big" in this one-chance letter. I don't think of myself as some know-all of the System. I do think I have an understanding of a lot of life-issue conclusions that it takes some people years to sift through. These are points and issues I wish someone had been there to tell me about when I was coming up. Often when the issue is in our face, we can forget to be rational, even if we already know and understand what we should do beforehand. When we have someone else looking out for us, they might remind us of the right thing to do. I hope that in this letter, I can sort of be there for you in that way.

If you don't realize it by now, I have a real love for you. I have dreamt of one day having an annual picnic where we all get together for a family reunion and share our stories. I would love nothing more than to hear how you made it through and what your plans for the future are. Maybe that will happen one day. Until then, I wish you all the best and want you to know that you are in my prayers. You are my brothers and sisters. If you have found any of the words in this letter to be helpful, then please share them with someone else in need. In that way we can all be big brothers and sisters to the only family that we know. We can be strong, for ourselves, and for each other.

I wish you good health and a long, happy life.

Sincerely,

Your brother, David Louis

P.S. I have intentionally left out religion from this letter. Although I hold spirituality in the highest regard, I have witnessed God being used as a crutch for blame, or as a cure-all where it is actually necessary for personal healing to take place. Research has confirmed the power of prayer. Please pray and ask questions. But please, turn to the Bible itself for answers (1 John 4:1), and not anyone's interpretation of it. Here are good places to start: Psalms 9:9, 10, John 17:3, 25, 26, and 1 Peter 2:21-25, respectively.

Chapter 23 – To All My Other Readers - Remember Terrell

"Unfortunately, it sometimes takes a tragedy to get everyone's attention."

—Sue Burrell, attorney with the Youth Law Center

I feel the system utterly failed me in only one regard—in one aspect that they cannot deny nor excuse: they didn't do a complete search for my family members. There is a new permanency agenda sweeping the country that asks social workers to locate 40 members of a child's family within a few weeks of their being placed in state custody. It is a program that I hope gets national support. I know that those efforts will help the youth know where they come from and often return them within the same family circle. I have seen it work first-hand with amazing results. If you are a social worker and would like to see a demonstration, please email me at heartgalleryhawaii@yahoo.com and I will give you further details.

My fight to prove that every life can have value is won every day I go to work. I am healed a little more every time I help someone else. As much as reaching back as a counselor has meant to me, there is one job I've had that has made me whole again. I founded a Heart Gallery for Hawaii.

Started by Diane Granito of the New Mexico Department of Child and Family Services in 2001, the Heart

Gallery Ideal is to connect foster children with no parents, or whose parental access has been terminated for safety or other reasons, with adoptive parents. Heart Galleries replace the typical "mug shots" in a case file with beautiful, insightful and even humorous portraits taken by professional photographers who volunteer their time and resources. The portraits they create are exhibited in prestigious art galleries and museums across the country which are attended by prospective adoptive parents.

Today, there are some sixty Heart Galleries in forty-six states. The Heart Galleries have made monumental positive impacts on adoption, finding homes for older foster children and sibling groups who are often forgotten and forced to age out of the System. In some states, the Heart Gallery exhibits have doubled or tripled the national adoption averages. Heart Gallery Hawaii has also shared in these successes.

The idea of the Heart Gallery underscores exactly what needs to be done so that when someone mentions "The System," the public, the providers, and the children stop cringing at what will be said next. The Heart Gallery provides an opportunity for children in the System to be recognized as real people, as individuals, with diverse personalities and a general need to be loved, like any other normal child.

I am going to bring up some negative things about the System before I put my pen away, but let me say something truly positive first. I have benefited greatly because of my experiences. The first step to healing my orphan heart was to acknowledge my past and accept it. Becoming an adult has meant reflecting on how I grew up, whom I have interacted with, and literally, what parts of the human spirit I admired and could use to make me whole. I have met so many people—children, adults, teachers, therapists, on the list goes on and on. At first, I became a chameleon, testing, learning, and feeling what it was like to display Sensei's strength, Phil's compassion, Darryl's insight and Lori's grace. Then I melded the best parts of all the people in my past and became a capable, knowledgeable, and passionate man. I have learned to be a friend, a husband, a father, an advocate, and, by reaching back, a one-of-a-kind counselor.

The head nurse on duty that day was Jennifer. She was a tiny young woman dwarfed by the nurses' station. She was fresh out of college and obviously intimidated by the reality of her position as a psychiatric nurse. I had just completed shift change and was preparing for group. I was putting together a written therapeutic activity when Jennifer flashed on a unit priority.

"David, will you go talk to Phillip? I heard that he's having a really bad day." It was a statement that was part request and part notification. I agreed to the assignment, I had a good rapport with Phillip. I opened the door and caught Phillip hiding a shiny object under his leg as he quickly sat down on his bed. I sat next to him and shared his gaze out of the window.

"What's up, Phillip?" A deep preparing breath and then, "We need to talk don't we?" We sat in silence for another moment and I tried again. "Don't you have something to say to me? You can tell me anything and you know I'll do what I can to help."

"You're just a staff, you can't understand. You don't know how hard it is!" After letting him relay a few choice words about placement and the staff, I gave time for the dust to settle. I put my hand on Phillip's shoulder and wrangled my own emotions before deciding to confide in him.

"But I do know what it is like, Phillip." He looked up at me with shock. I looked back out the window before continuing. "I grew up in the System. I never had parents and I was locked up a lot when I was your age."

"What?"

"I've sat where you are and stared out that same window and also thought of killing myself. Why not? What was

there to live for?" I could feel his gaze on me. I looked over to see tears in his eyes. He quickly turned his back to me. I continued, "But I didn't. I fought to make it to tomorrow. Now I have a family of my own, and I am sitting here with you, offering you all that I know, so that one day you can also get whatever you want out of life."

"But sometimes I get so...just...argh..."

"I know...I KNOW. I wanted to give up so many times. No one can understand how hard it is, going day to day with only yourself to rely on. And that's why I come to work every day. So that when it gets hard for you, you can give me some of the junk and tell me about what you're going through. And maybe I can help you through some of the tough days."

Phillip nods his head while staring at his feet. I can see that he is contemplating whether or not to let me help him. I wholeheartedly put out the offer.

"I just wish I could do more. But if anyone is bothering you, or you ever want to talk about anything; I'm here for you, okay?"

Phillip reaches under his leg and hands over a ground sharpened quarter of a metal picture frame. "Here... take this."

"Thank you Phillip. You know that you need to talk to the doctor about this." He gave me a quick look of betrayal. "But if you let me, we can talk to him together."

He looks back out the window, "Okay."

"Now, what do you say to a little game of 'Horse'?"

A grin rushes to his face, "Why do you wanna go and do that for? You know you're gonna lose?"

"Well, let's go blow off some steam and see about that!"

Within a few words, this is a literal example of who I became to those I work with in the System. Because I lived in every type of System placement, I have been able to be empathetic to whatever situation they are in, while remaining a therapeutically positive role model. It has been my pleasure and sometimes my pain. Simply put, I have been so successful because I help the youths I work with not feel so alone. I let them know that they have value, and I am able to prove that they can move towards positive goals in their lives no matter how bad a situation they are living through. Too often I hear horrendous stories of abuse and neglect that make my blood boil. I know that I am helping, but I feel like I am trying to wash every grain of sand at the beach one at a time.

There is only one thing that needs to be said about my childhood—it should have never happened. Child abuse and neglect is preventable.

In truth, System kids are financially the richest of all, inasmuch as their literal parents are the government. And just like a neglectful parent, the government chooses to focus on other issues instead of raising the kids they have taken in. "System kids" have only one major problem, and it is not child abuse. It is that their "parents" don't see them as, or treat them like, individuals.

Over and over I've recognized that look of desperation on the faces of the youths I work with. I can see that their hearts are being broken in the same ways mine was, or worse. As a staff, I can finally see the other side of the coin and I often don't like what I see. I work alongside many System staffers who dislike their work, or put up with their job as a reluctant stepping-stone to a better opportunity. I've witnessed staff saying despicable things about a youth they were frustrated with, and then acting to get back at that youth. When I've offered my insight, I have been shunned and outcast for taking the "kid's" side. It has been my experience that unless there is a personal reason why System providers (placement homes and foster parents) are there to help, there is a huge disconnect and the youths are often seen as problems or obstacles to be dealt with for a paycheck, and not as valuable human children. This leaves the juveniles in the System with not only pain from what happened in their biological family, but also the icy indifference of a clinical environment that is likewise legally restricted from offering a System child something as important as a daily hug.

This atmosphere creates System holes, abuse cycles, and leads to pain and devastation. It doesn't have to be this way.

No great changes have been made since I was the one being watched over, and I know that children in the System, and especially the victims of abuse, need help. Obviously one root issue is that the System is unnatural. Having permanent guardians who care for you on shifts, or who are getting paid to be your family, can't be expected to make any child grow up feeling nurtured and loved. There are countless studies that point to the absolute necessity of a stable home, the need for affection, and the long-term benefits of at least one parent, if not the ideal two. Bouncing around thirty or more placements, abuse, neglect, and injustice can be seriously reduced by simply attacking two solutions without the red tape that often bars outside interference. First, child victims of abuse (the entire Social Service population) need to be recognized as real, individual members of society, and second, the needs of orphans (and even all children in temporary government care) must be kept in the limelight until orphans can be connected with someone who wants to offer a permanent home (and more foster families can be found for temporary situations).

Although my thirty placements taught me that it was not uncommon for most of my roommates to have suffered child abuse, even severe child abuses, not every foster child has unloving foster parents. Likewise there are many staff and professionals who love their jobs, as I do, and are committed to helping those in the System. So, before I put a number on the problems of System life, I want to put out this precursor: There are many who do a phenomenal job caring for the "lost" children. There are many professionals who are the light in some young one's life. I know of many System providers who have dedicated their lives to helping orphans, foster children, or other children in crisis. I even know of loving, unselfish social workers and foster parents that adopted children from foster care. I don't want the content of this book to negate these wonderful people's efforts. I do not wish to create a hypersensitive climate where foster parents are blackballed because of false reports—and many System youths make those reports to gain attention or because they have crossed their own "closeness" boundary and subconsciously want to be moved. Rather, I need to shine a light on the overlooked children who get gobbled up by the System and have to live through unspeakable pains. I survived to tell my story, but the abuses noted in this book are not by any means rare. Justice for those in the System is too easily manipulated, and child abuse in general is a growing epidemic. I don't want ANY of my readers to think, "That was then, surely things have changed."

September 3, 2006. An Associated Press article was sent to me that was posted on CNN.com:

> **CINCINNATI, Ohio** (AP) — The foster parents of a disabled 3-year-old boy wrapped him like a cocoon and left him for two days in a closet, where he died while they attended a family reunion, a prosecutor said.
>
> The couple made several attempts to burn Marcus Fiesel's body and concocted an elaborate sham to cover up the boy's death, Hamilton County Prosecutor Joe Deters said Tuesday.
>
> "Marcus was wrapped in a blanket and wrapped in tape with his arms behind him—and this was not the first time," Deters said in announcing additional indictments against Liz and David Carroll Jr.

One sociologist commented, "You are more likely to get killed, injured or physically attacked in your own home by someone you are related to, than in any other social context." Child abuse is a closely guarded family secret, one that is protected and unreported whether the child lives with their biological family or not. But serious abuse is easier to hide by twisted caregivers, foster or "adoptive" parents, who just have to misdocument an incident or a mark on a child's body to cover their trail. Already battling severe low self-esteem, these children have no one to turn to for protection, no best friend, no family and therefore, no opportunity to have a voice. No one knows them as they are shuffled through home after home, which each having its own special measure of confidentiality. This equals out to a lack of consistency and follow-through that creates a gaping hole for abusers to perpetrate their physical, sexual, or emotional abuse crimes.

The fact that the System is so overwhelmed that it cannot properly monitor or follow through on most reports just adds to this dilemma. And as the numbers for drug abuse and teen pregnancy and births go up, the number of orphans who must navigate these trials of abuse all alone rises as well.

Today, in 2006, it is estimated that there are about 650,000 children in foster care, including some 150,000 who are orphans, a number that has nearly doubled in the last 15 years. Too many of them deal with the tortures I wrote about and worse, facing horrifying traumas at the hands of System providers. And only when the System can't maintain its "confidentiality" do a few of the ones who suffered ghastly deaths at the hands of their "parents" get pushed into the public eye. These are crimes that are happening in your community, sometimes even next door. Yet they continue on because someone thinks it's not their business; they don't want to be marked as nosy and interfere. Even when it is the media that pulls the covers off this issue, and a foster child like Terrell Peterson, who was brutally tortured and starved to death, makes a *TIME* magazine cover, their stories are only made a relative footnote to the 6 o'clock news. After a few days of shock and talk, everyone turns the page.

The article in the November 13, 2000, *TIME* magazine brought me to tears a dozen times. In my anger and sadness, I found the strength to detail in these pages what I went through, in the hopes there wouldn't have to be another newsmagazine article of such horror. On the cover is a photo of Terrell Peterson, and the story is entitled, "The Shame of Foster Care."

The feature article tells how Terrell lived a daily torture that was only finally reported in a medical examiner's autopsy. It stated that Terrell's feet and hands were severely burned, and tears on his wrists and ankles evidenced that he had been tied to a banister for most of his short life. When trying to complete the report, the medical examiner finally gave up trying to count all the cuts and abrasions. Terrell weighed only 28 pounds—and he had been six years old at his death.

When we read of another foster child like Octavius Sims, who was immersed in boiling water and beaten to death before his first birthday, all of America gasps, but then moves on. The plight of the orphan becomes overwhelming when you stop to think that these children have never known love, and when they are abused, it can only magnify their feelings of worthlessness. They deserve more than a sympathetic gesture. I know that abuse on the whole is hardly even acknowledged and children in so-called normal homes have suffered no less. I have held in my tears many times as I listened to a child solemnly tell me of how their uncle raped them or their mother seared their body with an iron.

It is projected that for every reported case of child abuse, 200 go unreported. This is an estimate that was solidified by a spokesman for The Child Welfare League of America when he stated, "The figures we have are only the tip of the iceberg." And what are those figures?

Each year there are around five million reported cases of child abuse in America. 400,000 of these are reports of verifiable sexual assaults filed by teachers and doctors. 142,000 of these children are seriously injured or maimed. The U.S. Advisory Board on Child Abuse and Neglect reports that 2,000 children die every year at the hands of their abusers, about six every day—a number that they say is estimated to be underreported by as much as 60%.

Please, stop reading and reflect on those numbers for a moment. To illustrate, I want you to think of the millions that have visited the Vietnam Memorial and have been overwhelmed by the chronological listing of the some 58,000 names on the wall. As a nod to Maya Lin, I wish to borrow her art. This whole book has around 140,000 words. Flip back through the pages and try to imagine that every word you see is a name, the first name of a child who was seriously injured, mutilated or maimed in the last year because of child abuse. Just staring at this page with that thought in my head weighs heavy on my heart. By completing this chapter you would have read the number of words equal to the number of U.S. children who were abused or neglected to their death in the last twelve months. THE DOCUMENTED STATISTICS FOR CHILD ABUSE ARE MIND-NUMBING.

TIME magazine commented, "...the incidence of physical and sexual abuse in the System is alarmingly higher than in the general populace." A study released in 2005 by Harvard Medical School and the Universities of Michigan and Washington, in cooperation with Oregon and Washington State agencies and Casey Family Programs (a major foster care agency), scientifically conveys the trauma of those who have been in the System. The report stated, "Foster care alumni experience post-traumatic stress at twice the rate of U.S. war veterans." It is easy to see why being in foster care feels like going to war, for many, including myself, have suffered abuses similar to those that have been outlawed, but secretly continued, in POW camps. Residing in a strange land and having your entire perception of the world changed to one of confusion, danger, or even terror at a moment's notice, is difficult for an adult soldier; how much more so can it be for a youth bounced around in the System? The major difference, of course, is that the adult enlisted to be put in harm's way, but the child didn't.

With so much behind me, I now want to put my name among the advocates for the rights of children. I write this hoping to involve you, the reader, hoping that you will convene to force sweeping impacts in many domains on behalf of the many orphans, foster children and all abused children. After reading my book, I need every one of you not to forget, but to remember. To ponder every day that there are at least six to ten children who were murdered, suffering abuses similar to Terrell's for God only knows how long—about one child physically beaten to death in America for every hour that the sun lights your neighborhood. Think of what their daily lives were like before they finally succumbed in death.

I have always loved to study history. I have been fascinated at human milestones and referenced timelines for myself so that I could grasp what was happening in one part of the globe versus another. And like most, I have reveled in tales of humanity overcoming overwhelming odds and conquering injustice. Civil rights issues have sparked the most heated human conflicts. The struggles of the past have always been answered with voices and outcries. People have rallied with peaceful demonstrations, violent clashes and even with large-scale wars. But in every social cause, no changes were made without that conflict, or without the cries of "injustice" and the refusal to accept that no one could change anything.

I have made you a witness to the atrocities of child abuse; now I need you to cry out. There is no way for children in the System to collectively yell, "More soup please." Victims of child abuse will not march on the Capitol, stage a sit-in, or band together in any way to affect the changes that could ensure their own safety. So I'm asking that you take a personal stand to be a voice for one child and never go silent until measures are taken.

When I think of all of those Washington lobbyists who represent Unions, large corporations, environmentalists and senior citizens alike, I am hope-stricken that maybe people will come forward to help these children. I beg those of you out there with connections to those powerful groups to likewise lend your support. For my part, I will continue being a part of the Heart Galleries, writing and speaking about the System and child abuse. I know if enough people come together, things will change. Join me in crying out for all those children who need a voice, I beg you.

I can only hope that my unfortunate years living these events, and the countless hours rehashing and retelling them, can have a positive outcome—a goal that surely my many former abusers, and today's current predators, would like to see fail.

Chapter 24 - Ten Rules for Foster Parents, Guardians and System Staff

Infused into relevant sections of this work, I placed reflections or rules I feel those involved in the Foster Care System need to implement in order to alleviate some of the major difficulties the System continues to experience. Having been in every type of out-of-home placement and now having worked in just as many, I hope that you will find these rules helpful if you are considering taking in a foster child, beginning a career in the System, or if you work in the System and feel stagnant in your current position. I've reprinted these rules here, accompanied by page numbers for quick referencing to the contextual narrative.

Foster Parent/Guardian Rule No. 1: *It All Starts with the Right Motive.* Page 7.

Check your heart closely. Do not look towards social services or parenting a foster child as a means to fill any void in your emotional life. Every child in the System wants a family of their own, but that doesn't mean it is going to all be "golden times."

Foster Parent/Guardian Rule No. 2: *Offer A "Home".* Page 26.

Check the boat! Take a close look at the hull, deck, and cabins before adding passengers. See if you really are up to the commitment; acknowledge both your own and the child's emotional precipitating factors and make sure that the fit is right. Don't be part of another pit stop or "placement failure."

Foster Parent/Guardian Rule No. 3: *Do No Harm.* Page 31.

If all you do is provide a child a roof and a hot meal, you have done something good. But if you want to help, give them some space to release and express their emotions without taking it personally, and respond with empathy and compassion. No matter what, don't add injury to the insult and shame of not having a family.

Foster Parent/Guardian Rule No. 4: *Measure Your Expectations.* Page 84.

Be reasonable. Be patient. Let them adjust, and give them time to accomplish the goals you set. Before you endeavor to teach anything, accept that some things will be easy, some will be more difficult, and sometimes, a child *does* forget.

Foster Parent/Guardian Rule No. 5: *Admit What You Bring and How it Will Affect Your Child.* Page 103.

Every day take an inventory of what you bring to the table when interacting with youth trapped in the System. Whether a personal belief, personality trait, or a mood—admit to what positive and negative impacts these will have on a child.

Foster Parent/Guardian Rule No. 6: *Be Approachable.* Page 191.
Don't expect gratitude. You are very often the only family that a System youth has. Put yourself in his shoes and think what it would be like if you felt like your parents hated you. Always have the door open and watch your body language.

Foster Parent/Guardian Rule No. 7: *Don't Be Intimidated or Frustrated by Defensive "Walls."* Page 267.

Whether you are meeting, working with, or permanently caring for a System youth, respect their right to have Walls. Grasp how hard it is for them to appear vulnerable, whether amongst their peers in placement or living with strangers, AND be everything you want and hope them to be. With time and trust, these walls will come down.

Foster Parent/Guardian Rule No. 8: *Listen Up!* Page 316.

There are few things more helpful than having someone who will be a good listening friend for you. If you ever have the privilege of a child offering you their personal story, insights, or perspectives, then, with all due respect, close your mouth, don't assume, and don't be pushy.

Foster Parent/Guardian Rule No. 9: *Be a Positive Role Model!* Page 332.

Every action and response will be observed, measured and often emulated. System kids already know the general rules or ideal of the System; instead, share the little things in life. Be a great communicator, for the curt response, "Because I said so," is either for violent adult inmates of prisons or someone else whose views you don't feel deserve to be recognized.

Foster Parent/Guardian Rule No. 10: *Never Forget Your First Interview.* Page 347.

Remember why you started on the path towards being involved in the System. I know that at some point the question was raised, "Why do you want to work with children?" And the only answer that could have allowed you to take a step forward was "Because I want to help children…" Your interactions will never be forgotten, and any lessons, good or bad, will stay with them.

A Special Note to Shift Work Staff and Other Institutional System Providers:

Never forget that *YOU* GET TO GO HOME. I have known too many colleagues who had it in for "that one kid" that got on their last nerve. I know that the job is difficult and many times very trying; but remember—YOU GET TO GO HOME! While you are at the movies, that kid is in placement; while you are out to dinner, that kid is in placement; and while you spend time with the ones that you love, that kid is in placement. Don't come to work looking for what Mister or Miss Troublemaker did while you weren't there. You have a unique opportunity to be the light of some kids' day—take it. Come to work with goals and never an agenda. Let's all endeavor to make youths in the System feel important and worthwhile, and not just a ticket to a paycheck.

Four Solutions for the System and Child Abuse

If I told you that the System is so broken that an adult can severely abuse a child for years without anyone stepping in to help, would you believe me? What if I told you that many child-care agencies regularly skip required monthly supervisor visits for periods lasting from six months up to *years*. Did you know that foster children are vanishing all over the U.S.? The hole is so big, that an adoptive parent took six children out of the country, abandoned them, and returned *without a question raised*!

I know it sounds like I'm telling you about a third-world country where Children's Right's are not as important as agriculture or livestock. But I am talking about the most affluent and powerful nation of our time—the United States of America.

On September 23, 2004, "Oprah" featured children who had suffered the aforementioned fate. An adoptive mother abandoned six brothers and sisters to fend for themselves on the streets of a Nigerian village. Only when a pair of American pastors visited the small village on a goodwill mission were these children discovered. They have since been returned to American soil—but only to again be left in the System that allowed them to be abandoned in a foreign country. It is blatantly obvious that things need to change if you agree that a child's safety is vital and that they are our future. We must not let this continue to be the existing status of the System.

At this time, I offer four suggestions that I know will make tremendous changes in the safety and care of System and abused children. I am presenting a new direction for us to turn, in as few words as possible, and I would welcome the opportunity to qualify my suggestions.

1. Proper background checking, legal history, and psychological/personality profile and testing of System provider applicants (foster parents or group and treatment homes) by an independent or private, bonded nongovernmental investigative company sworn under penalty of perjury to conduct a thorough and unbiased investigation.

A thorough, independent background check should be made of every provider, both currently existing and new ones as they apply, and all providers should have to be recertified annually. I propose that suitable psychological and/or personality profile testing should be given to all existing and newly applying System providers, professional, paraprofessional or otherwise, to identify any tendencies that are likely to operate to the detriment of foster children. Police and similar authoritative agencies require such testing and I believe the System could learn a lot from their respective examples. The testing would occur at least annually to take into account life changes the provider may incur, such as divorce, death of a spouse or other personal or business partner, arrests or warnings, a new job or a substantial rise or decrease in income. The results of all investigations and testing would be filed and reconsidered annually for as long as the individual or group home desires to work in the System. Providers would be required to sign a contract, duly witnessed and notarized, in which they promise, under penalty of prosecution, to never physically or mentally abuse a child in their care (and examples of the types of abuse, not intended as an all-inclusive list, should be clearly spelled out); to never withhold proper and sufficient nutrition, shelter at a sufficient level, quality and cleanliness; and to protect their bodily safety from dangerous animals, rodents, bugs, excessive dirt, as well as vengeful staff or other violent residents, child or adult; and to provide sufficient creature comforts that any usual child requires living in at least a middle-class home in his town, to grow up and become a happy, well-adjusted adult.

It is time to change the view that providers just need to brace for a job in the System and jump in. We need to look a lot more closely at them, scrutinize them legally, and do only what is best for the children.

2. A laminated or framed list of contacts

I would like to see a phone list of all family members, friends, professional contacts, social workers, teen care hotlines and every other genuine source of help posted as a requirement in every System kid's bedroom and maybe also in a common area. Too often children have to fight with providers who conveniently "forget" to get a probation officer or social worker's phone number upon request—often because they are hiding unacceptable or harmful behavior and acts on their own part. A clearly posted list will serve as a reminder to both parties to check and monitor their interactions or behaviors.

3. Provider accountability

I want System providers (placements) to be accountable to the "clients" they service, the foster children, and to the System that pays them. For the first part, I want to introduce the idea that when services are rendered to a child by a company, then for as long as that company is in existence, they would have to remain open to contact from the child and be required to furnish documentation (regarding reports filed about the child) to the social worker immediately upon the underage child's request, or to the recipient of said services (at age 18). That placement's phone number would be added to the required list of framed or laminated contacts. Secondly, if documentation isn't provided on a timely basis, or if the program/provider doesn't ensure timely supervisor visits, there will be no payment for any services rendered until the documentation is complete and all supervisions have been conducted. It is a travesty how some programs/providers use the government as some kind of bottomless piggy bank that they feel entitled to raid.

4. Local and State review and overhaul of social service agencies and personnel.

The System is too big—unfortunately, necessarily so. I have heard adages many times from those behind a microphone, stating: "Children are our most precious resource" or "Children are our future." So prove it. There are 650,000 children in foster care and surely double that number that pass in and out of state care within any given year. Abuse and neglect happen because our social workers are understaffed and underpaid, and they are stretched beyond their limits. It is unfair to the worker and the children they need to service. Please, double their pay (literally), offer college incentives to recruit more to the field, and limit the number of children they are legally allowed to have on their caseload at any given time.

One the other side of that same coin, regulate our social service workers with an outside agency that cannot possibly benefit by overlooking any holes or gaps in the care they are to provide. I have literally heard social worker supervisors admit that they have "good" workers and "bad" ones. Of course in my thinking, that should never be the case. Once a social worker slips up and a child is found to have been neglected or abused in any way, that worker should have their caseload cut in half immediately and put on probation that could result in reassignment to a different job in which they do not work directly with children, or they should just be let go so that their incompetence isn't repeated with another child.

Other aspects that need overhaul are: clear and standardized documentation, responsible and random or surprise supervisory visits (every foster child should always have a real person available to them to ensure proper care), stopping psychiatrists and drug companies from basically using foster kids as drug testers (i.e., guinea pigs) because no one is going to object to any prescribed medication, and reforms regarding the large issue of confidentiality. But surely things can change for the better if people care enough to make them change. Child abuse sufferers and System kids should never have to look for help—it should always be in place. If children can be moved up the ladder of priority so they are regarded as higher in importance than, for example, how we regulate meat production and distribution, then these children could thrive, be secure, and know that they have an opportunity to succeed in a land that is supposed to ensure that everyone has "certain unalienable rights" including "life, liberty, and the pursuit of happiness."

May God bless your efforts and mine. Thank you for "listening."

Epilogue

After learning to love myself, I was able to express love and build a family of my own. I live in Hawaii, and have been married since January 1998. My wife and I have two beautiful children together, a boy and a girl—one of which whom you've seen; my son is on the cover of this book. Tony has visited me in Hawaii, and I've achieved a level of closure on the first chapter of my life. I continue to search for my sister, Terry Martinez. I enjoy life and relish finally being part of my own family. That journey is another story altogether, but I wanted you to know that my dreams came true.

As far as professional goals; I have been a counselor and System consultant for more than ten years now. I offer my first-hand insights from both sides of the System coin in training sessions to other System providers and foster parents. I have teamed with hundreds of young people in various stages or cogs in the System. Heart Gallery Hawaii continues to be a staple recruitment effort as we continue to find permanent families for children waiting in foster care. I work very hard to promote the Heart Gallery Ideal and I am donating a portion of the proceeds from this book to help them.

Printed in the United States
63217LVS00001B/73-165

9 781601 450531